# PHANTOM AT WAR

To Alan & family
Very best Wishes
Andy & Sue.

Phantom's founder, Lt Col George Frederick Hopkinson, 1940.

# PHANTOM AT WAR

THE BRITISH ARMY'S SECRET
INTELLIGENCE AND COMMUNICATION
REGIMENT OF WORLD WAR TWO

BY ANDY & SUE PARLOUR

FOREWORD BY
SIR ROBERT MARK, GBE, KT, QPM.

CERBERUS

First published in 2003

PUBLISHED BY:
Cerberus Publishing Limited
Penn House, Bannerleigh Road,
Leigh Woods, Bristol BS8 3PF, U.K.
Telephone: ++44 117 974 7175
Facsimile: ++44 117 973 0890
e-mail: cerberusbooks@aol.com

© Andy & Sue Parlour, 2003

All rights reserved. No part of this book may be reprinted or reproduced or utilised in any form or by any electronic, mechanical or other means, now known or hereafter invented, including photocopying and recording, or in any information storage or retrieved system, without the permission in writing from the publishers.

British Library Cataloguing in Publication Data.
A catalogue record for this book is available from the British Library.

ISBN 1 84145 118 5

PRINTED AND BOUND IN MALTA

*'There is a heroism beyond all,
for which no Victoria Cross is ever given,
because there is no official enemy nor any sort of firing,
except one volley in the early morning at some spot where
the noise does not echo into the newspapers.'*

Rudyard Kipling (1865-1936)

We dedicate this book to our parents

Peter Cyril Hargreaves
*(Royal Air Force Hurricane Pilot 274 Squadron)*

Eira Keziah Hargreaves
*(Women's Land Army World War Two)*

William Frederick Parlour
*(Territorials, Royal Sussex and Royal Fusiliers)*

Margery Pamela Parlour
*(Factory Worker for the war effort)*

*To all the officers and men of the General
Headquarters Liaison Regiment 'PHANTOM'*

*and*

*to all the other men and women who
'did their bit' 1939-1945*

# Contents

                                                                                          Page

| | | |
|---|---|---|
| *Dedication* | | v |
| *Acknowledgements* | | viii |
| *Foreword by Sir Robert Mark, GBE, KT, QPM.* | | x |
| *Introduction* | | xii |
| CHAPTER I | Communications | 1 |
| CHAPTER II | Shadows of War | 7 |
| CHAPTER III | Dunkirk | 15 |
| CHAPTER IV | Phantom goes to War | 23 |
| CHAPTER V | Phantom Reborn | 29 |
| CHAPTER VI | The Battle of Britain | 39 |
| CHAPTER VII | The Postman Calls | 47 |
| CHAPTER VIII | The Reorganised Phantom Returns to Europe | 53 |
| CHAPTER IX | Phantom in Ireland and North Africa | 59 |
| CHAPTER X | Phantom and the Dieppe Raid | 73 |
| CHAPTER XI | Training Continues | 83 |
| CHAPTER XII | The Tide Begins to Turn | 87 |
| CHAPTER XIII | Into Europe | 97 |
| CHAPTER XIV | J-Service | 111 |
| CHAPTER XV | Italy and the Spring Offensive | 115 |
| CHAPTER XVI | An Air of Optimism | 121 |
| CHAPTER XVII | D-Day and Onwards | 127 |

*Page*

| | | |
|---|---|---|
| CHAPTER XVIII | Working with the Americans | 139 |
| CHAPTER XIX | Phantom 'F' Squadron and the Special Air Services | 151 |
| CHAPTER XX | Hitler's Answer to the Invasion of France | 189 |
| CHAPTER XXI | Closing the Falaise Gap | 197 |
| CHAPTER XXII | Arnhem | 209 |
| CHAPTER XXIII | Battle of the Bulge | 222 |
| CHAPTER XXIV | Across the Rhine and into Germany | 233 |
| CHAPTER XXV | Hitler Remains Defiant | 244 |
| CHAPTER XXVI | Victory | 253 |
| CHAPTER XXVII | Phantom Officers' Memories | 267 |
| CHAPTER XXVIII | Stories from the Men of Phantom | 295 |
| *Appendix One* | Military Historian Philip Warner's view of Phantom | *321* |
| *Appendix Two* | Letter from David Niven | *325* |
| *Appendix Three* | Development of Wireless up to WWII | *327* |
| *Select Bibliography* | | *333* |
| *Index* | | *335* |

# Acknowledgements

We would like to express our grateful thanks to the many people who helped us in the research for our book, especially Sir Robert Mark and the late Lord Cullen of Ashbourne for their memories and anecdotes, Colonel William Hewitt rtd. and Lieutenant Colonel T A Peter Luttman-Johnson rtd for their advice, guidance and contributions, Colonel David Gibson rtd, Major Mark Rammage rtd., Major John Randall rtd. and Captain Clem Skinner rtd for their contributions. All were officers in Phantom.

Henry Allen, Arthur Austin, Adrian Bazar, Stan Bennison, Cecil Bramley, John Campbell, Paul Holdway, Ron Jackson, Len Owens and Arthur Wood, men of the ranks who shared their special memories of Phantom with us.

Colonel Cliff Walters rtd., ex-Royal Signals, for his history of army wireless; Clive Richards of the Ministry of Defence Air Historical Branch; Tim Padfield, Paul Johnson and staff of the National Archives Public Record Office, Kew, for their assistance; ex-Typhoon pilot the late Flt. Lieut. Peter Watson RAFVR for his wartime recollections and Roy Willard for collating this information; ex-Mosquito pilot Flt Lieut. Bentley RAF for his recollection of Phantom; Chris Dove, Royal West Kent Regiment 1940-46, for the use of his war memorabilia collection; 'The Soldier' for permission to use quotes and photos; Shirley Harrison for extracts from her book 'The Channel; The Dividing Link'; Daniel Hearsum of Pembroke Lodge, Richmond Park, for his help and hospitality; Nick Pocock of Synxspeed Post Productions for his expertise and encouragement; John Brain, son of the late Major Geoffrey Brain, ex-Phantom; Ian Clark, military historian; Jeremy Beadle and Bruce Vigar; and the staff of the many libraries, museums and record offices that we visited during the five years of our research.

To our children Matthew, Melanie and Beverley for their continued support and our son-in-law Blair Stephenson for his computer knowledge and all his help, many thanks.

But the two men in particular who deserve our heartfelt thanks, not only for the background information into the beginnings of the General Headquarters Liaison Regiment and its important role in the Second World War but also for sharing with us their many memories of the war years they spent with this very special regiment in the service of their country, are Harry Binge and Ron Eaton of PHANTOM.

We would also like to express our thanks to those too numerous to mention for their valid contributions.

The compilers apologise to any copyright holders it has not been possible to acknowledge and thank them for any quotations and illustrations used. Every effort has been made to contact all copyright holders. The publishers will be glad to make good in future editions any errors or omissions brought to their attention.

Andy and Sue Parlour, July 2003.

Crown copyright material in the Public Record Office is reproduced by permission of the Controller of Her Majesty's Stationery Office. Document references WO215/10, WO215/37, WO215/47 and WO215/59.

# Foreword
## *by Sir Robert Mark, GBE, KT, QPM.*

I was surprised to receive the invitation to write this foreword. Firstly, because the Second World War finished more than half a century ago, and secondly, because my time in Phantom was no more than fourteen months in the rank of lieutenant. It then occurred to me, my police instincts stirring, that longevity was the answer. It is, after all, unlikely that many of those who served in Phantom are still alive.

It would have been more appropriate if this foreword could have been written by one of the few with the vision and determination to create the regiment and to nurture its growth. In deference to them I undertake this task encouraged by the thought that the book is essentially the worm's eye view of momentous events and in that particular context I am as well qualified as anyone.

My fourteen months with Phantom embraced training as a first line reinforcement at Richmond, duty with Phantom Regimental Headquarters in Normandy and at Waterloo, a short spell at Eagle Tac (XII US Army Group HQ) at Luxembourg, as a patrol with US VII Corps from Duren to Cologne, with US 9 Armoured Division across Remagen bridge to Siegen in the Ruhr and finally with US XII Corps of Patton's army across Northern Bavaria to the Czech frontier. As soon as the war finished I was recalled to 21 Army Group HQ at Bad Oeynhausen and compulsorily transferred to Military Government.

There were no formal farewells. Phantom was not a regiment likely to develop 'bonding'. We were split into penny packets and spread over an area several hundred miles wide. Socially, we were also widely dispersed. But we all got on surprisingly well. There was not, however, any corporate feeling such as that which permeated conventional units, battalions, batteries and so on. Of the several hundred members of the regiment I don't suppose I ever met more than a few dozen. On the other hand I had seen with my own eyes what the regiment was all about. I realised that the importance of its role, like that of the code breakers at Bletchley Park, was not likely to be understood by the public. It is natural and proper, too, that public attention during wars should be focussed on those who fight, die or suffer, rather than on those who make victory more likely by lessening or eliminating many of their difficulties in achieving it. For them, the ultimate victory is surely sufficient reward.

The book prompted in me an appreciation of the enthusiasm and dedication of its authors. It must have been a difficult task. I hope it gives them satisfaction to be told that, having read it, I now know a great deal more about Phantom than I did as a serving member and I suspect that is likely to be the reaction of most former members also. They will no doubt share the pleasure I derived from it.

Sir Robert Mark<br>Esher, Surrey

# Introduction

This is the story of perhaps one of the British Army's least known regiments of WWII – The General Headquarters Liaison Regiment, code-named PHANTOM.

Every commander in the field or at rear headquarters needs to have up to the minute information on the progress of the battle to enable him to plan his strategy. Communication, or lack of it, can sometimes decide the outcome.

One man had the foresight and inspirational thinking to realise this. Lieutenant - Colonel George Frederick Hopkinson served in France and Belgium in 1939/40 with the British Expeditionary Force until he was evacuated from Dunkirk. His experiences convinced him of the need for a special communication service. Immediately on his return to England, Hopkinson wasted no time in presenting his ideas to the War Office and the Ministry of Defence, and, with their approval, the General Headquarters Liaison Regiment, PHANTOM, was born.

PHANTOM was to serve in many theatres of World War Two, in Greece, North Africa, Italy and the Mediterranean, and its role was to be of paramount importance in the liberation of Europe. This elite regiment served with all the Allied forces and a special PHANTOM squadron worked with the SAS behind enemy lines. When General Urquhart was trapped at Arnhem, it was the PHANTOM radio patrol with him which provided the only link with the outside world.

It is not our purpose with this book to trace the operation of every army engaged in World War Two, merely to keep the reader informed of the month to month and year to year fight for victory on all fronts as we follow PHANTOM's involvement.

This book is about the men of PHANTOM and the memories of some of those who served in this elite regiment, both officers and other ranks. Some of the reminiscences are funny, some are sad, but hopefully the readers will enjoy reading the stories as much as the writers had in writing them.

Many of those who served with PHANTOM went on to achieve distinction in public life after the war.

*'To see and not be seen; to hear and not be heard.'*

Andy and Sue Parlour,
Thorpe-le-Soken, July 2003.

CHAPTER I

# Communications

*'The telegraph is a very important device for a commander leading whole armies.'*
NAPOLEON BONAPARTE, 1795.

In the history of military conflict one of the most important aspects of warfare has been the area of communication. News of what is happening at the front line can be vital to the overall strategic battle plan. How this crucial information reaches the commanders as quickly and as accurately as possible has changed continually over the years with the advancement of technology.

In 490 BC, during the Persian expedition against Greece, the only way for the Greeks under attack to summon help was to send a runner. Not really a very reliable method of getting information through as the courier was often intercepted and slain. When the Athenian general, Miltiades, sent his runner, Pheidippides, to beg assistance from the Spartans, he was lucky. Well, lucky in the sense that Pheidippides reached his destination, but not so lucky in the fact that the Spartans were in the middle of a religious festival and, despite Pheidippides' extraordinary run covering 150 miles in two days, they would not go with him until their celebrations were over.

Even without the help of the Spartans, Miltiades and his Greek army were victorious and Pheidippides was sent out from Marathon to run the twenty-four miles to Athens with the glorious news of their conquest of the huge Persian army.

Today's marathon, the long-distance race run over twenty-six miles, was introduced at the first modern Olympics in Greece in 1896 to commemorate Pheidippides' triumphant run.

In 1588, at the time of the Spanish Armada, beacons were lit to warn of the coming invasion. Phillip II of Spain had sent out 130 ships to invade England in retaliation for the English support of Protestant rebels in the Netherlands and for the execution, the previous year, of Mary, Queen of Scots.

The signal for seventy-six thousand men to muster was to be

given through a series of beacons set on high points along the coast. When, on the 20th July, the Armada was sighted in the English Channel off the Lizard, the beacons were set alight and blazed all along the Cornish coast warning of its approach. Under the leadership of Lord Howard of Effingham the Spanish were defeated, thanks partly to the early notification of the enemy's advance.

Two hundred years later a system of rapid communication was unveiled in Paris. Created by the engineer Claude Chappe, the optical telegraph was a truly revolutionary invention. The device was simple. Machines equipped with mobile arms were sited on towers built on high open ground. The arms could be moved into 196 positions, ninety-two of which represented the signs used in transmitting a message. The operator needed only to consult a codebook before sending information on to the next tower where it was read by another operator using a telescope and duly passed on. These messages could be transmitted at great speed.

Chappe's telegraph became a sensation in France. A small, and at that time unimportant, artillery captain wrote in his diary, 'The telegraph is a very important device for a commander leading whole armies.' That ambitious young military man was none other than Napoleon Bonaparte.

The system of signs that Chappe used with his optical telegraph apparatus, known as semaphore, was actually invented in 1767 by Richard Edgeworth, an Irish landowner with a genius for mechanics who displayed a remarkable talent for invention. It was not used extensively until 1791, mainly by the French at first, but it was soon after adopted by the Admiralty in England who could see its potential in 'ship to ship' and 'ship to shore' signalling using two hand-held flags at arms' length. This was ideal for short messages but the semaphore alphabet was somewhat slow for longer communications. Thus, the seamen soon invented a new code using flags of various shapes and colours which could be hoisted up a flagmast and seen from further away.

The next big step forward in communication came with the invention of the electric telegraph. The American Samuel Finlay Breese Morse, a sculptor and portrait painter of some distinction whose hobbies included electrical studies, worked out his idea for an electrical telegraph between 1832 and 1837. A shipboard conversation on signalling had given him an idea which he jotted down:

1) *An apparatus to send signals by opening and closing an electric circuit.*
2) *A receiver to record the signals as dots and spaces on a tape.*
3) *A code to turn the dots and spaces into letters and numbers.*

Morse spent a great deal of time trying to turn this brilliantly simple idea into a complicated means by which the government could send messages in secret code. When he realised that the dots and spaces could be heard as dots and dashes, he knew that he had hit on a revolutionary method of public communication. Congress was convinced of his ideas and Morse was granted funds for an experimental line between Washington and Baltimore.

At about the same time, in London, William Fothegill Cooke and Professor Charles Wheatstone were granted a patent by King William IV to develop their electric telegraph system. It consisted of five wires connected to five needles, any two of which could be moved simultaneously to indicate a letter on a diagram. With electricity running along wires, these signals were transmitted very quickly.

The military instantly took an interest in this telegraphy, a service which improved with Samuel Morse's code, and so too did the railway organisations. Very soon a network of wires, running mainly alongside railway lines, was laid down.

These advancements in communications seemed to have a domino effect and, shortly, a method whereby the human voice could actually be transmitted over a distance by wire was developed.

Alexander Graham Bell, a 24-year old Edinburgh born educationalist, moved to the USA in 1871. It was there in Philadelphia, while pioneering mechanical methods for teaching deaf children, that he invented his 'electric speech machine'. The message was generated by a vibrating diaphragm activated by the voice through a speaker system to a receiver that amplified the voice.

Bell's induction receiver, along with Thomas Edison's carbon transmitter, form the basis of the modern telephone.

The telephone, although a wonderful breakthrough in communications, was still very limited in its usage. Although it made conversation possible with people not only in this country but also in many others around the world, the need for wires and cables to transmit its signals made its value as a means of communication in times of war restrictive. With the coming of wireless telegraphy, pioneered by the Italian physicist Guglielmo Marchese Marconi, communication took on a new dimension.

Born in Bologna in 1874, Marconi came to Britain where he furthered the researches that he had begun in Rome. In 1901 the twenty-seven-year old finally confounded his sceptics who had sneered at his attempts at wireless transmission. On 11th December, Marconi was present at the receiving station at Signal Hill, St. John's in Newfoundland, when the first trans-Atlantic wireless message was received across three thousand miles of ocean from the transmitting station at Poldhu in Cornwall. Thus, Marconi proved that radio waves could bend around our spherically-shaped earth. A kite was the means by which the primitive aerial on the Newfoundland coast was raised to catch the wireless impulses sent out from England.

Marconi, with the help of his two assistants Kemp and Paget, carried on with his researches and was later to base his experimental systems at Chelmsford, Essex, where there is to this day still a Marconi factory producing electrical components for both military and civilian applications.

Wireless telegraphy was invaluable to the military. It could now send to and receive messages from the remotest parts of the Earth where wires could not practically, or possibly, be strung. From ships at sea to troops deep in enemy territory contact could be made on wireless sets. If these had been available during the Boer Wars in South Africa between 1899 and 1902, the British forces would not have had to resort to the early dispatch method of using runners such as the Greeks did with Pheidippides in 490 BC. The Boers continually cut the telegraph wires to hamper and confuse their enemy's progress. African native dispatch runners were an essential part of the system of field communications. Many native Africans were used to pass surreptitiously through the Boer lines surrounding the besieged towns of Ladysmith, Kimberley and Mafeking with coded messages concealed in their garments by British soldiers.

Of course many visual and aural signals have been used as a means of communication over the years in lands both near and far.

In 1876 when Captain Gray arrived with his cavalry troops at the Little Big Horn River, in Montana, USA, the sight that greeted him on the vast plain that stretched away to the mountains was horrific. The ground was strewn with the blue-uniformed corpses of the cavalry division that had been led by General George A Custer. Custer's body, easily recognised by his long fair hair, was found on the pinnacle of the hill where he had made his last stand. The flag of the Seventh Cavalry was still flying over him. The sole survivor of this massacre by the combined Sioux-Cheyenne Indian force, led by Chief Sitting Bull, cursed the day that traders ever sold mirrors to the Indians. 'This was the cause of our defeat,' the trooper declared, holding out several pieces of broken mirror. 'The Indian chiefs called their tribes together by means of these.'

Pieces of broken glass had been responsible for the defeat of Custer's famous Seventh Cavalry.

Known originally by the Indians as 'talking mirrors', the same basic methods were developed into a more sophisticated system. Heliographs were used by armies all over the world when and where there was sufficient light and sun.

Smoke signals were also a means of communication, used not only by the American Indians but also by the Russian Cossack guards during the Ottoman War in 1853. Smoke signals were used during daylight hours to be replaced by fire signals after the sun had set.

Moving on to aural signals, the speech of drums is very old. It was used considerably in Africa where drums were beaten to warn of approaching raiders looking not only for gold and ivory but also for natives to take as slaves.

In Europe, especially in the mountainous areas of Switzerland and Austria, yodelling could be heard echoing around the hills as a warning of impending danger. Yodelling is still used today, but now as a way of conveying messages from one to another, just as the Cretans use a system of whistling on their Mediterranean island.

One way of sending messages that has been utilized over many centuries is the employment of carrier or homing pigeons. They were used by the ancient Babylonians, Egyptians, Greeks and even the Romans. Homing pigeons could be seen flying over besieged cities, battlefields and military camps many, many years ago. Although their popularity waned with the development of more sophisticated means of communication, commanders of more modern day armies, remembering the Roman army regulations of allotting a certain number of homing pigeons to each legion, were to use them. Osier baskets full of air messengers appeared alongside the provisions and supplies of all armies marching through Europe. Even during the First and Second World Wars, pigeons battled their way through storms and gunfire carrying their vital messages.

CHAPTER II

# Shadows of War

*'I have nothing to offer but blood, toil, tears and sweat'*
SIR WINSTON CHURCHILL. MAY 13TH, 1940

On the German invasion of Czechoslovakia in March 1939, Britain and France pledged their support for Poland, predicting that very soon this neighbour of Germany's would become Hitler's next target. They were to be proved right – less than six months later.

On August 23rd, Hitler and Stalin, who had been sworn enemies for the previous six years, signed a non-aggression pact between Germany and the Soviet Union. The two sides agreed not to use force against one another or join hostile alliances with other powers. This virtually guaranteed that Germany could use military force to claim territory from Poland without fear of intervention by Russia. Hitler wasted little time. Nine days later the invasion of Poland began.

On the 1st September one and a quarter million German troops, with six armoured divisions and eight motorized divisions, swept into Poland. At the same time Stalin sent Red Army troops to occupy Eastern Poland. Within eight days the Germans had cut the 'Polish Corridor' and were at the gates of Warsaw. The Luftwaffe had knocked out the Polish railway system and shot their airforce out of the sky. Many Polish villages, towns and cities, including Cracow, a city of more than 250,000 inhabitants, were under German control. The city of Warsaw suffered two weeks of terror bombing before surrendering. In this short time an estimated 60,000 Poles had been killed, 200,000 wounded and 700,000 taken prisoner. The Polish government had fled to Rumania.

Meanwhile, on the 3rd September, only two days after the invasion of Poland had begun, the British and French governments declared war on Germany. Berlin had been warned that if Germany did not stop all aggressive action against Poland and begin to withdraw its forces from Polish territory by 11am on that date, Britain and Germany would be at war. At 11.15am, Neville Chamberlain, the Conservative Prime Minister, broadcast to the nation, announcing that 'no such undertaking has been received and that consequently this country is at war with Germany'. The French announcement followed at 5pm.

By that same evening one and a half million evacuees had been moved from Britain's cities to reception centres across the country. These in areas that were considered to be safe from the German air attacks that were judged to be imminent. Of these, 827,000 were school children travelling with their teachers and 535,000 were pregnant women or women with children under school age. The scenes at railway and bus stations throughout these cities were heartrending as sobbing youngsters were separated from their distraught parents. They had no idea where their children were being taken or when they would see them again. All they had was the promise that they would be informed of their whereabouts as soon as possible.

In Washington on the same day, 3rd September, President Roosevelt was emphatic, when he broadcast to the American people, that the US would remain neutral. One man who did not share his optimism was Dwight D Eisenhower. This American General, who five years later was to be appointed Supreme Commander for the Allied invasion of the continental mainland, was in the Philippines at the time. In his book 'Crusade in Europe', which was published in 1948, he expressed his fears at that time. 'The news of the invasion of Poland reached us and we heard that the Prime Minister of Great Britain was to make a radio address. With my friend, Colonel Howard Smith, I listened to the declaration that Britain and Germany were at war again. It was a solemn moment, particularly so for me because I was convinced that the United States would soon find it impossible to retain a position of neutrality.'

Despite Britain's and France's early entry into the war, they had not been able to prevent Poland from being overrun in just four weeks. Neither of these democracies was in any position to give very much help to the Poles and could, in the main, only watch their defeat and occupation from afar.

Britain's first air raid took place over Germany on the 4th September as German troops continued their advance into Poland. On the 7th French military units crossed the German frontier at three points, near Saarlouis, Saarbrucken and

Zweibrucken, but no serious clash of arms took place. A week later, General Gamelin, the Allied Commander-in-Chief, told a meeting of the Supreme War Council at Abbeville, in Northern France, that he was calling off any further military action. All was quiet on the Western Front.

On the 7th September, 1939, in London, the first meeting of the newly created Land Forces Committee took place. Sir Winston Churchill, the new First Lord of the Admiralty, proposed the creation of an Army of twenty divisions by March 1940. 'We must take our place in the Line,' he said, 'if we are to hold the Alliance together and win the war.' For the next six months there was a period of 'phoney war' during which time little actual fighting took place.

The war at sea had continued since early September, with serious loss to Allied merchant shipping in the waters around Great Britain caused by German submarines (known as U-boats), mines and air attack. Unarmed merchant ships of all nations were potential targets for the U-boats' torpedoes as a result of Hitler's orders to his submarine captains to open fire 'without question' on all neutral shipping. Norway, Sweden, Denmark and the Netherlands were all anxious. Norway's Foreign Minister revealed that fifty Norwegian merchant ships had been sunk since the war had begun, even though Norway was not a participant at the time – a situation that was not to continue for much longer.

At dawn on April 9th Germans disembarked at Copenhagen after being ferried across the Baltic Sea. The Danish King, Christian X, knowing that his army was in no condition to resist, ordered an immediate cease-fire. He explained in a broadcast to his people that resistance would be hopeless and that the German occupation had been accepted by the Danish government. Since Denmark had not resisted, it was not at war with Germany. It was still a neutral country.

Later that same night, aided by traitors who were led by Major Quisling, the Nazis moved on the Norwegian capital, Oslo. Vidkun Quisling, a Norwegian diplomat and Fascist leader, had founded the '*Nasjonal Samling*' (National Unity) in imitation of the German National Socialist Party in 1933. Now he saw his chance for power.

King Haakon rejected Hitler's orders to surrender and refused to have any dealings with the invaders. A difficult campaign followed.

On April 14th, British naval forces landed at Namsos, a seaport on the Folda Fjord, followed by a hastily organized expeditionary force. Four days earlier at the 'iron ore' port of Narvik, Captain Warburton-Lee, with his flotilla of five destroyers, wreaked havoc on the German defences before being forced to retire. Tragically, this heroic captain was killed in the heat of battle. He was awarded the VC posthumously for his outstanding deeds of bravery. A second attack followed, with Vice-Admiral Whitworth in command. As a result of this action, four German destroyers were shattered and sunk in Narvik Bay and, after a running fight and chase, another three were destroyed as well.

By the 17th a clash of armies had begun along the whole Norwegian coast, and Hitler was not feeling quite as pleased with himself as he had been a week or so previously. Thirteen thousand British troops were now ashore north of Narvik, as well as French and Polish troops. At the same time, Norwegian forces loyal to the King, refusing to submit to the new puppet government set up by Quisling, were preparing to fight. But it was not long before the Germans again began to get the upper hand and by the 20th April, his 51st birthday, Hitler was beginning to feel he was back in control. By the 26th the Allied units in the North of the country, having been unable to wrest Narvik from the control of the Germans, were starting to retreat. Narvik's iron ore was so vital to the Nazis' war-effort that they were determined to hold on to it at all costs. The following day Germany officially declared war on Norway. King Haakon and his government fled to England with many Norwegian soldiers, airmen and sailors who would continue the fight.

Quisling's government did not last long. After only fifteen days of power, this traitor, whose name would come to represent the betrayal of one's country, was replaced by the German Nazi Party official, Josef Terboven, on Hitler's orders. When the war was over Quisling was to be tried and executed for treason.

On the 10th May in London another government was set to fall. The Conservative Prime Minister, Neville Chamberlain, had told a restless House of Commons the story of Allied failure in Norway. As an outcome of the vote at the end of a two-day debate, Chamberlain had to go, in spite of a majority of eighty-one. Many Tories had voted with the opposition and this was, in effect, a vote of no confidence in their leader. Chamberlain's intention of forming a coalition government, bringing in the Liberal and Labour parties under his leadership, was rejected. The Labour Party leaders refused to serve under him, giving him no option but to resign his position.

Winston Churchill was promptly summoned to Buckingham Palace where King George VI invited him to form a new government. Churchill assured His Majesty that he would build an all-party team to achieve ultimate war victory. As well as becoming the new Prime Minister, Churchill also became Minister of Defence. In addition to these two positions, he was to head a special Defence Committee consisting of himself and the Chiefs of Staff of the three Armed Forces. The duty of this committee was to make the necessary day by day, or even hour by hour, strategic decisions.

One of the first decisions Churchill made, on the day that he became Prime Minister, was for British forces to occupy the Danish dependency of Iceland. Since the Germans had taken Denmark, Iceland had become an important strategic base that had to be denied to the enemy.

In his broadcast to the nation announcing his decision to resign, Chamberlain disclosed that Churchill had invited him to become a member of the new war cabinet and that he had accepted. Many, including the king, were sorry to see Chamberlain go.

But had Chamberlain been judged fairly? Had his signing of the Munich agreement on the 29th September, 1938, bought Britain precious time in which to rearm and build up her forces in preparation for the inevitability of war? Or had he really believed that ceding the Sudeten area of Czechoslovakia to Hitler would appease the military expansionist aims of the dictator and his government? This treaty had been co-signed by Chamberlain and the French Prime Minister, Edouard Dalalier, on the one hand and the Axis Power leaders, Hitler and Mussolini, on the other. (The Axis Powers was the name given to the pact of co-operation between Nazi Germany and Fascist Italy signed in 1936.)

Tragically, before the year of 1940 was out, Neville Chamberlain had died from cancer.

In his first speech to the House of Commons, Winston Churchill included these words: 'I have nothing to offer but blood, toil, tears and sweat. We have before us many, many long months of struggle and suffering. You ask what is our policy. I will say it is to wage war by land, sea and air with all our might and all the strength that God can give us, and to wage war against a monstrous tyranny never surpassed in the dark lamentable catalogue of human crime. That is our policy. You ask what is our aim. I can answer in one word: Victory.'

As early as September 3rd, 1939, the day that war was declared, the British Expeditionary Force was mobilized. (This army had first been established in 1906 and sent to France in 1914 at the start of World War One to support the left wing of the French armies against German attack.) By the 12th, some 158,000 men of the BEF with twenty-five thousand vehicles had been ferried across the Channel to take their place alongside the French Army under General Gamelin. A considerable achievement carried out with not a single casualty. Secret routes had been taken across Britain to prevent air attacks by the Germans on the road convoys. The men had moved in small groups, concealed by day and travelling by night.

One young soldier recalled that, on nearing the French coast, a seaplane came out to greet the troopships, sweeping round in circles until they reached Cherbourg Harbour. When he and his comrades finally stepped foot on French soil at 8am on a dreary and depressing morning, expecting to be met by a welcoming crowd with cheers and smiles, there was something of an anti-climax. 'The crowds assembled to welcome us consisted of a French naval sentry, some old women, a fisherman or two and three gendarmes. As a reception committee they were a decided failure. They vouchsafed us a disinterested glance or two, and then went about their business. And some of us had actually expected kisses!'

The British Expeditionary Force, made up largely of reserve forces and the Territorial Army, was taken to temporary barracks before being deployed at the front with its French allies.

Since 1929 the French had spent vast amounts of money building the Maginot line. This was a succession of casements interspersed with fortresses constructed of concrete and equipped with artillery to protect France's long border with Germany. By early 1940 the French had fourteen divisions manning this line, which only stretched as far as the Franco-Belgian border, and the BEF, commanded by Lord Gort, had four divisions positioned in Northern France as early as October 1939, a number which steadily increased to nine by May of 1940.

Now they waited. The Allies predicted that Hitler intended to use his main force to attack through the Netherlands and Belgium, as they did in the 1914 Schlieffen plan, then swing round Paris to catch the Maginot line in the rear. Their prediction was correct, but Hitler, wanting to build up his forces in the West and to avoid the winter weather, resolved to put back his plan until the Spring of 1940.

These plans, however, had to be revised when, in January, a German military plane with a *Luftwaffe* Staff Officer on board crash-landed in the Belgian town of Mechelen-sur-Meuse. Identified as *Major* Helmut Reinberger, he was carrying documents outlining the operational plans for a German airborne attack on the West. The information contained in these papers, including maps giving details of some intended saturation bombing of French airfields to begin on the 14th January, was passed on to the Dutch, British and French military headquarters.

When given the news of these lost plans, Hitler was believed to have bellowed, 'It's things like this that can lose us the war.' New plans had to be made.

With the Nazis already occupying Denmark and Norway, Hitler believed that the time was now right to continue to drive into Western Europe. This time he proposed an attack by his Army Group B in the North to trigger an Allied move into Belgium, while the Panzer divisions of his Army Group A would enter the Ardennes region with the intention of pushing their way through to the Channel coast. This would effectively sever the Allied forces from any support that was available to them in France. Hitler judged that if he could gradually push back the encircled troops to the sea, they would have to surrender. A plan that was to prove very successful, but with not quite the outcome that he had anticipated.

This attack, code named '*Fall Gelb*', was scheduled to begin on the 10th May. The day that the 'phoney war', or '*la Drole de Guerre*' as it was known to the French, came to an end.

The German '*blitzkrieg*', or 'lightening war', first seen in Poland the preceding September, came to the Low Countries with a ferocious suddenness. As dawn broke German bombers attacked the airfields not only in Holland and Belgium but also in France, effectively crippling the tiny Dutch and Belgian air fleets and severely damaging those of France and Britain. The Germans bombed railways and military strong-points and pushed forward their troops along a 150-mile front, gaining many key positions before the defenders could react. Parachutists landed in Rotterdam, Leiden and The Hague and gliders silently put down, carrying hundreds of German troops who seized the Belgian bridges across the Albert Canal.

Up until now the Dutch and the Belgian governments had refused to co-operate with the British and French armies for fear of provoking the Germans, even though they knew that sooner or later Hitler would attack them. Now, however, Queen Wilhelmina of the Netherlands and King Leopold of Belgium desperately sought the Allies' assistance.

The inactivity of the winter months and the cold, wet weather conditions had put a considerable strain on the morale of the British and French troops as they awaited the German attack, but when the order came they were ready to cross the Belgian border by 7am. Despite disarray caused by lack of communication on the Belgian side, by evening the Allied forces had reached their planned defensive line and set in motion their contingency plans to join up with the Belgian army.

The British government at once gave orders to the Royal Air Force for mines to be dropped in the River Rhine to cause maximum disruption to enemy shipping. Within an hour London learnt that German aircraft of the *Luftwaffe* had retaliated by dropping their mines in the River Scheldt. This vital waterway, which linked France, Belgium and Holland, was being used to supply the Allied forces.

Three days later, in spite of courageous fighting by the Dutch and after the loss of Rotterdam, General Henri G Winkelman, the Dutch Commander-in-Chief, fearing the complete destruction of Holland, surrendered. In his broadcast on Hilversum radio he announced, 'By vast superiority of the most modern arms, the enemy has been able to break our resistance, but ultimately the Netherlands will rise again as a free nation. Long live our Queen!'

Queen Wilhelmina, having been warned that she might be kidnapped by the Germans, left the Hague for Rotterdam where she crossed the North Sea to Harwich. That evening she was met at London's Liverpool Street Station by King George VI. She informed him that the Dutch people in the colonies would continue to fight alongside the Allies.

The Queen and her family were to spend the duration of the war domiciled at 'Laneswood', a large country house in the village of Mortimer situated on Berkshire's border with Hampshire.

CHAPTER III

# Dunkirk

*'The ring about the British, French and Belgian armies is closed forever.'*
GERMAN HIGH COMMAND, MAY 1940.

With the fall of Holland, Hitler could now concentrate all his efforts on Belgium and, in particular, his Army Group A's advance through the Ardennes and on into France. Here he would avoid the massive defensive fortifications of the Maginot line and would, hopefully, be able to drive a passage through to the English Channel.

By the 17th May, 1940, the Germans were in Brussels, Antwerp was about to fall and the French had started to withdraw their forces from the Belgian front, unfortunately without informing the British or the Belgians. This led to chaos. Especially when the French Seventh Army, pulling back from the mouth of the Scheldt, cut through the British and Belgian lines. Another situation caused by lack of communication.

The Allies desperately tried to regroup, and in committing themselves in Northern Belgium left the Germans the relatively easy task of advancing through the now practically undefended Ardennes. The French, confident of the impenetrability of this hilly wooded area, had left only a light screen of cavalry to defend it. The Panzers of Germany's Army Group A took little time to break through, push the cavalry aside and cross the River Meuse, despite Allied air attacks aimed at destroying the river's bridges. The Germans now had a virtually free passage to the coast, severing the Allies' links between their front line units and their bases and supplies in Western France.

By the 21st May, the Allied armies in Belgium were effectively surrounded and, in spite of a British counter-attack by tanks from the Royal Tank Regiment against Rommel's 7th Panzer Division, and the motorised *SS Totenkopf* divisions at Arras, they could do little to thwart Hitler's advance towards the English Channel. (The SS – *Schutzstaffel* meaning protection squad – was a Nazi organization founded in Germany in 1925, originally as Hitler's personal bodyguard.) Even the plan of General Weygand, the Allied Commander-in-Chief, for a counter-attack from the North and the South against the flanks of the corridor had come to nothing. It seemed that the Allies were powerless to stop the sweep of the mighty German Panzers.

The young King Leopold was rapidly coming to the inevitable belief that his Belgian Army could fight no longer and General Lord Gort gave orders for his BEF to fall back towards the Channel ports to form a new defensive line around Dunkirk.

A young officer with Y-Battery Royal Artillery, which was preparing to go into battle in the Ypres area, was standing in a farmyard at Nieppe, a village just inside the Belgian border, discussing with his Assistant Command Post Operator what was going to happen. Nobody seemed to know what was going on. They couldn't get a line on anything from anybody. The infantry didn't know much either, only that the official terminology had changed from 'side-stepping' to 'withdrawal'. When they had been at Vimy and had had to go back, they were just 'side-stepping' the Germans. Now there was no longer any attempt to keep up the pretence. 'It's withdrawal alright now – official,' said the ACPO. He had hardly finished his sentence before they found themselves under heavy shell fire. The drivers of the Y-Battery vehicles leapt from their seats and disappeared into nearby ditches. On re-emerging after the shelling had ceased, they were most concerned to find that one of their trucks had been destroyed. Not because it contained all the Battery records and the Office stationery, but because it also carried 125,000 cigarettes, the entire Battery stock. That was the real tragedy.

By the 25th May, Hitler's plan for the full destruction of the Allied armies in the West was on the point of fulfilment. The German corridor that had been driven down the Somme Valley had widened. Calais had fallen and only the ports of Dunkirk and Ostend remained as avenues of escape for the British, French and Belgian armies that were being forced back to the sea. They had been squeezed into an ever-shrinking pocket.

The fall of Calais had come only after a fierce struggle. Three thousand British troops under the command of Brigadier Claude Nicholson, many untried in battle, with the help of only eight hundred French troops and a handful of Dutch and

Belgians, had faced the impossible task of holding Calais. The British Expeditionary Force had been in no position to give them any aid for it was already in a precarious position itself – it had either to make a renewed effort to get through to the Somme, which General Gort believed impossible, or evacuate from Dunkirk.

By the 23rd May, when two Panzer divisions were close to Calais, Nicholson had repeatedly asked for more artillery, ammunition and food. The War Office in London had known of the desperate situation in Calais but ordered Nicholson to fight on. At midnight on the 25th May a minesweeper had fought its way into Calais Harbour with this message from Winston Churchill: 'Every hour that you continue to exist is of the greatest help to the BEF. The Government has therefore decided you must continue to fight. Have the greatest admiration for your splendid stand.'

And fight they did. By the time Brigadier Nicholson, the garrison commander, was captured on the afternoon of the 26th May, he and his small force had fought for four days against hopeless odds. His three thousand troops had been either killed or taken prisoner, including many wounded.

The German *General* Heinz Guderian, who had had much to do with the creation of the Panzer force and the *blitzkrieg* concept, and whose Panzer corps it had been who had broken through the French defences at Sedan, had hoped to ignore Calais and race for Dunkirk, but Calais had had to be taken. The four essential days of Nicholson's fierce resistance had bought much needed time for the BEF at Dunkirk. But had it been the defence of Calais alone that had saved the BEF or had it also been saved by German error?

With the BEF and the remnants of the French and Belgian units trapped in the Dunkirk pocket and with Guderian's Panzers closing in to strike the final blow, Hitler had suddenly and inexplicably ordered a halt.

When General von Runstedt had suggested that the armour should be halted until infantry support could be brought up, Hitler, delighted by the stunning victories of his German forces, but at the same time worried that the Panzers were being over-stretched, had agreed. So at 11.30am on the 24th May, Hitler had issued the order for all attacks in the perimeter of Dunkirk to be discontinued. Guderian's Panzers were to stop on the line of the Aka Canal. The Germans had estimated that there were one hundred thousand Allied troops encircled at Dunkirk, about a quarter of the true figure of four hundred thousand, and that it would be impossible for so many to be evacuated. The *Fuhrer*, therefore, had not felt any urgency in continuing the onslaught. By the time he rescinded his halt order the following day, he realised his grievous error. He had not appreciated that the BEF was preparing to evacuate and his army had lost 24 vital hours.

While the German Army paused, the British evacuation began.

As early as the 17th May, Churchill had ordered the British Admiralty to assemble a large number of vessels in case it became necessary to cross over the Channel to withdraw the BEF from France. When he went to see the King at Buckingham Palace on the evening of the 23rd, Churchill informed His Majesty that, if Weygand's plan did not succeed, he would have to order the BEF back to England.

As we now know, Weygand's plan did not materialize. Shattered by tanks and dive-bombers, the Belgian army was in chaos. With communications between the French and British in Belgium and the main French forces beyond all repair, the situation the Allies found themselves in was hopeless.

In his underground bunker deep in the cliffs at Dover, Vice-Admiral Bertram Ramsay received the radio signal from the Admiralty on the eve of the 26th ordering the emergency evacuation of troops from Dunkirk. OPERATION DYNAMO WAS TO COMMENCE.

Churchill had estimated that it would be possible to take off a maximum of forty-five thousand troops in two days. He had reckoned without the determination and courage of the British people. From Whitehall the call went out for ships and men to man them.

At Dover, Ramsay's fleet of destroyers and other units of the Royal Navy, including forty Dutch coasters which it now commandeered, were joined by an unbelievable flotilla of boats and ships of all sizes. London Fire Brigade boats, including the *Massey Shaw*, merchant vessels, large and small, colliers and coastal tramps were all seen alongside yachts, fishing vessels, pleasure boats and even dinghies as they assembled ready to make their way across the now, thankfully, calm sea towards the coast of France.

Among the boats that came from all along the south and east coast fishing ports and seaside resorts were two paddle-steamers, more used to carrying jovial holidaymakers than a retreating army. Sadly, they did not return. The *Brighton Belle* sank after colliding with a wreck and the HMS *Waverley*, previously converted into a minesweeper, was attacked on her return journey by twelve German dive-bombers. The single anti-aircraft gun on board was no match for the mighty *Luftwaffe* and the *Waverley* disappeared beneath the waves with three hundred troops on board.

Brightlingsea born and bred Basil Steady, who is sadly no longer with us, was a young first mate on a fishing smack that had been seconded to the Royal Navy. Its role was to supply the naval men who were based in this small Essex fishing village with fresh fish. Basil recalled making constant trips to get the men off the beaches of Dunkirk under incessant enemy fire. He always believed that he and his fellow fishermen were very lucky to still be alive at the end of the day after surviving several near misses. Brightlingsea considered itself to be particularly close to the Sussex and Kent cinque ports, of which Dover was one, being an associated member of the original five ports commissioned by Edward the Confessor to provide ships for naval defence.

It seemed that all along the Essex, Kent and Sussex coasts, and beyond, every conceivable craft joined the motley armada that made its way to France, and every able-bodied man with access to one risked his life to help save his gallant army.

The German High Command had arrogantly announced, 'The ring about the British, French and Belgian Armies is closed forever'. Had they forgotten about Britain's traditional ally – the sea?

Hitler, realizing the full extent of his failure to act when he had the opportunity, ordered a full-scale air and land assault on Dunkirk. The Allied troops, waiting on the crowded beaches for boats to take them off, were being battered continually by German artillery, dive-bombed by *Stukas* and strafed by Messerschmitt 109's of the *Luftwaffe*. The Royal Air Force was outnumbered but never outfought. It threw everything it had into the sky to try to give some protection to the rescue craft and the thousands of men stranded on the sands.

Because Dunkirk is set in a coastline riddled by shoals, sandbanks and narrow passages it made the rescue more difficult. It was impossible for ships larger than destroyers to reach the pier-head because of the shallow water, so columns of soldiers waded into the sea hoping to be picked up by one of the many small boats, such as Basil Steady's, that were ferrying troops back to the larger vessels waiting offshore.

Time and time again they unloaded the men and made their way back to the beaches to pick up more, all the while under relentless enemy attack.

British troops who were fighting rearguard actions around the perimeter of Dunkirk contributed much to the evacuation. Ninety-nine men of the 2nd Royal Norfolk Regiment held up an *SS Totenkopf* (death's head) company until their ammunition ran out. With no help available they were forced to surrender. Expecting to be taken prisoners-of-war and treated as such under the Geneva convention, they were slaughtered by their captors. Y-Battery and the other regiments in the artillery ring around Dunkirk were all the time sending shells crashing into the enemy masses that were still being stubbornly held by the infantry. Only when it was eventually their turn to withdraw to the beaches did these brave gunners cease firing and carry out the heartrending task of destroying their own equipment, lest it fall into enemy hands. All artillery and field-guns, such as 25-pounders, were to be spiked. All motorized vehicles were to be rendered useless. This was achieved by draining the oil from the engines and leaving the throttles jammed open until the engines either seized or blew up. Then the vehicles were set on fire.

The task of the remaining British defenders was not made any easier when, at 11am on the 28th, King Leopold ordered that the Belgian forces lay down their arms. (Although fighting continued for a further two hours at Ypres by a few units without channels of communication.) The previous day the King had sent his deputy Chief of Staff to ask the Germans for an armistice, but the *Fuhrer* had demanded unconditional surrender. The King had no option but to accept. His Belgian Army had fought valiantly for eighteen days, resisting wholeheartedly, but could hold out no longer.

One Divisional Commander who had to do some quick thinking after the Belgian surrender was 53-year-old Major-General, later Field-Marshal, Bernard Law Montgomery. During the night of the 27th he was ordered to move his entire 3rd Division into a gap to the left of the British front between the 50th Division and the Belgians. A dangerous manoeuvre that went without a hitch. In the morning he discovered to his astonishment that the Belgian army had gone! Montgomery had always maintained that there was no co-ordination between the operations of the BEF, the Belgians and the First French Army. A point now proved. The commanders of these armies had no means of direct communication except by personal visits.

In the early hours of the 3rd June, Major-General Harold Alexander, now in command of 1st Corps, the last to evacuate Dunkirk, toured the shoreline in a fast motorboat to make sure that no soldiers remained to be lifted off. Satisfied that he was the last, he returned to the quayside where he took a ship to Dover.

In the seven days from the 27th May, 338,226 men had been evacuated from Dunkirk. A most remarkable feat, but not without loss. Boats were sunk, planes shot down, and many soldiers, sailors, airmen and civilians lost their lives. Immobilized guns and tanks had to be left behind, and so did thirty-four thousand soldiers who had been taken prisoner-of-war by the Germans.

In his parliamentary speech on the 4th June, Churchill described Operation *Dynamo* as 'a miracle of deliverance'.

As soon as Dunkirk had been taken, the combined forces of the German Groups A and B turned south towards the Somme. The attack, code named '*Fall Rot*', commenced and the battle for France now moved rapidly towards its climax. With little real resistance from the demoralized French Army, the 136,000 British troops who still remained in Western France and 200,000 Polish soldiers, the overwhelming numbers of the enemy forced the Allies back. Even with the back up provided by the Royal Air Force, carrying out hundreds of bombing sorties on targets indicated by the French High Command, the German Army could not be stopped.

Hitler's plan now was to achieve what the Germans had failed to do in the First World War – to capture Paris.

By the 14th June, less than five weeks after its attack in the West had begun, the German Army was inside the gates of Paris and the French capital was on the verge of falling into Hitler's hands. Four days earlier the Germans had crossed the Seine and the French Prime Minister, Paul Reynard, had fled westwards with his government to Tours, leaving Paris in the hands of a military governor, *General* Hering.

After only two days Hering declared Paris an open city to save it from enemy bombing and Reynard resigned. He was succeeded by the 84-year-old *Marshal* Philippe Petain. It was Petain who asked for an armistice and accepted German terms on the 22nd June, 1940.

To add to their humiliation, the French were forced to sign

the armistice terms, in Hitler's presence, in the very railway carriage in the forest of Compiegne in which the Germans themselves had been forced to sign their surrender to the French in 1918.

As part of the peace agreement, the French under *Marshal* Petain were allowed to set up a government in the unoccupied zone in Southern France. This was to be responsible for the administration of the French colonial empire. The French naval fleet would not be allowed to pass out of French control and all the 1,538,000 French prisoners-of-war would remain under German control. This government would be known as the Vichy government of France. The name being taken from the spa town where it was based.

The following day, June 23rd, as Hitler triumphantly toured the sights of the capital, from which two million Parisians had already departed, the *Swastika* flew from the pinnacle of the Eiffel Tower. Hitler was now master of Poland, Holland, Belgium, Luxemburg, Denmark, Norway and France.

The Norwegian King Haakon and his government had fled to exile in England on June 9th, only two months after the German invasion of his country had begun. The previous day the British evacuation of Narvik had reached its conclusion and the German victory over Norway, coming at the same time as that of France, had been a severe blow to the Allies.

In less than ten months Hitler had taken seven European capitals. Now he was poised to take yet another – London.

CHAPTER IV

# Phantom Goes To War

*'The role of the force under your command is to co-operate with our Allies in the defeat of our common enemy.'*
LESLIE HORE-BELISHA, SECRETARY OF STATE FOR WAR,
TO LORD GORT. SEPTEMBER 3RD, 1939.

Two men who realised that communication, or the lack of it, played a vital role in whether a battle was won or lost, were General Montgomery, who we have already mentioned briefly in the previous chapter, and Lieutenant-Colonel Hopkinson.

Bernard Law Montgomery had qualified for the Royal Military College, Sandhurst, on leaving school in January 1907. On passing out eighteen months later, he put his name down for the Indian Army. Failing to gain a place in this his first choice, he was certain of a place in his second choice - the Royal Warwickshire Regiment. With it he learnt the foundations of his military art.

Montgomery's battalion served in India. First in Peshawar and then, for the last two years of its foreign service, in Bombay, before being returned to England.

By August 1914, Montgomery was a full lieutenant by 26 years of age. It was to take the experiences of the 1914-1918 war to show him what was wrong in the army.

After being wounded in France early on, Montgomery was evacuated back to hospital in England, taking no further part in the war for some months. During this period of enforced inactivity, he had time for reflection. Not being content to solely fight for his country and feeling a deep need to improve matters, he joined the staff and returned to the Western Front in France as a brigade-major.

By the end of the First World War Montgomery was Chief of Staff (GSO 1) of a division. To the enquiring mind of this ambitious young officer many things seemed amiss. Two matters in particular concerned him greatly. The lack of contact between generals and their soldiers and the need for greater all round communication.

During the last six months of this war Montgomery, in his own words, '...devoted much thought to the problem of how to get to Divisional Headquarters quickly the accurate information of the progress of the battle which is so vital, and which enables a general to adjust his dispositions to the tactical situation as it develops.'

A rather amusing episode, although one with potentially critical consequences, had occurred during the battle of the Somme in the summer of 1916. The Brigade Commander of an infantry division that was to lead a divisional attack, needed to know how best to utilize his rear troops. Brigade HQ was somewhat surprised to be informed that a pigeon would be employed to convey the necessary information.

The bird was duly delivered to HQ and on the day of the attack it was given to a soldier to carry. The idea was that when the moment was right an officer would attach a message to the pigeon's leg and the feathered messenger would be released to return to its loft at Brigade HQ.

The Brigade Commander waited anxiously for his first glimpse of the pigeon in the skies above. At last it was sighted and, sure enough, alighted safely in its loft.

Rushing the message to their Brigade Commander, the officers apprehensively awaited its contents. They were astonished to hear him read out: 'I am absolutely fed up with carrying this bloody bird about France!'

This incident, and many others, went a long way in persuading Montgomery of his convictions. He devised a system of sending officers with wireless sets up to the headquarters of the leading battalions from where they sent messages back by wireless to GHQ. This was the basis of the system, known as 'J-Service', that he was to develop in the Second World War. With the invaluable help of Brigadier Hugh Mainwaring, this communications link was to be used for the first time when Montgomery commanded the British Eighth Army in the desert during the Battle of Alamein in 1942.

His experiences as a Divisional Commander with the British Expeditionary Force in Northern France in the early days of World War Two, one of which we have already mentioned, further convinced Montgomery of the great need for improvement in this respect. He considered wireless communication within the BEF never to be efficient and that outside the BEF it was practically non-existent. This made inter-communication within the Allied armies only possible by the use of civilian telephone, supplemented by visits from liaison officers and by commanders and their staffs. As the German advance into France had begun to cut the land lines, telephone communication had ceased altogether and personal visits were then the only means of verbal intercourse. Lord Gort had established his GHQ in and around Habarcq, the headquarters of the various branches and services occupying thirteen villages covering an area of some fifty square miles. This dispersed system called for a cumbersome network of communications. It was difficult to know where anyone was and command from the top suffered from the very beginning.

The other man who was much concerned over the matter of communication in war was 44-year-old Lieutenant-Colonel George Frederick Hopkinson, MC. 'Hoppy', as he was better known, the son of George and Ada Hopkinson from Retford, in Nottingham, had served in the First World War as a reserve captain. He loved the army and made it his life. A small and stocky man with a great gift for extracting the maximum of loyalty and hard work from all ranks, he would never ask his men to do anything that he was not prepared to do himself. Those who served under him usually ended up being known as 'Hoppy's men', a label they were only too proud to wear. Hoppy never married, the Army being his one and only love which he happily devoted his life to.

Early in the days of World War Two, Lieut-Col. Hopkinson was sent to No. 3 Air Mission as a Military Observer. This RAF Mission was under the command of Wing-Commander J M Fairweather, DFC. With Poland already occupied by the Germans and in sure certainty that Holland and Belgium would be Hitler's next targets, No. 3 Air Mission was set up in readiness to liaise with the Belgian General Staff when the invasion came. The BEF under Lord Gort was waiting on the Franco-Belgian border ready to strike at the appropriate moment. With Allied troops then in Belgium, the Mission's role would be to pass back information about the position of these troops from Belgian GHQ to the Advanced Air Striking Force HQ. On this information would be laid down what was known as the 'bomb-line'. A line separating the opposing armies. A line behind which the Allies would be safe when their own air forces struck at the enemy.

Because the Belgians, as neutrals, had been reluctant to provoke a German attack, it had been difficult for the British Forces to develop contingency plans with them before the inevitable happened. The need to be well-informed and alert to the position of the enemy when the time did come was vital.

What exactly Hopkinson's part as Military Observer was intended to be is difficult to say, but he and Fairweather, or 'Fairy' as he was popularly known, soon realised that the Mission needed restructuring. The information from Belgian HQ would be insufficient on its own to enable the Mission to fulfil its role and they agreed that ground reconnaissance officers would be required to supplement this information. Soldiers, not airmen, would have to be used for this task - a group of men specially trained, highly-mobile and skilled in communications. To Hoppy communication meant wireless. His idea of liaison, very much like that of Montgomery, was based on wireless, mobility and flexibility. At the beginning of the war the Army was not very wireless minded. The Royal Corps of Signals did a wonderful job, but in a way that only a large organization could. They used wireless only until such time as they could get the telegraph wire up. Their role as a linesman too meant that they had less time to concentrate on wireless training.

Now the '*Hopkinson* Mission' came into being. When it started out it consisted of only Hoppy himself, a driver, a clerk and a batman. By the end of October 1939 they were working very closely with No. 3 Air Mission at Valenciennes, France, where this original Mission had established itself. To quote officially, 'It was provided for the purpose of obtaining, in conjunction with No. 3 Air Mission, information regarding the progress of the battle in Belgium during its early stages, and of transmitting that information to the Air Office Commander-in-Chief, British Air Forces in Europe, with a view to assisting him in the direction of air operations in that battle.' Hopkinson's Mission, which was initially at Aldershot, grew rapidly.

The seeds had now been sown for the remarkable new intelligence unit that would form the basis of the elite General Headquarters Liaison Regiment that was to be born out of the aftermath of the miracle of Dunkirk, but was for now known by the name that the combined Missions, under Fairweather's command, adopted for themselves - PHANTOM.

During the following six months new units arrived to join the ever-growing mission. A troop of the 12th Royal Lancers, under the command of Captain J A Warre, was one of the first sent out from England to be attached to the Mission. The 12th Royal Lancers were Light Cavalry and, as such, were equipped with armoured cars. An armoured car troop of about thirty men, in Guy scout cars, could move rapidly to and from trouble spots and their cars could carry wireless sets that were sufficiently powered to transmit over long distances. Soon others were to join Hopkinson and his men as they trained in preparation for their task, including motor-cyclists who came from the Queen Victoria's Rifles and the reservists from the Royal Tank Regiment. The Mission's combined strength was to be fifteen officers and 110 other ranks. By the time Phantom was to see action for the first time, when the German advance into Belgium began on the 10th May, 1940, Hopkinson had under his command a well-organized and highly-trained unit.

Motorcycle and wireless training had been given top priority and all the men were now highly proficient in both these tasks. Hopkinson was adamant that the motorcycle would be the only vehicle on which the liaison officer would remain mobile and that wireless telegraphy was the way forward in communication within the Army. General fitness was also considered of great importance and many hours had been spent on the parade ground, doing drill and physical training exercises.

Fairweather was now based at Belgian Headquarters at Willebroek, near Antwerp, with a detachment to maintain contact with the RAF. Hopkinson, with the rest of Phantom, made up the Advanced Report Centre. This ARC consisted of an HQ of four wireless detachments - one being with Fairweather, one with GHQ BEF, one an Armoured Car Squadron of two armoured car troops, equipped with No. 11 wireless sets, and one an Intelligence Section.

The Advanced Report Centre, working very closely together, carried out forward reconnaissance, contacting the Belgian Army when necessary to find out exact details of enemy positions and to transmit this vital information back to Fairweather, who would inform the RAF. Once they knew precisely where the advancing enemy troops were they could use their air-power accordingly.

As the German forces steadily progressed it became increasingly difficult for the Advanced Report Centre to maintain the headquarters that they had set up at Mielen-sur-Aelst, near St Trond, and they were forced to move their base several times. In spite of this, they were still able to retain contact with Fairweather.

As we now know, despite every effort, the British, French and Belgian armies were unable to stem the tide of the advancing German army, whose tanks, under *General Guderian's* command, were proving to be their ultimate weapon as they speedily pushed their way through the Low Countries.

The Allied forces were compelled to withdraw in haste. They were unable to do anything against the mighty power that bore down on them. The combined Missions, under Fairweather and Hopkinson, by managing to maintain contact with each other and with the Air Commanders, played a vital role in the successful retreat to Dunkirk of the British Expeditionary Force.

Finally, on the 27th May, Fairweather, now at Bruges, ordered the Intelligence Section to join him in preparation for their own evacuation to Britain. The first detachment embarked on the evening of the 29th from Ostend, followed by the rest of the Phantom party on the 31st from La Panne, near Dunkirk.

Tragically, Wing-Commander Fairweather was not to make it home. He and the whole of his No. 3 Air Mission were wiped out when the boat they had boarded, the *Aboukir*, was hit by a torpedo launched from a surface German E-boat and sunk eight miles off the Belgian coast. In total ten Phantom officers and twenty-two Phantom soldiers went down with her.

Of the military on board this merchant ship, one who did survive was Second-Lieutenant Norman Reddaway. Luckily for him, he was on deck when the torpedo struck and, being an exceptionally strong swimmer, was able to get away. He used a bit of wreckage as a raft until he was picked up by a destroyer and landed at Dover.

In a War Office memorandum written by Phantom Captain John Jackson after he returned from Dunkirk and the fall of France, he briefly outlines Phantom's performance in France.

> *'The ability of Phantom to beat other information channels in France had been proved beyond doubt. It had continued to be not only the quickest channel, but frequently the only source of information available to the Commander-in-Chief. If this service was useful in France, it must be indispensible in the imminent battle to defend our shores.'*

CHAPTER V

# Phantom Reborn

*'You may wish to consider the possibilities of employing reconnaissance and liaison units in the arrangements for the defence of Great Britain.'*

LIEUTENANT-COLONEL HOPKINSON, JUNE 7TH, 1940.

It is probable that the foundations for the reformed Phantom unit were laid on the windswept Romney Marshes on the Kent coast. It was here, and around the Kent ports of Ramsgate, Margate and Dover, that many of the BEF evacuees, returning to Britain in the aftermath of Dunkirk, were based, including the remnants of the combined Fairweather-Hopkinson Mission. The BEF had been reduced to a disorganized rabble. Most of its heavy weapons had been abandoned in Flanders, the soldiers returning with only the equipment they could carry, and only a handful of fighting units existed in this country.

At least a month elapsed before many of the BEF were either re-united with their existing regiments or seconded to others. Some went to newly-reformed units – such as Phantom.

On his return from France, Lieut-Col Hopkinson wasted no time in putting forward his ideas for the reformation of Phantom to the appropriate ministry department. He sent the following letter, re-printed in full, to the Deputy Director of Military Operations on the 7th June, 1940, recommending the continuation of an organization, similar to the Hopkinson Mission, for the defence of Britain.

DDMO.

1. You may wish to consider the possibilities of employing reconnaissance and liaison units in the arrangements for the defence of Great Britain, as suggested in the last paragraph of my report on the activities of the Hopkinson Mission.

2. At Major-General MacDougall's request, I reported at GHQ Home Forces on 5th June, to explain the system which had been employed in the operations in Belgium and Northern France.

General MacDougall agreed that the question should be considered.

3. I have not had the opportunity of finding out what arrangements already exist for the collection and dissemination of information in this country, but some organization on the following lines might be found suitable for incorporating in the existing arrangements.

4. It is realised that time must elapse before a complete organization and full equipment can be established, but a great deal can be done at once by improvisation, by using motor cars in place of armoured vehicles, by the extensive use of motor cycles and by making use of local resources. One essential is efficient wireless equipment, without which the scheme would be of little use.

5. The object of the organization is the production of accurate information at GHQ Home Forces and at the appropriate RAF Headquarters regarding the points at which enemy attacks are being made on Great Britain, the scale of those attacks and their subsequent progress.

6. The organization might consist of a headquarters, located at GHQ Home Forces, and four reconnaissance and liaison units, one located in South-East England, one in East Anglia, one north of the Humber and one in reserve in the Midlands.

7. Each of the four units would consist of:
    (i) Headquarters
    (ii) Intelligence Troop (of six to ten officers mounted on motorcycle combinations, with despatch riders)
    (iii) Motor Cycle Squadron (of six troops each of three armed motorcycle combinations, with a proportion of solo motorcyclists)
    (iv) Armoured Squadron (of six troops, each of three scout cars, one with a wireless set, one with a Bren gun and one with an anti-tank rifle)
    (v) Signal Squadron, with four mobile No. 9 sets for communication to GHQ and RAF, five or six mobile No. 11 sets for use of the Intelligence Troop and Motor Cycle Squadron and a No. 11 anchor set for working to the armoured troops.

8. Other information headquarters and units could be supplied with information under arrangements to be made locally, but the main object of getting information from the battlefield to

GHQ and the RAF in the shortest possible time should not be lost sight of. The reconnaissance units therefore should be controlled by their own headquarters which would be located at GHQ and operating under the orders of the C-in-C.

9. I have taken the liberty of sending copies of this minute and the report to General MacDougall.

7th June, 1940.<br>
Lt-Colonel,<br>
General Staff.

This is the first known letter to the War Office requesting the formation of a new elite signals reconnaissance unit.

Hopkinson's request obviously met with serious consideration and enthusiasm for only a week later the following letter, written by the Chief of the General Staff of the British Expeditionary Force in support of Hopkinson's ideas, was on its way to the Under Secretary of State at the War Office.

Subject:- Hopkinson Mission. Re-mobilization.
GR/7/1/SD.
The Under Secretary of State
The War Office (DMO & P, MO 4)

It is understood that Lieut.Colonel Hopkinson has already been instructed to assemble the survivors of his Mission with a view to their future employment. During the recent operations, the Mission was of considerable value, not only in its original purpose of obtaining information for the RAF, but also as a reconnaissance and liaison unit working for GHQ. It is considered desirable that a unit of this kind should be included in the new battle order of the BEF and the following proposals are put forward on the assumption that War Office approval will be given for Lieut. Colonel Hopkinson's detachment to be armed and equipped for despatch to France at an early date.

The task of obtaining and transmitting ground intelligence for the RAF Headquarters in the field – the task for which the mission was designed – should be accepted as a BEF responsibility. The work should be carried out by a military reconnaissance and liaison unit, with perhaps one RAF officer attached, and not a mixed RAF and Army mission. Such a unit would carry out similar tasks for GHQ, by whom it would be controlled and administered. RAF requirements would be met by a close liaison between HQ, BAFF and the officer commanding the unit.

The unit should be known as 'GHQ Reconnaissance Unit'. The withdrawal of the RAF Mission would necessitate certain additions to the establishment of the unit. Certain modifications would have to be made as a result of recent experience. Provision must also be made for expansion or for the creation of further units as may become necessary. This a question requiring further consideration. In the meantime, and in order to avoid delay, it is suggested that re-mobilization should be proceeded with at once, on the basis of the existing establishment for No. 11 (Hopkinson) Military Mission.

In order to enable the unit to operate in France at the earliest possible moment, a high degree of priority must be given for the supply of its personnel and equipment. For certain items improvisation must be accepted.

If this proposal is approved, it is suggested that Air Ministry be asked for their concurrence, and that Lieut. Colonel Hopkinson should deal with the War Office direct.

GHQ (S.D)<br>
Chief of the General Staff,<br>
Nobel House<br>
British Expeditionary Force.<br>
13th June, 1940<br>
<br>
Copies to:- The War Office (MO 7)<br>
Lieut Colonel Hopkinson

Hopkinson's proposals were taken very seriously indeed and he was promptly asked to reconstitute Phantom as No. 1 GHQ Reconnaissance Unit, as part of the defence forces under the direct command of GHQ Home Forces. The unit was formed at Lechlade in Gloucestershire from the nucleus of the Hopkinson Mission.

Initial training began immediately. Obviously, as with any new unit, teething troubles occurred, but these were quickly resolved and Hopkinson's unit rapidly began to take shape. So much so, that from the following secret memo in War Office records, we can see that the Army chiefs were impressed enough, only five months later, to question whether, perhaps, the same methods of reconnaissance and information gathering could be employed by the Army in general.

## SECRET

## THE COLLECTION AND TRANSMISSION OF INFORMATION IN BATTLE

1. The object of this paper is to examine the possibilities of applying to the Army in general the methods employed by GHQ Home Forces in obtaining information through its GHQ Reconnaissance Unit.

2. The ever-increasing speed with which the military situation changes in warfare of today demands corresponding acceleration in the means of collecting and transmitting information. In the British Army, this demand is not being satisfied. Experience in the Belgian campaign and in exercises during the past five months has shown that commanders of formations do not get the accurate timely information which they so badly need; neither does the RAF get the information required to enable it adequately to support the Army. There is no doubt whatever about that.

3. The root of the difficulty, of course, is to be found in the system of expecting troops and staffs, whose main preoccupation lies in the direction of the enemy, to send back information through the usual channels, in the course of which it is sifted, collated, edited and otherwise delayed at each stage of its journey until eventually it arrives at its destination too late to be of any real use. Delays can be reduced by various means but this system can never completely satisfy our requirements. Some form of short-circuiting, with all its disadvantages, must be resorted to.

4. The problem, so far as the GHQ Home Forces is concerned, has been partially solved by superimposing on the normal system an independent information collecting service provided by the GHQ Reconnaissance Unit, equipped with armoured and un-armoured reconnaissance troops, liaison officers, mobile wireless sets and aircraft. The sole duty of this unit is to send to the Commander-in-Chief the very latest news of events in the more important sectors of the battle field. Its role might be compared with that of an RAF Reconnaissance Squadron operating under orders of GHQ. A note on this unit is attached at Appendix 'A'.

5. The information obtained by this means from headquarters of formations and units, from troops already in contact with the enemy, from the RAF, from civilian sources and from actual reconnaissance of the enemy's dispositions and movements, must, of course, be used with discretion. It is unfiltered

information. Much of it may have to be discarded as unconfirmed reports. Some of it may enable events to be anticipated. Occasional items may be of great value.

6. If this is true, then the information should be made available at destinations other than GHQ. Arrangements have already been made to enable headquarters of the Corps concerned to intercept it. But a much wider distribution would be made effective by broadcasting reports in cipher from high power transmitters and intercepting them on small portable receivers – a method already in use in the *'Beetle'*.

7. Furthermore, if this system, notwithstanding its limitations, is considered sound, then its application to the Army as a whole seems to be justified. This would involve the creation of new units or the conversion of existing units to the new role. It is suggested that a further five units, similar to the existing one, be raised for employment under GHQ Home Forces and that reconnaissance units for the Army overseas be raised on a scale of one per two divisions of The Field Army.

8. The characteristics, generally speaking, should be the same as those of the existing unit. That is to say, it should be designed for reconnaissance only, not for 'protective reconnaissance'; it should contain a high proportion of officers and small armoured vehicles fitted with wireless. An organization into five reconnaissance groups is suggested and a high-power transmitter for broadcasting information must be added to each unit. A liberal allotment of small portable receiving sets could best be held by the Unit for issue to formations. (In the organization for Home Forces, the broadcasting portion of the existing 'Beetle' system might well be absorbed into the new organization.)

9. The six reconnaissance units at home might be disposed roughly as follows:

No. 1 Unit: West of England, South Wales
No. 2 Unit: Hampshire, Sussex and Kent
No. 3 Unit: East Anglia
No. 4 Unit: Lincolnshire, Yorkshire, Durham & Northumberland
No. 5 Unit: Scotland
No. 6 Unit: Ireland

With the exception, perhaps, of the Units in Scotland and Ireland, GHQ should retain control of each unit. The success of the system depends largely on its freedom to operate, collect its information and distribute it, unhampered by the necessity of obtaining approval from commanders and staffs who are preoccupied with more important matters. In other words, the intention is to extract information from the 'usual channel' and to feed information into it, but not to be absorbed by it.

Control by GHQ could be exercised by the Intelligence or Operations Staffs. The setting up of a separate organization to control the four Units is not considered necessary.

The headquarters of each Unit would be suitably located in its area, the site being chosen with a view to good conditions for broadcasting. The five reconnaissance groups of a unit would obtain their information and transmit it to Unit HQ, as is done in the existing GHQ Reconnaissance Unit. At Unit HQ the information would be edited, encyphered and broadcast. It would be intercepted by headquarters and units, including GHQ, decyphered and delivered.

Control of the four units operating under GHQ would be exercised by direct wireless links between GHQ and the unit. These links would be used for controlling and issuing orders to the reconnaissance units and would be available for transmitting information in the event of failure of the broadcasting system.

Units in Scotland and Ireland could probably best be controlled by the Army Commanders concerned.

10. The Middle East, where distances may be greater and communications less developed, seems to provide even bigger opportunities for the useful employment of reconnaissance units of this type. The composition of the unit might be similar, and provision on a scale of one per two divisions seems suitable. The system of broadcasting information might well be employed. The question of control is a matter for further consideration. Wireless sets of a longer range might have to be substituted.

11. Various objections are apparent in the proposed scheme.

    (a) It may be said that the unit cannot fight for its information. That is true. It has little or no offensive power. It can, however, use its armoured protection to enable an officer to reconnoitre as far as and around the areas occupied by the enemy. It can also get into close touch with troops already in contact with the enemy.

    (b) The existing GHQ Reconnaissance Unit consists of selected personnel. This is a decided advantage. Additional units would to some extent forfeit this advantage. They would be raised by converting existing units of another type or from training and holding units. A long period of training would be necessary, particularly for wireless operators. This, of course, is true.

(c) The third and biggest objection to the proposal lies in the fact that, though much of the information will originate at the various headquarters, on occasions, military information will be broadcast on the responsibility of a Lieut Colonel commanding a reconnaissance unit without its having been seen by the formation commander concerned, without its having been collated at a formation headquarters and without any expression of opinion by any commander. The proposal may not commend itself in some quarters for these reasons. But similar objections never appear to have been made to the system by which an aeroplane pilot reports direct to headquarters of higher formations, and there is a distinct similarity between the two systems.

In any case, the recipient of the information will be fully aware of the conditions under which it has been obtained and can attach to it whatever weight it seems to justify. Again this information is only intended to be supplementary. It will be confirmed or refuted sooner or later through the usual channels.

Above all, the old system has failed, and something must be done to meet the deficiency. The proposal put forward does provide a possible solution.

24th October, 1940.

The following report from War Office records shows the organization and duties of Phantom as originally laid out:

### GHQ RECONNAISSANCE UNIT

Notes on the organization and duties of the Unit.

The GHQ, Reconnaissance Unit originated in a small reconnaissance detachment, known as 'The *Hopkinson* Mission' which was formed in France in November 1939 for the purpose of obtaining information regarding the progress of the battle and of transmitting that information direct by wireless to HQ, BAFF and to GHQ, BEF. The Mission carried out these duties during the invasion of Belgium and France. On return to England it was reconstituted as the GHQ, Reconnaissance Unit under GHQ, Home Forces.

The purpose of the Unit is to provide the Commander-in-Chief with an additional means of obtaining information concerning events which are of sufficient importance to require the employment of reconnaissance troops reporting direct to GHQ instead of through the normal channels. The Unit is not intended to replace the normal means of reconnaissance and the normal flow of information. It is designed to enable GHQ to obtain the information regarding certain events on the battlefield more quickly than the normal channels could provide it. It should be noted that the reports received at GHQ by this means are unfiltered and contain information on which Commanders of formations may not have had the opportunity of expressing their views. The role of the Unit may be compared with that of an RAF, Reconnaissance Squadron operating under the orders of GHQ.

The Unit is organized into a Headquarters and six Reconnaissance Groups. Five of these Groups each consists of four subaltern officers patrols. Each patrol is composed of an officer on a motorcycle, an armoured Scout Car with a No. 11 wireless set, two despatch riders and a truck for stores. The sixth Group has no Scouts Cars or Wireless; it consists of a headquarters and four motorcycle patrols commanded by subalterns. The headquarters of each Group is connected by wireless to units Headquarters situated at GHQ. The remainder of the unit consists of a small intelligence and liaison section at Unit Headquarters, a pigeon loft, administrative personnel and a flight of three aeroplanes. The Unit's code name is: 'PHANTOM'.

The Reconnaissance Groups and, to a lesser extent, the Officer's Patrols are administratively self contained and can operate for long periods up to a distance of four hundred miles from the Unit to the Group and fifty miles from the Group to the Patrol.

The methods employed in obtaining information include actual reconnaissance on the ground, liaison with formations and units, visits to RN and RAF headquarters and personal contact with Civil Defence organizations. A Reconnaissance Group entering a Corps Area will send an officer to Corps Headquarters to report the proposed action of his group and to inform the staff on which wireless frequencies and call signs the group will be operating. This officer will give a copy of the Unit cipher to the Corps Staff, so that, if desired the Unit's wireless reports may be intercepted. The Reconnaissance Group will keep the closest possible touch with formations and Units and will ensure that any information it may obtain is made as widely available as possible.

The aeroplane flight is employed purely for intercommunication purposes within the unit. The aircraft are not yet fitted with wireless. Contact with groups and patrols is made either by landing the aircraft or by message dropping and ground signalling.

Although light aircraft are mentioned as being part of Phantom's organization in the above report they were, in fact, never used. The normal method of air to ground reconnaissance was carried out by Army Air Reconnaissance and the Royal Air Force.

CHAPTER VI

# The Battle Of Britain

*'It will take between a fortnight and a month to smash the enemy Air Force.'*

GENERAL STAPF, GERMAN HIGH COMMAND,

SPRING 1940.

Hitler, now the master of Poland, Norway, Denmark, Holland, Belgium and France, could not believe that Great Britain, with her forty-six million people, would continue to fight. But fight they did. Winston Churchill's voice was the voice of the nation when he announced Britain's determination to resist the Nazi onslaught.

The only parts of Great Britain that the enemy ever occupied were the Channel Islands of Jersey, Guernsey, Alderney and Sark. The decision to demilitarize these islands - which lie only a few miles from the French coast - had been taken by Churchill's government early in the month of June 1940. There was no way that they could be defended without huge loss to civilian life.

Many British-born nationals rushed to leave their island homes, crowding onto the few available boats in order to reach the British mainland before the inevitable arrival of the Germans. When the invaders came on the 30th June, white flags of surrender were flying over British soil. Thousands of leaflets had been dropped by the *Luftwaffe* ordering a peaceful surrender. White crosses were to be painted on the airport runway, the main square and a car park. If these signs were not observed then the German's threat of heavy bombardment would be carried out. The governor-general of the islands had no choice but to yield to the enemy's demands. When he met the German High Command terms and conditions for the surrender of the islands to German occupation were agreed and signed. The occupation of the Channel Islands had begun and was to last for nearly five years.

The islands were turned into fortresses and a large underground hospital was built on Jersey. This was to take care of the German casualties of war who were being ferried there from areas of conflict in Europe, and later from the Russian front. The fortifications and the hospital were built using thousands of enforced workers and slave labour, including prisoners-of-war, many of whom perished on these islands. A slave camp for eighteen thousand had been set up on Alderney.

Even today, visitors to the Channel Islands can see the large reinforced concrete gun emplacements erected by the Nazis, and can understand why they placed so much importance on flying the *Swastika* over British soil and the great propaganda coup that it achieved.

As early as the 14th May, 1940, Sir Anthony Eden, Secretary for War, broadcast an appeal inviting all able-bodied men between the ages of seventeen and sixty-five, and not already enlisted in the services, to join the Local Defence Volunteers. The response was overwhelming. Men, young and old, anxious to do all that they could to protect their country, besieged police stations all across the land offering their services. Everyone of them determined to be well-drilled and armed ready for the invasion that was now deemed imminent. Many of these men were veterans of the First World War, and some even of the Boer Wars of the late nineteenth and early twentieth centuries.

Within five months, 1,700,000 men had stepped forward. Armed at the outset with only a meagre assortment of weapons - a few rifles and shotguns, knives, home-made coshes, broom handles and pitchforks - these volunteers were more than willing to use them to the end if the occasion arose.

An LDV training school was set up at Osterley Park, near London. This was run by Tom Wintringham, the former commander of the British volunteers in Spain who fought as part of the International Brigade against General Franco's Fascists in the Spanish Civil War of 1936.

Subsequently, the LDV, on Churchill's insistence, was renamed the 'Home Guard'. With their newly-supplied uniforms these men, once described as 'a motley crew, but handy with molotov cocktails', were quickly knocked into a well-equipped home army.

One spin-off of the Home Guard was the Auxiliary Unit. An employer in the early 1960's of one of the authors, Andy Parlour, was a member of the Home Guard in Essex. Albert Cocks tells us in his book, *'Churchill's Secret Army 1939-45'*, how he became a member of the Auxiliary Unit.

'Quite by surprise I was invited to attend a secret meeting. Arriving at the residence of a local schoolmaster, I found I was one of a half a dozen lads of the village there. We were ushered into a room where we were introduced to two gentlemen in military uniform and by their bits and bobs it was obvious they were high ranking officers of the regular army. They soon put us at our ease by explaining that they contemplated forming an underground resistance movement, a sort of private commando force. We were told in the event of this taking place it would be necessary for those taking part to conform to the Official Secrets Act. It would also be necessary for us to know every local hedge, ditch, culvert, drainage system; every inch of local moors, railway routes, bridges and all of this to cover a five mile radius of one's place of residence. We were informed that previous to this meeting each one of us had been recommended by our commanding officer in the Home Guard plus various other sources not divulged, and being locally born and bred country boys we were considered fit and proper persons.

We were conscious of the possibility of any enemy invasion, conscious also of the responsibility we were accepting, but the situation was critical and at that time one could not shirk any responsibilities, however unpleasant or difficult they may be.'

Although, thankfully, they were never actually called upon to take up arms against the Germans, the Home Guard and the Auxiliary Unit would, nevertheless, have posed a potent threat had the jackboot of the Nazi regime ever set foot on mainland Britain.

Back in Germany, Hitler still hoped that Britain would make peace but, should they refuse to do so, he had already set in action plans for the invasion. Operation *Sealion*, as it was known, was still only to be regarded as a last resort.

Meanwhile the *Luftwaffe*, under the command of *Reich-Marschall* Hermann Goering, was stepping up its offensive on coastal shipping around British shores. On the 10th July, 1940, they mounted their biggest attack to date on a convoy off the south-east coast. The RAF was quick to respond. Spitfires and Hurricanes immediately took to the skies and, although outnumbered by their adversaries, quickly won the day, driving off the attackers who only managed to hit one ship.

The first requirement for invasion was complete air superiority and Hitler's plans to destroy the RAF began in earnest in early August 1940. *General* Stapf, convinced of the *Luftwaffe*'s ability to master the skies, arrogantly declared, 'It will take between a fortnight and a month to smash the enemy Air Force'. How wrong he was.

What came to be known as the 'Battle of Britain' commenced with intense fury. The *Luftwaffe* began full-scale attacks on RAF bases and installations along the south coast and beyond. Many of these attacks were foreseen with the advent of early-warning systems such as radar stations, whose ability to spot the approach of enemy warplanes enabled many of our Spitfires and Hurricanes to scramble and be airborne in readiness to take on the *Luftwaffe* in the skies before they could reach their targets on the ground. All along the south coast of Britain the keen eyes of members of the Observer Corps gave valuable assistance in spotting and identifying the approach of all aircraft, be it friend or foe.

The Observer Corps, which had been founded in Kent in 1925, gave sterling service throughout the whole of the war and was, in fact, granted a 'Royal' prefix, being from the 9th April, 1941, officially renamed the Royal Observer Corps. In a broadcast made by Air Commodore Goddard in 1941, the Observer Corps' contribution to the air battle was again praised.

> *'Of all our air defences, I think the searchlight and balloon crews and the Observer Corps have about the most thankless tasks. No-one knows how much is owed to the balloon and searchlight men for the moral effect they exert on the enemy. We do know occasionally, when bits of aeroplane get washed ashore with cable wire twisted round them, that some balloon crew has earned a good night's sleep. We know, too, but less tangibly, the fending-off effect of our searchlights as well as their power to reveal the black Boche when he comes low enough. But do we all realise that the Observer Corps has been the foundation of our Fighter Defence? That Corps of veteran volunteers must have taken a quiet pride in their vital but little known part in the Battle of Britain.'*

The balloons referred to were the barrage balloons used as a deterrent against low-flying raiders; the cables of these moored balloons were excellent. Collision with one of the cables could rip off or very seriously damage the wing of any Service aircraft. In those days, the Balloon Barrage made accurate bombing of targets in misty weather or in low cloud too dangerous for anybody but a suicide raider. It earned the whole-hearted respect of both the German Stuka dive-bomber pilots and the low-flying hit-and-run fighters.

Unable to gain mastery of the skies, Goering turned his attentions to bombing civilian areas. His idea was to sap the morale of the British people and bomb them into surrender. This in fact had the counter-effect of stiffening their resolve.

On the 24th August, 1940, the *Luftwaffe* bombed London for the first time since the *Kaiser's* airships had attacked the capital in 1918. The next night Bomber Command retaliated by sending eighty-one aircraft to bomb targets in Berlin. And so the tit-for-tat raids went on.

But it was not Londoners who became the first British civilian victims of the Second World War. Earlier in the year, on Tuesday the 30th April, a stricken German bomber had crashed into the home of Dorothy and Frederick Gill in the south-east coastal resort of Clacton-on-Sea in Essex. Their home in the town's Victoria Road had been completely demolished and the couple killed outright. The German aircrew also perished and were buried with full military honours in Clacton's Burrs Road cemetery.

It was against the background of bombing and the fear of invasion at any time that the GHQ Reconnaissance Unit was being re-organized. Colonel Hopkinson, by September 1940, had amassed a band of forty-eight officers and 407 other ranks. Working under direct command of GHQ Home Forces, Phantom consisted initially of a headquarters and four scout car groups, a group being made up of four officer patrols. Each patrol had for its transport a Daimler scout car, a 15-cwt truck and three motorcycles, and could be self-supporting for forty-eight hours. The patrol, comprising an officer and six men, kept in contact with its group headquarters by wireless and despatch rider. The group headquarters then passed any relevant information through Regimental HQ to GHQ Home Forces.

The groups were deployed mainly in coastal regions and it was their task to determine any early signs of invasion and to pass this information on as quickly as possible. As early as June 1940, Hopkinson's officers and men were making reconnaissance reports of beaches throughout the country on which the Germans were likely to attempt a landing.

Lord Croft, Parliamentary Under-Secretary to the War Office, suggested that the enemy might attack frequently and at many points.

> 'We hope to get early information of his intentions but in this uncertain world, and under cover of dark nights, sea mist and fog, we must be ready for any emergency. For that reason it is essential that every possible landing place should be covered by fire-power.'

It was to this end that Phantom patrols were working diligently.

Pill-boxes and blockhouses constructed of reinforced concrete, barbed-wire entanglements, anti-tank obstacles, army lorries, tanks, artillery, machine gun nests and all the paraphernalia of land warfare began to make their appearance.

Andy Parlour's father, William, then a 27-year-old Lance Corporal with the Royal Sussex Regiment, was in charge of a bren-gun unit defending the airfield at Shoreham, near Brighton, where the regiment was based. The men were also employed on the sea-defences, helping to prepare forty-gallon drums filled with a highly-flammable mixture of petrol and paraffin. These were to be anchored to the sea bed by chain and would rise and lower with the tide flow. Thousands were put into place along the south coast where the German invasion, Operation *Sealion*, was thought most likely to take place. The idea was that when German landing craft reached the middle of these defences, fuses and tracer bullets would be fired to ignite these floating oil-drums and so '*Set the Channel on fire!*' would have been the order of the day. The results would have been devastating, inflicting tremendous casualties on the enemy.

Although the invasion could have come at any point around Britain's coast, intelligence reports stated that the most likely area, because of its close proximity to the continent, would be from Ramsgate in the east to Portsmouth in the west, with the main beachheads at Shoreham, Eastbourne, Hastings, Dungeness and Folkestone; Shoreham especially targeted for the large airfield facilities it would provide. (Intelligence were to be proved correct when, after the war, the plans for Operation *Sealion* were uncovered.)

Back in Germany, Hitler's tentative plans to fix the launch of Sealion for the third week in September were going ahead. He gathered considerable shipping in the German, Dutch, Belgian and French harbours all the way from Hamburg to Brest, with very large numbers of German troops awaiting the order to go aboard. But still he was reluctant to take the final step until the RAF had been all but wiped out. A large-scale operation by sea appeared to him to be extremely hazardous with the RAF still a potent force. At the same time he knew that he could not keep his ships waiting about indefinitely while every night they were being attacked by British bombers and often shelled by Royal Navy warships waiting in the Channel.

By the morning of the 17th, some twelve per cent of the Nazi invasion barges and transports had been damaged or destroyed and the German Navy was under no illusion about the fate of the remainder if Hitler were to order them to put to sea. His decision, announced that same afternoon, was recorded in the War Diary of the German Naval Staff as follows:

> 'The enemy air force is still by no means defeated; on the contrary it shows increasing activity. The weather situation as a whole does not permit us to expect a period of calm. The Fuhrer has therefore decided to postpone OPERATION SEALION indefinitely.'

Two days later, on the 19th September, on Hitler's instructions, the great invasion fleet began dispersing to safer areas, without even attempting so much as a single raid on the coast of Britain.

It is remarkable therefore that on the 4th October, when Hitler met Mussolini at the Brenner Pass, he declared, 'The war is won. The rest is only a question of time.' Amazingly, only eight days later, the *Fuhrer* was to issue orders to abandon Operation *Sealion* altogether.

'*Never in the field of human conflict was so much owed by so many to so few.*' These were the words used by Churchill when he addressed the House of Commons on the 20th August, 1940, praising the skill and courage of the men of the RAF. By now the planes of the RAF were being flown by men of many nationalities. Those of the British Empire were joined by pilots from all over the free world, including flyers from the occupied countries of Europe, and American nationals who, although their country was not directly involved in the war, felt the fight against the fascist dictatorship of Hitler and Mussolini was well worth the sacrifice.

The few had won the 'Battle of Britain' and now the second winter of the war was beginning. The Luftwaffe, driven from the daylight skies of Britain, concentrated all their efforts on night bombing. Hitler's aim was to flatten London.

The cruel, wanton, indiscriminate bombings of London had reached a crescendo on the 7th and 8th September with mass attacks believed to have been directed by Goering himself. German planes had swarmed over the British capital dropping bombs, incendiaries and land-mines at an alarming rate. The densely populated East End had suffered most. There the docks and railway yards had been set ablaze and private dwellings demolished. Over four thousand fire-fighting appliances from all over London had been brought into service to tackle the blazes.

Now the attacks were to continue throughout the long

autumn and winter of 1940/41. Historic landmarks were devastated. The church of St Giles Cripplegate, which had survived the Great Fire of 1666, and where Oliver Cromwell had married, was amongst those obliterated and so too was the Church of St Clement Dane, the children's church which sang of oranges and lemons. The ancient Guildhall, built in 1411 was completely burnt out and lovely old buildings in the Temple were disfigured. The House of Lords and the Tate Gallery both received direct hits, but fortunately did not suffer extensive damage. Three bombs hit Buckingham Palace, but again no serious damage was sustained, and St Paul's Cathedral was saved only by the bravery of the Bomb Disposal Section who courageously removed a huge time-bomb from its west end.

Another cathedral, that tragically did not survive the ravages of the Nazi bombers, was the beautiful fourteenth century Coventry Cathedral. On the night of the 14th/15th November the enemy dropped 450 tons of bombs on this great Midland city and razed it to the ground, boasting that it was a reprisal raid for British attacks on Munich.

And so the attacks went on. Targets in Hamburg, Bremen, Berlin, Emden and Rotterdam were on the receiving end of the RAF's bombs, while Bristol, Birmingham, Manchester, Liverpool, Portsmouth and, yet again, Southampton were among the major victims of Goering's bombers. But still Britain would not be defeated and stood defiant, its people stoically accepting the enemy bombing as night after night they sought the safety of underground shelters. The *Blitz*, which had begun in the summer of 1940, continued until the night of the 10th May, 1941, when an all-out attack on London by over five hundred bombers marked the last raid of the '*Spring Blitz*' of 1941.

Nearly forty thousand people had died in the air raids on Britain but still the British people would not be beaten into surrender. The fight went on.

CHAPTER VII

# The Postman Calls

*'We were soon to learn what PHANTOM was all about and why we were told - WE ARE SOMETHING SPECIAL.'*

RON EATON, SPRING 1941.

Not much has been written about Phantom in the years since the war and it still remains very much an unheard of regiment, even by those who benefited from its work at the time. The stories that have been told have, on the whole, come from officers, but before we come to some of their recollections we would like to relate the experiences of two young men who found themselves members of this elite unit.

In 1940, 26-year-old Henry 'Harry' Binge was working for the upholsterers Greaves and Thomas in Clapton, East London, a job his uncle had secured for him, starting as an apprentice, ten years earlier. On leaving school, Harry had found himself employment working at a furniture shop for 12/6d a week, but all he seemed to do was *'shift furniture about'*, so, fed up with this, he joined a company that specialised in billboard advertising where he was responsible for *'mixing the inks and filling in the colours'*. Not finding this work very fulfilling either, when his uncle managed to secure him a position at the upholstery firm he himself worked for Harry jumped at the chance.

In May the phoney war had come to an end with Hitler's invasion of Holland, so Harry knew that sooner rather than later his call-up papers would be dropping on the doormat.

Working on the same floor at Greaves and Thomas was a young man, six years Harry's junior, Ron Eaton. One day Ron turned up at work with the news that he had received his call-up papers that very morning, only to discover that Harry's had arrived too. These two young men were both to report to the Blandford Forum army camp in Dorset to commence training on the 24th June, 1940.

When the due date arrived, Harry and Ron, having bade farewell to their families and friends, set off. Carrying their suitcases and with their rail passes in hand, they made their way with some trepidation to Waterloo Station where they were to board the Dorset train. Excited but at the same time apprehensive about what lay ahead of them, the two workmates settled down to the journey ahead.

On arrival at Blandford Forum Station they, and a few other conscripts who had joined them at various stations along the way, were met by a recruiting sergeant who piled them and their belongings into an army truck for the short run to the 309 Infantry Training Centre that was to be their home for the next five or six months. Here Harry and Ron were to join the Royal Berkshire Regiment.

In Ron's own words,

> 'Blandford was the usual basic training unit that was supposed to make you a soldier in three months. After the novelty wore off, it was a pretty humdrum existence. The only exciting day was on the firing range which was situated on the south coast. We had finished our firing and were sitting around on the grass when a plane came in from the sea, losing height and with smoke coming out from one of its two engines. We suddenly realised that it was a German Dornier Bomber and we hit the ground as it passed just to the left of us at about a height of a hundred feet and crashed into the next field. We were not allowed to go to the crash-site but we were later told that the crew miraculously all survived, although with serious injuries.
>
> One morning towards the end of our basic three month training, the sergeant asked the parade for volunteers - all those with driving licences to step forward. By this time we had learned that these kinds of requests usually meant that you found yourself cleaning latrines, working in the cookhouse, or worse. This was army sergeants' humour. Harry and I looked at each other and decided to take a chance. We stepped forward along with two others and were delighted to find that we were being transferred to the Motor Transport Section. Harry became a truck driver and I became a DR (Despatch Rider) on a motorcycle. Shortly after this, the guys we had trained with were sent to the Royal Norfolk Regiment and eventually to Singapore. I heard later that they had been captured by the Japanese. There but for the Grace of God go us!'

Harry was already a driver before the war, having passed his test in 1937, so driving a truck was easy for him. But it was not only trucks that he was required to drive, he also found himself acting as chauffeur to the top brass. Harry recalls, 'We didn't really have anything to do with the infantry after this, we were driving all the time. It was a cushy job, we didn't even have to wear army boots, soft shoes were the order of the day.'

Unfortunately for them, their stay at the MT Section was soon over. In November 1940, Harry and Ron were transferred to the Norwich Barracks, the home of the Royal Norfolk Regiment. 'Life at Norwich was regular army,' recalls Ron. 'Dress inspections before you could leave to go out on the town, kit inspections, barrack room inspections, and the usual route marches.'

'And freezing cold,' adds Harry. 'Crawling about in the ice and snow. What a shock to the system after our time at Blandford. We were nearly on the verge of going AWOL (absent without leave),' he laughs, 'when we heard the rumour circulating that a new regiment was being formed. 'Cor blimey', I thought, 'anything's got to be better than this', so when the call went out for drivers and anyone with special trades, Ron and I again stepped forward and were accepted.'

After a short leave, during which time Harry returned to his widowed mother's home in Field Road, Walthamstow and Ron to his family in Leyton, they received their new papers and instructions. They were to report to Richmond in Surrey.

Ron recalls, 'We were a party of five that arrived at Richmond Station, four from the Royal Norfolks and a sergeant from the Signals Corps, Sergeant Charles McDevitt. McDevitt and I became friends from the day we met and were to meet again several times over the years, after the war and after his retirement from the Army. We were met at the station by an army truck driver who would take us to GHQ. The first thing we noticed was the patch sewn on his sleeve. A white 'P' on a black square. We asked him what it stood for and he replied, 'PHANTOM'. We looked at each other in some disbelief. That didn't seem the type of name a British army unit would be given. Our silence was answered by the truck driver with the comment , 'WE ARE SOMETHING SPECIAL'.'

By the end of January 1941, the GHQ Reconnaissance Unit had changed its name to the General Headquarters Liaison Regiment and its 'groups' had become 'squadrons'. Via a short stay at Kneller Hall in the Whitton/Twickenham area of Middlesex, it had moved its headquarters from Lechlade, Gloucestershire, to Richmond, Surrey. Why Richmond? Situated as it was on the western outskirts of London, within easy reach of the North and South Circular roads and access to all trunk roads, it was ideally placed for all logistical movements and for all squadrons wherever they were deployed. The Richmond region was not subject to heavy bombing, being on the extremities of London, and as such was considered a reasonably safe area. Its large park, which was firmly closed to civilians, was to become the regiment's home base and training ground. Richmond was also not far from the War Office and only a short distance from St Paul's School where the Home Forces' headquarters was based.

Harry's memories of their arrival at Richmond are of the way in which they were treated. He takes up the story from here.

*'We were taken to the Richmond Hill Hotel and shown inside. We entered the foyer of this large plush building where we were met by an NCO and noticed that he and all the other uniformed men were wearing the mysterious white 'P' on the black background shoulder patch. There seemed to be an air of relaxation, not like the usual hustle and bustle of an Army HQ. We stood there with our equipment and rifles and were told to our amazement, 'You won't need all that stuff here, put it in that room over there.' We were allocated our billets in nearby private houses and told to have a freshen up, a shower and a change of clothes, before reporting to the hotel's dining room, where there would be a hot meal waiting for us. And what a meal it was! Roast pork and all the trimmings. A bit different from the usual cookhouse food.*

*We were soon to learn what Phantom was all about and began to realise what the driver had meant when he'd said, 'We are something special'.'*

Training now began in earnest at GHQ Richmond. New techniques in radio wireless communications had to be learnt, but Morse Code was given top priority. This brilliant code, pioneered by Samuel Morse in the 1830's, had to be mastered. Hour upon hour, day after day, was spent memorising letters and numbers as dots and dashes until the trainees could transmit and receive messages in double quick time. This proved to be one of the most taxing of tasks.

Driving was another ability of the utmost importance and Richmond Park, once the hunting ground of kings, was the perfect location for practising driving skills.

One of the largest and most beautiful of the metropolitan parks, Richmond covers an area of 2,358 acres. It is undulating, hilly in parts, and consists of oak groves, plantations and great stretches of bracken fern, as well as numerous lakes and ponds. Once known as Sheen Chase, the park was enclosed in 1637 by Charles I for hunting purposes.

Its wooded areas were ideal for training Phantom drivers in all types of vehicles as these parts very much resembled the terrain that would be encountered by Phantom in France, Holland and Belgium after the invasion of Europe.

Daimler Dingo armoured cars, equally as fast going backwards as forwards, Ford and Bedford 15-cwt and four ton trucks and motorcycles were all there to be mastered. The trucks would be loaded with the normal Army supplies, plus vital communication equipment such as radios, aerials and masts, in fact everything that would be needed to sustain a patrol on a mission, to simulate battle conditions.

The skill to ride the BSA M20 and the more powerful Norton motorcycles at high speed across any type of ground had to be acquired. To be an army motorcycle despatch rider required the utmost daring and determination to ensure that the messages being carried got through to HQ. In the event of the breakdown of wireless communication for any reason, including the 'jamming' of radio signals by the enemy, the ability to get messages back quickly was essential. Many vital decisions in battle situations could rely heavily on Phantom's swift actions.

The DR with Phantom was often required to perform other duties, such as scouting ahead to seek out suitable locations in which to set up base and foraging for food and fresh water when the need arose.

One training exercise held near Pembroke Lodge, the Regimental HQ in Richmond Park, called for every patrol member to drive a 15-cwt truck through an imaginary minefield marked out by a series of pegs joined by white tape. Harry Binge recalls one such trial and the surprising results.

> 'Every man in the patrol had to be a competent wireless operator and a proficient driver, able to drive everyone else's vehicle. One day we all had to take part in trials in the park. I had to manoeuvre my truck through a narrow zig-zag corridor. I thought that I had done quite well, just touching one peg and slightly moving it sideways. After this our mechanical skills were put to the test. We had to leave our trucks and stand aside while something was done to immobilize them. I was lucky. I spotted the trouble with mine straight away. The mechanics had changed the plug leads over.
> 
> Some time later, Major David Niven, the actor, who was the commanding officer of Phantom's 'A' Squadron, hired the local cinema one Saturday morning and we all went along for a special showing of one of his films. 'Batchelor Mothers' it was called, co-

*starring the American dancer and actress Ginger Rogers. While we were all there, it was announced that they were going to hand out the prizes for the truck trials. I had almost forgotten about them. Anyway, I was surprised to hear my name called out. I had come second. I was asked to step up onto the stage where I was delighted to receive a medal from the founder of the regiment himself, Colonel Hopkinson, and Major David Niven.'*

The medal, in a presentation case which bears the makers name, F Phillips - Medallist - Aldershot, is of brass decorated in black and white enamel. The distinctive white 'P' of Phantom on the front has inscribed below it 'GHQ Liaison Regiment' and on the back are the words 'MT Driving Test. March 5th 1941. 2nd. Pte. H W Binge'.

*'I was always very proud of that,' boasts Harry. 'The chap who came first only got a bottle of Scotch.'*

Soon, the party of five who had arrived at Richmond together, Charles McDevitt, Harry, Ron and the two others, became part of the same patrol in the newly-formed 'G' Squadron, commanded by Major Terry A Watt who had come from the Life Guards. They had barely settled down as a squadron at Richmond before word came that 'G' was going to Northern Ireland, in case of an enemy landing in Eire. Here they would be attached to the British Army Garrison.

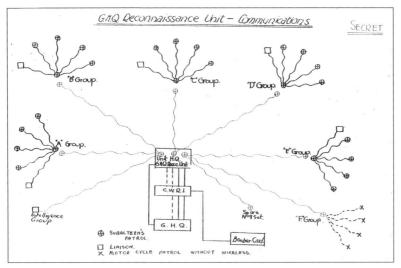

Diagram drawn by Lt Col Hopkinson, 1940.

Phantom in France 1940 (pre-Dunkirk). Lt-Col. Hopkinson with pipe & Lord Charles Banbury on right.

Phantom shoulder patch. Front and back of medal presented to Harry Binge March 1941.

309 Training Unit, Blandford. Ron Eaton *(left)* & Harry Binge *(right)*, 1940.

Trooper Henry 'Harry' Binge. Phantom ID 1941.

*l to r:* Capt Charles Webb with wife Biddy; Capt. Charles Stuart-Liberty with his wife; Capt. John Randall. 'G' Sqn, Northern Ireland, 1941/3.

Capt. John Randall on exercise with his patrol, Northern Ireland, 1941/3.

'G' Sqn mealtime, Northern Ireland, 1941/3.

'G' Sqn relaxing on exercise, Northern Ireland, 1941/3.

'G' Squadron Phantom in Northern Ireland, 1941/3.

Captain Mick Millar, Northern Ireland, 1941/43.

Captains John Sadoine (with dog, Trigger) and Mick Millar, Northern Ireland, 1941/3.

'E' Squadron Phantom, Edinburgh 1942. Pte John Campbell 6th from left. back row.

Radio Operator Adrian Bazar, 'F' Sqn, Phantom/SAS, 1942.

Captain John Randall & Trigger, Northern Ireland, 1941/43.

Suez, August 1943. Cpl Bill King *(left)* & 'Joe' Owens.

Len 'Joe' Owens at his radio, 1944.

CHAPTER VIII

# The reorganized Phantom returns to Europe

*'We must leave exactly on time...From now on everything must function to perfection.'*
BENITO MUSSOLINI, ITALY'S FASCIST DICTATOR,
SEPTEMBER 1939.

Benito Mussolini, the Prime Minister and Dictator of Italy since 1922, first took Italy into the war in June 1940. He had promised his Axis Power partner, Hitler, that he would enter the war on the 5th June but, despite his pleas, Hitler would not allow Mussolini to join him in the fight for France, rejecting his help because he wanted a complete German victory over France. Mussolini was determined to snatch some of the spoils of Hitler's victories and to fulfil his dream of turning the Mediterranean Sea into an Italian lake. After the fall of Paris, Hitler welcomed Italy's participation in the war for Europe.

Italy was already quite a power in North and East Africa. Libya had been under Italian rule since 1912 and in 1935 Mussolini's Fascist troops had marched into Ethiopia, forcing the *Emperor* Haile Selassie to flee his homeland and to seek exile in England. (Here the *Emperor* lived in Bath, assuming the name of Mr Smith for fear of attempts on his life.) On the 7th August, 1940, Italians crossed over the Ethiopian border into British Somaliland with tanks, artillery and aircraft. Despite resistance by the Camel Corps, made up of British Empire troops, the towns of Hargeisa and Zeila were soon captured and by the 19th the capital, Berbera, was to fall. For sixteen days six thousand Imperial troops had fought gallantly against thirty thousand Italians before being forced to withdraw.

Mussolini now turned his attentions towards Egypt.

Britain, by treaty rights, maintained small armed forces in Egypt, as she also did in Palestine, Iraq and other territories in the Middle East, over all of which General Archibald Wavell, one of the most noble-hearted of men, was Commander-in-Chief.

The Middle East, with its great oil-fields, its control over the sea, air and land routes to the Indies and Australasia and its close proximity to politically sensitive areas, was of immense importance to Britain and the lands of the Commonwealth and South-east Europe who, after the fall of France in June, faced the enormous strength of the Nazis and Fascists alone.

While the bulk of the British Army, scantily armed with old weapons after Dunkirk, hourly awaited the expected German invasion of England, only a small force of thirty-six thousand men stood guard in Egypt.

On the 12th September, the Italian *Marshal* Graziani, hoping to add Egypt to Italy's crown, crossed the frontier with about a hundred thousand men, supported by an air force greatly outnumbering that of Britain. He set up camp at Sidi Barrani, within the frontier but still some seventy miles from the main British positions. At the same time, Mussolini took the decision to further enter the European war by invading Greece. This was much to the annoyance of Hitler who regarded it as a grave strategic error, laying open as it did, to a great extent, Italy's Libyan flank to British counter-attack. Hitler himself favoured a further advance into Egypt to seize the British naval base at Alexandria.

Mussolini, however, would not be swayed by Hitler's objections and, in late October 1940, the Italian invaders, operating from Albania, began their advance into Greece, only to be driven back over the border to where they had begun four weeks earlier, by the Greek Army. On the 22nd November, after a great Greek victory at Koritza, Albania's largest town where the Italian headquarters was situated, many prisoners and guns were taken. These weapons were soon to be used against their previous owners. The Greek Army was far hardier and better able to hold its own in the mountains and snows than the Italians were.

Back in North Africa, the British troops, superior in morale, equipment and training, launched an attack on the Italians in the Western Desert. Under the command of Lieutenant-General O'Connor, a brilliant but unconventional Irish-born leader, they attacked Graziani's base at Sidi Barrani, taking thirty-eight thousand prisoners and putting the remaining Italians to flight, pushing them back over the Egyptian border into Libya. By February 1941 the British and Commonwealth troops had taken not only the seaport of Derna but also the major ports of Tobruk and Benghazi, very important conquests. The RAF's bombing of Italy's bases in Libya, that had started at the beginning of January, greatly contributed to the Allied army's success.

A week later Rommel's *Afrika Korps* arrived in Tripoli, but more of Rommel later.

In Berlin on the 19th February, 1941, Hitler issued a warning to Greece to end the war with Italy or face Germany fighting alongside the Italians. King George I of Greece (who was in fact William, the third son of Britain's late King Edward VII and grandfather to our present Queen Elizabeth's husband Prince Philip, Duke of Edinburgh) did not heed Hitler's warning.

Britain, who in 1939 had given a guarantee of support to Greece in the event of it being invaded, had in the winter of 1940 sent what aid she could, including a Phantom Group.

Sir Winston Churchill had sent the following message of support to the Greeks: 'We will give you all the help in our power. We fight a common foe and will share a united victory.'

The Phantom Group which was chosen by Lieut-Col Hopkinson to go to Greece was 'A', then commanded by Major Miles Reid who had joined them from the Royal Engineers. Major Miles Reid had fought throughout the First World War, had rejoined in 1939 and served as a Liaison Officer with the French during the battles in Belgium. 'A', although as yet not fully trained, was undoubtedly more prepared than any of the other Groups. Its objective, according to Hoppy's directive, was to provide GHQ Middle East with accurate and up-to-date information regarding operations in which the Greek Army was engaged and the Group was to repeat its messages to Regimental HQ in Great Britain for transmission to the War Office. Phantom needed to have the maximum possible freedom of movement in this theatre of war and access to formations and units of the Greek Army to carry out its task. This it would prove to achieve with unparalleled success.

There was great excitement at headquarters Richmond as Phantom prepared to return to Europe for the first time since Dunkirk. The Group, with Major Reid, who had been based at Chilham Castle in Kent, sailed from Liverpool on the 13th November, 1940. When they arrived in Alexandria, Major Reid added 'non-desert worthy' scout cars to his tally of vehicles that he had brought with him before continuing on to Cairo and from there, hopefully, to Greece. When they arrived in Cairo it transpired that no-one had been informed of their coming and that no-one even knew who Phantom was. An interview was hastily arranged between Major Reid and Field-Marshal Wavell who, believing in flexible military thinking, approved the plan of Phantom's support in Greece. But first he insisted on a brief period in the desert to gain experience.

While with General O'Connor's Western Desert Force, Phantom soon learnt that the wireless scts that it had been provided with were not suitable for use in the desert so, while O'Connor and his troops were pushing back the Italians westwards, Reid and his men returned eastwards to Alexandria to modify their radio equipment. After its problems had been ironed out, Phantom Group 'A' finally arrived in Athens at the end of December 1940.

Hitler, in carrying out his earlier threat to Greece, signed his directive No. 25, the simultaneous invasion of Greece and Yugoslavia, in March 1941.

By the 17th April, Yugoslavia had fallen and Prince Paul, the Yugoslav regent, signed a pact with the Axis having seen his neighbour, Bulgaria, accept German occupation two months previously and both Bulgaria and Turkey also sign a non-aggression pact under German pressure.

Despite this, stiff resistance to the German occupation of Yugoslavia continued by the partisans under the command of *Marshal* Tito, who would never succumb to the control of Hitler's forces and after the war would, in fact, become Yugoslavia's first Communist Prime Minister in 1945.

Now Greece was in grave danger. German troops had crossed the Greek border to join up with their Italian Fascist allies who were pressing hard against Greek, British, Australian and New Zealand troops. The Phantom patrol that was by now in Eastern Macedonia flashed the first news of the German invasion, code named 'Marita', on April 6th using the agreed code words 'BULGE-BOCHE'. The Greeks had fought valiantly against the Italian army, having held out since October the previous year, but now against the combined enemies their task was impossible.

Meanwhile, Major Reid's Phantom Squadron, as it was now known instead of Group, was playing a major role in communications. Many vital decisions were made and battle plans laid on information supplied by Phantom. This information included enemy troop and vehicle movements as well as the Allied forces' battle positions and exactly where the action was taking place. Another important task undertaken by Phantom was to ascertain the number of enemy prisoners-of-war taken and their regiment identification. This enabled Command to calculate the remaining strength of the enemy forces and so deploy their own men accordingly. Co-operation with the RAF and the small but brave Greek Air Force in laying down the bomb-line was essential to continued air support.

Despite every brave effort by the Allied forces, Greece was soon surrounded. German troops were well-established on the Bulgarian frontier and Albania was in the hands of the Italians once again. Now that Yugoslavia had fallen, the Allied forces had nowhere to retreat except the sea. Operation Demon, the evacuation of British, Australian, New Zealand and Polish troops, began on the 24th April, the day after the Greek Army surrendered to the German and Italian invaders. The evacuation from eight small ports continued for six days. In all, nearly fifty-one thousand troops were taken under strong naval escort to Crete. Again, reminiscent of Dunkirk, heavy weapons, trucks and aircraft had to be immobilized and abandoned.

On the 26th, Major Reid and his Phantom detachment, consisting of Sgt Averill and seven men, while playing a paramount part in the safe evacuation of troops from Greece, found themselves in a very tricky situation. With German parachutists landing all around them, and realising the futility of trying to maintain wireless links, they took up arms against the enemy. Heavily out-numbered, they fought long and hard before, running critically low on ammunition, Major Reid took the difficult decision to surrender, but not before destroying all their equipment, wireless sets, papers, maps and code-books, to prevent confidential information from falling into enemy hands.

Two Phantom members, tragically, died as a result of the fighting. Private James Donald Anderson and Private Francis Bowen Beardsall were attempting to drag a box of ammunition to their position when they were seen by the enemy and were fired on. Twenty-one–year-old Anderson, who had joined Phantom from the Royal Army Medical Corps, was killed outright, and Beardsall, 28, who had come from the Leicestershire Regiment, died as a result of his injuries on the 29th May while in captivity.

The men of another Phantom patrol, along with their officer, Captain Hamar, had better luck. They managed to make their way down to the coast and board a boat to safety.

Major Reid's Phantom Squadron had played a very brave and important role in Greece and many valuable lessons had been learnt during its operations there. These lessons were later to prove beneficial when Phantom, in conjunction with Montgomery's 'J' Service, the Eighth Army's own liaison detachment, was in action in the North African Campaign. Amongst these lessons learnt was the very important discovery that different wireless sets were required to operate under different conditions. Also, the need to short cut the method of wireless communications was essential to get the messages back to command headquarters as quickly as possible, partly to overcome the problem of the enemy jamming the air-waves. More use was also to be made of motorcycle despatch riders.

At Major Reid's request a second detachment of Phantom had been prepared to join him in Greece. This Group, consisting of five officers and fifty men, set sail from London on the 19th March, 1941, but, by the time they arrived in Egypt, Greece had fallen. With no specific task, 'H' as 'A' was now officially re-designated, was left very much to its own devices. Signal training continued and, for a time, this section of Phantom became more of a long range signals reconnaissance unit than the liaison squadron it was intended to be.

Back at Phantom's headquarters in Richmond, its progress in the Mediterranean had been closely monitored by its commanding officer, Lieut-Col. Hopkinson. A new 'A' Squadron was in the process of being formed and the newly-created 'G' was on its way to Northern Ireland.

CHAPTER IX

# Phantom In Ireland And Africa

*'Herr Hitler will do his utmost to prey upon our shipping and to reduce the volume of American supplies entering these islands.'*

WINSTON CHURCHILL, 9TH FEBRUARY, 1941.

German air raids on Northern Ireland, although few, were enough to remind the people of the six provinces that they were part of the United Kingdom and would be treated as such. On the 15th April, 1941, a particularly heavy raid on Belfast, Northern Ireland's capital, destroyed a considerable amount of commercial, industrial and private property and left 500 dead and 1,500 injured, mainly civilians. Three weeks later, on the nights of the 4th and 5th May, as part of a concerted move against British ports, Belfast was bombed again. Although the destruction this time was less severe, it nevertheless caused considerable damage.

Belfast was a crucial port in the Battle of the Atlantic which had been raging since the beginning of the war. The danger to Britain's shipping routes had become more severe after the fall of France in June 1940 and all ships passing to the south of Ireland were exposed to German submarine, surface and air attack. From the beginning it was apparent that the outcome of the war very largely depended upon Britain and America keeping control of the great Atlantic sea lanes. In spite of their immense casualties, the men of the Merchant Navy, escorted in the Atlantic approaches to Britain by the limited resources of the Royal Navy, still plodded their tramp-steamers back and forth across the Atlantic. Oil tankers and merchant vessels carrying many tons of countless varieties of food and munitions, machinery and raw materials braved the sudden encounter with Germany's U-boats. As vital as it was for Germany to strangle Britain's sea-borne traffic, it was equally vital for Britain to prevent her.

Apart from the U-boats, Germany's great battle cruisers *Scharnhorst* and *Gneisenau* were causing much destruction. As they, after being systematically bombed during April and May 1941, sought safe haven in the French port of Brest, the news was announced that Germany's new battleship *Bismarck* was sailing out into the Atlantic to join the battle. Accompanied by their new cruiser *Prinz Eugen*, *Bismarck*, with its eight 15-inch guns, posed a potentially devastating threat. The British battle cruiser HMS *Hood* and the battleship HMS *Prince of Wales* at once sailed from Scapa Flow to intercept their expected passage. On the evening of the 23rd May they found their quarry. In the early hours of the 24th they opened fire and scored hits, but the enemy's shooting was more successful and the *Prince of Wales* was hit and lost contact. The *Hood*, show ship of the Royal Navy, received a blow in the magazine and exploded immediately. With the exception of three, all of her 1,500 crew were lost. These included civilian workmen, still on board when she had been hastily ordered to set sail.

The *Bismarck* had to be stopped. For four days she managed to shake off her pursuers as, damaged by a hit from the *Prince of Wales*, she tried to make her way to a French port. Admiral Sir John Tovey, the Royal Navy's commander-in-chief, guessed that this was the course she would take and ordered a naval squadron to come up from Gibraltar. This force included the large air-craft carrier HMS *Ark Royal*.

The *Bismarck* was eventually sighted five hundred miles west of Brest and the hornets of the *Ark Royal*, despite rough seas, managed to take off and, after several false flights, torpedoed her. Now it was the turn of the battleships *King George* V and *Rodney*. They pounded the crippled *Bismarck*, withdrawing before the threat of German U-boats and the Luftwaffe arrived. It was left to the torpedoes of the battle-cruiser *Dorsetshire* to finish her off, which they did successfully on the morning of May 27th, 1941.

The German's now abandoned their plans to win the Battle of the Atlantic with surface ships, but the U-boat campaign was to continue for some considerable time. It was aided by the planes of the *Luftwaffe* whose long-range aircraft, the four-engine Focke-Wolf Fw 200 'Kondor', operated from Stavanger in Norway and Merignac, near Bordeaux, in France.

It was not only Northern Ireland that suffered from German bombers. Eire (Southern Ireland), despite its neutral status, was also hit at irregular intervals by bombs falling on villages and isolated spots. This random destruction was apparently the penalty that Eire paid for being on the flight path between two warring nations. Whenever bombs fell on Eire the Germans were quick to play down the consequences, blaming pilot error or the weather. But the bombs that fell on Dublin, Eire's capital city, on the 31st May, 1941, could not so easily be dismissed. The Germans offered the customary excuse, suggesting that the mistake was due to high winds. Thirty-four people died and the North Strand area of Dublin lay in ruins. For the people of Southern Ireland, Germany's excuses were wearing rather thin.

However, the fact remained that Eire was a neutral country and, with its border with Northern Ireland, it was felt by the British government that any enemy attack would come through a landing in the South. It was partly for this reason that Phantom was sent to Northern Ireland.

By the Spring of 1941 'G' Squadron was fully prepared for its journey by sea from the port of Liverpool to Belfast and from there the short journey to Lisburn, the town that was to be its operational headquarters for the duration of its stay in Ireland. Major Terrence A Watt, ex-Lifeguards, was the commanding officer of the six patrols that made up 'G'.

Ron Eaton recalls,

*'On our arrival at Lisburn we started some very intensive training. Everybody had to take Morse code training, in coding and deciphering and map reading. The composition of German units and their insignias was another very important lesson we had to learn. It was vital that we could instantly recognise these. There were different categories of Bailey bridges etc. which we had to be familiar with. All of this I found a lot more interesting than the normal army training which we were still doing.'*

Harry Binge particularly remembers the initial difficulty he had with Morse code.

*'Morse code. From morning to night. All the time Morse code. I thought I'd never get the hang of it. It was never spoken as dashes and dots, you know, that took too much time, it was das and dits.*

*A dash was three times as long as a dot. The ones I had the most difficulty with were the Q and the Y. Now a Q is 'da da dit da' and a Y is 'da dit da da'. I didn't think I would ever get the hang of it. It took ages. Then, all of a sudden, it clicked and once it did you never forgot it. Like reading music really, once learnt never forgotten. We had some men in our Unit who had come from the Royal Corps of Signals and one particular chap could listen to Reuters (the telegraphic news agency), which was really fast, and tell us what it was all about. I soon learnt to read it pretty quick myself, particularly figures. These were very important as there were a lot of map references to be deciphered and transmitted. We trained on all sorts of things, anything that was written, especially newspapers. We even played card games in Morse, a popular one being Rummy.'*

Each Phantom squadron was made up of patrols. A patrol consisted of an officer and a junior NCO and five other ranks. Each patrol had a Daimler Dingo scout car fitted with a No.11 wireless set, three motorcycles, either BSA M20's or the more powerful Norton fitted with the Villiers engine, and a 25-cwt. truck to carry patrol baggage and sufficient supplies to make a patrol self-supporting for 48 hours. Each patrol worked back, by wireless and despatch rider, to its group headquarters, the rear link thence to Regimental Headquarters being run by the regiment's own Royal Corps of Signals personnel.

Harry remembers his patrol officer, Capt. Webb, as being 'a very nice guy'. Working closely as they did in their small groups it was essential that the men all got on well with each other, and with their officer. Harry and Ron's patrol was a very happy one. Despite the rigorous training procedure there were many light-hearted moments. On one occasion just Harry and Ron, with Capt. Webb, had been out on an exercise for three days. Unwashed and unshaven the three of them were looking pretty scruffy when Capt. Webb suddenly announced, 'I think we've got time. I'm going to make a phone call to a lady friend of mine, and if I'm not very much mistaken I think I can get us a dinner.'

Without further delay he made his phone call, which obviously received a favourable response because Harry, Ron and Capt. Webb, with Harry driving, immediately set off in their armoured car. They had driven through the countryside for only a few miles before, on turning a sharp bend in the narrow country lane, they saw before them a huge white mansion set on a hill at the end of a very long tree-lined drive. 'This is it!' cried Capt. Webb excitedly.

As they drew up before the great house Capt. Webb jumped out and, as he bounded up the steps to the huge oak door, he told Harry and Ron to go round to the side door where they would be looked after. And looked after they certainly were, and in style. They were ushered into a room where they were invited to sit at a very large highly-polished table laid out with beautiful silverware. During the hour or so that followed the two young men were attended by 2 or 3 servants who waited on them hand and foot with as much food and drink as they could possibly manage.

'We must have looked a funny sight sitting there,' Harry laughingly recalls. 'Dirty and dishevelled in our khaki battledress, seated at that big posh table, being waited on. The funny thing is, we never did find out who the Lady of the house was, or how Capt. Webb came to know her. Or even what the two of them got up to while Ron and I were safely out of the way!'

So the training went on. Day after day, week after week. 'We must have visited every town in Northern Ireland during our eighteen months there. We were even issued with passports. It seems ironic that, in the event of a German invasion of Eire, we would have to show our passports to the Southern Irish border officials before crossing the border and tackling the enemy!' laughs Harry.

Partly to prevent boredom setting in and partly to give all the men some experience of war as they waited patiently for their turn to see action, all members of the squadron were sent to one of the other armed services for a week. Harry and another member of his patrol were attached to the Navy for a week. Capt. Webb arranged for them to join a destroyer that was escorting a convoy round the British coast. This exercise was primarily to learn the Navy's way of radio and wireless communication and to become familiar with their equipment.

'I was in the Navy for a week on a destroyer, HMS *Vanity*,' says Harry. 'The food was wonderful and someone gave up their hammock for me. That was the real experience, sleeping in a hammock. We didn't actually see any enemy action but we knew that the U-boats were about. I remember that we called in at Southend and went ashore in a Liberty boat. But that's about all I do remember. I got the worse for drink and had to be carried back to the ship.

I remember one of the other patrol's radio operators, I think his name was Bill Reynolds, telling me how he and his patrol officer, Lord Banbury, were assigned to the RAF and went with them on a bombing raid over Germany in a Lancaster. After they had released their bombs and turned for home, Lord Banbury tried to get up out of his seat but, because of his size, he was well and truly stuck. Amidst all the noise of the enemy flak and the plane bumping about there was Bill and one of the aircrew desperately trying to pull him out of his chair. Goodness knows what would have happened if they had all had to bale out quick!'

By the early summer of 1941 the situation in the Eastern Mediterranean had changed significantly. Greece had fallen to the Axis powers and the island of Crete, where half the troops evacuated from Greece had been sent, itself fell into enemy hands. Unable to take this island from the sea, which Admiral Cunningham's naval fleet controlled, German *Fallschirmjager* (paratroops), as part of Operation *Merkur*, dropped from the skies and captured the island between the 20th and 27th May. British and Commonwealth troops were again forced to abandon their struggle and evacuate. Many left from the north coast port of Heraklion, while the larger part of the Allied troops crossed over the mountainous area of the island to reach Sphakia in the south. From there they were safely shipped to Egypt's Alexandria. Major-General Freyburg's thirty thousand troops had fought hard in the defence of Crete, but German air-power had eventually won the day.

Back in the Western Desert the fortunes of the Axis powers were changing for the better with the arrival in Tripoli, on the 12th February, 1941, of the German *General* Erwin Rommel. Adolf Hitler had personally chosen Rommel to rescue the 'wretched Italian Army', as Hitler called it, who within two months had lost 130,000 prisoners-of-war, 380 tanks and 845 guns to the British. Two days after Rommel's arrival came Hitler's new *Afrika Korps*. It took them only until the 12th April to push back the Allied troops to within 100 miles of the Egyptian border.

The ground that the Italians had lost was now back in the hands of the Axis troops. The main reason that Rommel met with so little resistance was that many of General Wavell's army had been withdrawn to help defend Greece.

Rommel now faced the fiercest battle of the campaign so far. At Tobruk on the 14th April he was forced to withdraw as his light tanks came under the constant fire of British anti-tank and heavy artillery. A second assault, supported by Stuka dive-bombers, began on the 30th, but again with little success. It seemed that Rommel's dramatic charge across Libya had been brought to a temporary halt. The British garrison at Tobruk could be supplied by sea as long as the Royal Navy controlled the Mediterranean and so Rommel faced the prospect of a long siege. Two weeks later his *Afrika Korps* pushed the Allies back across the Egyptian frontier, but still they could not take Tobruk.

The *Fuhrer*, however, was delighted with what Rommel had achieved. Originally sent to the Western Desert to aid the Italians in their fight to hold back the Allies from Tripoli, the German general and his *Afrika Korps* had attained much more than was thought possible in so short a time.

Now Rommel and the German Naval Staff felt that it needed only a sharp push to destroy Britain's Middle East defence system. They were devastated when Hitler refused them the extra forces needed to carry out this offensive. Hitler's thoughts were now on Russia, for he had made up his mind in early 1941 that Russia, with whom he had signed a non-aggression pact in August 1939, would be his next target.

On the 28th April, *Count* von der Schulenberg, the German Ambassador in Moscow, met with Hitler in Berlin and assured him that there was no danger of an attack on Germany from the Soviets. This news was of no interest to Hitler. His mind was already made up. He cited two reasons for his decision to attack Russia. Firstly, that Russia was preparing to attack Germany in the summer of 1941 and, secondly, that Britain's refusal to acknowledge defeat was due to her hopes of Russian and American intervention, and that Britain had actually entered into an alliance with Russia against Germany. He was wrong on both counts, and he knew it. His true reason for invading Russia was pure greed. Not only did he relish the thought of conquering more lands, but he also wanted the raw materials they possessed, such as coal, iron and oil, to feed the massive German war machine. He also wanted the forced labour that the peasants of this vast country could provide.

At 4am on the 22nd June, 1941, without warning, German troops poured across the Russian border on four fronts. At the same time the *Luftwaffe* attacked major Soviet cities, including Sebastopol and Kiev, and targeted enemy airfields, destroying Russian aircraft on the ground. Operation *Barbarossa* had begun. Hitler's objective was to take Moscow before winter. The Russian Red Army was taken completely by surprise, but it took only six weeks to organize itself and slow down the relentless speed of the German advance towards Moscow, which was by now half-way from its goal.

In Britain, Winston Churchill declared, 'We shall give whatever help we can to Russia and the Russian people.'

Throughout the summer and autumn of 1941 Hitler was entirely occupied with the fighting on the Eastern Front. The Mediterranean, North Africa and Rommel had to wait. His decision to divert *Luftwaffe* strength to Russia aided Britain's Mediterranean Naval War against Italy. Without the constant threat of air attack Britain's fleet, under the command of Admiral Sir Andrew Cunningham, was able to reinforce its strategic naval base on the island of Malta and to carry out its immediate task, to sever Rommel's supply route from Italy to Libya and to open Britain's trade route from Gibraltar, via Malta, to Alexandria. This to a large extent it achieved.

Until Phantom's active service began in North Africa, the Long Range Desert Group (LRDG), which had been operating in the Western Desert for most of the war, was responsible for nearly all of the reconnaissance, intelligence and communication work carried out behind enemy lines. Although not essentially a combat group, they did attack the enemy whenever the opportunity presented itself. When Rommel's *Afrika Korps* pushed back the British Eighth Army as far as the Egyptian frontier, the Special Air Services (SAS), which had been carrying out commando raids behind enemy lines, had to rethink its tactics and suggested to the LRDG that they might like to add transporting the SAS raiders to their list of tasks. Although not extensively involved at this time, Phantom, with their specialised radio techniques, were nevertheless used by both of these elite groups.

The SAS regiment had been formed in 1941, the brainchild of two young Guard's lieutenants, David Stirling and Jock Lewes. They were formed as a small-scale fighting force suited to raiding and reconnaissance deep behind enemy lines, intelligence gathering and close-quarter combat. In the Western Desert they raided enemy airfields and logistical centres, destroying the enemy's fixed bases and supply routes. Supply lines were vital in the desert campaign. As supplies ran short campaigns petered out. Both British and German supplies had to be transported by sea or air, and then continue their journey overland along extensive supply routes to reach their destinations. The ability of the British SAS regiment to cause disruption to the German supply lines played a large part in the Allies' eventual victory in North Africa.

Originally the SAS groups were parachuted into the desert to reach their targets, but as parachuting was rather hit and miss, being very dependent on suitable weather conditions, Stirling came up with the idea of working with the LRDG. His suggestion that the LRDG transport the SAS raiding parties was met with the reply, 'Tell us where you want to go and we will take you there and bring you back.'

Over the next few months this new partnership wreaked havoc within German and Italian territory.

Much has been written about the LRDG and the SAS over the years. One such story, from Robin Hunter's 'True Stories of the SAS', illustrates the courage, bravery and tenacity of this regiment whose motto is 'Who Dares Wins'.

'LRDG patrols carried the SAS far behind enemy lines, letting them off to raid airfields and providing transport for wild raids along the coastal road - shooting up any camp or transport park that loomed up in the night. Before long the SAS patrols were in action every night, the crash of their bombs and the glow of the fires they started becoming familiar features of night-time in the desert. Many SAS soldiers found raiding very much to their taste and became one-man waves of destruction once loose behind the enemy lines. Paddy Mayne attacked the fighter airfield at Sirte, destroyed twenty-four aircraft and took the time to gate-crash a party in the German Officers' Mess and spray the revellers with bullets from his tommy-gun before destroying one final aircraft on the way out by tearing out its control panel with his bare hands.

Jock Lewes raided a roadhouse and transport park, shooting the drivers and placing bombs on twelve petrol and tank transporters; Bill Fraser took a small patrol into the airfield at Agebadia and destroyed thirty-seven aircraft - all this without the loss of a man. The Germans and Italians, quite understandably, became seriously concerned.'

On Thursday the 31st December, 1941, Jock Lewes was killed. Returning from a raid mounted on an airfield at Nofilia, Lewes and his party were attacked by a lone Messerschmitt Bf 110 fighter. The aircraft came in low and, from its aerial fire, Jock Lewes was hit in the leg and badly wounded. He died within minutes. An air of despondency descended over the SAS when they heard of the tragic loss of one of their founder members, a man who was greatly respected by all who came in contact with him.

David Stirling managed to avoid capture until the last week of January 1943. He had been returning alone across the desert after a raid on an enemy base when he was betrayed by a young Arab who had befriended him. Offering to lead him to food and water, the traitor led him straight into the arms of the Italians.

We will read more about the SAS later, when it was realized

that their operations in Europe were to need a more sophisticated and organized wireless communication system and an approach was made to Phantom HQ. In February 1944 Phantom's 'F' Squadron was to be reformed for such use.

Phantom's 'H' Squadron, made up of the remnants of the party which returned from Greece and the second echelon sent out from London in March, was based at the camp of GHQ Troops Royal Signals at Mena in Egypt for several months. During this time it had very little communication with Phantom HQ at Richmond, being left very much to its own devices. It wasn't until Operation Crusader began on the 19th November, 1941, that 'H' was to again see active service in the role for which it had been trained.

With the arrival in Alexandria in May 1941 of new tanks and aircraft, General Sir Archibald Wavell, Commander-in-Chief of the Middle East, felt strong enough to mount another attack on Rommel's forces who held their position on the Egyptian-Libyan border. This operation, which involved the 4th Indian Division, aided by the 4th Armoured Brigade who were equipped with Matilda tanks, and the 7th Armoured Division, was code named '*Battleaxe*'. It was to last for only three days as Rommel counter-attacked with his 15th Panzer Division.

As part of the operation, on the 15th June, the Allies attacked the enemy's position at Halfaya Pass, but the defenders were better prepared than Wavell had anticipated. The *Afrika Korp's* 88-mm dual purpose anti-tank and anti-aircraft guns were waiting. The first news that came back from the 4th Brigade read, 'They are tearing my tanks to bits.' So high was the muzzle velocity of the 88-mm that it was lethal to every type of Allied tank, its heavy projectile arriving well before the roar of the gun that fired it was heard. Of the thirteen Matildas that went into battle that day only one survived the attack.

By the fourth morning the British forces were back where they had started. Operation *Battleaxe* had cost the British ninety-one tanks and 1,000 casualties, and Wavell his job. Winston Churchill replaced him with General Sir Claude Auchinleck, Commander-in-Chief in India.

Auchinleck immediately set about transforming the Western Desert Force into the Eighth Army, whose command was given to Lieutenant-General Sir Alan Cunningham. The new army was divided into the 13th Corps, which included the New Zealand Division and the 4th Indian Division under Lieutenant-General A R Godwin-Austin, and the 30th

Armoured Corps under Lieutenant-General C W M Norrie. It was with the Eighth Army that Phantom was to be put to its original use again and to realise its full potential. Communication in the desert was by wireless alone, only along the coast were there telegraph lines that had been erected by the men of the Royal Engineers and Royal Corps of Signals.

On the night of the 18/19th November, 1941, with the long-awaited arrival of his new supplies, Auchinleck launched his Operation *Crusader*. The Allies now had 700 tanks against Rommel's 320 and 700 aircraft against 320 Axis war planes. The basis of the operation was that the 13th Corps would pin down the enemy troops who were holding the frontier positions, while the 30th Corps swept around to destroy Rommel's armoured forces and push their way through to reach the garrison at Tobruk. The 'Rats of Tobruk', as the besieged Australian and New Zealand forces had named themselves as they lived amongst the ruins of this vital seaport, had endured four months of bombing by the *Luftwaffe* and the Italian Air Force.

Night-time ferries had brought fresh supplies to the Rats, as well as the very welcome reinforcements of British, Polish, South African and Indian troops. To ease his own supply crisis, Rommel desperately needed the port of Tobruk, which had been held by the Allies since they had taken it from the Italians at the beginning of the year.

With the Eighth Army went Phantom. On the 18th November, 'H' Squadron, now under the command of Major Dermott Daly (Major Brian Franks having been sent home to England due to ill health), moved its headquarters forward with 30th Corps as it prepared to go into battle. It left a rear link patrol under Captain Donald Melvin, one of the five officers who had come out from Britain with the second echelon, at Army HQ at Maddalena.

Captain Edgar Herbert's patrol was to join Brigadier Jock Campbell's 7th Support Brigade. Campbell was rather surprised at its unexpected arrival, not having been notified of its coming, and nearly had the patrol arrested! Lieutenant Carol Mather's patrol was with the 4th Armoured Brigade and Captain Graham Bell's No. 3 patrol was attached to the New Zealanders.

Each of the nine Phantom patrols was equipped with two 8-cwt wireless cars and one 15-cwt truck. As the four day tank battle raged around Sidi Rezegh, Phantom kept in touch, with a constant flow of messages being radioed back to their HQ and thence to Army HQ where Melvin's patrol was still stationed. Not enough emphasis can be put on the importance of communication in battle situations.

Phantom's No. 9 or No. 11 wireless sets were adequate for medium to long range transmission but for even longer distances they were up-graded. The Phantom wireless operator needed the high qualities that his training had afforded him to pick up weak signals against a background of atmospherics and interference. This was known to the experienced signal-man as 'slush'.

In the heat of battle messages would be coming in thick and fast, in both Morse code and the spoken word, from the commanders of the forward tanks. All of these, once deciphered, would be passed to the officer of the patrol. Based on all the information supplied from his operators, the officer would then decide which reports were of the most importance and send them back to rear HQ, either by direct radio transmission from Phantom or by motor cycle despatch rider. These messages were vital to convey to Army HQ and the overall commanders the information necessary for them to map out the various phases of the battle-plan as new situations developed. Speed was essential. Previously information from the battlefront had taken much longer to reach the decision makers. Therefore, by short cutting the former procedures, the GHQ Phantom Liaison Regiment was now proving invaluable in the way that its founder, Lieutenant-Colonel Hopkinson, had envisaged.

In Berlin on the 28th November, Hitler heard that the German siege of Tobruk had been broken. The British armour had recovered sufficiently from Rommel's counter-attack to link up with the New Zealanders who had broken out from the Tobruk Garrison. Despite heavy fighting around Sidi Rezegh, where heavy losses had been imposed on the New Zealanders, Rommel could do nothing to prevent a British and Imperial entry into Tobruk on the 10th December.

It was the Phantom link that carried the Corps Commander's first message. 'Godwin-Austin to Cunningham – Tobruk is as relieved as I am. The Press may now be informed.'

The news of the relief of Tobruk was met with great joy and excitement by those back home in Britain who, up till now, had had little to celebrate. It lifted morale. This was the first major overseas victory of the combined British Empire and Allied forces. This jubilation was, however, sadly to be short lived.

After Tobruk Rommel, short on supplies, had decided to withdraw. As he and his *Afrika Korps* retreated westwards, Derna and Benghazi changed hands yet again. It looked as if the Axis forces had suffered a major defeat, but Rommel was not to be defeated. By the 21st January, 1942, he had begun a counter-offensive. The Eighth Army, for a short time under the command of Major-General Neil Ritchie, only managed to hold on to Tobruk until the 21st June when it again fell into enemy hands. Now that he had the port that he so desperately needed to keep his army supplied, Rommel was ready for his advance into Egypt. General Auchinleck took the decision to command the Eighth Army himself and fell back to take up a defensive position at El Alamein.

At Derna on the 30th June, two Italian aircraft landed. One carried Mussolini and the other carried his horse. So confident was he of an Axis success in Egypt he was all set to lead his victorious army through the streets of Cairo on his white Arab charger, like a Roman emperor. He was to be sorely disappointed.

During Operation *Crusader*, Phantom had established its value. Unfortunately, during Rommel's counter-offensive, Major Dermott Daly, who had proved himself a worthy commander of 'H' Squadron, had been captured by the enemy and found himself a prisoner-of-war. 'H' now withdrew to its base at Mena to re-group and reform before being deployed to the Middle East where, in Iraq, the British garrisons in this nominally independent country, were coming under attack. Here Phantom was to provide much improved signal and radio communications.

One particular incident that occurred during the North African Campaign is worth recalling. Although at the time only considered important by those directly involved, it was later to prove significant in ground to air co-operation in wireless communication, especially after the Allied invasion of Normandy. This was known as the Cab-Rank system. The incident concerned a lone RAF Hurricane pilot who was patrolling at about 6,000 feet over the desert and running dangerously low on fuel. He had decided that it was the right time to return to his base when, all of a sudden, he picked up a Mayday distress call coming in over his radio transmitter. The pilot at first thought that it was coming from another patrolling aircraft but it soon became apparent from the message that it was coming from a single British armoured car that had been out on a reconnaissance mission. It was being pursued by a more heavily armed *Afrika Korps* half-track and its crew.

The British commander of the armoured car had broken radio silence but, unable to contact his own base, had sent out a distress call that the Hurricane pilot had, luckily, picked up.

Once given the map references and co-ordinates, the Hurricane was quickly on the scene and put the German half-track out of action by strafing it with cannon fire. Both the Hurricane fighter plane and the armoured car then returned safely to their bases.

CHAPTER X

# Phantom and the Dieppe Raid

*'The democratic way of life is at this moment being directly assailed, either by arms or by the secret spreading of poisonous propaganda.'*
PRESIDENT ROOSEVELT, 6TH JANUARY, 1941.

Soon after dawn on the 7th December, 1941, wave after wave of Japanese warplanes began to bomb America's deep-water base on the island of Oahu in the US Pacific Ocean Protectorate of Hawaii. Pearl Harbour was taken completely by surprise. Within two hours 366 Japanese bombers and fighters destroyed four American battleships as they lay at anchor and fourteen smaller craft. The enemy also attacked Pearl Harbour's airfields, adding nearly 200 aircraft to their tally of destruction. Two thousand four hundred people, many of them civilians, were killed.

The following day the American president, Franklin D Roosevelt, denounced this act of treachery and, as Commander-in-Chief of his country's armed forces, took all the necessary steps for the mobilization of their services. He stated, 'I ask that the Congress declare that since the unprovoked and dastardly attack by Japan on Sunday, December 7, 1941, a state of war has existed between the United States and the Japanese Empire. With confidence in our armed forces, with the unbounded determination of the people, we will gain the inevitable triumph, so help us God!'

Except for a single Pacifist vote, both houses voted for war unanimously and without discussion.

Adolf Hitler was ecstatic. In a long speech to his people he welcomed Japan into the war. In it he stated, 'Now it is impossible for us to lose the war. We have an ally who has not been vanquished in three thousand years.'

Just over a year previously, on the 25th September, 1940, the United States had announced a further loan to support China's General Chiang Kai-shek in his struggle against Japan. Two days later Germany, Italy and Japan signed a tripartite agreement extending the Rome-Berlin Axis to the Far East, after which all three were referred to as the Axis Powers. This agreement created a New Order in Europe and Asia, each pledging to help the others if any of them were attacked by a power not already involved in Europe, ie. by the United States of America.

On the same day the Japanese bombed Pearl Harbour they also attacked three other American Pacific islands – Guam, Wake and Midway. Determined to show their strengths and their intentions, air attacks also took place on the British bases of Singapore and Hong Kong.

In Britain, Prime Minister Churchill announced that the Japanese had begun landing in British territory in Northern Malaya. He also paid tribute to the people of China who had long battled against Japanese domination, declaring friendship for the Chinese people and assuring their great leader, Chiang Kai-shek, that, henceforward, they would fight the common foe together.

On Christmas Day, 1941, Hong Kong fell to Japan. After a seven day battle against overwhelming odds six thousand British Empire troops surrendered. The Governor of Hong Kong, with only one day's supply of water left after the enemy had captured their reservoirs, had applied for a truce, but to no avail.

A similar fate was to befall Singapore. After a fierce struggle and with their water supply lost to the enemy after repeated bombing, Singapore surrendered on the 15th February, 1942. Over sixty thousand soldiers, British, Indian and Australian, were taken prisoner. (More than half of them were to die while prisoners-of-war.)

The loss of these two British Crown Colonies served as a severe blow to the people of Britain who were already reeling from the loss of their aircraft carrier HMS *Ark Royal*, battleship HMS *Prince of Wales*, both who had played a part in the earlier sinking of the *Bismarck*, and battle-cruiser HMS *Repulse*.

The *Ark Royal* had gone to the bottom of the sea a few miles east of Gibraltar on the 13th November, 1941, after an unseen U-boat had torpedoed her. Miraculously, with the loss of only one of her 1,600 crew.

The brand new *Prince of Wales* and the old but serviceable *Repulse* were both sunk on the 10th December. The *Repulse* went first after a swarm of Japanese aircraft showered them with bombs and aerial torpedoes. The *Prince of Wales*, hit four or five times, went down soon after her.

The Japanese had dealt the Allies a resounding blow in the first stages of the struggle for the Pacific. From the Allied point of view communications at that time had proved very difficult. Many vital and important messages were being lost due to the vast distances that they had to travel to reach the Far East. Not all of these messages that were being transmitted by radio over the oceans and across mountainous and jungle terrain were getting through to their destinations. The Armed Forces locally mostly had to rely on short wave radio sets which were obviously not suited to jungle warfare. As in the Boer War, fought in South Africa at the turn of the century, much use had to be made of native runners and pigeons to take messages to and from headquarters and their combat units.

Due to the speed of Japanese success in overcoming the forces of the British Empire, culminating in the fall of Singapore, no Phantom squadron was made ready in time to be deployed to the Far East.

By March 1942 the Japanese were in a very strong position. The whole of Malaya had been overrun, Borneo, Java and Celebes occupied, and very soon the Japanese were to add the Solomon Islands to their tally. From their foothold in New Guinea they were menacing Australia. The Northern Territories and North Western Australia experienced air raids and a concerted but mainly unsuccessful submarine raid was made on Sydney Harbour in May. Few doubted that the principal Japanese goals were India and Australia and the creation of a new empire. The Nipponese Army was now set to seal off China from all available help and to advance on India through the Burmese jungles.

Meanwhile, back in Europe, a joint British and Canadian commando raid took place on the 19th August, 1942, on the French port of Dieppe. The aim of the raid was to practise techniques for an eventual invasion of Northern Europe. Operation Jubilee, as it was code-named, was planned as a 'reconnaissance of force' to test the enemy defences on a well-defended 11-mile stretch of the French coast around the town of Dieppe. The choice of Dieppe as a suitable site for an amphibious operation was geographically hazardous. Instead of an open smooth-sloping beach with easy access to the land behind, Dieppe has a steeply-angled shoreline with only a two-mile stretch of it practicable for the type of landing planned. To the east and the west of the town high cliffs rise from the sea. On the top of these cliffs, only five miles either side of the town itself, at Varengeville-sur-Mer and Berneval-le-Grand respectively, the Germans had sited heavy defensive gun emplacements. It was below these two villages that landings were to be made in order to knock out the batteries and so protect the main forces landing at Dieppe itself. The problem was, that to silence these batteries, the invaders had to first scale the steep 150-foot cliffs leading to them.

Five thousand Canadians and a thousand British, as well as fifty American Rangers and as many Free French, took part in the raid on Dieppe. They were accompanied by a Phantom squadron.

'J' Squadron, under the command of Major the Hon Jakie Astor, was chiefly an experimental one. It had in May that year started training on commando lines, patrols from other squadrons having joined it for combined operations training, so it was the obvious choice when the regiment was called upon to play its part in this assault. Up till now, 'H', originally in Greece and now in North Africa, was the only Phantom squadron to have seen active service.

Capt. Alastair Sedgewick's patrol was to accompany No. 4 Commando landing on two beaches at Varengeville (code name *Orange*) while Lieut Michael Guy Hillerns' (who had joined Phantom from the Devonshire Regiment) was to be with No. 3 Commando landing at two points below Berneval (Yellow). Capt. Julian Fane's patrol was to land with Brigade HQ in the main Canadian attack on Dieppe itself (Red and White beaches). This main attack proved to be a disastrous one. Two other landings on headlands immediately to the east and west of Dieppe at Pourville (Green) and Puys (Blue) did not have a Phantom patrol with them.

A fleet of 252 ships, including eight destroyers, had sailed from four of England's south coast ports on the evening of the 18th August, arriving off the French coast at 3.30am the following morning. HMS *Calpe* and HMS *Fernie* were detailed as command ships. Just before 5am five thousand men were ready to go ashore in assault craft, but by then the element of surprise had been eliminated. The No. 3

Commando force to the east had run into an escorted German convoy and the gunfire that followed alerted the German land forces. Aerial photographs had shown that Dieppe was strongly defended. At every possible landing site the Germans had placed 59-mm coastal defence guns. Of the twenty-four landing craft only ten managed to land twenty-seven tanks and there was trouble getting these past the obstacles on the beach. The Canadian infantry never effectively crossed the sea wall, being pinned down against barbed-wire on the beach by terrifying enemy fire. Capt. Julian Fane's Phantom patrol did not even get as far as the beach. The landing craft that his patrol was on, was to suffer a severe hit and had to return to its parent ship.

Lieut Michael Hillerns' patrol with No. 3 Commando, who as we know had been engaged in enemy fire in the Channel, managed to land but with only sixty commandos remaining after the sea fight. Despite enemy machine-gun and sniper fire they managed to reach the top of the cliffs. Phantom's job was to get on the air. Lance-Cpl. William Ley Craggs (who had joined Phantom from the 2nd Batt. Rifle Brigade) tried without success to make wireless contact himself but he could hear the patrol with No. 4 Commando passing messages. Before Craggs could make contact at all, the order came to withdraw and as he made his way back down the gully to the beach he was tragically killed by machine-gun fire. Driver Richardson and Cpl Masterson were wounded. The remains of the patrol destroyed their code books and radio lest they fell into enemy hands.

When they reached the beach they sheltered from the heavy enemy fire in caves. With no alternative means of escape Lieut Hillerns took the brave decision to swim out to a drifting boat. Unfortunately, he was hit by machine-gun fire from the cliffs and died instantly.

The No. 4 Commando's phase of Operation *Jubilee* was the most successful. Commanded by the legendary Lord Lovat, who had had a short spell as an officer with Phantom in its early days, it briskly and efficiently silenced the battery at Varengeville, having first successfully landed and scaled the cliffs. Capt. Sedgwick's Phantom patrol was able to set up its radio and, unlike Lieut Hillerns', successfully pass messages. It competently reported the action as follows:-

0614    4 Commando on Bridgehead OK at 1530 hrs. SGB

|  |  |
|---|---|
| | reported an attack by enemy on her convoy of 'R' craft which had been scattered. |
| 0630-0700. | 4 Commando demolished enemy ammunition dump and engaged over six-gun battery. The RAF were engaged over target. The Commando which was intact, put in a further attack at 0630 hrs. There was no contact between the commando and the troops on their left though the Camerons had landed. Our troops were pinned down on White and Red beaches and unable to land at Blue. |
| 0735-0730 | 4 Commando withdrawal delayed. Information later. |
| 0745 | Will advise when embarking. Identify now. Identify. |
| 0800-0744 | Half embarked. Remainder follow. Will open up in boat. |
| 0840-0835 | Now in MGB with OC 4 Commando and wounded men off shore one mile. |
| 0859 | To CCO from OC 4 Commando. Everyone of gun crews finished with bayonet. |

After less than six hours the commander of the raiding force, the Canadian Major-General John Hamilton Roberts, ordered the survivors to withdraw. Out of a total force of 6,100 men just over one thousand died and 2,340 were captured. Of these, the Canadian 2nd Division, supplying most of the troops, had lost nine hundred men killed and nearly two thousand taken prisoner. Lieutenant Edwin V Loustalot, of the 1st Ranger Battalion, became the first American to be killed in land fighting in Europe in this war.

Three Victoria Crosses, 'for conspicuous bravery in the face of the enemy', were awarded during this raid. To one of the British commandos, Captain Pat Porteous; to a Canadian officer, Lieutenant-Colonel Merritt; and to a Canadian chaplain, John Foote, who spent many hours tending the wounded while under fire on the beach. When the time came to embark he carried them to the boats but refused to leave himself, preferring to become a prisoner-of-war so that he could carry on helping the wounded men.

The RAF had given excellent air support but lost 106

machines to the Germans' forty-eight, and the guns of the Royal Navy had been ineffective against the heavy guns of the enemy shore batteries, one destroyer and thirty-three landing craft were sunk.

What lessons did the Allies learn from the disaster at Dieppe? The raid had been designed as an exercise to test the enemy forces and gather intelligence about their defences. This it certainly achieved. Lord Mountbatten, the chief of Combined Operations, believed that it had shown that, to succeed, overwhelming fire support, including close support during the initial stages of an attack, was crucial. The decision not to use airborne troops had also contributed to the raid's failure. Dieppe convinced the Allied commanders that the planning for any future cross-Channel invasion needed a massive force, one that could not possibly be assembled before 1944.

A lesson had been learnt by Phantom too. Because it had gone into action determined to prove its merit, and to meet the particular needs of this raid, extensive changes had been made to the normal organization of the squadron. As such this did not represent a normal detachment. This proved to be a big mistake.

Jakie Astor's brother, Michael, who was also a member of Phantom but did not take part in this raid, tells us in his book, *'Tribal Feeling'*, how he felt while awaiting news of his brother's safety:

> *'I waited anxiously for his return. When I thought of him in danger, his effervescent wit, which acted on people like a tonic, seemed less important than his honest and generous spirit. He turned up after that eventful raid, un-perturbed. He had commanded his landing party from the destroyer HMS* Calpe *which, as well as bombarding Dieppe, had shot down a German fighter. 'We couldn't stop to pick up the pilot,' said Jakie 'He bailed out at about two thousand feet. And in any case his parachute didn't open.' '*

Major David Niven, as commander of 'A' squadron, had the heartbreaking task of writing to the families, wives and girlfriends of the men lost from his squadron who had joined 'J' for the raid. From his book, *'The Moon's a Balloon'*, we read how he kept thinking of a scene from the film *'Dawn Patrol'* as he wrote and re-wrote the letters. In the film, the Commanding Officer was going through the same agonizing ritual when the adjutant who had been watching him for a while said gently, 'It doesn't matter how you word it, Sir, it'll break her heart just the same.'

Before we go any further let's learn how the renowned Hollywood actor, David Niven, came to be a member of Phantom.

His military career had originally begun when, on leaving his English public school, he had enrolled at the Royal Military College at Sandhurst where he was known as a 'Gentleman Cadet'. By the summer of 1928 he had graduated from Sandhurst and had been commissioned into the Highland Light Infantry. After four years, mostly spent on Malta, and bored with Army life, Niven resigned his commission and sailed for Canada.

Between 1932 and the outbreak of World War Two, David Niven carved a niche for himself as one of Hollywood's top movie stars, so most of his colleagues were surprised when he insisted in 1939 on returning to England, where he volunteered his services to the RAF. They rejected him. 'We do not encourage actors to join this service,' he was told. Having found Army life rather dull the first time round, he was reluctant to become part of it again but, when he was invited to join the Rifle Brigade, probably one of the most famous of all the British Army's elite light infantry regiments, he accepted.

When some time later Niven heard that volunteers were being called for to form a new elite force of a highly secret nature, he put his name down. He was accepted and became a Commando. In September 1940 he was promoted to captain and became liaison officer between MI 9, the War Office Department responsible for the Commandos and their operations, and the units themselves.

There he was to remain until, out of the blue, he was ordered to join 'a new and highly secret outfit within the Special Services' at its Richmond Park headquarters. After a short period of intensive training David Niven was quickly promoted to major and given command of Phantom's 'A' Squadron, a position he was to hold for more than two years until the Spring of 1943 when he left Phantom to join the Chief of Staff to the Supreme Allied Commander (COSSAC).

In March 1942 Phantom consisted of 900 men of all ranks, and the squadrons were deployed thus:

'A' under Major Niven was working with the 'V' Corps on the South coast behind Poole Harbour in Dorset. The Corps Commander at that time was General Bernard Montgomery. David Niven later recalled, "'A' was my pride and joy. My second-in-command was a sardonic Irish newspaper man and the patrol officers included a Cameron Highlander, a Frenchman, a Lancastrian, a weight lifter, the assistant Bursar at Eton College, an amateur steeplechase jockey and an interior decorator who frequently called me 'dear' instead of 'sir'. The squadron Sergeant-Major was a Scots guard and the seventy other ranks were made up of bank clerks, burglars, shop assistants, milkmen, garage mechanics, school masters, painters, bookmakers, stockbrokers and labourers.'

'B' was down in Kent with 'XII' Corps.

'C', which was stationed near Grantham in Lincolnshire, was available to work with either the 'IX' Corps in Northern Command or with 'II' Corps in Eastern Command.

'D' was with the Canadians in Sussex.

'E' was in Scotland under the command of the expeditionary force that was to go to Tunisia. It had been based in Edinburgh for some time in preparation for its detachment to North Africa.

'F' was with the 'XI' Corps.

'G' was still in Northern Ireland.

'H' was, as we know, in North Africa.

'J', under Jakie Astor, was camped in reserve at Cliveden, his family home. (The Dieppe raid was still five months away.)

Harry Binge remembers a member of 'J' Squadron telling him of an amusing incident that took place at Cliveden.

One day Jakie Astor had taken this man's patrol up to the big house. Lady Astor, his mother, ordered the men to take their boots off before entering the house. This they did. Jakie settled his men in a comfortable room before going off in search of the butler. On his return he announced that he had sent the butler down to the cellar for some bottles of wine. It duly arrived and when the first lot of bottles had been finished off, Jakie sent the butler back down for more. This went on for some time until the butler eventually came back empty handed with a message from her Ladyship that they were to have no more. 'You can tell her Ladyship to go and... herself!' was the slurred reply from her now very merry son, much to the amazement, and amusement, of his equally merry men.

CHAPTER XI

# Training Continues

*'Are you 100% fit? Are you 100% efficient?
Do you have 100% Binge?'*
MAJOR DAVID NIVEN, CO 'A' SQUADRON PHANTOM.

Back at Phantom's headquarters in Lisburn, Northern Ireland, the men of 'G' Squadron were still training hard. Not only had they to be ultra-efficient in wireless communications and competent drivers, being adept at emergency mechanical repairs, they also had to be extremely fit mentally and physically. Cross country runs and assault courses were undertaken week after week, and PT on the parade ground, when not out on training exercises, was a daily event. All this coupled with gym work and weight training made for a super-fit, cohesive unit. But not all of the men were that keen.

One way in which Harry Binge found he could evade the rigours of this training procedure was to use his expertise as an upholsterer. One day he was approached by one of his officers who, having been made aware of Harry's skill with a needle and thread, asked him to sew badges on his uniform and those of his fellow officers. This Harry eagerly agreed to. Anything to get out of PT. Harry's success at this particular duty escalated into a much larger task when he was given the job of re-upholstering all the well-worn chairs on the camp. The search was now on for a suitable material. The regimental sergeant major came up with an inspirational idea. Down at the quartermaster's stores, stacked up in the corner, was a pile of pale blue blankets. Where they came from no-one knew, but the Sergeant Major deemed them to be 'just the thing' for the job in hand.

The rest of the squaddies looked on in envy as Harry sat in a nice warm workshop carrying out his trade, while they continued with their training in all weathers. All of a sudden, men were stepping forward all claiming to be upholsterers in civilian life. The sergeants and officers were quick to cotton on to this ruse and Harry was left to his own devices. He laughingly recalls how funny it was to see row upon row of chairs upholstered in pale blue blankets. 'It certainly brightened the place up,' he chuckles.

One amusing episode, that potentially could have had disastrous consequences, occurred when 'G' Squadron was for a short time billeted in the market town of Lurgan, a few miles south-west of the main Squadron Headquarters at Lisburn. Harry and his five other patrol members were being inspected in readiness for guard duty. This inspection was being conducted by a captain and an NCO. On the base was a drill sergeant, in Harry's words, 'a horrible little man', who seemed to Harry to have it in for him.

Ron Eaton recalls, 'All the time, whether it be on the parade ground or anywhere else on the base, all you seemed to hear was this little Sergeant bellowing out Harry's name: Binge, button your tunic up. Binge, straighten your belt. Binge, clean your boots. Binge, put your beret on properly. Binge this, Binge that. This is probably where the amusing quote used by David Niven came from: 'Are you 100% fit? Are you 100% efficient? Do you have 100% Binge?' I must admit that Harry was not the smartest of soldiers, but he was, nevertheless, one of the best drivers and radio operators in the squadron.'

Carrying on the inspection, Harry was ordered to present arms to the officer. This he did. The Lee Enfield .303 calibre standard issue rifle was duly inspected, or so they thought. The bolt action slid into place. Harry was then told to pull the trigger to test the empty chamber. To everyone's astonishment, there was a loud retort. The rifle fired, the bullet just missing the officer's head. The Drill Sergeant, Harry's tormentor, was now off duty and happened to be watching the parade from the balcony of a near-by grain store in the middle of town, this at the time being used as a billet by Phantom. The speeding bullet hit the wall, only inches to the left of the horrified Sergeant's head, taking half a brick out. Silence descended on the entire town centre for a few moments. Civilians and uniformed men alike were standing in a state of shock. Of all of the people it could have happened to, it had to be Harry.

There was, of course, an official enquiry conducted by the Commanding Officer who remarked that, although Private Binge had actually pulled the trigger, the Officer on duty carrying out the inspection was somewhat negligent in the respect that he had failed to ensure there was not a live round in the breech before the bolt action was replaced and the trigger pulled. An official reprimand was given to all concerned.

Ron, who had witnessed this incident, even today chides Harry, 'I reckon you meant that, Bingey!'

One aspect of training that most of Ron and Harry's patrol enjoyed was compass instruction and map-reading. 'We often had to go out on compass and map-reading marches,' reflects Harry. 'Sometimes over a distance of up to fifteen miles. Some of these marches would end up not back at base but at previously selected sites. We would then have to practise wireless communication between our positions and those of our HQ which had been set up at another site, possibly twenty miles away. These exercises had to be conducted in the darkness of night as well as during daylight hours.'

Despatch riding, another important facet of Phantom training, often took place over extremely difficult terrain. Northern Ireland was an ideal location for such training, not only for motorcycle despatch riding but also for driving armoured cars and trucks. Tuition in driving was given all over the province. In the towns and villages, in the mountainous regions and over the gently sloping countryside, where streams and small rivers often had to be crossed. Driving over whatever ground Phantom would be faced with under battle conditions had to be mastered. All this was part of the preparations for the day when the Allies would invade enemy-occupied Europe where similar terrain would be encountered.

> *'In the summer of 1942 we lost our Squadron Leader,' remembers Harry sadly. ' Major Terry Watt was killed when flying over to England from Ireland for an Officer's conference. His plane hit the side of a Welsh mountain. His death was a terrible blow to 'G' Squadron. He was very popular with the men of all ranks. A firm man but at the same time very fair, you always knew where you stood with him. He certainly motivated us. I remember a Major Light taking over from Terry Watt. He was a good man too.'*

At the end of October 1942 'G' Squadron was returned to Richmond. 'Our reason for being in Ireland, a threat of German invasion by sea or air, had now evaporated,' explains Ron. 'Our stay in Richmond was not very long. We were sent on to Penn Street in Buckinghamshire for dissolution, for the disbandment of 'G' Squadron. Penn Street was a holding unit for Phantom, for the people who had been disbanded like us. There was a big re-organization of the Regiment going on at that time. They now planned to have two main squadrons, large ones. Normally a squadron had been five to six patrols, but the two new squadrons, 'A' and 'B', would have as many as twelve or thirteen patrols in each. We operated as 'G' for a while at Penn Street, but after two or three months we were really split up. I was sent to 'A' Squadron and Harry to 'B'.'

These two young men who had worked together in civvy street and had received their call up papers on the same day in the early summer of 1940 had now, for the first time, to go their separate ways. They had shared many adventures over the past two and a half years, especially during the last eighteen months in Northern Ireland where they and their fellow patrol members had become a very efficient and cohesive unit with a great sense of camaraderie.

'I lost touch with Harry for a while after this,' continues Ron thoughtfully. 'Although I did meet up with him a couple of times in France after D-Day. My life now carried on with 'A' Squadron up near York. The usual training. Now we kept wondering when the second front was going to be. We just seemed to be training all the time. I think we must have been some of the best trained troops in England. I went on a two week mountain course in Scotland, which was a nice break, and I did a course on demolition. This was kind of exciting. Blowing up railway lines and poles that were meant to look like trees, but pretty big ones. Learning to do these things was very stimulating and I can imagine how people get a real bang out of it. Several months later, returning to England, we moved down to a little village about twenty miles outside Oxford, and still the training went on. Nothing very exciting happened during this time, things were getting boring. Everyone was looking forward to the second front.'

CHAPTER XII

# The Tide Begins to Turn

*'Now this is not the end, it is not even the
beginning of the end,
but it is perhaps the end of the beginning.'*
PRIME MINISTER CHURCHILL.
10TH NOVEMBER, 1942.

July and August 1942 were critical months for the defence of Egypt. When the British Eighth Army, pursued by the *Afrika Korps*, retreated in disorder into Egypt, things looked extremely black for General Auchinleck. While he ordered a temporary halt at Mersa Matruh, the bulk of his forces withdrew to El Alamein, 150 miles further east. No sooner had they arrived than they were attacked by Rommel's panzers. General Auchinleck rallied his troops with the words, 'You are fighting the Battle of Egypt. A battle in which the enemy must be destroyed. You have shown that you can stick it, and I know that you will stick it right out.' And stick it out they did. Rommel was forced to withdraw and dig in. The British 8th Army had fallen back on the Alam Halfa ridge. This was the fortified line that ran between El Alamein on the Mediterranean Sea in the north and the Qattara Depression, an area of soft sand, to the south. Rommel, the tough Nazi general, could not now use his usual mode of attack - sweeping around the enemy positions. He was forced by geographical features to face the combined Allied forces head on.

Throughout July the two armies skirmished for the ridges that would give them some advantage, but by the third week of July Auchinleck was forced to call off his attack. The First Battle for Alamein had halted Rommel's advance but failed to remove the threat to Cairo.

The British now had the advantage of being near to their base whereas Rommel and his army were operating far from their main supply base in Tripoli. The enemy had a long supply line that was regularly being targeted by British bombers. By the end of August Rommel was becoming desperately short of oil. One of his great petrol stores at Mersa Matruh had been destroyed soon after it had been set up, but still he issued orders for another advance on Cairo. Again he failed to reach his goal. By now the British 8th Army was under the leadership of Lieut-Gen. Bernard Law Montgomery. He had been specially selected by Winston Churchill to take over command from General Auchinleck on the 13th August, 1942, after Churchill's first choice, Lieut-Gen. William Gott, had been shot down while flying to a meeting and killed. Montgomery was more than happy to be serving under a man he knew well and greatly admired, the new C-in-C of the Middle East, General Sir Harold Alexander. Auchinleck had been removed from this command too.

When Rommel's attack came on the night of the 30th August, his panzers fell straight into Montgomery's trap. As they and his motorized infantry were lured forward towards Alam Halfa Ridge they found themselves enmeshed in minefields and confronted by the determined defence of British, Australian, New Zealand, Indian and South African troops. Rommel was forced to withdraw. Montgomery had won his first desert victory and Rommel had lost the last chance of his.

What Rommel did not know was that his attack had not taken his enemy entirely by surprise. By their reading of *Enigma* messages, the British knew the German's plans for the ensuing attack. Over two years previously, a team of scientists, mathematicians and chess masters, under the leadership of Professor Alan Turing and based at Bletchley Park in the Hertfordshire countryside, had been working to solve the secrets of the German *Enigma* enciphering machines. In May 1940 their first great breakthrough had come, and a year later came a second when on May 8th, 1941 two British Navy destroyers, HMS *Bulldog* and HMS *Aubretia*, part of the Third Escort Group in the Atlantic, tangled with a German U-boat, the U-110. The U-boat was forced to the surface and, with its entire crew, was captured. A Royal Naval boarding party was sent on board and was able to seize important enemy secret code books and equipment before the Germans had a chance to destroy them. From that time on decoded German messages had ably assisted vital Allied decisions during the duration of the war, unknown to the Germans. Phantom was to play an important role in the forwarding of some of these messages that they themselves had picked up with their high powered radio equipment when in battlefront situations. Their Squadron HQ's passed these intercepted messages through Army HQ onto Bletchley Park for the experts to decode.

The summer of 1942 marked the peak of Axis achievement in the war. Gradually, the tide began to turn. The Axis master-plan, that had been conceived on such a grand scale, was slowly being undermined. As we know, in North Africa Rommel had blown his last chance of gaining Egypt and in Italian East Africa Mussolini's Fascists had been defeated.

On the 19th January, 1941, a British attack against the Italians in Eritrea, Somaliland and Ethiopia, the Horn of Africa, by a force of 30,000 had opened up another war front. It took this force less than five months to achieve their objective. By the 25th February, Mogadushu, the capital of Italian Somaliland was in British hands, and by the end of March the Italians, under *General* Frusci, had been forced by British and Indian troops, ably assisted by the Royal Air Force, to withdraw south out of Eritrea into Ethiopia. The conquest of Eritrea had been completed when the Italian armies were finally and totally defeated with the capture of Asmara and the surrender of the naval base at Massawa on the 1st and 5th of April respectively. It was also on the 5th that the Italians had been forced to evacuate the capital of Ethiopia, Addis Ababa, - thus ending the Italian domination of East Africa.

The Germans, in the first year of the war on the Eastern Front, had torn into Russia with a vengeance, but the people of Russia and their Red Army had rallied to the defence of their motherland. Their iron will to hold on to Stalingrad at all cost, at last, halted the German advance and marked the beginning of the end of Hitler's dreams. Many bloody battles had taken place and millions of Russians had died but, after untold suffering, they gradually began to drive the German invaders out. September 1942 marked the turning point and the bitter winter of 1942/43 aided the defenders who were much better equipped to fight the cold. German losses in the four-month battle for Stalingrad were staggering. An estimated 300,000 men had been killed or died of starvation and cold and 91,000 captured.

The war in the Mediterranean was continuing but the island of Malta, with an area of only ninety square miles, continued to be a constant thorn in the side of the Italian naval fleet and the Axis strategists. A British Crown Colony since 1815, Malta was an important base, situated as it was halfway between Sicily and North Africa. Its strength in numbers of Royal Air Force planes was always tiny, but its twenty-odd Blenheim and Beaufort torpedo-bombers, eight Glenn Martin Baltimores and thirty Wellington night-bombers, played the major part in strangling the supply route to the Germans in Libya. Malta, desperately short of food, petrol and munitions, and with their anti-aircraft gun barrels worn smooth from constant use, could some days put only five Spitfires from its force of eighteen in the air to defend against the bombardment of the Junker Ju 88s and Messerschmitt Bf 109s, which were based only eighty miles away on Sicily. Hawker Hurricanes also played an invaluable part in the defence of this tiny island.

On April 15th, the epic endurance and bravery of the Maltese people was rewarded when King George VI signed the award of the George Cross, the highest decoration for civilian valour, to the Island Fortress.

When Italy had declared war the Axis powers had anticipated that Malta would early on fall into their hands. How wrong they were. The destruction went on all through 1942, and towards the end of the year Rommel wrote to Hitler: 'I have personally warned *Feldmarschall* Kesselring of the tragic consequences for my lines of communication between Italy and Africa if he does not succeed in establishing air superiority over Malta.' This task Kesselring did not achieve. The Battle of Malta ended in victory for the Allies on the 1st January, 1943.

In the summer of 1942 the tide was also turning in the Allies favour in the war in the Pacific. The Japanese, like the Germans, had overstretched their forces. Buoyed up by early successes, and with defeat unimaginable, they thought their march to victory was unstoppable, but the Americans, having now steadied themselves, were in a much stronger position to begin striking back. In the first week in June, in one of the greatest battles ever to be fought at sea, the Battle of Midway, the US Navy warships, together with aircraft operating from carriers, sank four large Japanese aircraft carriers and badly damaged three battleships. As the

Japanese fleet withdrew, American commanders, with the memory of Pearl Harbour still fresh in their minds, rejoiced in their triumph. Very soon British, Commonwealth and American forces began to fight back in Burma, almost a year after the Japanese had overrun it.

By the autumn of 1942 Hitler's ranting, raging and table-top fist-banging could not alter the fact that the German advances in Russia and North Africa had been brought to a halt. The man who had begun by peddling third-rate sketches in the back-streets of Vienna was, at this point, the undisputed master of the greater part of continental Europe, with vast armies threatening the Volga, the Caucasus and the Nile, but this was as far as his empire was to expand. The initiative had now passed out of Hitler's hands, never to return. Throughout the First World War Hitler had served as a *'Meldeganger'*, a runner whose job was to carry messages between Company and Regimental HQ, and, although he was not actually to fight in the trenches, there is little doubt that his was a dangerous job, never being very far from the Front. In October 1916 Hitler was wounded in the leg and, for the first time in two years, was sent back to Germany. It was his experiences during this war and the years following it that drove him on in his quest to become Chancellor of Germany in 1933 and leader of the *Third Reich*. In 1939, on the outbreak of World War Two, Hitler had declared himself War Lord.

The third struggle for El Alamein is remembered as one of the world's outstanding battles. It began at 9.40pm on Friday the 23rd October, 1942, when General Montgomery's British 8th Army, aided by the light of a full moon, attacked the German lines at El Alamein. The artillery bombardment that they unleashed took the enemy completely by surprise, leaving them stunned and bewildered. Nearly 900 field and medium guns opened fire, in Montgomery's words, 'like one battery'. Within a few hours, before the enemy had had time to react with any significant retaliation, the British infantry had pushed forward three miles and gained their first objectives. This feat could not have been achieved without the courage and fighting spirit of Anzac, Free French and Indian troops who fought bravely to the left and right of the main British force. The overhead co-operation of the RAF also worked perfectly with the ground attack.

*General* Erwin Rommel, who was in Germany on sick

leave when the offensive began, rushed back to Africa. His stand-in, Lieutenant-General Georg Stumme, had been killed in the initial bombardment. Rommel had been instructed by the *Führer*: 'The position requires that the El Alamein position be held to the last man. There is to be no retreat. Victory or death!' His General, ignoring these orders, withdrew his troops towards Mersa Matruh on the 2nd November after twelve days of vicious fighting which saw the Allies break out into the desert beyond the Alamein line. Rommel left behind the Italian forces to delay the enemy.

By late afternoon on the 4th November Rommel was in full retreat, having lost half of his men and well over 400 tanks. The following day Montgomery set off in pursuit of his prey. The 'Desert Fox', as Rommel was known, endeavoured to make a stand at several vantage points but was overcome by the surge of the Allied forces. It was not until he reached the Mareth Line that Rommel, at last, reached an effective defensive position. Here he prepared to make a stand. (The Mareth Line was a chain of antiquated block-houses that the French had originally built to check any Italian invasion of Tunisia from Libya.)

In Britain on November 8th, church bells, silent since June 1940, rang out to celebrate victory at El Alamein. The bells of Westminster Abbey were broadcast by the BBC to occupied Europe – and Germany! (A great propaganda coup.) On this Sunday morning, for the first time since the war had begun just over three years previously, there was a feeling of optimism in the air for, on this day also, Operation *Torch* began. Allied troops landed in French North Africa in Morocco and Algeria. Rommel found himself in a sandwich position with the 8th Army on one side and the 1st Army on the other.

In the Western Desert a period of consolidation followed. This respite allowed the commanders of the 8th Army to take stock of the situation and the Transport Corps and its officers to bring up fresh supplies. On the 23rd January, 1943, the leading troops of the 8th Army entered Tripoli. They had covered nearly 1,400 miles in three months. Tobruk and Benghazi had changed hands yet again, on the 13th and 18th November respectively. The loss of Tripoli marked the end of the Italian African empire. It now ceased to exist. Regions that had belonged to Italy for a third of a century passed out of its hands. Moving westward into

Tunisia, Montgomery and his army came up against the Mareth line on the 24th February.

The Allied forces that determined to drive the Germans from French North Africa formed what was up until then the largest amphibious invasion force in the history of warfare. 300 warships, 370 merchant ships and 107,000 men launched Operation *Torch* on the 8th November, 1942. Commanded by the American Lieutenant-General Dwight D Eisenhower, the operation got off to a good start, despite the early opposition of the Vichy-French authorities in North-West Africa. At Casablanca in Morocco, Major-General George Patton's Western Task Force of 25,000 men came under attack from Vichy-French air and ground fire and at Oran, Major-General Lloyd Fredenhall's Central Task Force of 39,000 men had to fight hard to establish beachheads. In Algiers, Major-General Charles Ryder's Eastern Task Force of 43,000 men, after heavy fighting, were able to land on three beaches. After just three days Admiral Jean Darlan, commander of the French forces, surrendered.

At the annual Lord Mayor's Luncheon in London on the 10th November, 1942, Winston Churchill declared, 'Now this is not the end, it is not even the beginning of the end, but it is perhaps the end of the beginning.'

Within seventy-six hours of the launch of Operation *Torch* Allied troops were in control of 1,300 miles of the African coast, and within eight days the 1st Army was just eighty miles from Tunis. With General Sir Kenneth Anderson's British First Army went Phantom's 'E' Squadron, commanded by Major Mervyn Vernon. The operation that began swiftly soon slowed as incessant rain turned the African desert to mud, bogging down many army vehicles. Overstretched supply lines and reinforcements of German troops newly-arrived in Africa, further hampered the Allies' progress. One of General Anderson's main aims was to seize Bizerta and Tunis in Rommel's rear, but this he failed to achieve before the Germans, having recovered from the initial surprise of the landings, took possession of both cities. With incredible alacrity they had arrived there first by transporting large numbers of troops, supplies and light weapons by air.

'E' Squadron was in the middle of the action. In spite of the atmospheric conditions, good radio contact was maintained at all times. Phantom distances were increasing and the long-range training was proving its worth. Most patrols were fifty miles from Squadron HQ, which was itself 150 miles from the Anchor Detachment that was with Army HQ. Phantom was well regarded and the fact that the squadron had a direct radio link with England was most impressive. So valued was the work of Phantom that soon another squadron was requested by the First Army. This time Major Warre's 'K' Squadron was made ready. Tony Warre, you will remember, had joined Phantom in the early days of the war when his troop of 12th Lancers had joined Hoppy's original mission in Belgium. He had taken over the newly-formed 'K' in 1942 and on Friday the 19th February, 1943, Warre and his squadron found themselves on board the SS *Buissevain* docked on the Clyde at Glasgow. The following Wednesday, at about midnight, they set sail for North Africa.

One of Phantom's officers with 'K' Squadron was the actor Hugh Williams, better known as 'Tam'. In the middle of 1941, at the request of film director Michael Powell, Tam had been released from the army to make a series of morale-boosting films 'to assist the war effort'. Newly-married, for the second time, Tam was only to happy to get back to the film studio. Over the next eighteen months he starred in films such as '*Ships With Wings*', '*The Day Will Dawn*' and '*One of Our Aircraft is Missing*'. At the end of 1942 Tam was back in the army, but not with his old regiment the 8th Battalion of the Devonshires. With the influence of an old friend, Major John Hannay, Tam now became a member of Phantom. John Hannay was at that time second-in-command to David Niven, fellow actor of Tam's, who was still commanding 'A' Squadron.

The SS *Buissevan*, with the officers and men of 'K' Squadron on board, sailed into Algiers on the 5th March, 1943. Here they disembarked and, carrying their gear, marched a mile or so to a designated transit camp. Three days later they made contact with 'E' Squadron. Major Warre's job was to liaise with American forces under the command of General Patton, who were preparing to attack Gafsa, and to work with them in covering the news of the battle. This they did most successfully. Their contact with the RAF, plotting map references and co-ordinates of enemy positions and movements, and transmitting them back to Phantom HQ, was particularly helpful to the outcome of the ensuing battles. Especially in air to ground strikes.

With General Patton's US II Corps threatening the rearguard of the German troops, Montgomery's attack on the Mareth Line was launched on the night of March 20th. By now, Rommel was no longer in command. He had handed his Army Group over to *General* Jurgen von Arnim and flown to Europe to see Hitler, having concluded that it would be suicide for the Axis forces to continue to fight on in Africa. Furious at what he called Rommel's 'pessimism', the *Führer* barred his General from returning to Africa, sending him instead on sick leave.

The Battle of Mareth proved not to be an easy one as the Germans fought ferociously to defend their position, but eventually *General* Messe and his forces were out-manoeuvred and by the 27th the Mareth Line was turned and Messe led his army along the coast road in retreat. By the middle of April the last of the German and Italian forces in North Africa were holed up in an enclave around Tunis.

When the 1st and 8th Armies finally met at 1st Army HQ near Souk-el-Arbra in April, both Phantom Squadrons were present. A large part of Montgomery's experienced troops was lent to the 1st Army and the final break-through began. Phantom's No. 3 and No. 6 patrols from 'K' were with the leading Allied troops when they arrived in Bizerta on the 7th May. Bizerta and Tunis fell within a few hours of one another. Axis troops had continued to fight stubbornly all along the front but could not hold out. Von Arnim withdrew his remaining troops to Cap Bon where, having nothing left to fight with and unable to escape by sea or air in any large numbers, he surrendered the remains of his Army Group. Admiral Cunnningham's Royal Navy had made evacuation by sea impossible and the planes of the RAF were commanding the skies. 300,000 men laid down their arms. The North African campaign was over.

A victory parade was held in Tunis on the 20th May, 1943. Pipers of the 51st Highland Division led the march through the streets of the city where the salute was taken by Generals Anderson, Eisenhower and Giraud. A patrol from both 'E' and 'K' Phantom Squadrons were invited to take part, for the victory was theirs as well.

The North African campaign had been a great success for Phantom. The Chief of the General Staff Home Forces paid the following tribute to their work:

'The two Phantom squadrons under 18 Army Group have

done excellent work. Their information was accurate and, owing to their excellent communications, up-to-date. On battle days about seventy-five per cent of the information coming in was from Phantom.' Praise indeed!

The use of the jeep by a Phantom patrol, introduced by the Americans, was considered far superior to the use of the existing motor-cycle, so the jeep would, from now on, replace the motor-cycle wherever and whenever possible - one of the lessons learnt in North Africa. Another was that patrol leaders, until now usually Lieutenants, needed to be Captains. A rank that would allow them easier access to operations rooms and a higher standing at any army headquarters.

CHAPTER XIII

# Into Europe

*'His death was felt keenly by the whole division for he was much respected.'*
PETER STAINFORTH, OFFICER, AIRBORNE DIVISION,
SPEAKING OF MAJOR GENERAL HOPKINSON,
FOUNDER OF PHANTOM.

As the summer of 1942 had marked the high water line of Axis aggression, so the summer of 1943 marked the onset of the ebb in Hitler's war. Attack and advance were giving way to defence and withdrawal.

January 1943 saw a renewed bombing campaign by the Allies on German cities, ports and industrial areas. On the 27th American bombers - eighty-four Flying Fortresses and seven Liberators - made an unescorted daylight raid on the naval base at Wilhelmshaven and three days later the Royal Air Force marked Nazi Germany's tenth anniversary by bombing Berlin, not once but twice, in their first daylight air raids on this great city. On March 2nd, Berlin was again devastated when it suffered its biggest raid of the war so far. The heavy bombers of the RAF delivered 8,000 tons of high-explosive bombs from the night sky causing massive destruction. The following night it was the turn of London to suffer a tragedy.

Britain, in the early days of the war, had not been prepared for the destruction that the *Blitz* would cause and the ferocity with which it would come. London had received the most aerial bombardment from the *Luftwaffe* and its people had soon come to realise that having the world's largest underground railway system was to save many lives. As soon as the air raid sirens were heard many people quickly made their way to their nearest Underground Station. Others, either by choice or because they were unable to move far because of age or illness, stayed at home seeking safety under stairs and in cellars, or in Anderson shelters. These shelters, named after the Rt Hon. Sir John Anderson, the Home Secretary at the outbreak of the war, were built in the back gardens of many homes. A simple hole was dug in the ground and its sides and roof were shored up with timber and covered in corrugated tin with soil and sandbags heaped on top. These home-made shelters, surprisingly, gave good protection from Hitler's bombs.

One of the largest of the Underground Stations was Bethnal Green, right in the heart of London's East End. An horrendous accident occurred there on the evening of the 3rd March, 1943, that caused the deaths of nearly two hundred people.

Londoners were expecting a reprisal raid after the RAF's attack on Berlin the night before. On the evening in question, German bombers had been sighted over the south coast of England. Destination London. The air raid sirens sounded at about 8.15pm and the East End inhabitants left their homes. Within a few minutes over a thousand people had entered Bethnal Green Underground Station by the one and only entrance, and many more were queuing to get in. The usual crowd had been swelled by the audiences of two cinemas and the passengers of three double-decker buses. Just after 8.30pm, as the sound of anti-aircraft guns, which were situated in nearby Victoria Park, were heard unleashing a salvo skywards, panic set in. The people mistakenly took this noise to be the sound of bombs dropping around them and they surged forward to gain shelter. A woman carrying a child stumbled and fell on the dark stairway and many more fell on top. The mass of bodies was further crushed as more people, not realising what had happened, tried to shove their way in.

It took the rescue services and civilian helpers, including the author's father, Bill Parlour, more than three hours to clear the casualties from the tangle of human bodies and to remove the corpses of those who had been suffocated or trampled to death in the stampede. Nearly two hundred men, women and children died in this terrible tragedy, but what made it all the more poignant was the fact that it had been a false alarm and no bombs had actually fallen.

The Allied air raids continued and the Ruhr city of Essen, in Germany's industrial heartland, became the target of Lancasters, Halifaxes, Stirlings and Wellingtons, as the RAF desperately sought to knock out the armament and industrial factories sited there. At the same time, Russian long-range bombers made individual attacks on Danzig and Königsberg from the East.

Meanwhile, in the South Pacific Seas, on February 10th, six months after first landing on Guadalcanal, it was announced that American forces had cleared this small island of Japanese forces. It had been a terrible blow as Japan attached the highest importance to the strategically placed Solomon Islands.

In the North Atlantic on the 24th May, *Grossadmiral* Karl Doenitz, who had replaced *Grossadmiral* Raeder as commander-in-chief of the German navy, accepted failure. 'The Battle of the Atlantic' had become a disaster for the Germans. Radar and the successes in breaking the *Enigma* codes by the men and women at Bletchley Park had made life increasingly difficult for them. During the first twenty-two days of May, Doenitz had lost thirty-three U-boats and now recalled what he had left to the less dangerous waters of the South Atlantic.

On the Russian front the war had not been going Hitler's way either. January 31st had seen *Feldmarschall* Friedrich Paulus surrender to a Russian lieutenant in Stalingrad, after one of the greatest and bloodiest battles of the Second World War. On the 2nd February, the last pockets of German resistance in this ruined city had surrendered. Column after column of German prisoners had been marched away and in Germany two days of mourning had been decreed. Five days later the Russians retook Azov and a few days after that they recaptured Krasnodar in the Kuban. A major coup had come when the Red Army captured Kharkov, Germany's main base in southern Russia, only to lose it again in a counter-offensive by the Germans. But still the Soviet troops marched on. In early March Stalin had been awarded the rank of Marshal of the Soviet Union, hailing him as 'the greatest strategist of all times and of all peoples.'

By May, in less than six months, Stalingrad and Tunisia together had cost the Axis the loss of well over half a million men.

These successes in the first few months of 1943 boosted the morale of the British people. A thanksgiving service for victory in North Africa was attended by the royal family. The King and Queen were accompanied by their two daughters, the Princesses Elizabeth and Margaret. Once more the sound of church bells, silent since the beginning of the war with orders that they were only to be rung as a signal of enemy invasion, could be heard ringing out over the land. The cabinet had decided that 'in the light of changing circumstances' the ban could be relaxed on Sundays and special occasions.

Sport in Britain, nearly all cancelled at the outbreak of war in 1939, enjoyed a revival. Racing and greyhounds had continued, mainly due to gambling, although many racecourses with their open tracts of land were being used for the war effort. The Grand National was not run for five years, but the Derby, which had moved from Epsom to Newmarket in 1940, was as popular as ever. Those lucky enough to attend in June 1943 saw *Straight Deal* win this premier classic event. Greyhound racing thrived as an afternoon entertainment for night workers and the sport became so popular that some meetings became all-ticket events. Ernest Bevin, the Minister of Labour, encouraged the game of cricket and when the Prime Minister, Winston Churchill, attended football matches the campaigners against sport admitted defeat. 'Sport,' declared Churchill, 'nurtures cheerfulness.' Incidentally, the suspension of the FA Cup made Portsmouth, winners of the cup in 1939, the longest ever holders as this competition was not to be played again until 1946. A special War Cup in the spring of 1940 had been won by West Ham United. They beat Blackburn Rovers 1-0 at Wembley in front of a crowd of 42,399, which included survivors of the previous week's retreat from Dunkirk.

By the summer of 1943 the war had not been won by any means but the tide was strongly flowing in the Allies' favour.

During the last week of July and the first week of August RAF Bomber Command was to launch Operation Gomorrah, a major bombing offensive on Hamburg which destroyed much of its industrial capability and razed the city to the ground.

The pace was beginning to quicken now for Phantom. Between the 23rd February and the 6th March, 1943, Exercise Spartan had taken place. This exercise, which took place in the Home Counties, had been the first in which Phantom had been employed in its proper role, having had four squadrons deployed at Corps level and two mobile anchor detachments (MADETS) with Army HQ and RHQ at General Headquarters. Spartan was the fullest scale exercise the British Army had ever carried out and its theme was the liberation of Europe.

The 1st Canadian Army played the part of the 6th German Army and the men of the Berks, Bucks and Oxford regiments played the part of the British Army. In this exercise Phantom was to receive information from both sides, an unreal position. For this reason the exercise clearly demonstrated the value and importance of Phantom. A satisfactory feature was the success of the MADETS which were being tried for the first time for the purpose of this exercise.

The four squadrons employed by Phantom on *Spartan* were

A, B, C and D. Patrols of one officer and five or six men of other ranks were now given the use of a new wireless set, the No. 22. This proved to be far superior to the former No. 11 which was apt to fade out. The new sets and their operators worked well together, especially over long distances, and neither let the other down.

One positive result of this exercise was the impression that Phantom made on the Canadians. From that time onwards Phantom was to achieve maximum effect when working alongside the Canadians, both before and after D-Day.

Phantom was next to see action again in July 1943 with the Allied invasion of Sicily.

Even before the final defeat of the Axis powers in North Africa, the Allied leaders were turning their thoughts towards their next move. At a secret meeting in Washington in May 1943, Churchill and Roosevelt, after several days of discussion, had agreed that Italy would be their next target. Roosevelt had favoured an immediate invasion across the Channel to liberate France and the Lowlands but Churchill opposed this saying that more time was needed before the Allied troops would be ready for a campaign in North-west Europe. Churchill convinced Roosevelt that it would be best to try to knock the Italians out of the war first and so they set the date for the invasion of France for no later than May 1944.

Before landings could be made in Italy the large island of Sicily, with its fifty or so enemy airfields, would first have to be taken. A combined American and British operation, code named Husky, was planned for July 1943. Air and naval bombardments neutralized the outlying islands of Pantelleria and Lampedusa in June in readiness for the invasion of Sicily. By the time the enormous sea-borne fleet approached the south-eastern coast of Sicily on the night of the 9/10th July, four thousand planes of the Allied Air Force, under the command of Air Chief-Marshal Tedder, had knocked out many of the enemy defences. The island's aerodromes and harbours had taken a severe battering and Messina, the port on the tip of the island facing the Italian mainland, alone had received 5,000 tons of bombs.

British and US airborne forces were to precede the soldiers who would land early on the 10th, but things did not go quite as planned as high winds scattered both the British gliders and the American paratroops.

In one of the leading gliders was Phantom's founder, George

Hopkinson, now a Major-General. Hopkinson had left Phantom in the late autumn of 1941 to command the gliderborne brigade of the 1st Airborne Division. Peter Stainforth, one of his officers, recalls in his book, *'Wings of the Wind'*, Hoppy's arrival on Sicily: 'Our Divisional Commander, Major-General Hopkinson, who flew to Sicily in the leading glider, came down in the sea himself but managed to swim ashore, making, like Julius Caesar, a less dignified landing than intended.'

The sea-borne landing, thankfully, went more smoothly. The enormous invasion fleet, comprised of 2,590 ships, both large and small, carrying 180,000 men, took part in Operation *Husky* under the command of Admiral Cunningham. Under him, Admiral Sir Bertram Ramsay was in command of the landings with 237 merchant vessels and troop transports and 1,742 amphibious motorized landing craft to bring ashore the men, tanks and supplies. This was, up till then, the largest sea-borne invasion in history, larger even than Operation *Torch* the previous November on North-west Africa.

General Patton's US 7th and General Sir Bernard Montgomery's British 8th from North-west Africa, under General Alexander's command, were the two Armies involved. The British Eighth comprised the XIII Corps and the XXX Corps, which included the 1st Canadian Division. It was with the former that patrols from Phantom's 'H' Squadron were to go.

In April news had arrived at 'H' Squadron's base at Alexandria from Phantom's regimental headquarters at Richmond, that a Special Assault Detachment, commanded by Captain Sedgwick was on its way out from England. Forty members of 'H' Squadron were to join the Assault Detachment at Suez, with all to be under the command of Major Grant, 'H' Squadron Leader. With the confirmation of the date for the assault on Sicily, training began in earnest. The men would have to be fit for the task ahead, so physical training played a large part in their preparation. Military exercises began and it became clear that for Phantom to be efficient its patrols needed to be in the craft of the commander of the leading formation when the landings began and that they would need their own transport.

By dawn on the 10th July, 150,000 British, Canadian and American soldiers were safely ashore, with a further 320,000 preparing to join them over the following two days. The enemy was taken somewhat by surprise. Not until the last moment did the defenders realise that Sicily was to be the invaders' target.

A brilliant Allied deception, involving the use of a corpse with false documents which was allowed to be found by the Germans floating in the sea, had convinced Hitler that Sardinia was to be the invading convoy's destination - although Mussolini had all along suspected Sicily would be. When it became clear that the convoy was bound for Sicily, an unseasonal storm, which delayed the invasion for only an hour, convinced the Italians that landings could not take place and many of them stayed in their beds. They awoke to surrender in their hundreds.

Patrols from Phantom's 'E' and 'K' Squadrons, commanded by Captain Julian Fane, MC, had embarked from Sousse in Tunisia for Sicily on the 8th July. The three patrols, under Lieutenants Cuming, Laurie and Adam who were all Scotsmen, were happily deployed to the 51st Highland Division. 'H' Squadron was with XIII Corps. One patrol was to go in with each assaulting battalion, one was with each brigade HQ, a detachment with each division and the control party was to be with the Corps HQ on board HMS *Bulolo*. Difficulties arose here when Phantom's Signals Officer, Captain Adam (no relation to Lieutenant Adam), and the ship's Signals Officer, who had control of all the wireless sets on the ship, clashed. With the sets down below receiving no signals and thus no information, Adam smuggled a No. 48 set up to the toilet above where he got a perfect reception, although not much information was coming through from those ashore.

In the assault itself the duty of the patrols extended little beyond the reporting of the initial phase of the battle and, with the arrival of the 8th Army's 'J' Service, which carried out a role very similar to its own, Phantom was withdrawn. Although they had served a purpose, Phantom's Major Grant was disappointed with the results, feeling that the squadrons had not really been of much use in this invasion.

By the 17th August, after just 38 days, Sicily was in Allied hands. Bitter fighting had seen the Allies push the enemy north. The Americans narrowly beat the British to the historic city of Messina, where they found the retreating Axis army had crossed the Strait of Messina to the toe of Italy.

The fall of Sicily opened the way for the invasion of the Italian mainland which was, by now, no longer under Mussolini's control.

On the 19th July, Hitler had summoned the Italian dictator to Feltre in Northern Italy to discuss the current war situation.

A most unsatisfactory meeting from both the German and Italian point of view. Hitler did all the talking and Mussolini listened in silence. Hitler had long felt that the co-operation between their two Armed Forces was becoming increasingly strained and that his Alliance partner had lost the will to fight. Benito Mussolini left the meeting to return to Rome. Here he found buildings in this ancient city burning after enemy bombing, and a feeling of revolt from both the people and his own government.

Within a week of his return, Mussolini was dismissed by Italy's King Victor Emmanuel III and placed under arrest. At a meeting of the Fascist Grand Council, Mussolini's conduct of the war was severely criticised and a resolution to return Italy to a constitutional monarchy with a democratic parliament was carried. The veteran *Marshal* Pietro Badoglio was asked to form a non-Fascist government with its authority based on the Crown and the Army.

From the day that Badoglio became Italy's premier, he was determined to take his disillusioned country out of the war. On the 3rd September, 1943, the fourth anniversary of Britain's declaration of war with Germany, Italy's *General* Giuseppe Castellena, signed a secret armistice with the Allies in Sicily. US Lieutenant-General Walter Bedell Smith signed for the Allies. On this same day Western Allies launched Operation Baytown, the invasion of mainland Italy. At 4.30am that morning, under cover of naval fire, formations of the British 8th Army, commanded by General Montgomery, crossed the Straits of Messina to land at Reggio di Calabria, on the tip of Italy's toe, and all along the shore to San Giovanni. The shells of the monitors, cruisers and destroyers which had rained down on the beaches along this coast ensured that the Allies met with little opposition. The remains of the two German Panzer divisions in the area had left and the Italians, having little stomach for the fight, put up no resistance.

By nightfall on the 3rd the Canadians had seized Reggio aerodrome and the first Allied landing on the mainland of Hitler's Europe had been made. On the 8th another landing, this time at Taranto, gave the Allies a base behind the Italian toe. Again there was little opposition, but it was to be a different story at Salerno.

The announcement of the unconditional surrender of Germany's former partner was made on the 8th to coincide with the major Allied landings at Salerno, Operation

*Avalanche*. Soldiers in the convoy approaching Salerno heard the voice of their Commander-in-Chief, General Eisenhower, announce the Italian surrender over the ships' Tannoys. The ensuing high spirits of the troops were not to last long though as, this time, the Allies were met by much stronger German opposition. Salerno, a few miles south of Naples on Italy's west coast, was in the middle of the German lines. Three Panzer and several infantry divisions fought fiercely to repel the invaders. It was not until the 18th that the crisis was over, and two days later Montgomery's 8th Army, pushing up from Calabria, made contact with the Allies at Salerno.

After withdrawing from Sicily, Phantom's 'H' Squadron was in three parties that reassembled in Egypt in the middle of August. It spent the autumn of 1943 training in Syria where it was joined by members of 'K' Squadron, which was disbanding and leaving North Africa. 'K' had been put under the command of Captain Julian Fane in July as Major Tony Warre, who had been one of the founding members of Phantom back in 1940, left to return to his regiment. Now in October some of its officers and men joined 'H' and the rest sailed for England, but not before they heard the devastating news from Richmond that their founder and former commander, for whom they all had the greatest respect and affection, had been killed in action in Italy.

Major-General Hopkinson, had led his division, cruiser-borne, as they sailed to establish a bridgehead at Taranto on the 9th September. As a divisional Commander, Hoppy was always to be found well up with the forward troops. Three days later, in an operation just outside Castellaneta, a town 15 miles inland from Taranto, he was killed by a stray bullet, although some reports said it was from a sniper's rifle, while watching an attack on a road-block.

An air of despondency and gloom now descended on all the men of Phantom. Respected by all he commanded, Hoppy, as he was affectionately known by his men of all ranks, had been sorely missed when he had left the Phantom regiment two years previously. A soldier through and through, he never took a wife. He always said his marriage was to the British Army. As a commander, he would never expect his men to do anything that he would not do himself. Lieutenant-Colonel George Hopkinson, MC, had joined Phantom in November 1939, originally as a Military Observer to Wing-Commander Fairweather's Air Mission. He had come from the North

Staffordshire Regiment where he had previously been part of Major-General Sir Richard Howard-Vyse's mission, whose task it had been to liaise with General Gamelin in Paris. As a qualified pilot, Hoppy knew only too well the importance of ground to air reconnaissance and co-operation, being able to see battle developments from both a soldier's and an airman's perspective. Among his many talents was his adept horsemanship and his ability as a sailor. Although not the tallest of men, Hoppy was solidly built and extremely fit. Harry Binge recalls that on one particular cross-country run Hopkinson, leading his squadron, went off at a tremendous pace leaving his men far behind. They all thought that he would never keep it up, but how wrong they were. He was back at base long before they all straggled in!

There are many stories that have been told about Hoppy, some of which we now relate to you.

David Niven, long time Squadron Leader of 'A', remembered Hoppy as 'a short square officer with a fertile imagination and a great gift for extracting the maximum loyalty and hard work from all ranks. Before he was killed in action in Italy, he built up a unit that again and again proved its worth in the liberation of Europe.'

When in 1941, just prior to leaving Phantom, Hoppy realised that his men were becoming increasingly bored with all their training, he sent them whizzing all over England. 'Keep the men interested,' he would say. 'Think up some novel employment for them. Turn night into day. Make up some front line conditions.'

The Hon. Michael Astor, who was with Phantom from the early days, tells us in his book *'Tribal Feeling'*, how Hoppy once tried to change his plans for him as he was about to go on leave by suggesting that he should use his time in having his appendix removed. 'But why, Sir?' I asked him. 'I think my appendix is all right.' He answered, 'But when you go into battle you will be a better risk as an officer if you don't have an appendix. I had mine out on leave in India.' To miss a battle because of an appendix would have been a disappointment George Hopkinson would not have wished on anybody.

On one occasion, in the second winter of the war, Hoppy was the guest of a few of his junior officers in London, including Michael Astor. After dinner Hoppy invited them to drink a glass of port with him in the United Services Club and, realising that he might be late back, he asked Michael to ring up the duty officer at Richmond to let him know. Astor got on the telephone and the corporal in the orderly room explained that the duty officer could not be found. 'This is ridiculous,' Astor answered. 'Who is the duty officer?' After a moment the corporal sheepishly replied, 'You are, Sir.'

Realising that his absent-mindedness had put a blemish on the evening, Astor hurried back to the orderly room at Richmond and the lapse gave Hoppy the excuse to return to regimental headquarters rather than to go on to a night-club. At two o'clock in the morning he visited Astor in the orderly room and after a few minutes light-hearted small-talk, he finished on a military note. 'Try turning out the guard at four o'clock this morning.' 'Yes, Sir,' Astor replied. 'Good night, Michael.' 'Good night, Colonel.'

Michael Astor knew that somehow he would have to stay awake until four o'clock. He could not let his commander down again.

Captain Norman Reddaway, who had been with Phantom from its beginnings and had been evacuated from Dunkirk with Wing-Commander Fairweather (who did not make it home), commented on Hopkinson's vision: 'From the beginning Hoppy realised that the set-pattern of World War One was unlikely to be repeated. In a future mobile war he felt that the set-front signals system would be inadequate and that it was therefore essential to find a substitute relying on radio and reconnaissance. His single-mindedness was completely dedicated to this idea. He was only interested in the future.'

It was not only the officers of Phantom who sang Hopkinson's praises, it was also the men. Harry Binge well remembers receiving his medal from Hoppy and David Niven at the Richmond cinema in 1941 and laughingly recalls how they nearly never made it.

Hoppy had arranged with David Niven for the officers and the men of Phantom to watch Niven's latest film 'Bachelor Mother', in which he co-starred with Ginger Rogers. This Saturday morning treat, Hoppy felt, would make a welcome break from the tedium of constant training. Several hundred officers and men were duly marched down Richmond Hill to where the cinema was situated. Harry remembers how the officer in charge, who he thinks was a Lt Brook-Hart who he later served with in Northern Ireland, decided to take a short cut. 'We started to march down a side-road. Very shortly it turned into a scene like that from the TV series *'Dad's Army'*, for at the end of the cut was a six foot high solid brick wall. The men at the front were soon being squashed against this wall by the men at the back who, not realising that they were in a cul-de-sac and not being given the order to mark time, kept on marching - completely unaware of the chaos ahead. There was one very red-faced officer that morning, I can tell you.' This incident appealed to Hoppy's sense of humour.

Peter Stainforth, an officer serving with Hoppy's Airborne Division when he was killed, reflected, 'His death was felt keenly by the whole division for he was much respected.'

Lieutenant-Colonel Vladimir Peniakoff, a Belgian born of Russian parents, was the commander of Popski's Private Army which worked alongside Hopkinson's First Airborne Division. He remembers Hoppy in his biography, 'Popski's Private Army': 'We were attached to First Airborne Division and training hard. I talked over my plans with General Hopkinson who commanded our airborne troops. Once convinced of their feasibility, he grew enthusiastic, for he was that kind of man, and he and his staff helped us to the limit of their power.'

Peniakoff goes on to say, 'General Hopkinson had been killed at Massafara, outside Tarranto, on a visit to his outposts. He was a man who couldn't bear to remain behind when he ordered his men forward, and a sniper shot him through the head. A well-beloved leader in his picked division, according to his men he was just what a general should be. It might seem a pity that he should have been killed, not on one of the airborne missions for which with great fervour he had prepared himself and his troops, but on a humdrum routine tour of inspection of his grounded troops; but it is a fit end for a soldier to lose his life in the punctilious performance of his less spectacular duties.'

Today, Phantom's founder, George Hopkinson, lies at rest in the Bari War Cemetery in Italy, some thirty-five miles north of the spot where he was killed. He is remembered with honour thus: 'George Frederick Hopkinson, MC, OBE. Major-General, North Staffordshire Regiment, who died on Sunday, 12th September 1943. Age 47.'

It was Phantom's 'E' Squadron, by then commanded by Major the Hon. Hugh Fraser, which was to go to Italy. A message from Major-General Hopkinson, which proved to be the last to his old regiment, had arrived on the evening of the 8th September from Airborne HQ, requesting that a Phantom Squadron be ready to leave the following afternoon with all its gear for the first part of its journey to Italy - the 200 mile trek to Bizerta. A week later the squadron embarked on the cruiser HMS *Aurora*, with four of its jeeps but minus its scout cars and wireless vans which were to follow.

As they crossed the Mediterranean the officers and men of Phantom witnessed the magnificent sight of the Italian Navy making its way to the Maltese port of Valetta where it was to surrender.

By the time the *Aurora* arrived off Taranto on the 12th, the men of Phantom knew what their task was to be. General Downes had decided that a mixed reconnaissance force should check out the area beyond the line that the landings at Taranto and Brindisi had formed across the heel of Italy. The reconnaissance force would consist of a group of Popski's Private Army, a squadron of the 2nd SAS Regiment under Major Roy Farran, the Airborne Division Reconnaissance Squadron and 'E' Squadron Phantom.

Popski's Private Army (PPA) had been raised in October 1942 by Lieut-Col. Vladimir Peniakoff, known as Popski, and it had engaged in intelligence-gathering and hit-and-run attacks behind enemy lines in North Africa. Now it was to harass the Germans in Italy.

In his biography Popski remembers the meeting with Phantom, 'We reached the coast shortly after dawn, slept for a few hours in an olive grove, then drove to Bari where we found a few of our troops, odd specimens like us: Hugh Fraser with his 'Phantoms' and also a detachment of 2nd SAS under Roy Farren, who had driven up brazenly through German positions in a train from Taranto. They could deal with local reconnaissance and this confirmed me in my resolve to penetrate deeper to the north.'

Phantom's orders were to deploy towards Bari, further up the coast from Brindisi. The squadron had had to off-load onto a minesweeper to get into Taranto Harbour and in the darkness had assembled on the quayside. With the news that a German armoured division was advancing on the town, it withdrew to an olive grove on the outskirts of the town where it spent the night. It was the following morning as the men were sorting out their equipment that had been unloaded in heaps beneath olive trees, that they heard the devastating news of Hopkinson's death.

The patrols of 'E' were given their orders to patrol behind enemy lines and to keep contact with the withdrawing enemy forces, so they set off in their jeeps, which they now had two of as well as a motorcycle, carrying as much of their wireless apparatus as they could to start a communication system. It was no easy task to obtain reliable information concerning enemy movements. When the first Phantom patrol, that of the now Captain Denys Brook-Hart, arrived in Bari, the town was in a state of confusion, the Italian 19th Corps had set up its headquarters there. As the two had been at war until only a few days before, the atmosphere was rather strained and so the Phantom patrol set up its headquarters in an olive grove outside the town. Two days later CO Hugh Fraser and further patrols from 'E' joined it, and they moved their HQ to a vineyard on the outskirts of a small village to the west of Bari. It was from here that they successfully conducted their reconnaissance and intelligence-gathering operations behind German lines.

Although until recently enemies, the Italian people were only too eager to help the Allies. Not only did they shower them with gifts of fruit and wine, they were also quite happy to help them in any way they could in their fight against their now common foe, the Germans.

For three weeks Phantom continued to work with the V Corps and the Americans but, having proved its worth yet again, Phantom was withdrawn from Italy in mid-October. In spite of its great success, Montgomery had arrived with his 8th Army and, yet again, wanted his 'J' Service to take Phantom's place.

CHAPTER XIV

# J-Service

*'It was important that the Brigade Commander should receive early information of the progress of his forward troops.'*
BRIGADE-MAJOR MONTGOMERY.
BATTLE OF THE SOMME, 1916.

As mentioned in Chapter Four, Hopkinson was not the only one who had come up with the idea of a liaison unit. General Montgomery had also developed his own form of information service. In his memoirs he recalls, during the Battle of Alamein, the beginnings of his 'Staff Information' service:

*'This was an organization for intercepting the signals sent out by our own forward units and relaying them to Army and Corps HQ. We called the service 'J', for short. It was used for the first time in this battle. It was invented by a most able officer on my staff called Hugh Mainwaring; he was unfortunately captured with a reconnaissance party near Mersa Matruh early in November, and then I had to find another officer to operate 'J' Service.*

*Receiving wireless sets 'listened' on division, brigade, and armoured corps forward controls and broadcast the information obtained. This cut down the time-lag between the origination of information by the forward troops and its receipt at Army and Corps HQ. 'J' gives to a higher commander a good indication of the fighting spirit of his troops and, incidentally, although this was not its prime purpose, it could also help in spotting obvious breaches of security. It had the overall effect of tightening the entity of the Army; bringing it all closer together. Wireless links became intimate links between men engaged on the same enterprise. It ended the remoteness of the staff.*

*It will be remembered that as a GSO 1 in 1918 I had devised a system of getting to Divisional HQ quickly the accurate information of the progress of the battle which is so vital. Then I used officers with wireless sets. The 'J' Service invented by Hugh Mainwaring was a great improvement on my earlier attempts.'*

Lieut-Col. Hugh Mainwaring, reputed to be of a dour and humourless nature, was the Eighth Army's Intelligence Officer.

He often briefed his senior commanders on the preceding twenty-four-hour operations on information gathered, much of which was supplied by his 'J' Service.

When a reconnaissance party was sent forward by Montgomery to select a site for his headquarters in the Mersa Matruh area, Hugh Mainwaring, and, incidentally, Dick Carver, Monty's stepson, were members of this party. As they approached Smugglers Cove, just to the east of the town, the reconnaissance party was captured. They had been led to believe that all enemy forces had been cleared from the region by that time but, delayed by heavy rain that bogged them down in the desert, the Allied forces had failed to reach this area. Monty himself could have been captured at Smugglers Cove had he not bumped into an enemy rearguard that was trying to hold off the advancing British while they cleared Mersa Matruh. Bringing up the rear with his own small escort he had been about to turn off and follow his reconnaissance party down the same road when they ran into an engagement that was going on a few hundred yards in front of them. Very quickly his party retreated to a safe position.

'J', although very similar to Phantom, was essentially a listening service. Its signal operators listened in to everything on the air from its Army's forward units, and from enemy positions too. It developed a system of analysing the wireless traffic of its units in combat. While it was Phantom's task to obtain official information from forward HQ that was often delayed by coding, 'J' received chatter from tank commanders in the heat of battle about events as they happened. This they could pass on very quickly.

By January 1943 'J' Service had one Royal Signals officer and forty-nine other ranks, and was a unit of Royal Signals. Delighted with its success in the Battle of Alamein, Montgomery continued to rely on its information as the campaign across North Africa moved on. It was particularly successful during the Battle of Mareth that commenced on the 20th March. Here Rommel had made one last stand. Montgomery addressed his Army with the words: 'We will destroy the enemy now facing us in the Mareth position, drive northwards until we finally reach Tunis and not stop until the enemy has either given up the struggle or been pushed into the sea.' As we know, the Mareth Line was in the possession of the Eighth Army by the 28th and, with the First and Eighth Armies having joined forces, Tunis, the stronghold of the German *Afrika Korps*, fell on the 7th May.

A detachment from 8th Army 'J' had joined 1st Army at its HQ at Souk El Abra and received information from both armies, very successfully.

As in Sicily, when Montgomery arrived in Italy with his 8th Army it was his 'J' Service that he wanted to work with, and Phantom was once again withdrawn.

By now it had become apparent that 'J' was at its most useful when listening in to armoured formations and interpreting their actions and positions in battle while Phantom was able to collect information from areas where wireless silence was in force and then, using its motor-cycle despatch riders, pass it back along special channels.

Subsequently, 'J' Service would become part of Phantom, but not yet. Its incorporation into Phantom would not officially come until December 1944, in Europe, but in the months preceding D-Day, June 1944, Phantom was adding many of 'J's methods to its own intelligence gathering and communications network. In fact, three patrols from 'B' Squadron would eventually be selected to form a 'J' Troop for that squadron, and the same was happening in 'A' Squadron.

On the 17th March, 1943, Lieut-Col. Alexander Macintosh took over as Phantom's third Commanding Officer. Lieut-Col. Derrick Hignett, who had commanded Phantom since Hoppy's departure to the 1st Airborne Division in the autumn of 1941, was unhappily forced to relinquish his position on health grounds. Macintosh came to his post just after Operation *Spartan*, during which Phantom's Second-in-Command, Major Morgan, and Major Russell of 'B' Squadron had been asked by General Gammell to read up about 'J' Service, of which they had never heard, and decide almost immediately whether they could provide the same service during this very important operation. Of course, they readily agreed and found the experiment to be highly successful.

Now the question of 'J' Service was being very closely examined by Phantom. It was felt that as the Service existed and could not be ignored, it would be better to use 'J' than try to oppose it. Its similarity to Phantom meant that it could satisfactorily be used by others, thus weakening Phantom's own standing. An experimental 'J' Troop was formed, mainly from existing Phantom members, and was deployed for the first time during Exercise *Columbus* which took place in the last week in May. *Columbus* was an exercise in which, for the first time, the British and the Americans were on opposing sides. 'L' Squadron was deployed with four patrols on the American side and one patrol plus the new 'J' Troop on the other. Again the experiment was extremely useful, indicating that 'J's methods could successfully be integrated into Phantom's.

During the summer of 1943 the future role of Phantom was being seriously considered. Earnest discussion was taking place at Henley-on-Thames where most of the regiment was camped. The outcome was that Phantom squadrons would in future serve army HQ's instead of corps HQ's and fewer but larger squadrons would be needed. As a consequence, from the 1st September, 1943, the old 'B' and 'D' Squadrons would become the new 'A' Squadron, commanded by Major Russell with Major J M Hannay second in command, and the old 'A' and 'C' would become the new 'B' Squadron under Major Pattrick with Major J E Dulley second in command. A Phantom squadron when deployed to an army would be made up of nine patrols – plus a 'J' Troop.

A War Office Committee sat in judgement on Phantom in the middle of September and, after much deliberation and scrutiny of its work in North Africa and Italy, it was decided that Phantom, in its new form, should be allowed to carry on, but that it should be made a unit of the Reconnaissance Corps. Very soon the Reconnaissance Corps, with Phantom, was to be merged into the Royal Armoured Corps. Another decision concerning Phantom's future was that it should be fully prepared to work with the Americans.

At the end of 1943 the Phantom Regiment consisted of five squadrons. The new 'A' and 'B' were at home training intensely for the great invasion of Europe. 'F' was in Scotland with 1 Corps, which we will read about later, and 'H' was still training in Syria awaiting its orders for Italy. 'E', after its withdrawal from Italy in October, was to disband and its personnel returned to England. 'K', still in North Africa, was also disbanded, many of its members going to reinforce 'H' and the remainder embarking for home at the end of November. The other squadron still in existence was 'L'. Having had no battle experience, this squadron had been sent to Scotland in July to replace the old 'C', although it was not to join 1 Corps. Training in the mountains and taking part in exercises all over Scotland, frequently with the 52nd (Lowland) Division commanded by Major-General Neil Ritchie, occupied most of this squadron's time. Obviously, wireless communication in mountainous areas was not easy and experiments were carried out using different sets and aerials.

1943 had not been an easy year for Phantom but the regiment had come through it with flying colours.

CHAPTER XV

# Italy and the Spring Offensive

*'I doubt if there are any other troops in the world who would have stood up to it and gone on fighting with the ferocity they have.'*

GENERAL ALEXANDER, SPEAKING OF
THE DEFENDERS OF MONTE CASSINO.

Less than five weeks after his country capitulated, Italy's new leader, *Marshal* Badoglio, declared war on his former Axis partner, Germany. The declaration did not make Italy one of the Allies, but Badoglio called on all Italian soldiers to take up arms and fight the Germans to the last man. On the 31st October, 1943, the First Motorized Group was the first Italian unit to join the US 5th Army as a co-belligerent, and in Rome the vindictive attitude of the Germans who still occupied this ancient city was forcing the Italian population to create a resistance movement.

The war in Italy during the last two months of 1943 was much determined by the weather. Steady remorseless rain turned the small summer rivers into fast-flowing torrents. Mountain tracks became impassable as the deluge washed away great chunks of the rocky hillsides. The Allied advance in the appalling mud continued, but at a much slower pace, as the Germans raced eastwards to counter a major threat to the *Gustav* Line. During the previous six months the Allies had captured Sicily and about a third of Italy, including Naples and the Foggia airfields – a major coup.

One of the last great battles of the Italian peninsula commenced in the middle of January 1944. With Mussolini no longer in control and the government in the hands of the Socialists, the Germans soon realised that if the whole of Italy was to fall into the hands of the Allies, the doorway into the underbelly of the German Fatherland would be open wide and Hitler's *Third Reich* would surely fall. This was too harsh to contemplate and a last great stand to protect Germany's southern approaches against the advancing combined armies of the free world would be made at Monte Cassino.

With its Axis partner in Europe now effectively 'on the other side', Germany stood alone, with a determination never to cede even one inch of ground without putting up the fiercest possible resistance. When its armies were forced to fall back, they did so strategically, leaving behind them a trail of destroyed road and rail bridges that spanned the many rivers and valleys in these mountainous regions, thus slowing their enemies still further.

The *'Gustav* Line' stretched from coast to coast through seemingly impassable mountains. Many strong defensive points were built by the Germans on mountain tops with panoramic views over the hills and valleys below. Early in December Allied troops had taken the summit of Monte Camino and in the middle of the month the crucial town of San Pietro had been taken, but not without tanks, artillery, mortars, phosphorous grenades, and the guts of the young American infantrymen. At the end of December British and Canadian forces had taken the eastern coastal town of Ortona after a five-day struggle, but in front of Cassino a renewed American attack could not dislodge the German forces.

The *'Gustav* Line' was at its strongest in the West, covering the Liri Valley and the path to Rome. Towering over the town of Cassino was the 13th century Benedictine Monastery. At a height of 1,700 feet above the town, it was a spectacular building which had suffered many attacks in its turbulent history. But none of the like that was to come. The monks, along with their priceless art treasures and ancient manuscripts, had been evacuated with the help of the German Army.

The first attack on Monte Cassino was launched on the 12th January. Led by the French Corps progress was made, but not enough. The determined German defence and the appalling winter weather made the capture of the town of Cassino impossible. By the time the First Battle of Cassino was called off on the 11th February, 14,000 Allies had been lost. Four days later, the Second Battle of Cassino commenced with a massive bombing campaign on the historic monastery. A most controversial decision. The New Zealand Corps which had the task of assaulting the heights, in the belief that it was being used as an observation post for German artillery, asked for it to be bombed. Although there was no absolute proof that it was being used for this purpose, the bombardment, nevertheless, went ahead. Six hundred tons of bombs dropped by 142

Phantom Assault Sqn Combined Ops Patrol, North Africa, 1943. *l to r:* Vic Trew; Frank Richardson; 'Joe' Owens; 'Croom' Johnson; Bill Randle.

Sgt Arthur Wood Phantom/SAS Sqn, 1944.

> 1st S.A.S. Regiment
> A.P.O.,
> England.
> ..........June.. 1944
>
> Dear Mrs Wood,
>
> The following information is available regarding your husband, Cpl A. Wood, 5442642
>
> He was dropped by parachute into France on 11.6.44 and up to the time of writing was quite safe and well. You may take it for granted that he is safe unless you hear to the contrary from us. He will not be able to write to you for some time but will be able to receive your letters so please keep writing.
>
> Cheerio, keep smiling and don't worry,
>
> Yours sincerely, G. Rose. R.S.M.
>
> To:- Mrs A. Wood,
> 94 Appleyard Crescent
> Norwich, Norfolk

Letter sent to Mrs Arthur Wood from 1st SAS. 12th June, 1944.

> Officer Commanding,
> "F" Squadron,
> G.H.Q. Liaison Regt.
> 1st July 1944.
>
> To:- Mrs. M. Wood, 94, Appleyard Crescent, Norwich, Norfolk
>
> Dear Mrs. Wood
>
> Your Husband, Cpl. Wood, is fit and well, and I am in constant contact with him.
>
> It is still not possible for him to write to you and this is likely to be the case for some time. I am sending on all letters addressed to him, so do keep on writing.
>
> Yours sincerely,
> J A Darwall Smith - Capt.
>
> Army Post Office,
> England.

Letter sent to Mrs Arthur Wood from 'F' Sqn, Phantom. 1st July, 1944.

Phantom Corporal servicing radio equipment, Phantom HQ Northern France, 1944.

Corporal Alf Askew *(left)* with Trooper Harry Binge, 'B' Sqn No. 23 patrol, Brussels, 1944.

Capt Millar *(centre front)* with No. 23 patrol J Troop, Brussels, 1944.

An 'L' Sqn patrol, France, 1944.

Bedford 'Q' truck – Phantom Radio Vehicle. *(Photo Ken Rimmell)*

'L' Sqn's Peter Bloomfield, 1944.

'A' Sqn, No. 12 patrol's White Armoured Radio Scout Car, France, 1944.

Phantom Radio Operator at work.

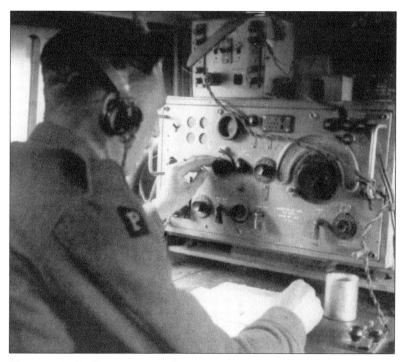

Phantom Radio Operator at work.

Phantom at work, Verdun, 1944. Attached to General Omar Bradley's Army Group. (Note Swastika still on wall.)

'B' Sqn. No. 23 patrol J Troop with Kite patrol, Brussels, Winter 1944. Harry seated on jeep centre front.

Phantom/SAS leaving for Operation Houndsworth, 10th June, 1944. Taken by Major the Hon. Jakie Astor, CO 'F' Sqn, at Fairford Airfield, Glos.

American B-17s, B-25s and B-26s reduced this beautiful building to a shattered ruin.

This attack claimed the lives of the Bishop, who had decided to remain, and over two hundred civilians who had sought shelter in this medieval Christian shrine.

After this attack the Germans felt justified in moving into the rubble which enabled them to establish a still firmer defence, repulsing the assault by the New Zealanders and the 4th Indian Division. By the 20th the Second Battle of Cassino was over.

A month later General Mark Clark, commanding the US 5th Army, tried again. On the 15th March, a massive air and artillery bombardment destroyed the pleasant valley town of Cassino in preparation for another assault by the New Zealanders. At the same time a new assault was being made on the Cassino monastery, or what remained of it, but after a week of bitter fighting the Allies could still not dislodge the Germans from their mountain fortification. As each aerial and artillery bombardment started, the German defenders retreated into the deep cellars, caves and tunnels which had been hewn out of the solid rock centuries before when the monastery had been built, only to re-emerge, practically unscathed, ready to repel any further attacks by their enemy. By the 23rd March, it was apparent that no real progress was being made and, with heavy losses sustained, the third battle was brought to a close.

Three major assaults had failed to dislodge the Germans from the *Gustav* Line at Cassino so crucial planning went into the fourth and, as it turned out, the final offensive.

On Thursday the 11th May a huge army comprising British and Empire, Polish, American and French Colonial troops advanced northwards. This time it took only a week to force the Germans from their stronghold. Polish troops finally seized the monastery on the 18th May, 1944.

A family friend of the Parlours, Harold Young, who was serving with the British 8th Army alongside the Canadian 1st Corps, remembers, when finally entering the ruins of the monastery, going down into the vast cellars below. The sight of row upon row of barrels and bottles of wine in racks greeted their tired eyes as they grew accustomed to the dim light afforded by their torches. Ignoring warnings that the retreating Germans could have booby-trapped the cellars and their contents, the battle-weary soldiers were soon having quite a celebration.

Phantom was not involved in the early attacks on Monte

Cassino, but 'J' Service was. It had been seen early on in Italy that in order for 'J' to serve its purpose, of listening in to battle situations, it would have to be re-organized. The speed at which the advance of the Allied army moved meant that very quickly the leading troops were out of the range of 'J's intercepting receivers. The hilly nature of the countryside also interfered with radio transmission. Therefore, the Service was divided into two smaller units with one going along with the advancing forward troops and the other staying back halfway between the front and HQ to where the information was relayed. The re-organization was successful and nearly all the up-to-date information that was being received by the Army was coming from 'J'.

By the end of October 1943 the Americans had developed their own type of 'J' Service. Known as SIAM (Signals Intelligence and Monitoring), this was soon taken over by the Eighth Army and a link was formed between the two armies. As there were now many British divisions in the American 5th Army, the decision was taken to form a new 'J' Squadron, and so on the 1st February, 1944, No. 2 'J' Squadron was born. This was to be commanded by Major Allen. Both 'J' Squadrons were to be self-contained units and to carry out intercept and liaison work, based on Phantom operational procedure.

During the long arduous battle for Cassino both 'J' Squadrons proved their worth, passing countless messages. Their work was particularly successful during the third attempt to take Monte Cassino. No. 1 'J' worked with the 8th Army and No. 2 worked with the 10th Corps and the New Zealand Corps.

By the time Monte Cassino was taken Phantom's 'H' Squadron had arrived in Italy. Landing in Taranto in March, it moved its headquarters to Casserta in early April. The following month patrols were being made ready for the attack on the *Gustav* Line which was due to begin again on the 11th. Detachments were sent to the headquarters of both the British and American Armies and patrols to each Corps of the Eighth Army – the 5th, 10th, 13th, Polish and Canadian. Their main task would be direct liaison for General Sir Harold Alexander, Commander-in-Chief of the Italian campaign. Major Grant and his Phantom Squadron were delighted that, after months of training, they were at long last going to see action.

When the battle for Cassino began the British 8th Army was no longer under the command of General Montgomery. On the

24th December, 1943, he had been woken with a signal from the War Office. He was to return to England to succeed General Paget in command of 21 Army Group, the British Group of Armies preparing for the 'second front'. In Montgomery's own words: 'Though sad of course to leave the Eighth Army, I was naturally delighted to have been selected for the great task ahead: the full-scale invasion across the Channel which would truly avenge Dunkirk.' Montgomery's place was taken by Lieut-Gen. Sir Oliver Leese who assumed command on the 1st January, 1944. Leese had been one of Monty's Corps Commanders for the campaign in Sicily and was a long-time trusted friend and highly-regarded military tactician. Major-General Sir Harold Alexander, Supreme Allied Commander of the Mediterranean theatre, was sorry to see one of his ablest of Generals leave.

With the successful conclusion of the Cassino battles and with the *Gustav* Line at last broken, the vital link could now be made with the American Major-General John Lucas, who had landed at Anzio with his combined troops on the 22nd January. This amphibious landing, behind the *Gustav* Line yet only thirty-two miles south of Rome, was code-named Operation *Shingle*. When the Allied army stormed ashore the beaches were undefended. Anzio was deserted. The inhabitants had been evacuated and there was no sign of a German anywhere. By the end of the day nearly fifty thousand men, with three thousand vehicles, had established a beachhead. Now Lucas made the mistake of delaying his break-out. He decided to wait for more supplies of tanks and heavy artillery and to consolidate his position. He had missed his opportunity and his actions, or rather lack of them, ultimately lost him his position of command. By the end of the day the Germans had rushed up reinforcements and were able to contain the invasion force for several weeks. In the middle of February, although the situation had improved slightly, it was not enough to save Lucas and he was relieved of his command. The American Major-General Lucien Truscott took over.

After four months of being pinned down at Anzio, the break-out came on the 23rd May. Within two days Truscott's forces had linked up with the advancing Allied forces from Cassino and were on the road to Rome. A Phantom patrol from 'H' Squadron, Captain Webster's, played a major role in reporting the break-out and the positions of Allied forward movements.

By nightfall on the 25th an American forward patrol entered

the village of Velletri, only twenty-five miles from Rome. US forces took the village and surrounding area on the 30th and thus pierced the new defensive line, known as the *Caesar* Line, that the retreating German Army had established. Scizing the initiative, General Mark Clark pushed on, and when the Americans triumphantly entered Rome on Sunday the 4th June they found all the bridges intact. As they crossed the River Tiber and entered St Peter's Square they could see that the Eternal City had been left unscathed by the Germans. *Feldmarschall* Albert Kesselring, commander of all the German forces in Italy, had declared it an 'open city' rather than risk its destruction in prolonged fighting and aerial bombing.

Two million overjoyed Romans crowded the streets, welcoming the Americans with flowers and bottles of *Chianti*. The carnival atmosphere was only silenced by the pope's speech: 'Yesterday Rome was trembling for her sons and daughters. Today she is able to look with renewed hope and faith to her salvation.'

The spring offensive of 1944 in Italy, Operation *Diadem*, had cost the Allies dear, with over fifty thousand casualties. The Germans had suffered over ten thousand killed and wounded. Twenty thousand more had been taken prisoner in the successive battles.

CHAPTER XVI

# An Air Of Optimism

*'A good man to serve under, a difficult man to serve with and an impossible man to serve over.'*
GENERAL EISENHOWER SPEAKING
OF MONTGOMERY, 1943.

As the fighting continued overseas, at home late 1943 saw Britons preparing for their fifth Christmas of the war.

With the German U-boats in the Atlantic on the run, increased supplies of food and day-to-day items, as well as war materials, were getting through to our fortress island. From the outbreak of the war Germany had done its best to starve Britain into submission but as 1943 came to a close things were looking up. With the battle for the Atlantic now all but won, Britain's vital ocean supply route from the Americas was proving a much safer passage. Allied losses had fallen dramatically from an average of 650,000 tons per month throughout 1942 to only 18,000 tons of shipping sunk in April 1943. Food rationing, introduced as early as January 1940, still continued, but there was now slightly more choice available. Items up till now only obtainable on the black market were filtering their way through to the shops and, with the Mediterranean – Mussolini's Lake – now firmly under the control of the Allies, even fruits such as bananas and oranges, rarely seen in Britain since the beginning of the war, could be bought – although at a price!

Ken Keeble, a long time friend of the authors, lived as a young lad near Barking Creek, East London. He remembers a cargo ship, which was moored there, receiving a direct hit during a German night bombing raid and tons of fresh oranges spilling into the water. For days afterwards he and his mates would fish them out and clean and dry them to sell to everyone in the neighbourhood. 'We made quite a bit of pocket money and were very wealthy kids for several weeks,' Ken laughingly recalls.

Tobacco and alcohol, for some the very staples of existence, were never rationed. Nevertheless, they were in short supply and the price demanded for them rocketed. A bottle of Scotch which had cost 12s 6d (63p) in 1939, fetched £1 5s 9d (£1.28) three years later and the price of a pint of beer had gone up from 6d (3p) to 1s 3d (7p). Now, with the United States Armed Forces firmly established in the British Isles, having been arriving since January 1942, cigarettes with famous American brand names such as Camel and Lucky Strike were widely available. It was not only cigarettes that the Americans brought with them. Luxuries such as chocolate, chewing gum and nylon stockings for the ladies arrived too. Freely handed out, these tempting gifts were a great publicity coup on the part of the Americans. Sceptical Britons, feeling invaded by foreigners despite fighting a common foe, were very soon won over by the generosity and friendliness of these young men. In fact, many British girls were to marry American servicemen and return to the United States to settle with them after the war.

It was not only food that was rationed. In June 1941 clothing coupons had been issued as clothes rationing was announced by Oliver Lyttleton, President of the Board of Trade. Utility clothing, introduced in 1942, was designed with an eye on the economy of raw materials. Gone were the pleats and flounces that required yards of cloth as in came straight skirts – their hemlines raised in the name of the war effort. And for men and women alike, single-breasted jackets and coats became the fashion as double-breasted were banned.

The BBC television service, the world's first to transmit regular programmes, had been inaugurated in November 1936 but closed down in 1939 with the outbreak of war, so the radio was the choice for home entertainment. Frank Sinatra, who had ousted Bing Crosby from the top of the radio hit parade, could be heard, along with the classical strains of the BBC Symphony Orchestra and the American big band sound that was sweeping the country.

In dance halls the craze of 'jitterbugging', introduced by American servicemen, was taking over from the more traditional dance steps. And at the cinemas one could either watch war films such as Zoltan Korda's *Sahara* starring Humphrey Bogart, fresh from *Casablanca* in which he co-starred with Ingrid Bergman, or, for pure escape from the war, *Jane Eyre* with Joan Fontaine in the title role opposite Orson Welles' melodramatic Rochester.

People also flocked to the theatres to be entertained by the Forces' sweethearts – singers Gracie Fields, Anne Shelton and Vera Lynn, amongst many others.

There was an air of optimism as families all over Britain, some lucky enough to have procured a traditional turkey or goose, sat down to Christmas dinner in 1943, convinced that it would be their last eaten in wartime. The previous evening it had been announced that General Dwight David Eisenhower (Ike) had been appointed Supreme Commander of the Allied Expeditionary Force preparing for the cross-Channel invasion of France and that General Sir Bernard Law Montgomery, at Churchill's insistence, would command all Allied land forces until Eisenhower had set up his headquarters in France. With the knowledge that this invasion, to rid the world of the evil of the Nazi doctrine forever, would surely now take place very soon, the British people looked forward to celebrating the following year's festivities with their loved ones who were now away from home.

Planning for the invasion before the appointment of Eisenhower and Montgomery had been in the hands of the British Lieutenant-General Sir Frederick Morgan, Chief of Staff to the Supreme Allied Commander (COSSAC). As early as July 1943 Morgan had advised that the landings should take place in Normandy.

Since 1942 British Intelligence had been studying photographs of the French, Belgian and Dutch coastlines, that had been taken by camera-carrying reconnaissance aircraft of the Royal Air Force. They had examined the defensive positions of the Germans all along the Atlantic Wall, a network of coastal fortifications built as part of Hitler's plans for an impregnable 'Fortress Europe'. They had studied both tide and current tables and the phases of the moon. They had analysed soil and sand samples, collected by Secret Service frogmen who had swum ashore from midget submarines under the cover of darkness, and they had checked that the beach gradients were neither too steep for the disembarking amphibious vehicles nor too shallow for the landing craft.

From the three thousand miles of coastline in Western Europe, from Holland round the shores of France to the Italian mountain frontier, the area of possible assault was narrowed down to the three hundred mile stretch between Flushing in the Netherlands and Cherbourg on the French Contentin Peninsula. This was the only sector that could be adequately covered by fighter aircraft based in Great Britain. The area chosen must have harbours and ample beaches across which the assault forces could be reinforced until ports could be captured. Analysis ruled out all but two areas; the Pas de Calais or Normandy, between Le Havre and Cherbourg.

Many considerations had to be weighed up and balanced

between these two options before the final decision could be made.

The Americans favoured Calais because it offered a more direct route to Germany, although it was more heavily defended, and a shorter crossing for the assault forces prone to sea-sickness. The British preferred Normandy because its defences were weaker and because it could be cut off from the rest of Europe by bombing the bridges over the Seine and Loire rivers. In the end COSSAC recommended the Caen sector of Normandy; on the grounds that the Caen beaches were weakly defended and excellent for both a landing and a logistic build up and that the German airfields in the Caen area were limited and would be easier to neutralize.

COSSAC's recommendation was to be accepted by Churchill, Roosevelt and the Combined Chiefs of Staff at the Quebec Conference in August 1943.

Eisenhower's deputy for Operation *Overlord*, the largest ever seaborne invasion, was to be Air Chief Marshal Sir Arthur Tedder, who had earlier been his deputy in the Mediterranean. Air Chief Marshal Sir Trafford Leigh-Mallory was given command of the Allied air forces and Admiral Sir Bertram Ramsey command of the naval forces. On his arrival as Supreme Commander, Eisenhower replaced Morgan and his COSSAC staff with his new Supreme Headquarters Allied Expeditionary Forces (SHAEF) which was based at Bushy Park, near Hampton Court, west of London. Here Eisenhower's American Chief of Staff, Major-General Walter Bedell Smith, was to oversee a headquarters of 750 officers and six thousand men.

Eisenhower and Montgomery, in accepting Normandy, planned a landing force far stronger than Morgan had recommended and took the decision that the landings would be made across a front of forty miles on five beaches. These to be code-named *Utah*, *Omaha*, *Gold*, *Juno* and *Sword*. At Montgomery's insistence airborne troops would be used on both flanks to prevent interference during the early moments of the assault phase when the invaders would be at their most vulnerable.

German Intelligence failed to forecast the date, place or strength of the cross-Channel invasion, thanks to an elaborate deception plan by the British to encourage the belief that the main forces would come ashore at Calais.

Phantom's 'A' Squadron HQ, based in Dover, was to play a significant part in this deception. Patrols transmitted and received radio signals to and from imaginary Allied forces, knowing only too well that German receiving stations only a short distance away across the English Channel would be listening in.

'Operation *Fortitude*' succeeded in convincing German Supreme Command that General Patton was to land his assault troops in the Pas de Calais region.

Patton's 1st United States Army Group (FUSAG), which did not in fact exist even after the invasion, was given dummy bases, training grounds, a communication network, plans, orders of battle and a specific target – the French coast between Calais and Boulogne. German *Enigma* messages, decrypted at Bletchley Park, revealed that, for the Germans, FUSAG, as well as a fictitious 12th British Army, was a reality.

Field-Marshal von Runstedt was convinced that the main landing would be in Calais and so was the higher command of the army in Germany, although Hitler favoured Normandy and so, surprisingly, did Rommel. The location was not the only thing that Rommel and his immediate senior could not agree on. Rommel felt that an invasion could only be halted at sea and on the shore. Runstedt disagreed. Thinking Rommel's judgement faulty, he chose to rely on a plan of delivering a powerful counter-offensive to crush the Allies after they had landed – at Calais! The British Secret Service even fooled Heinrich Himmler, Hitler's head of Intelligence. After the war, in German files captured by the Allies, 250 reports from Himmler's men were found predicting the time and place of the invasion. All but one of them was wrong!

The British Broadcasting Corporation was to play a vital communications role, sending out coded radio messages which were to be picked up by the French Resistance and by Allied agents previously dropped into occupied France, including some SAS along with their Phantom radio operators. These agents worked with the Free French of the Interior and the Maquis and the messages only made sense to those who knew their true meaning. Two of the most important messages sent by this means were 'It is hot in Suez' and 'The dice are on the table'. The former, the *Green* plan, would put into effect pre-arranged plans for the sabotaging of railway tracks and equipment and the latter, the Red plan, the cutting of telephone lines and cables. When these alerts were received the underground leaders knew that the actual day of invasion was only hours away.

On the 17th May, Eisenhower selected Monday June 5th, as the tentative D-Day (later known as *Deliverance Day*), but the final decision would depend on the weather. Minimum conditions acceptable to all three services required that the forecast for D-Day and the following three days be quiet. On the 3rd June, with the invasion date still set for the 5th June, SHAEF meteorologists informed Eisenhower that a gale, the worst in twenty years, was on its way into the English Channel. Eisenhower had no choice but to order a postponement of the invasion – but only for 24 hours. A second day's delay would mean a postponement until mid-June or even July. Finely-tuned plans could not be kept in suspension for that long. In constant contact with his meteorologists who were predicting that the weather would improve, Eisenhower considered, 'I am quite positive we must give the order. I don't like it, but there it is. I don't see how we can do anything else.' Tuesday, June the 6th, was set as D-Day.

Denis Edwards, then a 19-year old private with the 2nd Battalion Oxfordshire and Buckinghamshire Light Infantry attached to the British 6th Airborne Division, was one of the first to set foot in occupied France. Just after 11pm on the 5th June, 1944, six plywood and fabric-clad Horsa gliders, each carrying thirty men (including the two glider pilots), joined an RAF bomber force and were towed to the French coast where, minutes after midnight, they were cast off and crashed-landed between two inland bridges on the East flank of the Allied invasion – due to commence at dawn. The Caen Canal runs from the coast at Ouistreham up to Caen eight miles inland. Running parallel with the canal about 500 yards to its east is the River Orne. At a point about four miles inland both are crossed by bridges. Denis was in the first of three gliders to land beside the vital Caen Canal suspension bridge. It had been wired for demolition by the Germans and was defended by permanent guards. The task of Major John Howard and his men was to capture this bridge intact, while the other section was to attack and hold the other bridge crossing the Orne, until paratroops from the 6th Airborne dropped from the sky and Lord Lovat's Commandos, who were amongst the first to storm ashore at Normandy, arrived to relieve them. It was a remarkable achievement. This small force held firm against a determined German counter-attack for several hours in the knowledge that once the Germans realised where the main invasion was really taking place, they would rush reinforcements from the east. By denying them access over the bridges, the enemy would be forced into a detour down to Caen, thus buying the Allies valuable time.

The greatest military invasion of all time, to rid Europe of the evil of Naziism, had begun – and Phantom was well prepared to play its part.

CHAPTER XVII

# D-Day And Onwards

*'Believe me, Lang, the first twenty-four hours of the invasion will be decisive... the fate of Germany depends on the outcome... for the Allies, as well as Germany, it will be the longest day.'*

FIELD-MARSHAL ERWIN ROMMEL TO HIS AIDE, APRIL 22, 1944.

Britain, in the early months of 1944, was an armed camp of over 3.5 million soldiers, sailors and airmen, comprised of British, Canadians, Australians, New Zealanders, all British Empire and Americans, as well as French, Poles, Belgians, Dutch, Norwegians and Czechs who had escaped from their occupied countries. All were well-trained and eagerly awaiting the second front.

Before the great fleet of warships, transports, landing craft and supply ships could set off on their hazardous mission, the Royal Navy and Allied Air Forces swept a passage through the seas of enemy mine fields and cleared the skies of German planes.

During May alone Anglo-American forces unloaded twenty thousand tons of bombs upon railway networks and river bridges, destroying communications between the German coastal armies and their bases further inland. Not just in Normandy but also in the Pas de Calais region as further proof to the enemy that Calais was to be the object of the main assault.

Since October 1943, with the preparations for a cross-Channel invasion advancing, the code-name '*Mulberry*' had been chosen for a huge prefabricated harbour made of concrete. From the night of 5th/6th June, this marvel of engineering ingenuity that had secretly been built by 37,000 skilled workers, was towed across the Channel in sections by 85 tugs to facilitate the landing of men and supplies upon the beaches of Normandy until a French port could be captured intact. In fact, there were to be two floating *Mulberry* harbours. One off St Laurent for the Americans and the other off Arromanches. Until these could be put in place, shelter was provided for the unloading craft by sinking lines of obsolete ships to form breakwaters at each of the main assault sectors.

By dawn on the 6th June, eighteen thousand British and American parachutists were on the ground in Normandy and at 6.30am the first troops landed on the beaches. First the Americans on '*Utah*' and '*Omaha*' followed by the British on '*Gold*' and '*Sword*' and the Canadians on '*Juno*'. By midnight one hundred and fifty-five thousand Allied troops were ashore.

In her book '*The Channel: The Dividing Link*', author Shirley Harrison describes the moment that the French and the Germans realised that the invasion was under way.

> '*When the intelligence chief of the French Resistance movement in the Bayeux area received the now famous coded message 'It is hot in Suez', he set off on his bike to spread the news. Cafe owners, butchers and grocers stood by ready to destroy communications. Just before dawn the first of the invasion fleet was spotted, in black comedy, by a German soldier sitting in a door-less privy overlooking the sea. By then it was already too late; the Germans had been sure the invasion, if it came at all, would head for Calais.*
>
> *On the other side the assembly area around the Isle of Wight was a Piccadilly Circus - 5,000 boats were on their way. You could have walked on their decks all the way to France.*'

Shirley goes on to describe the colossal *Mulberry* harbour at Arromanches and its vital importance:

> '*The port itself was the size of Dover and the capacity of tonnage equal to that of Gibraltar.*
>
> *At the same time as the building up of the outside breakwater, pierheads were established to unload the ships. These were floating platforms made of steel, at each corner of which were spud legs, four in all, which were lowered to the bottom of the sea where they were adhered by pressure while the platform slid up and down according to the tide. The total length of the seven pierheads was 2,300 feet. They were linked to the shore by floating roadways made of small concrete pontoons reunited together by Bailey bridges; the total length of each was about 4,000 feet. There were four floating roads; one for light vehicles such as ambulances, command cars and jeeps, one for empty lorries going to the pierheads, another they used to come back when loaded; and one for heavy duty such as tanks, bulldozers and cranes.*
>
> *In addition to these unloading possibilities, there were numerous*

barges as well as about 180 Dukws *(amphibious vehicles) plying constantly between the ships and the shore.*

*Sometimes there were up to 280 ships at the same time in the harbour, so that on June 12th, (six days after the landing) 326,000 men had been put ashore, as well as 54,000 vehicles of all sorts from jeeps to kitchens and tanks of 40 tons, and 110,000 tons of various goods.*

*To protect the harbour from aerial attack, a formidable defence by heavy machine-guns and bofors-guns had been established not only along the shore but on the ships and pontoons as well.*

*This was the prefabricated harbour which from the start contributed so much (and was one of the main factors) in the liberation of Europe.'*

Another important factor was the constant supply of fuel made available by the Pipe Line Under The Ocean (PLUTO), which was laid down by the Royal Engineers and pumped fuel direct from England to Normandy beneath the waters of the Channel.

Much has been written about D-Day and the Normandy landings and we leave it to others to tell the full story of *'the longest day'*. We would like now to relate the experiences of Phantom in general and of Phantom's Corporal Ron Eaton in particular in the days leading up to the invasion.

In his own words Ron explains: 'We were based in a little village about twenty miles outside Oxford, and still the training went on. Nothing very exciting happened during this time and things were getting boring. Everyone was looking forward to the second front. Then suddenly in May, about three weeks before D-Day, we were all dispersed to the Units we would be attached to for the invasion of France. We had the 51st Highland Division and as we had a Scots officer in charge of our patrol, Captain John Mackenzie, that fitted nicely with him. The rest were myself, Ted Rourke our Corporal, Paul Holdway, Andy Black, 'Brad' Bradbury and 'Nobby' Clarke.

We spent the next three weeks getting ready for the second front. We had to check all our gear, especially the radio gear, and towards the end we had to waterproof our vehicles. This was a long, tedious job of slapping greasy plasticine round everything. All the electrical things, like the plugs, the leads, the generator and the magneto had to be smothered and, round by the gearbox where the breather was, we had to attach a long pipe from the carburettor up the side of and above the armoured car so that the engine could breathe under water. This was quite a long job and we had to test it in a homemade tank. We had to go down into the water, through the water and out the other side. If nothing happened you were okay!

We were by now in an army camp just outside High Wycombe, living in Nissan huts, and every morning Reveille was played on the bagpipes. This was customary for a Scottish regiment but was a new experience for us - one which we rather enjoyed.

Then things really began to happen. We had to load everything up and make our way down to the camps near to our departure points. I couldn't believe it when I found out that the 'S' camp (the identification letter for such camps) that we were going to was situated only fifteen minutes from where I lived in Leytonstone, East London. At this particular point Epping Forest comes down and joins Wanstead Common, known as the Flats by Eastenders, right opposite the 'Green Man'. This pub is on a big crossing and the camp started practically on its doorstep. All camps were called S3, 4, 5 or whatever. I'm not sure what number we were but I do know that once we were in it we were not allowed out. They had armed guards patrolling the barbed wire fence. We were told that if we were caught outside we would be arrested until after the invasion, and our families too, but I don't know if this ever happened to anyone. To me it was where I used to play as a kid, in the forest and in the big open air swimming pool.

The camp was like a big fairground, a hive of activity. There was music playing all the time, interspersed every now and then with loud speaker messages for people to report to here or to report to there. ENSA (Entertainers National Servicemen Association) put on a show for us every night, the weather was fine, just as well as we were living in tents, so it wasn't too bad. Only for me it was hard because I couldn't get out to see my family who were living so close.

After a few days we had to take our vehicles down to the East India Dock, in the Pool of London, to be loaded into the ships that we would be going across to Normandy in. We drove down there and after our lorries were tucked away we came back, under guard, to the camp. Another two days went by and we were given some French francs, I don't remember how much, before we were again loaded into lorries and taken down to the docks where, this time, we went aboard the ship. It was a liberty ship. I remember the name of it, it was called *Samark*, the SS *Samark*. We were taken to our accommodation which was very, very tight, it was all hammocks three or four high. It was terrible. The latrines were out on deck in wooden huts.

We set sail on the 4th June. We sailed down the Thames and when we got as far as Southend they dropped anchor inside the defensive boom. We were just one of hundreds of ships, big and small, and we just lolled around there for another day. Then on the 6th we started out in the early morning. It was kind of overcast. As we made our way out of the Thames, we had a line of steamers behind us. No landing craft, they were all tramp steamers, like the liberty ships. The night before we had seen the gliders being towed across ready to start the invasion, but we weren't supposed to be there on D-Day, we were supposed to get there on D+1 and we were on schedule. It was like a haze as we went through the Straits of Dover, we couldn't see France.

We thought after going through the Straits that we had escaped an air-attack by the Germans but all of a sudden shells started arriving from the enemy coastal defences. Not a lot but enough to make you jump. They were big shells and they sounded like trains going through the air and splashing in the water. They were more concentrated behind us and hit the rear of a ship two back from us. It was still underway though and the last I saw of it, it was making for the shore. I guess they were going to beach it. That was the last bit of excitement - for that day anyway!

The water was getting quite choppy by now and the escort of MTB's (motor torpedo boats) that we had as protection were hitting the water so hard it was going right over them. It was a slow procession of ships that arrived on the morning of D+1 and dropped anchor off shore. Our vehicles were to be lifted off by Derrick crane, dropped into the landing craft and taken ashore. Then we would 'await landing', as they say. All around us were hundreds of ships, it was very mind-boggling. We knew we wouldn't be off our ship right away because our armour was on the bottom deck, so we were able to view everything else that was going on. We saw rockets being fired from tank landing craft and we saw the battleship HMS *Warspite* come in between us and the next ship dropped at anchor just along the coast. She just glided in at about 2 knots, stopped and, all of a sudden, her big 15 inch guns opened up. The noise they made was unbearable. They flattened the sea all around with their blast. They only used a couple of salvos then she backed slowly out and continued down the coast a bit.

That's the last we saw of *Warspite*. I guess she pulled in somewhere else and blasted a few other places.'

HMS *Warspite* was the most battle-scarred British battleship of World War Two. She had also fought in the First World War. She shook off a jinx that had dogged her since 1918 and won a reputation for enjoying good luck. During the evacuation of Crete in 1941 she had been seriously damaged but she survived and went to America to be repaired. She was again badly damaged two years later, this time by enemy glider-bombs during the Salerno landings. Even after being sold for scrap after the war she cheated the scrapyard, for a while, by running aground on the Cornish coast when her rudder malfunctioned, in exactly the same way as it had during the Battle of Jutland in 1916.

Ron continues, 'The same thing as happened with *Warspite*, happened again a little later with the battle-cruiser HMS *Norfolk*. She just glided in, stopped, let loose one barrage of shells after another and then glided out again and went off somewhere else. Other than that there were also some false alarms. There were guns going off, anti-aircraft guns. I didn't see any enemy planes but I understand they were further down the beach.

Towards dusk we still hadn't disembarked so we knew it wouldn't be happening until the next day. The naval personnel, known as boat-marshals, who were responsible for unloading the ships, had by now reached the lower level, so we went down into the darkness of the hold to unhook the chains securing our vehicles and equipment. While we were doing this, out of the blue came the sound of what I could only assume were German dive-bombers. It sounded like there were only two or three of them. The ack-ack of our anti-aircraft guns opened up. Just one or two at first then all of a sudden the whole lot of them were firing skyward from the ships all around us. It was a terrific sight, all those tracers lighting up the sky as the enemy planes started to dive. We were on the bottom deck looking up at all of this through a square of light and, being down there, the sound was magnified. It seemed as though the planes were going to come straight down at us through the patch of light we could see - but they didn't. They disappeared pretty quickly and, just like someone turned off a switch, the firing stopped. That night there were a couple more raids, but nothing really to keep us awake.

The following morning the unloading started again. With so

much activity going on you had to be on your guard or you were likely to get hit, not only by enemy fire but by your own men. There had already been one accident, fortunately not to any of us but to the toilets that were built on deck. This truck was being winched out of the hold and they didn't lift it high enough. The crane driver swung it round and smashed the whole row of latrines overboard into the sea. Luckily there was no-one sitting in there at the time!

After about an hour, up came our armoured car all set to be dropped into the landing craft. Then it was our turn to go over the side. We had to climb down a Jacob's ladder with all our gear on our back plus a Sten gun slung over our shoulder. Because we were forward on the ship, as you climbed down the ladder it hung away from the ship where the hull sloped inwards. It was kind of hairy. It was starting to get rough and the landing craft was hitting the side of the ship and then going away from it about six feet or so. You had to time your drop or you would end up in the sea. Fortunately, you had people ready to grab hold of you in case you didn't make it. Anyway, we all got into the landing craft okay and it made its way towards the beach where the ramp was dropped. The first vehicle, a jeep, went down and practically disappeared beneath the waves, for the sea was by now getting rather choppy. When it finally reached the bottom, the water was about six inches from the top of the hood of the jeep so the three guys scrambled out and sat on the top. As they were quickly pulled off, the landing craft was deftly manoeuvred round their floundering vehicle which was left to be recovered from the shell hole it had plunged into.

Meanwhile, the guy who was next in line was having problems with his jeep, which was towing an eighteen pound anti-tank gun. They asked our patrol officer, Captain Mackenzie, if we would take his gun ashore for him and it was duly hooked on behind my armoured car as I was next to go. Well, I wasn't too pleased with this added weight as it was a pretty steep ramp and you've only got two feet and you are trying to do three operations at once. You have got to ease the thing down until it gets into the water, slipping the clutch all the time, then let it go. If you go in with too much of a rush you might swamp everything and yet, at the same time, you mustn't let the engine revs go down too low. Anyway I managed it. Eased it down and in I went. The force of the water was so great it rolled up to the windscreen and a big spout of water shot up into the armoured car through the hole in the floor where normally there should be a gun-post mounting. Anyway, the car slowly began to sink. As it hit the sand I instinctively put my foot down, giving it full throttle, and the water slowly started to slide away and get shallower as we made the beach, pulling the gun behind. Our other patrol vehicle successfully made the beach too.'

The beaches on which the invaders, including Phantom, landed were littered with burnt out and destroyed army trucks, jeeps, tanks, beached landing craft and naval vessels of every description. A testimony to the ferocity that had welcomed those who had landed on '*Sword*' Beach on D-Day, the 6th June, and which still continued, albeit more intermittently. Stretcher bearers were running to and fro carrying the dead and injured to the first aid posts and field hospitals that had been set up on the foreshore to care for the many Allied casualties. Doctors and medics were working flat out to save the lives of these brave men.

Ron and his patrol had to negotiate this mayhem. Beach marshals directed them onto the taped off paths that had been cleared through the minefields and defences. Phantom drivers had practised this many times over in training, but this time it was for real.

> '*Directly we landed, with shells dropping all around us from the enemy batteries, we jumped out, unshackled the gun and got off the beach as quickly as possible,*' Ron recalls. '*It was a very dangerous place to be. As we set off along the road, we were amazed at the sight that met our eyes. Amongst all the chaos of the smoke and exploding shells, there stood a little old man dressed in black, holding a tray on which were finely balanced a bottle and three small glasses. As we came alongside him, he greeted us thankfully as liberators and offered us a glass of Calvados, a strong apple wine. It was pretty potent and we all felt better for it.*'

The German defenders had been quick to react to the invasion of the Allied forces and were continually bombarding the landing areas. Ron's captain decided that they should drive some little way inland, so Phantom's 'A' Squadron No. 12 patrol moved on. It came to a halt beside a battery of guns. As the divisional headquarters of the 51st Highland to whom they were attached was not ashore yet, the patrol had no-one to work with so the men dug their foxholes and spent the afternoon and evening where they had stopped - beside the gun-battery. Probably not a very wise decision.

Ron recalls, 'About dusk a plane came over. You could always tell when it was a German plane because the drone of their engines was invariably out of synch. All of a sudden there was the shrill sound of a bomb dropping. Just one. We jumped into our holes as the noise came nearer and nearer. They couldn't have seen us, it must have been the guns they were trying for. All around us was open ground and we were digging with our fingernails with all our might. Then there was a terrific thump and crash and all I remember is that I had stars in my eyes. After a few moments all was quiet. We pulled ourselves together and climbed out to take a look. There was a great mound of earth all around the shell hole. Although we were only about five yards from the impact of it, miraculously, not one of us was hurt. The night was uneventful after that.'

The following morning the 51st still hadn't all come ashore so Ron's patrol as yet didn't have a real job to do. It was now that General Headquarters realised that they had made one grave error. They had not supplied a Phantom patrol for the 6th Airborne Division which had dropped at the extreme end of the British Sector in the early hours of D-Day. Capt. Brook-Hart's Phantom patrol kept up a shuttle service between them and advanced 3rd British HQ, a distance of about ten miles, until the mistake could be rectified. A formal request was now made from Command for Phantom to provide communications and No. 12 patrol was duly despatched to the 6th Airborne who had set up their HQ in a Château. With the map references and locations it had been given, Phantom set off to provide the service that it had spent the last three years preparing for.

Ron continues, 'We drove down this small road surrounding the chateau alongside a high stone wall, which must have been at least twenty feet tall, until we were directed into an orchard where we were to set up our base. Two sailors from the Royal Navy, who were there to direct the shell fire from their ships off the Normandy coast by radio, helped us to dig our foxholes. We thought, 'Hello, this is very nice of them,' only to be told that they were doing it with good reason. The German gunners had zoned into this area and it was a veritable hot spot. No sooner had we finished the hole than all hell let loose. We endured two hours of constant bombardment. I think it must have been coming from a small German artillery placement. They were shelling us with mortars and firing eighty-eight millimetre field-guns at us. It sounded like this was our baptism of fire!

After an attack of this kind is over, everything goes quiet. There are no birds singing, everything is so shocked. All we could hear was water running, but we were in the middle of an orchard and there were no streams nearby. We soon realised it was coming from the radiator of our armoured car, a lump of shrapnel had gone right through it. You can close the vents down on it so that it has an armoured front, but I had left them open. I wasn't expecting the bombardment so hadn't thought to close them, with the result that there was a jagged hole right through the radiator. There were some other scratches on the armoured car itself, but luckily none of us was hurt.

Later that day there was another attack. This time the Germans were within two hundred yards of headquarters, which seemed to be the object of their attack. As we had been instructed in training that it was imperative that our code-books and maps did not fall into enemy hands, our officer took the decision to destroy them. We were advised to get out, leave our site, abandon our vehicles and go back down the lane a little way. Here we took up a new defensive position facing outwards. There was a big field surrounded by high hedges and this we were ordered to hold. At that point we had some trouble communicating. The patrol in the next sector, that of Captain Denys Brook-Hart, could hear us sending messages to control, but, unknown to us, control was not picking us up, so Brook-Hart sent over his NCO, Sergeant Vic Stump, on a motorcycle to pick up our messages to re-transmit. On his way to HQ, Vic was blown off his motor cycle by a shell near the Benouville bridge and never came back. We later heard that he had not been badly hurt and had managed to hitch-hike the rest of the way to Divisional HQ.

The next day, there were some German snipers concealed in the trees and hedges, but you just couldn't see them, all you could hear were the bullets buzzing past, sounding like bees. Not a lot of them, but enough to make you keep your head down. Using farmyard walls as cover, you couldn't stand up above them for fear of giving the snipers a target to aim at. We had been told by the troops already there that they were 'bloody good shots'.

Later that same day there was a night attack. We could hear the Germans shouting out orders in the woods ahead of us. They were engaging our paratroopers who were on the outskirts of the perimeter. It was very scary to be so near the action. We felt very isolated, as though we were out there by ourselves.

We were pulled out after this because our division, the 51st Highlanders, had finally managed to all come ashore and we were to rejoin them. Apparently, the day after we moved on, the 6th Airborne moved their Divisional Headquarters back as it was too hot there.'

The first Phantom message to be received back at Squadron Headquarters Control (SHC) at Dover, for direct transmission by secure land line to Invasion Headquarters at Portsmouth, had come from Captain Denys Brook-Hart's No. 5 patrol at 0815hrs on D-Day, while still on board ship.

Brook-Hart's patrol carried one No. 22 set with amplifier and two R.107 receivers. The 22 set and one receiver were mounted in a White scout car and the other receiver was in a jeep. The net was one-to-one working, from patrol to SHC, Dover. Brook-Hart and his patrol managed to get ashore at 1250hrs on the 6th June, landing on Sword beach between Ouistreham and Lion-sur-mer and successfully reached the advanced HQ of 3rd Division, to whom they were attached, by 1600hrs. Before landing, the Phantom captain had been sending messages from the landing craft, the last one before closing his set at 1250hrs read: '061250 P. 10 Landing now.' His patrol re-opened its sets on land at 1530hrs that afternoon. On D-Day alone No. 5 patrol handled twenty-one in and twenty-six out messages.

One of the other two Phantom patrols to take part in the landings on D-Day itself was Captain Keith Salter's No. 8. The party, that came ashore on '*Gold*' beach, consisted of only two driver-operators, Hovey and Lane, and Salter himself. Their jeep, in which was installed their No. 22 set, pulled a trailer carrying two motor-cycles. For them, everything had not gone according to plan. The LCT (Landing Craft Tank) they were in was hit by a shell, putting its engines out of order. Two jeeps and a half-track had already floated out to sea before several men managed to swim ashore and, with the aid of a cable made fast to a beach recovery tractor, winch the LCT near enough to the shore to enable the remaining men and vehicles to be safely unloaded.

Salter's task was to make it to Meauvaines, a village about one and a half miles inland, to report to 50th Division Tac HQ. They signalled SHC at 1545hrs to say they had arrived safely. '061545. P.12. No. 8 patrol with 50 Div. I am located with 50

Div. Tac HQ at Meauvaines, 893852. Safe.'

The third Phantom patrol to actually land on French soil on the 6th, was that of Captain Ian Balfour-Paul. The officer and his men were delayed in landing but managed to intercept the radio traffic and plot the course of success from their craft. At 1900hrs, while still afloat, they sent off the following message: 'Landing held up by congestion on the beach. Will not be landed before possible 2300hrs.' They were to come ashore on Juno and work with the Canadian 3rd Infantry Division, whose objective for D-Day was the Bayeux-Caen Road, linking up with the British 9th Brigade Group at Le Carpiquet.

CHAPTER XVIII

# Working With The Americans

*'Get me one of those limey Phantom
patrols over here double quick.'*
COMMANDER US ARMY SIGNALS CORPS.
AMERICAN SECTOR NORMANDY BEACHES,
D-DAY, 6TH JUNE, 1944.

In the build up to the Normandy invasion, the American army was offered the services of Phantom, but declined. It considered its own signals, communications and liaison services to be quite sufficient. By early afternoon on D-Day itself, this proved not to be the case. The call went out from the Commanding Officer of the American Signals Corps, 'Get me one of those limey Phantom patrols over here double quick.' And to his own Signals Corps he instructed, 'Give them any assistance and equipment they want.'

We now publish in full for the first time the War Office memos covering Phantom's operations with the Americans for the early days after D-Day, the 6th June, 1944.

PHANTOM OPERATIONS IN THE US SECTOR
OPERATION *'OVERLORD'*

ORGANISATION

GHQ Liaison Regiment, usually known by its code name 'PHANTOM', is a British Organisation which had its beginning during the withdrawal across France in 1940.

ROLE OF PHANTOM. The role of PHANTOM is (1) To obtain accurate and confirmed information regarding the positions of forward troops, the progress of current operations, and enemy intelligence, and to transmit this information by the quickest possible means to higher headquarters requiring such information. (2) To provide lateral liaison where required between divisions, Corps and Armies.

NORMAL METHOD OF CARRYING OUT ROLE. An

officer's patrol, working at Divisional HQ or forward thereof, obtains the information required from the most reliable source available to it and transmits it in High Grade cipher DIRECT to Phantom Sqn HQ, which forms part of the Army HQ. The information is there deciphered, checked for accuracy and ambiguity, and is then passed to the operations branch of the Army HQ. While this information is being transmitted to Phantom Sqn HQ at Army, a Phantom detachment at the headquarters of the Corps to which the division belongs is intercepting the radio net, thereby making the information available to the Corps Commander. At the same time, the Phantom patrols with the two flanking divisions can intercept and decipher this information and thus put their respective Division commanders in the picture as to what is happening on their flanks. By this method the Army commander, the Corps commander, and the two flanking Division commanders get the benefit of this information which normally should be cleared within half an hour of time of event. At Sqn HQ the messages are sorted out and retransmitted, where necessary, to Army Group HQ.

THE BASIC ORGANISATION. GHQ Liaison Regiment in Western Europe consisted of two Army Sqns, one Reserve Sqn, one sqn working with the Special Air Service and a Regimental Headquarters.

The Army Sqn is designed to work for one Army. It consists of an officer's patrol at each division HQ, an officer's patrol at each Corps HQ, a 'J' or monitoring section listening to forward radio nets, and Sqn HQ situated at Army HQ controlling all radio nets and passing the information to Army HQ.

The Regimental HQ is situated at Army Group HQ. It consists of an administrative section, an operations section and a signals section.

ORGANISATION WITH THE US ARMIES. When it became necessary to deploy PHANTOM in the US sectors it was not possible to cover the front to the same degree as in the British Army. As only one reserve sqn was available, it was decided to deploy patrols only as far forward as Corps HQ. By breaking up the existing Sqn HQ and controlling the Corps patrols from Regimental HQ, it was possible, with the personnel thus released, to provide receiving detachments for 12 Army Group Main HQ, 12 Army Group Tac HQ, First Army HQ and Ninth Army HQ. These detachments were also in direct communication with Phantom Regimental HQ.

The Corps patrol consisted of one officer (Capt) and six enlisted men including one NCO. The officer was trained as an operations staff officer and had a working knowledge of radio and cipher. Three of the enlisted men were operators and three were cipher clerks, two of them also functioning as drivers, a third as a motor mechanic and another as a cook. The patrol could be self supporting for a period of three to four days. The patrol transport consisted of one 3/4 ton truck 4x4 (White) 'Scout Car', one 1/4 ton 'Jeep' and trailer. The Scout Car was fitted with a 25-watt (2-6 M/C) transmitter and two receivers. The remaining space in the scout car was used as a small operations office. Other main items of equipment included code and cipher material, batteries, charging engine, cooking utensils and weapons.

The HQ detachments varied in size according to the amount of traffic that they were required to handle. The Phantom Detachment at 12 Army Group Main HQ consisted of three operations staff officers (one Capt, two Lieutenants), four radio operators, six cipher clerks, three teletype operators and a radio repairman. The Detachment operated in a tent or room in the headquarters and had as its main items of equipment one transmitter (25 watt No. 12 set) operating from the HQ radio pool by remote control, two R-107 receivers, one teletype machine, cipher material, and a map board showing the whole Allied front. The Detachment was not self supporting. Other Detachments were equipped on the same basis according to requirements.

## METHOD OF OPERATION

THE PHANTOM CODE. The one-time-pad cipher principle employing a special PHANTOM vocabulary and phrase book, was used throughout operations. The system is High Grade and could be handled at great speed by experienced clerks. The control and issue of one-time-pads was dealt with by Regimental HQ. Much of the success of Phantom was due to the secure, convenient and quick cipher system.

THE US CORPS PATROL. The Corps patrol normally established itself on a suitable radio site in the vicinity of Corps Headquarters, but at a distance great enough to ensure no interference from other sets. Contact was maintained at frequent intervals with Phantom Regimental HQ. The duty of the patrol officer was to keep in touch with the situation as reported to the

G-2 and G-3 sections of the Corps HQ. He would be familiar with the plans and intentions of the Corps. As soon as any information became available which he considered worthy of report, he would compose a message giving the situation. Before transmission this message was shown to some competent officer of the section concerned and confirmed. The message was then enciphered and transmitted to Phantom Regimental HQ. When necessary this patrol would intercept the radio signals of flanking Corps patrols in order that the information might be made available to the Corps HQ. Periodical sitreps were received from the Phantom Regimental HQ regarding the situation on other fronts.

REGIMENTAL HQ. Regimental HQ was situated near 21 Army Group HQ. Its function was:-
1. To receive messages from First Canadian Army Sqn, Second British Army Sqn and the American Corps patrols and pass the information to 21 Army Group Main.
2. To clear messages to American HQ Detachments as required.
3. To pass necessary information from American patrols to British Army Sqns.
4. To control all the radio nets to all U.S. Corps patrols and HQ Detachments and British and Canadian Army Sqns.
5. To control the cipher security.
6. To write sitreps three times daily on the whole front for the benefit of Corps patrols which otherwise would not obtain that information.
7. To control the policy of the regiment.

THE US HEADQUARTERS DETACHMENT. The duty of the Headquarters Detachment was to make available to its Formation Headquarters any PHANTOM information of value to it. The Officer in charge of the Detachment informed Phantom Regimental HQ what traffic he required. After a message had been received and deciphered, a detachment officer would check the message on the map and from his knowledge of current operations, he would then edit it and have it typed, and delivered to the sections concerned. If the officer was in any doubt as to the clarity or truth of the message he would have it checked for cipher error, transmission error and if necessary check it to its source, before passing it on to his formation HQ.

## LINKS WITH U.S. FORCES.

EARLY PHASES. When the initial landing took place on D-Day there was no PHANTOM with the U.S. Forces. Several patrols were landed with the early waves of the British Army and by about noon on D-Day a considerable amount of information was available, giving the situation at the beaches. By the afternoon of D-Day it became evident that unless some form of radio liaison were set up on the beaches, the lack of information would make it extremely difficult for the C in C to control the course of the battle.

Permission was immediately obtained to deploy PHANTOM on the US beaches.

At the time there was one Sqn of Phantom – 'L' Sqn – which was not committed. It was in Scotland training and equipping for mountain warfare and taking part in the cover plan, which previous to D-Day, succeeded in drawing several enemy divisions to Norway. Orders were issued to 'L' Sqn to concentrate in the Portsmouth area. In the meantime two patrols were hastily made up out of available personnel and equipment at Regimental HQ. On D-plus-one, a patrol commanded by Capt. Macintosh-Reid was operating from VII US Corps beach in direct communication with Tac HQ at 21 Army Group. By D+4 the first elements of 'L' Sqn arrived in the Portsmouth area and as they became available were sent to join the US Corps. It was then decided to make a complete sqn to cover the US Sector and twenty-one American enlisted men and one officer were detailed by SHAEF to form the monitoring section of the Sqn. This detachment joined the sqn in the Portsmouth area where it underwent instruction and training. It was soon realised, however, that it would not be economical to form a separate sqn for the US sector, and it was decided to use the American personnel to work alongside the British and form part of the patrols and HQ detachments that would later be required to give comprehensive coverage of the front. By D+12, PHANTOM was operating from V, VII, XIX and VIII US Corps. As the remaining Corps became operational, Phantom patrols were despatched to cover their front. On D+16 a small headquarters Detachment was sent to FUSAG in London. It opened a teletype circuit with the Phantom radio centre on the South coast over which all information of interest to FUSAG was passed.

Before we continue with the 'American Adventure' we must

return to England three months prior to D-Day and to Harry Binge and his patrol, now code-named '*Kite*'. A year previously, in March 1943, Lieut-Col. Alexander Macintosh had taken over as Phantom's Commanding Officer from Lieut.-Col. Hignett who had had to relinquish command due to ill health. Hignett himself had taken over from the regiment's enigmatic founder, Colonel George Hopkinson, when he had left to join the 1st Airborne Brigade. It was Macintosh who decided that 'B' Squadron patrols, other than being known by their numbers, could take on the identity of British birds.

Harry remembers, 'Our patrol, No. 23, 'B' squadron, adopted the name '*Kite*'. Other patrols in our squadron used - *Harrier*, *Kestrel*, *Eagle*, *Tern*, *Fulmar*, *Gull*, *Merlin* and *Gannet*. Our officer was Captain Michael Millar, who had joined Phantom from the King's Own Yorkshire Light Infantry. He was a schoolmaster in civvy street. Rather a reserved man, but very fair and a fine leader of men. We all had a good relationship with him. The rest of our patrol was made up of Corporal Alf Askew, Corporal Ron Eagle, who was one of our Despatch Riders, Private 'Robbo' Roberts, who drove the armoured car and also doubled up as the patrol chef, Private 'Duggie' Douglas and Private 'Darkie' Watson who, with myself, were the main radio operators and also drivers. Darkie could also ride a motorcycle.'

In February 1944, Captain Michael Millar's patrol relinquished the code-name '*Kite*' when selected to become one of the three patrols of Phantom 'B' Squadron's 'J' Troop. The other two patrols being those of Captain Michael Astor and Captain John Waring. As stated in Chapter Fourteen, when Phantom's role was redefined in the summer of 1943, it was decided that a squadron, when deployed to an army would be made up of nine patrols – plus a 'J' Troop. The name '*Kite*' was passed on to Captain Peter Ling's No. 20 Phantom patrol 'B' Squadron.

Harry continues, 'Our patrol, still No. 23 but now part of 'J' Troop, was to go into France with the 2nd Canadian Corps so, in March 1944, we joined them at Staplehurst, near Maidstone, in Kent. After about a week, we moved with them a few miles to Eastling Wood. Now a stint of intensive training began in 'J's methods. Exercises in map reading took up a lot of the time as well as more wireless practise. We had to waterproof our vehicles ready for the landings and sort out all the equipment that we would be taking with us. By the time we were finally given our orders to move, we were getting really fed up. The invasion had taken place on the 6th June, and now, nearly two weeks later, we were still in England. We were itching to get some of the action. This is what we had been training for for nearly four years.'

Early on the morning of the 19th June, Captain Millar's patrol, in convoy with the TAC HQ 2nd Canadian Corps, moved to Purfleet Marshalling Yard on the Essex side of the Thames.

> 'I remember that it was a stifling hot day. As we drove across Tower Bridge and turned right, we couldn't believe the wonderful reception we got from the East Enders as we passed by. It made me very proud as I was a cockney, born and bred in the East End of London. I often wondered what the Canadians thought of all this. They certainly enjoyed the send off.
>
> The following afternoon, we boarded a Liberty Ship and thought that this was finally 'it' - but it wasn't.'

Harry's patrol was in the same convoy as the new '*Kite*' patrol, No. 20, under the command of Captain Peter Ling, and was to work in a close liaison role with it. Although Phantom officers were not encouraged to keep diaries because of the secret nature of their duties, some, nevertheless, did write notes. Captain Ling kept a brief account of '*Kite*' patrol's venture into Europe. He describes the events:

JUNE 19th 1944. Hot weather. 15mph all way. Magnificent reception from people in East End of London. Marshalling Camp filthy with dust. Morale of all men pretty low. Several false alarms on moving.

JUNE 20th 1944. Boarded Liberty Ship about 5pm. Many British Infantry and Royal Army Medical Corps men aboard.

JUNE 21st 1944. Sailed to just off Southend and remained anchored there 6 days. Extremely hot. Troops packed like sardines aboard. One water bottle full per day for drinking and washing. Pack rations. Organised concerts, PT and lectures to keep morale up. Tempers got frayed.

JUNE 27th 1944. Sailed at night to within 2-3 miles of French Coast.

JUNE 29th 1944. Vehicles transferred to landing craft. Landed at Corcelles-sur-mer at 3pm. Kept comparatively dry. Patrol split up during landing. Met at Amblie with TAC HQ. Three DR's with M/C's in Canadian truck arrived late. Truck lost way. 'B' Squadron HQ arrived and camped only one mile away.'

Harry remembers, 'After coming ashore on '*Juno*' beach, we spent the next couple of days contacting the Canadians who we were going to be working with. We made visits to officers of the units we were most likely to be assigned to, to introduce ourselves and to explain just what our task would be. A kind of selling ourselves, really. Also, to inform them that, when we required provisions for an assignment, we would have to be able to draw supplies and rations from their various quatermasters without having to spend time explaining just who we were.

After about a week we moved with '*Kite*' to Camille where we joined the rest of the Canadian Corps. Here our patrol camped in a field in front of heavy British artillery overlooking Caen. The men watched the bombing and shelling of this great city as Operation *Goodwood*, the liberation of Caen, began. Phantom's work now began in earnest as radio operational traffic passed through at a terrific rate.'

Meanwhile, Corporal Ron Eaton's patrol had rejoined the 51st Highlanders who, with the 4th Armoured Brigade, left the 6th Airborne Division's bridge-head east of the River Orne and turned towards Cagny, six miles east of Caen. It was to form part of the force that would make up the encirclement of the city. Ron's patrol was to provide the radio link back to 'A' Squadron HQ. He relates the happenings. 'After we left the 6th Airborne we made contact with the headquarters of the 51st. This wasn't too bad as we moved back a little way from the front, although at night you could hear the German guns. They would bring up SP's (self propelled guns) to shell our HQ. During the day they would use 88mm anti-aircraft guns as artillery. This was a little scary as its heavy projectile arrived well before the roar of the gun that fired it was heard. If you could have heard the shell coming you could jump into a hole or take some form of cover, but the first you knew of its arrival was a big crack above your head.

Anyway, we were there for a few more nights until the 51st moved their HQ. They started to take over the lines from the 6th Airborne and another Division. Then came a series of attacks to break out and take Caen. It was supposed to have been taken on the first day of the invasion but now, some days later, this objective had still not been achieved. The Germans had really fortified it, bringing up their best armoured divisions to face the British. It was a real slogging match. At that point the front was only about eight miles from the Normandy landing beaches, so we didn't have far to go in the constant moves we had to make.

All the time we were keeping communications between the front line and rear HQ.'

Operation *Goodwood* commenced on the 16th July. This was to be an Anglo-Canadian onslaught, to finally kick the Germans out of the city of Caen and to provide the breakout that the Allies so desperately sought. Defence probing forward patrols of the Canadian Forces, who had been on the outskirts of the city for several weeks fighting their way through nests of German suicide squads, now took part in the main assault that was about to begin. The attacks were continually backed up by the Royal Air Force and the United States Army Air Force, whose bombers dropped thousands of tons of high explosives on this ancient city. The German ground forces also faced regular attacks by low-flying rocket-firing RAF Typhoons, whose fire power inflicted devastation upon armour, light artillery and troops. These flying machines were to become the most feared airborne raiders that the enemy faced and struck with awesome power.

By the time Caen had finally fallen to the British on the 20th July, the city had been reduced to a pile of rubble. Miraculously, the Abbey containing the tomb of William the Conquerer had escaped relatively unscathed. This had provided much shelter for the civilian inhabitants of the town who, having suffered so much during four years of German occupation, welcomed their liberators with a fervour that was undiminished by their personal losses.

Harry Binge's Phantom patrol, being one of the first to enter the ruins, followed the bulldozers of the Royal Engineers as they cleared a road through the debris. From amongst all this devastation people were starting to appear. 'How anyone could have survived this carnage, I will never know,' Harry exclaims. It was here that Harry was to briefly meet his old mate Ron, who informed Harry that new patrols were being formed and that his own patrol, No. 12 'A' Squadron, was off to join the Americans.

The American Forces had landed on '*Omaha*' and '*Utah*' beaches in the early hours of the 6th June. After landing on '*Utah*' the objective of Major General Collins' United States VIIth Corps was to cut off the entire Contentin Peninsula at its base, before driving north to seize the port of Cherbourg. Despite the artificial harbours, the Allies knew that it was essential to establish a permanent port on the French coast without delay. This peninsula, thirty miles long and more than twenty miles wide, is hilly with two main roads leading to the town of Cherbourg. One near the east coast and one near the west. The Germans had marked the flanks of the Allied landings by the deliberate flooding of the lowlands and marshes from which many of the Allied paratroopers suffered on the night of D-Day. The flooding on the American flank almost cut across the base of the peninsula, turning green and open water meadow into treacherous swamp land. The small port of Carentan, on the eastern road, was surrounded with water, but the American troops managed to by-pass the floods and gain higher ground. After fierce fighting Carentan fell.

Defeating the German defenders was made all the more difficult by the hedgerows and small lanes, which were ideal for enemy snipers hidden in the foliage and for the concealment of tanks, armour and artillery, both light and heavy. As Supreme Commander of the Allied Forces, General Eisenhower had noted, 'The Germans were aided by the Normandy countryside.' Most of the attacks in the Contentin Peninsula had to be made through such hedgerow country where it was at its worst. This was known as 'Bocage' - an obstacle to advancing armies and perfect for defending armies. The hedgerow was a tangled mass of trees and brambles growing to a height of fifteen feet. This often on top of a mounded ditch, often ten feet wide in places, with banks on both sides three or four feet deep. So in many cases the German defenders had natural trenches already provided. The 'Bocage' divided the countryside into a quilted patchwork-like design of small rectangular fields, originally built centuries before as borders to fields and a natural shield to protect animals, crops and local communities from the Channel winds and storms.

General 'Lightening Joe' Collins opened his assault on the outer defences of Cherbourg on the 22nd June. The defenders put up a hard contest but, against the American ground forces and constant air and naval bombardment, *Generalleutnant* Karl-Wilhelm von Schlieben was forced to surrender four days later. Despite orders from Hitler that they should fight to the last man.

For the American troops who landed on '*Omaha*' beach just after 6.30am on D-Day, things went disastrously wrong. They had expected little opposition but the entire first wave found themselves pinned down on the beach by a determined foe. As more troops hit the beach, confusion grew. Radio and signalling equipment had been lost, so those waiting offshore had no idea what was going on. All morning the fighting went on with heavy casualties being inflicted on the Americans, but before noon, with determination and brute force and the help of both British and American Naval destroyers, the battle had turned in their favour. By nightfall, although they had not achieved their perhaps over ambitious target, to secure an area six miles deep and eighteen miles long, they had made significant progress. The troops of 'Bloody Omaha' had done an incredible job against all odds.

As we have read early in this chapter, the Americans had soon realised their error in not accepting the services of Phantom. Two patrols were hastily assembled to join them. The first under Captain Mackintosh-Reid was attached to VII US Corps, who had with him as liaison officer, the US Army's Major Maurice Frary.

The second was led by Captain Maurice Macmillan, son of the future Conservative Prime Minister, Harold Macmillan. His patrol was allotted to the V US Corps. Landing on the 12th June, it was on the air that same day, sending vital messages back to SHQ as the Americans fought their way south.

With the Contentin peninsula now in their hands, the Americans were preparing to breakout from Normandy but before Operation *Cobra* could take place the ancient town of St Lô had to be captured. It stood at the centre of the road system in that part of the province and was therefore vital to both the German and American armies. Since D-Day the town had been under constant air attack and by July it had been reduced to rubble, but still the German resistance could not be weakened and the Americans were forced to fight every inch of the way. In the end, American determination and air bombardment began to crumble away the defender's will and on the 18th July, they entered St Lô.

In this battle as in others, Phantom embarrassed Intelligence Officers and completely flummoxed many Allied commanders by the extent of their knowledge. Imagine the surprise of a US colonel who, after thirsting for hours for news of a particular formation after the break-through at St Lô, was casually told by a Phantom officer, pointing to a map, 'There you are, Sir, your 5th Armoured Division is now twenty miles south of here.' 'And how the goddamned hell did you find that out?' the colonel asked with amazement. 'Phantom, Sir.' was the reply to his question. This news was confirmed twelve hours later.

Now US General Omar Bradley could launch Operation *Cobra*.

Ron Eaton takes up the story. 'By the time Caen had fallen, the Americans were ready to break out as well and our role changed again. The 51st Highland Division came out of line for a while so my patrol was moved on to join the Americans. We now formed a nice co-ordinated and cohesive Phantom unit.

It was great being with the Americans because they operate a little differently - and the food was wonderful. I loved the American food and couldn't get enough of it. They didn't like to have their headquarters too far forward and kept their radio people away from headquarters. They used to call it 'radio city'. When you are transmitting on a radio set you are sending out a signal which can easily be picked up by German Intelligence who could be listening in. They in turn could pass the information on to their artillery or air force and so we could come under enemy fire from ground or sky. With the British Divisional HQ the communications were right there near their front, but with the Americans you had to go up the road a mile or so to get to their communications centre - radio city.

The first division that we went to was next to a British Division. As the two different armies were going forward alongside each other, one was sometimes going faster than the other, so there was always a great danger that they would see each other in front of them and, thinking that they were the Germans, would attack them. On many occasions we had to give a warning out to tell the British that they were shelling the Americans. This proved just how vital our role was and how important were the messages that we were transmitting back to Squadron Command HQ.'

One of the main tasks of Phantom in a situation such as this was to establish the bomb-line. The establishment of this line, which divided the Allied attacking front forces from the defenders, was, in effect, to stop the shelling of its own infantry and leading armoured assault vehicles from its own heavy artillery and from air attack by Allied 2nd Tactical Air Force. This was possibly one of Phantom's most crucial roles.

Having informed the reader of the contribution made by Phantom's 'A', 'B' and, subsequently, 'L' Squadrons in the early weeks of the invasion to liberate Europe, the next chapter brings the reader up to date with the exploits of 'F' Squadron - which was about to go into action with the SAS.

CHAPTER XIX

# Phantom 'F' Squadron & The Special Air Service

## PHANTOM/SAS BEHIND ENEMY LINES.

*'Phantom proved that it was possible to combine a first-class standard of soldiering with a professional ability to communicate from inhospitable sites.'*
COLONEL DAVID STIRLING, CO-FOUNDER OF THE SAS.

After the amalgamation of Phantom had taken place in September 1943, 'F' Squadron was sent to Scotland. Here it was to join 1 Corps at Largs, in Ayrshire. The original idea was that when the planned invasion of France took place, Phantom would go in with 1 Corps' assault troops, playing its normal role of reconnaissance and liaison, sending back messages from the battle-front to HQ by wireless.

'F' was still commanded by Major the Hon. Jakie Astor. One of his officers was Captain John Hislop who, before the war, had been a noted amateur steeplechase jockey, a favoured pastime that he still continued whenever he got the opportunity. Hislop had joined Phantom at Richmond in March 1941 when he had been assigned to 'A' Squadron, then under the command of Major David Niven. When 'A' had its out-station at Stourhead House, Mere, in Somerset, the home of Sir Henry Hoare, a race horse owner, and his wife, Hislop was able to take advantage of the large stables there. Within a year of joining Phantom, John Hislop took part in a novice chase at Cheltenham riding a little bay gelding that he had ridden on several occasions before the war and had, indeed, won on. This time his mount, Overseas, was not to make him a winner. He failed to clear one of the fences, throwing his jockey to the ground. Hislop received a serious injury to his leg and as a result was out of action, both as a jockey and a soldier, for many months.

With the promise from Tom Reddaway, the Adjutant of Phantom, that a place would be available for him with Phantom when he was fully fit again, Hislop began his long journey of recuperation. It was not until March of 1943 that he was pronounced fit enough to join the Phantom training squadron at Penn Wood and from there he was assigned to 'F' Squadron.

Hislop and Jakie Astor, an amateur jockey and owner himself, were already well-acquainted. In fact, the two friends had travelled to Cheltenham together on the fateful day that Hislop had suffered his accident. John Hislop was more than happy to serve under Jakie and his second-in-command John Darwell-Smith, a schoolmaster in pre-war days. The Squadron Sergeant-Major at the time was SSM Harrison, who had taken part in the Dieppe raid as part of Jakie Astor's 'J' Squadron in August 1942. Here he had been forced to swim for his life when he ended up in the sea. Two other officers with 'F' at that time, whom Harry Binge remembers from his days in Northern Ireland, were John Sadoine and Lord Charles Banbury.

Harry recalls, 'One of our officers was a rather temperamental character. Sadoine was his name. He called himself a Baron, I don't know if he really was but he looked like he was important. He was a tall, thin man with a slightly foreign appearance. He was always short of money, always overspending. I was very friendly with his batman who had a hairdressing business in civvy street and was quite well off. He told me that his captain was always tapping him up to borrow money until his monthly allowance arrived from his mother.'

In fact, Captain John Sadoine's father was a Belgian baron and his mother an Englishwoman. He had a reputation for being rather a volatile and difficult officer but an extremely efficient and reliable one when in action.

An episode concerning Lord Banbury still amuses Harry and Ron to this day. 'Many of our officers came from well-to-do families and many of their fathers had served as officers in the First World War. They were always trying to outdo each other and striving to prove that they had the best patrol. Competition was very evident. One memory is of Lord Banbury, a very jolly man and well thought of by the men of all ranks. Whilst training in Ireland, when his patrol was issued with two motorcycles painted in dull army camouflage colours, Captain Banbury, not thinking them good enough for his men, decided that he was going to make them something special. He had his men strip off all the matt paint, for they were to be chromed. When they were finished they looked magnificent, all shiny and bright, like showroom bikes. The only trouble was, they could be seen from miles away. Not only in the daylight but at night-time too. With the moon shining brightly, they stood out like beacons.'

Lord Charles William Banbury, who had succeeded to the title Banbury of Southam in 1936 on the death of his grandfather, had been with Phantom from the beginning. Born in 1915, after the death of his father who had been killed in action in 1914, Lord Banbury had been a member of Hopkinson's Mission as part of the BEF in France in 1939, and was evacuated from the beaches of Dunkirk.

In Scotland, 'F' began assault training in earnest. The squadron worked in six patrols. Cross-country walking, with everything they needed for a 72 hour operation on their backs or, if they were lucky in a jeep, formed a large part of their preparation for France.

When General Montgomery was authorized to take on the intended invasion of occupied Europe, his change of plan, shifting the use of 1 Corps, meant that 'F' Squadron's original role was now redundant. While taking part in an exercise, *Eagle*, in February 1944 at Aldershot, 'F' was visited by Lieutenant-Colonel A A McIntosh, Phantom's Commanding Officer. The news he brought was that he had been asked to provide Phantom communications for the SAS. As a Signals and Reconnaissance Squadron for the SAS, their task would be to parachute into France with an advance party of SAS behind enemy lines, set up operational bases and relay a constant stream of information back to England. Once a suitable Dropping Zone had been located, the main party would go over.

As the only available squadron, and in view of the training that it had received in Scotland, 'F' was duly assigned. As working with the SAS involved parachuting, for which only volunteers could be used, McIntosh had to know as soon as possible how many would respond so that he could inform the War Office. Only those whose build prevented them from parachuting were not asked. One of these was Lord Charles Banbury, whose ample physique precluded him from such action. The response was overwhelming and within a few days the volunteers were sent on a concentrated parachuting course at Ringway, near Manchester, before joining the SAS at its headquarters at Auchinleck, Ayrshire.

Another officer who did not feel that he was fully able to take part in parachuting operations was Captain Denys Brook-Hart. Denys had joined Phantom in the winter of 1939. He had been on duty in the London dock area when he and six friends in his company were asked if they would like to volunteer for a new special unit. As anything seemed better than guarding a coal heap on a bitterly cold December night, the seven of them stepped forward. Denys served with Phantom when they went into action in Belgium in May 1940 and returned safely to England. Joining the unit again at Lechlade after a brief leave, Denys achieved his long-held ambition to become a Despatch Rider. Unfortunately, a nasty accident occurred while he was on duty when his motorcycle hit a tank. His leg was saved only by the skill of a Canadian orthopaedic surgeon.

When he returned to Phantom some months later, Denys was to join David Niven's 'A' Squadron where he was to remain for two years before joining Major Mervyn Vernon's 'E' Squadron in the January of 1943. With 'E', Denys Brook-Hart was to see action in North Africa and Italy before returning to England for Christmas 1943. In January 1944, he joined Jakie Astor's 'F' Squadron only to leave it when it was assigned to work with the SAS. Although his leg was well-healed, Denys had serious doubts about his ability to perform in parachuting operations and so he requested that his patrol should be given some other assault role. He was to see action in France with 'A' Squadron.

In his book, *'The SAS at War 1941-1945'*, Anthony Kemp explains the difficulties that the SAS was having with communications.

'Communication with parties in the field was naturally vital, both for operational control and for organizing resupply. Bearing in mind the technology available at the time, this presented considerable problems. The base signals layout was established at Moor Park where HQ SAS Troops set up its tactical headquarters. This consisted of a number of 12-hp transmitters installed by the BBC, each of which could transmit to five outstations. The latter consisted of Jedburgh sets, which had a sufficient range, though low power, and which were attached to parties in the field. Instructions to individual parties were also passed on broadcast channels to officers who were issued with small MCR 100 receivers. Messages were sent using the codeword SABU followed by a number which represented the officer concerned. It was not possible to provide for communication between parties or larger groups operating in the same area. If they wished to talk to one another, one had to send a message back to base, who would then retransmit it to the other. In August there were at one time twenty-five separate parties in the field, passing about a hundred in and out messages back to base each day. Encoding and decoding naturally took time and, in addition, there was considerable traffic that had to be passed via the BBC. Finally, the age-old method of military communication, carrier pigeons, was resorted to, with indifferent results.

The SAS Brigade war diary recalls the frustrations of the period. Limited air time restricted communications with the field to the laying on of air operations, the passing of immediate intelligence reports and brief operational orders. 'Once a party was committed, little was known of its movements here and little control could be exercised over them... The need for a very high standard of telegraphese and faultless ciphering was apparent. Most messages arrived either mutilated or much too long – in the case of 4 French Para., normally both.'

The base stations at Moor Park were operated by Royal Signals personnel, but there were insufficient signallers available to man the sets in the field, all of whom would have to be trained to SAS standards. Therefore in April, 'F' Squadron GHQ Liaison Regiment, 'Phantom', was attached to the brigade, commanded by Major the Hon. J J 'Jakie' Astor. This unit had been founded in 1940 to provide reliable communications direct from the front line back to higher formations. The various squadrons were subdivided into patrols, commanded by a captain. Two patrols each went to 1 SAS and 2 SAS. The French and Belgians had their own signals organization, but the operators were trained by 'Phantom'.'

It was not only the men of 'F' Squadron who were asked to volunteer their services to work with the Special Air Service. 'A' and 'B' Squadrons were also asked for volunteers to join them to drop behind enemy lines and work with the French Resistance in covert operations against the enemy. This would include working with other nationalities, such as Belgian and French members of the SAS. Ron Eaton recalls that when the men of his squadron were given 24 hours to think it over, much deliberation went into the duties that it would entail and the dangers that it would imply. The following morning on the parade ground when asked for their decision, nearly all of Ron's squadron stepped forward. Those who were accepted went on to more intensive training, ready to work with 'F' Squadron when required.

During their parachute training at Ringway, one or two members of 'F' dropped out, discovering that they did not have what it required to jump from a plane, but most enjoyed the experience tremendously.

After the preliminary ground training, which mainly consisted of learning how to roll on landing, the men took to the air, but not yet in a plane. Jumping from a secured balloon at seven hundred feet through a large hole in the floor of the basket preceded parachuting from a Whitley bomber, the plane introduced for their training. This again entailed dropping through a hole, but this time the aperture was in the belly of the fuselage, and if the men weren't careful they hit their face on the far side of the small opening as they jumped. An incident they very soon learnt to avoid. The experience of jumping from a side door did not come until they were eventually to go into action. These training jumps were made not only in daylight hours but also in the hours of darkness under moonlit skies. For many of these young men their first night drop was a scary ordeal, jumping from the relative safety of their plane into the darkness below.

Other training with the SAS was not without problems. One Belgian and two French SAS companies, some being ex-Foreign Legionnaires who were particularly battle-hardened from their days in the French colonies in Africa, had to be taught the use of wireless. The task of teaching fell to Jakie Astor. He surprised everybody with the way in which he managed to make himself understood, breaking through the language barriers. All those about to go into action realised that team work was paramount and that victory in Europe would depend very much upon international co-operation, remembering that they were still up against a highly organized and resourceful enemy.

This new role for Phantom meant that lighter equipment had to be carried for easier movement. The wireless sets which were now to be used were Jedburghs, known as *Jed* Sets. These were more portable. They didn't require a battery but were powered instead by turning a handle. This operated a magneto which generated the power required.

Organization of 'F' Squadron was now a headquarters and four patrols. Two were to join 1st SAS, commanded by the legendary Colonel 'Paddy' Mayne, and the other two were to be with 2nd SAS which was commanded by Colonel Brian Franks. Franks had been the first Squadron Leader of Phantom's 'H' Squadron in Egypt, but had left Phantom to join the Special Air Service. The patrols of Captain John Sadoine and Lieutenant Tom Moore joined 1st and those of Captain John Hislop and Lieutenant Peter Johnsen went to 2nd. The French and the Belgians had their own Phantom trained signals units which also worked back to 'F' Squadron HQ. Apart from continued practise on their new wireless sets, Phantom training now consisted of crossing the countryside by night and taking part in attacks on bogus aerodromes, they had to be up to SAS standards. They continued in Scotland until the operational headquarters of 'F' Squadron and the SAS moved to Moor Park, just north of London, home of the Airborne Forces whose command they were now under.

This intensive training, day after day, pulled together the combined resources of all fighting services in preparation for the planned invasion that would rid Europe forever from the tyranny of Nazi Germany.

The objective of the SAS in France was to harass the enemy and to cause the maximum confusion. Lessons learnt from their previous experiences in North Africa were to prove their worth. Parties of the SAS were to join forces with the *Maquis*, the French Resistance fighters, whose task was to disrupt German supply routes and communications and prevent German reinforcements reaching the Normandy battlefields from Germany and Southern France, while the Allied armies established a firm beachhead and built up their forces for the breakout.

In the weeks just before and just after D-Day, patrols of Phantom's 'F' Squadron with SAS soldiers were dropped or infiltrated into France behind enemy lines to team up with the one hundred thousand guerrilla fighters, both men and women, of the *Maquis*. These soldiers were fully armed and equipped with jeeps for easy movement. They established firm bases in the many forests that covered the area and from here they carried out their reconnaissance and sabotage operations. One of their main jobs was the location of targets, such as railway lines, fuel trains, ammunition dumps, German troop and armour concentrations and, most importantly, headquarter fortresses. Phantom would then report the map references and co-ordinates back over the net and the targets would be prioritized and attacked by the Royal Air Force.

A military commander once said, 'Communications channels are as important to an army as are blood vessels to the human body.' This is very true. The first thing that the Germans did when they occupied a country was to make sure that they had control of the railways. The SAS and the Resistance fighters in France were greatly helped in their task of disruption by the courage of the railway employees. These men and women were in an excellent position to watch the movements of the enemy forces and, if they were unable to sabotage the trains themselves, to pass this information on to the *Maquis*.

Railway workers risked their lives day in and day out to disrupt the Germans' progress about the countryside. One way in which they managed to slow down the transportation of troops was by changing the points, thus sending whole trainloads along the wrong rails. This caused chaos.

The first two Phantom patrols to drop in France were those of Captain John Sadoine and Lieutenant Tom Moore with 1st SAS, just after D-Day, on the 8th and 11th June, 1944, respectively. Their operations were successfully completed and the communications worked perfectly. That of Tom Moore, Operation Houndsworth, is described in more detail later in this chapter by Phantom's Sergeant Arthur 'Chippy' Wood.

On the night of 13th August, as part of Operation Loyton, Captain Hislop's Phantom patrol of four together with six SAS soldiers, commanded by Captain Druce, left Fairford aerodrome in Gloucestershire and successfully parachuted into their intended drop zone close to the village of La Petite Raon, near St Die, in Eastern France. A ten hour walk through the mountains, guided by members of the *Maquis* who had met them, led them by evening fall to a *Maquis* encampment on top of a wooded mountain. The aim of Operation *Loyton* was to establish a secure base 300 miles behind enemy lines in the Vosges mountains for more SAS troops and equipment to be dropped into. They hoped to establish a blocking force across the communication lines in the Vosges to severly hamper any Germans who were retreating east from Paris. Unfortunately, things did not go as planned. By the time Loyton was operational, the area was already crawling with the enemy. Word reached the mountain hideout that the Germans had discovered their drop zone and as a result were pouring more troops into the area. The decision was taken to move on after only having been there for four or five days. The SAS and Phantom patrol, aided by the *Maquis*, had to keep on the move continually, travelling by night, for the Germans were very much aware of their presence.

The party that had left the encampment split into two groups. One of them ran into a German detachment which spotted them hiding in a small hollow and opened fire. They were forced to run for their lives, leaving behind all their equipment and belongings, including the rucksack in which their radio was packed. Luckily, Capt. Hislop had the code-book and crystals on him, without which the radio was useless to the enemy.

Hislop's sergeant, Gerry Davis, who had set off before him, was missing, as were some of the SAS. It was later learnt that they had been captured and shot in cold blood, because they refused to talk.

It was some time before Hislop's party managed to get in touch with England through the French Underground movement but, when it did, the news was that further supplies would be arriving. After five or six nights spent waiting anxiously by the drop zone, the plane arrived, carrying not only supplies and a new radio transmitter, but also Lieutenant Peter Johnsen's Phantom patrol with twenty SAS members.

This was a very pleasant surprise, for Hislop had not been informed of their coming. Among the SAS was the colonel of 2nd SAS himself, Brian Franks, who immediately took charge of operations. The Phantom patrol included Sergeant Len 'Joe' Owens whose story is told later in this chapter.

Restocked with a plentiful supply of food, arms and explosives the SAS, along with the Maquis and the Phantom patrols, were now able to operate with some success again. Over the following few weeks they played havoc with German communications and troop movements until, during the first two weeks of October, Franks concluded that, with the onset of bad weather that made re-supply almost impossible, it was time to curtail the mission. News duly arrived from England confirming his request to bring an end to the operation. Their orders were to make their way back through German lines to rendezvous with the most forward American troops. These they found were a division of the US 7th Army under the command of Major-General Patch across the River Meurthe. Here they reported to Phantom's Captain Tam Williams whose patrol had been attached to Patch's liaison group.

Operation *Loyton* was over. Only half of the eighty men who went as part of this combined mission came back. 'F' Squadron lost three men killed in action. The sacrifice of these men was not in vain for their joint efforts, in this and other such operations, had kept the Germans in a permanent state of awareness. German forces, who should otherwise have been deployed fighting troops on the American and combined Allied front, had had to be withdrawn to deal with the exploits of the SAS and Phantom.

During the two months that *Loyton* was in progress Paris had fallen to the advancing Allies and in late October news was filtering through from the Free French Army Headquarters that *General* De Gaulle was ordering the French Resistance movements to disarm.

The other large scale operation carried out by the SAS behind German lines in France was Houndsworth, which was due to begin on the night of the 5th June, 1944. Phantom's 'F' Squadron was again to play a major role. We now relate the story of Sergeant Arthur Wood, of how he joined the army, became a member of Phantom/SAS and his part in Operation Houndsworth.

'I was born in Norwich in 1921 and grew up in this great capital of the county of Norfolk. I left Thorpe Hamlet school when I was fourteen and went to work for the firm of Boulton and Paul, who at that time were making aircraft. I joined them as an electrical plater. When the company moved to Wolverhampton I found work in the local foundry which, when war broke out, started to make war components. This was a reserved occupation and as such I did not have to go to war, but the work I was doing was not good for my health, so I thought I would be better off in the Army! I was by this time a married man living in a village close to Norwich, so in September 1940 I walked into the local recruiting office to volunteer my services. Having previously been in the TA 4th Norfolks, I was given my old Army number and was sent to the local drill hall where I was provided with a uniform.

After my initial six weeks training at Aylsham, twelve miles from Norwich, I was posted to a small airfield where I was put on guard duty, but soon I was on the move again, this time to Coltishall airfield – and more guard duty! Despite this I was enjoying the Army; the outdoor life, and the discipline. This was just after the Battle of Britain, and Squadron Leaders Tuck and Bader were there at that time.

The 70th Battalion Royal Norfolks, which I was serving in, was basically for young Norfolk lads, so when I reached my 20th birthday I was given three choices as to which regiment I would like to join – the Grenadier Guards; the Royal Corps of Signals; or the Norfolk Regiment. Being six feet tall I thought I would be well-suited to the Guards, but instead was assigned to the Signals. I suppose because I had done some radio work when I had been in the TA. Now I was off to Huddersfield up in Yorkshire where I trained to be a wireless operator. During my six months there I learnt morse code, to send and receive, how to repair radio sets, and general wireless work, which I thoroughly enjoyed. After qualifying in 1941, I was sent to the General Headquarters Liaison Regiment, and that is how I came to be in Phantom.

For a time I was operating radios at the Richmond Headquarters of this great regiment until I was sent down to Dorking in Surrey to a radio station on Leith Hill, 900ft above sea-level and the site of an old hill fort. Here my three comrades and I, under a Lance Corporal, were the link between Phantom's 'G' Squadron in Northern Ireland and 'H' Squadron in the North African desert. We had to be on the air at certain times to take the messages, which were all in code so we had no idea of the content.

From Leith Hill, which was part of HQ, I was sent to 'J' Squadron commanded by Major the Hon. Jakie Astor and often went down to Cliveden, the family seat of the Astor family. Two of Lord and Lady Astor's sons were officers of Phantom, Jakie and his younger brother Michael, and both were very friendly down-to-earth men. It was while at Cliveden that Lord Banbury, another Phantom officer, taught me to drive – in an Austin pick-up truck! Banbury was a big man who was loved by all his men.

With 'J', my patrol was on the move all the time, I was working as a wireless operator from a Scout car back to base. The squadron was attached to other branches of the British Army, and at one time to Combined Operations. We worked with the Commandos in Scotland and went with 1 Corps which was to be involved in the invasion of France. These were exciting times, we did beach landings, with suitcase radio sets, and climbed mountains with all the equipment that was needed.

In February 1943, 'J' Squadron, to avoid confusion with the 8th Army's 'J' Service, became 'F' Squadron. Seven months later our squadron was to be disbanded and we were to be sent to other squadrons – or volunteer for parachuting. Having no idea what our ultimate role would be all eighty of us stepped forward, and so, still as 'F', we found ourselves back in Scotland, this time at Auchinleck in Ayrshire. Here a PE instructor had to toughen us up before we began our parachute training at Ringway, now, incidentally, the site of Manchester Airport. Back in Auchinleck we were put into patrols of five – an officer, an NCO, and three wireless operators – and sent to various squadrons of the SAS. My patrol was posted to 'A' Squadron 1st SAS. 'F' Squadron became SAS PHANTOM, and our role was to provide signals for this very special service.

My patrol, No. 2, which consisted of Lieutenant Moore,

myself (Corporal Wood), Rifleman Ralli, Trooper Harris and Private Brinton, was posted to the squadron of 1st SAS which we were to go in with. This was at Darvel, still in Scotland.

Towards the end of May 1944, we were all taken down to Fairford in Gloucestershire, little knowing that the long-planned invasion of Europe was less than two weeks away. Here we were put in barbed-wire compounds, for now security was paramount. We were briefed as to where we were to drop and shown maps of the area. After the 6th June, D-Day, every night a truck would come and take a patrol away, our turn came on the 10th June. We were taken to an airfield where we drew our parachutes, picked up our wirelesses with our kit bags and got aboard a plane, but not before our CO came along and took a photo of us all. Our party consisted of Major Bill Fraser, two or three of his men, my patrol and Colonel Hastings of SOE.

I remember we took off at 10.30pm, crossed the Channel and the Normandy beachheads and flew on over France to the Massif Central area, where we were to drop 150 miles south of Paris. When we arrived, however, low cloud obscured the drop zone (DZ) and we couldn't see the reception committee, or rather the pilot couldn't, but we went ahead anyway and found ourselves spread out over a large area. Major Fraser and two of his men had dropped a long way off and we didn't see them until a week later! Luckily, our patrol officer found us, and took control. At first light, about 3.30am, we buried our parachutes and decided what to do. We didn't know where we were but moved east, looking for a disused railway line on our map. We never did find it! After six days, moving early in the morning before people were about or late in the evening, we were cold, wet and hungry, so our officer took one man with him and went into a village. I was one who stayed behind, where we lit a fire to dry out. It attracted an old peasant farmer who came along and we were able to make him understand who we were. He went away and returned with his two sons. They in turn went off, only to return an hour later in a truck with the local Maquis, who we should have met up with in the first place. We had been in touch with the UK by radio every day so they knew that all was well with us but we were having difficulty finding a base. However, we did find a base and brought in the rest of the squadron, about eighty in all, I think. That was our task, you see, as an advanced party, to set up a base. Well, now we were able to set up a camp and an ammo dump and we settled in.

We were in the middle of a field one day, reporting back to

the UK at one of our scheduled times, when a battle started near us between the Germans and the local Maquis. We abandoned our radio and took cover and the rest of the squadron joined in and helped. The Germans didn't know that there was an SAS Squadron there, so they got a nasty shock! As a result our sergeant major, Reg Seekings, was shot in the head. He had won the Distinguished Conduct Medal in the Western Desert with Col. David Stirling. I remember him, with a bullet lodged in his head, walking into camp with the back of his battledress soaked in blood. They couldn't operate on him in case it did more damage, so he carried the bullet in his head right through our mission. And he survived!

Once we were established we divided into three camps. Our Major was in the headquarters near the village of Monsauche, where I was, and the two out-stations were at Dijon and Chateau Chinon. Our only link with them was via England as we had no direct link. The aim of our operation, Houndsworth, was to stop Rommels Panzers, which were in the south of France when the invasion took place, from moving up to Normandy. When this task was complete we took out other targets, including an oil refinery, and radioed information about train movements back to England. The RAF soon flew in and sorted these out.

One of my tasks was to re-supply and it worked that in the morning I would receive a message such as 'One plane, ten containers to blue DZ, estimated time of arrival 0100 hours, running in from north to south, recognition letter P. Acknowledge.' About half an hour before time of arrival I would take another operator up to the DZ with my *Eureka* which worked to the *Rebecca* in the plane. If a plane flew over and I didn't get a high-pitched noise through my headphones I would let it go. When I did get the high-pitch I would send my recognition letter on Morse key, and the three men with me would light up a small flare path with sand soaked in petrol and the supplies would be dropped by parachute.

On one occasion a Frenchman came along and said that his chateau had been taken over by Rommel as his headquarters. Major Fraser decided that two or three jeeps would go to the chateau. I would go with them and another wireless operator to lay on an air raid. In the confusion the other two jeeps would go in and capture Rommel. He said we would all get a medal if we survived. I think it was such a hair-brained scheme that the 'powers that be' back in Britain vetoed it straightaway. The RAF did come in and bomb the Chateau from our map references, but Rommel was not there at the time.

We lived in the forest for three months until the Germans had retreated into Germany and Paddy Mayne came down on the 6th September and relieved us. Paddy Mayne knew of our work, usually 16 hours a day. We had been in touch with England every single day, decoding and encoding the messages, sending them over the air and arranging the re-supplies at night. He sent a message back to England saying that my wireless patrol had made the whole operation a success, because of the way we had done our job. We were all 'Mentioned in Dispatches', except our patrol officer.

During our time in the forest we had been constantly on the move, but with help from the French underground we were always one step ahead of the enemy. It was cat and mouse all the time. Although there was a garrison of Germans on the other side of the mountain we weren't bothered by them much, until the latter part of the operation when we moved camp at least five times. We had two very good *Maquis* groups in the area who were very active and kept us informed, but there were others who were not so good. They tended to skulk in the woods, so we decided not to involve them in our operations. Anyway, we worked quite independent of the Maquis and so we didn't really have much co-operation with them as such. The *Maquis* was really the realm of the SOE who were in the area. They were dealing with them and the French underground more than we were. We were there on our own, doing our own thing.

Once one of our out-stations met a German staff car and in hand-to-hand fighting they killed two of the officers and took the driver prisoner, he was brought back to our camp and stayed there until we went back to England. He was treated quite well and helped the cook, well when I say he helped the cook all our food was tinned and heated up on a wood fire. On another occasion when the men who were out met up with Germans and there was hand-to-hand fighting we had men shot. One had a bullet through his shoulder, one through his ankle, one broke his pelvis when the jeep he was in overturned, and we had a broken femur from a bad parachute landing, but the worst was when a jeep was out looking for an airfield so we could evacuate our wounded. They went round a bend in the road and alongside the road was a German convoy. They couldn't turn round so accelerated past the convoy, but when they had passed it a German machine-gun opened up from the rear and Captain Bradford and Private Devine were both shot and killed. A sergeant who was on the jeep got bullets in his back and had his fingers blown off, but still managed to evade capture and, with two others, made his way back to base to tell us what had happened. That was the worst incident as far as casualties were concerned.

Our living conditions in the forest had been pretty basic and uncomfortable, sleeping in sleepingbags on the ground, and, in the early stages we didn't have any medics so it was a little bit difficult at first, but after a while two did join us, but until then any of our seriously wounded, who could not be evacuated, were operated upon on a kitchen table in a village home by a French surgeon. That was all the medical attention that we could have.

I was never nervous, I didn't have time to be because we were so busy, we had a job to do and we got on with it. All of this time we were in uniform, battledress with a red beret, but with no insignias. We were armed with a .45 revolver and an American carbine rifle, and all carried water purifying tablets. Very important they were. We didn't really have any problems with the radios all the time we were out there. The arduous thing was that the messages had to be put into code and the messages received had to be encoded, which took a considerable amount of time. While two men operated the wireless the other two would do the coding and encoding. We used to take turns at that. It was a five letter code, all groups of five letters. I still have the silk handkerchief that I used in France with a table on and lots of short phrases that could be put into code using just three letters, and we used this and a code book to put all the messages into code. The corresponding code book was in the UK at base.

In my opinion Operation *Houndsworth* was a great success, it achieved all it set out to do and more besides. It pinned down the German troops who would normally have been in Normandy, they were in the area looking for us. The railway lines were destroyed and the oil refinery was destroyed and numerous other smaller targets were destroyed. In fact the main railway line in the area that carried the German forces was blown up over twenty times. Many Germans were killed or wounded, and some taken prisoner. Over thirty bombing raids by the allied air forces were carried out on information supplied from Phantom SAS.

On the 6th September, we commandeered a number of old cars from the area, and escorted by Paddy Mayne and his jeep, we travelled overland to Arromanches and we got on board ship and came back to Newhaven. From there we travelled by rail to Victoria Station where our commanding officer, Major Astor, came down to meet us. He took us back to Moor Park, the main base in England at that time. Major the Honourable J J Astor was a wonderful CO and a very nice man. At Moor Park I was called to Major Astor's office where he congratulated me on the job we had done on Operation *Houndsworth*, and sent us on a month's leave. When we came back he called me into his office again and said that he didn't think that he would send my patrol on any more operations because we had done enough, but I was to keep my patrol fit. We went on long marches, lived out in the open and worked our wireless.

When the Allies were crossing the Rhine the SAS were involved in an entirely different role. Instead of parachuting they were mobile with jeeps and crossed the Rhine. We were sent out to join them. The idea would then be that we were forward of all the other troops doing reconnaissance, finding out what Germans were in the area and relaying the messages back, and any pockets of resistance to mop them up. This is what the 1st and 2nd SAS were doing all across Germany. I was involved in that as well. The Germans were now in full retreat and some days we were moving ten to twenty miles a day. It was a little bit difficult once we'd crossed the Rhine, but the American Airborne Division and the British Parachute Troops had made a bridgehead where we crossed, and after a while it wasn't quite as arduous as it might have been.

When we'd finally reached Hamburg and the peace was signed on Luneburg Heath a message came through to the SAS to say we were to return to England immediately. We returned and were then flown out to Norway. The idea was to round up some of the hundreds of thousands of Germans still left in Norway. It was up to us to round them up and send them back to Germany. The Germans realised that it was all over for them and they came quietly. They never gave us any problems whatever. When this was done the war would be over for us, too. First we were at Bergen then my squadron went up to a small town on the Sogne Fjord called Vadheim, near where there was a large German camp. We also went to Stavanger.

Our patrol at the end was the same as I had started with, Lieutenant Moore and the three originals, Rifleman Ralli,

Trooper Harris and Private Brinton, but they had expanded my patrol in Germany to ten men and they were with me in Norway as well. Lieutenant Moore was a captain by now and had been awarded the Military Cross after France, and I had been promoted to sergeant and awarded the *Croix de Guerre*. I was also awarded, along with many others, the honour of being permitted to wear the SAS wings for working behind enemy lines with this special force.'

One of the other secret and dangerous SAS Phantom operations involved Lieutenant Charles 'Jock' McDevitt. As you may recall McDevitt, as a sergeant, had arrived at Richmond Station along with Harry Binge and Ron Eaton early in 1941, having come from the Royal Corps of Signals. Later he left to go to a Signals Officer Cadet Training Unit (OCTU) where he gained a commission and returned to Phantom as an officer. It was at his own request that he rejoined this regiment and later he was to join 'F' Squadron.

Ron and McDevitt had become firm friends from the day they first met and remained so throughout the war and afterwards, meeting many times over the years after McDevitt's retirement from the army. Ron remembers Jock telling him of how he parachuted behind enemy lines into occupied France in 1944, not long after D-Day.

On the night of the operation, McDevitt and his patrol had nervously dropped through the hole in the floor of the modified RAF Stirling bomber, which had flown them to their destination, into the darkness below. Their task was to make contact with the leader of the *Maquis* of an area of the Compiegne region, some fifty or more miles east of the River Seine, and to send back to England over the radio news of his groups' activities.

When Lt McDevitt hit the ground, he desperately searched around for the rest of his patrol, aware that without another man he would be unable to operate the wireless because, with the Jedburgh sets, another pair of hands was required to turn the handle of the dynamo to power the set. McDevitt's rallying call, that was supposed to be a low chirp but sounded more like a loud squawk, brought the others scurrying from their concealment in the undergrowth. Fortunately, the only injury suffered in the drop was a twisted ankle by one of the men.

Awaiting first light, the patrol snatched a few hours sleep in a clump of trees. At dawn, McDevitt and one other set off in search of the *Maquis*, who should have been expecting their arrival, while the rest rounded up the supplies that had been dropped with them. Both parties were unlucky. The Resistance leader could not be located and one of the food containers was missing. The loss of the contents was not too drastic but, if found by the Germans, the container would alert them to a British landing.

A few inquisitive French peasants, who had started to appear as if from nowhere, were taken into Phantom's confidence and urged to help in their search for the missing box. Their numbers quickly swelled and very soon the identity of this small party of men was discovered. But they had no need to worry. The locals were delighted to greet the British, showering them with gifts of food and helping them in any way they could.

The missing container had not been found by the time the Phantom party was due to make its first call to England at 10am. To everyone's great relief they were informed by base that the elusive container was not in fact missing, it had failed to drop from the plane and was safely back in England.

With one mystery solved, the party was packing in preparation for its continued mission, to find the *Maquis*, when mumblings of 'M. le Cure' came from the locals gathered round them. As a young priest on a very old bicycle with a face as black as thunder came flying along, the crowd separated and gave way to him. The priest was extremely angry, not only with the assembled peasants but also with the soldiers. Declaring himself to be the leader of the *Maquis* who Phantom were seeking, he demanded the names of all the French villagers who were present, with threats that if any one of them spoke of the 'situation' they would be shot! He then turned his anger on McDevitt and his men, demanding to know why they had not jumped to his lights. Obviously, a blunder had been made but now it could be remedied.

A large horse-drawn farm cart heaved into sight and the party with all their belongings was quickly stowed away under a tarpaulin and a bumpy ride, at last, brought them to their hideaway – the village church. Up in the belfry, they found themselves sharing their shelter with four Frenchmen who had escaped from the Germans while en route to a labour camp and had been given refuge by the priest. While waiting for le Cure's return, the Frenchmen told them of the exploits of the priest. Over the past four years, this man of the cloth had been a constant thorn in the side of the enemy, wreaking havoc with their convoys and troop movements as he led raids on roads and railway lines, blowing them up and destroying vital supply and communication links. When the priest returned, now calm, he proudly showed McDevitt his secret hide-outs and his arsenal of weapons. McDevitt thought it strange that a religious man such as he could treat killing so casually. When he later questioned the priest about this, McDevitt was amused to hear him say, 'I am first and foremost a Frenchman, and anyway as I kill them, I also absolve them!'

Over the next two weeks, although constantly in danger themselves, Lt McDevitt and his Phantom patrol worked ceaselessly, collecting and sending all the available information about the work of the priest's Resistance movement back to England. This vital intelligence was passed on to the forward Allied troops in the area as they continued their advance across France.

Ron Eaton recalls how proud he was when he heard the news that Jock McDevitt, his friend and fellow Phantom member, had been awarded the *'Croix de Guerre'* by the French for his work with the SAS and the French and Belgian partisan movements. Lt McDevitt stayed in Phantom, was promoted to Captain and eventually to Major, and was in fact the last Commanding Officer of No. 3 GHQ Liaison Regiment when it was attached to the 7th Armoured Division, of the 21st Army Group. Part of the British Army on the Rhine. Phantom was stationed at Bunde, Westphalia, Germany, from 1945 until the regiment returned to the UK in July 1948.

Company Quartermaster Sergeant Leonard 'Joe' Owens, MM, Royal Signals attached to Phantom 'F' Squadron/SAS now tells the story of his army life and his role with the SAS.

'I was called up in January 1941, and having expressed a wish to go in the Navy, as was inevitable in those days, found myself posted to the Army, and a unit stationed at Prestatyn in North Wales, in what had originally been a holiday camp.

Having passed through the various stages of training, I was sent to the GPO Wireless Training School at Sheffield, to be trained as a wireless operator. While there my friend was a lad called Tony Breirton who was six feet, four inches, and as I am only five feet, four inches we presented an odd couple as we went round the various pubs in the town. On returning to the TC, I applied to be transferred to the Navy, which created a good deal of head shaking on behalf of the orderly office. However, strangely enough, shortly after a notice appeared on the board inviting applications for 1) The Commandos or 2)

Combined Operations, and as this sounded more like it, I immediately put my name down for option 2. Eventually, the postings came up and while many were sent to Signals Units at Catterick and Ossett, I found myself directed to the RTO at St. Enoch's Station, Glasgow, for onward routing to the Combined Operations Training Camp at Inveraray, Scotland. On arriving at Glasgow, I and like characters were put into the back of a 3-tonner and transported up over the 'Rest and be thankful' and around Loch Fyne to the camp at Inveraray. Here we went through intensive training, jumping on and off all sorts of ships and landing craft, by day and by night. This was a rough old place inhabited by all sorts of Army, Navy and Air Force units who were billetted in Nissen huts just outside the town.

Eventually, I found a cushy billet running the Signals Dispatch Office with a Petty Officer at HMS *Dundonald*, which was a Naval shore establishment near Troon, but cushy billets were not prone to last in those days. I was soon informed that a special assault unit from an outfit called Phantom had applied for assault trained wireless operators and that I had been posted to this outfit. As they were about to leave for the Middle East I was sent on ten days embarkation leave. Transferred with me were Signalmen Frank Richardson, 'Croome' Johnson and Oscar Ash.

On return from leave we were taken by truck to Greenock and by drifter out to HMS *Bulolo*, which was a specially adapted HQ Communications ship. Having gone aboard this was the first time we had any contact with this strange sounding unit named Phantom.

I now jump to July 1943. We took part in Operation *Husky*, the Allied landings on Sicily, and then the unit was ordered to reboard HMS *Bulolo* for withdrawal to Malta. There was a great deal of satisfaction, I think, for our little unit had integrated well with our Phantom companions.

Arriving on the island of Malta, we were billetted in tents on the airfield where we were heavily bombed. And if anyone ever tells you that schrapnel will not go through tent canvas, don't you believe them! Here we were informed that the unit was to split up. Some were to continue up through Italy while the remainder would be withdrawn to the UK. Sadly, our little group was split up, two of three of my companions being sent with the Phantom detachment to Italy, while I was listed as returning. We were not happy with this arrangement, but such were the fortunes of war in those days. The group of Phantom we were with were a happy lot, some of whom had been in the Middle East for some time. We set off in a landing craft for Sousse on the Tunisian coast. This harbour had been bombed and was full of sunken ships, there appeared to be chaos everywhere. Eventually, by truck and by cattle-truck on a train, we trailed across North Africa to Algiers, where we were again billetted in tents. This time on the local race course, Maison Blanche. Algiers is a very, very large city with bars, theatres and, of course, the local *Casbah*, where all sorts of carnal delights could be experienced – so I was reliably informed!

At the end of November we boarded the troopship *Samaria*, which was an ex-Cunard liner, and sailed for the UK. Some weeks later after a hellish storm in the Atlantic, where it was plain Phantom would never make sailors, we sailed up the Mersey towards Liverpool, in mist that was so thick one could not even see the famous Liver Birds above it. Passing a wooden jetty, that I knew to be Langdon Dock, out of the mist was visible a British policeman, whereupon the whole ship's company lined the rails and joined in that well-known phrase 'All coppers are bastards!' To his credit, the constable raised his helmet in salute and was cheered as we passed. And so we disembarked at Liverpool landing stage to be greeted by a band, and tea and buns by the Red Cross. We then boarded a train at the riverside station for the south, and Phantom HQ at Richmond. Here we were issued with the medal ribbon of the Africa Star, which usually caused some interest in the local pubs, and were sent on disembarkation leave.

Our next billet was someone's ancestral home – Dynes Hall, near Halstead in Essex, but before we were sent there we were stationed for a few days at Stroud in Gloucestershire. One evening we sallied out to the local pub, *The Woolpack*, only to be told that there was no beer! Never mind, there was plenty of rough cider, and after a night on this the whole unit could not have fought its way out of a paper bag!

But back to Dynes Hall. Here for me my whole situation changed. We were paraded and informed by Major the Hon. J J Astor that he had been asked to form a Signals Section for the SAS. As this was a volunteer job, anyone who did not wish to step forward was quite entitled to do so. Eventually, we were told that enough people had volunteered and that was the direction in which our future lay. Immediately, we were sent on a parachute training course at Tatton Park, near Manchester.

With me at this time were Sergeant Gerry Davis, Signalman

Peter Bannermann and Private Jock Davis who, sadly, were to be killed on Operation *Loyton*. Corporal 'Chippy' Wood, who was to receive fame on Operation *Houndsworth*, when he received the '*Croix de Guerre*' with star and was 'Mentioned in Dispatches'. A couple of lads who were handy with the ladies, Signalman Skipworth and Trooper Plum, and to some extent that famous Norfolk swede-basher, Trooper George Harris, whose nickname in the unit was 'Fruit' for some odd reason. Bomber Panchen and Lance Corporal Hopper I remember too, and also Lance Corporal Trew, who was known to some in our unit as TF, which I will leave to your imagination to elucidate!

I think I suffered bouts of fear the whole time I was at Tatton Park, and particularly terrifying were the drops from the static balloon, where one was taken up to about 800 feet – and then deadly silence. One could look down through the hole and see the ground and then, on the word of command, push oneself out, being careful not to bang ones head on the other side of the hole. This was known as 'ringing the bell'.

Night drops, too, were a bit dicey and one Sunday afternoon, with quite a brisk breeze blowing, we were told that a Brigadier would be coming to observe a parachute drop. I don't think the instructors were too happy with the conditions, but it went ahead anyway, and it was on this that I received my only minor injury – coming down I twisted my knee.

Eventually, we passed the course, received our parachute wings and returned to Dynes Hall. Here we were made up into patrols and I was attached to Lieutenant Peter Johnsen who would be working with the 2nd SAS. Also in my patrol were Signalman Peter Bannermann and Troopers Plum, Highland and Bateman. We were given a 15cwt truck which 'Fan' Bateman kept in perfect working order and pristine condition, and were sent on exercises with our opposite numbers in the SAS. Major Astor had it firmly in his mind that to become familiar with and integrate with one another we should live and work together, and so learn to trust one another. Now we were sent north to Scotland, for training in an area bordered roughly by Largs in the north and Ayr to the south. We roamed over the Scottish hills carrying our Bergen rucksacks, which weighed 70 or 80-lbs, on exercises conducted on SAS lines, which went far beyond what we would have dared to do as ordinary soldiers in the British Army.

Once when we were exercising in the area of Newton Stewart, which is border country, we were informed by radio that we should abandon the exercise and go to a place called Glentrool Lodge where it had been reported that they had seen someone descend by parachute up in the hills. We were sent to investigate this alleged sighting and set off up into the hills, through streams and heather, but having arrived and searched the whole area of the hills above the house, nothing was found – either German or British. By chance, our patrol officer, Lieutenant Johnsen, knew the family who lived in this ancestral house so we were invited to stay for dinner. An extraordinary scene could be observed of soldiers, soaked to the waist, sitting round a large ancestral table with silver service, being served by a butler and servants. We were very grateful and after having our clothes dried departed on our merry way. Officers sometimes come in useful!

Another interesting exercise with the SAS was to infiltrate as many official buildings in the Glasgow area without being seen or challenged. If we were caught we were in possession of passes of immunity from arrest, by either military or civil authorities. We managed to get in and out of numerous establishments in Glasgow and were never challenged. These were, of course, recorded. Try as we may though we were not able to fiddle to retain these passes, which would have been worth a King's ransom to any soldier. They were all numbered and had to be strictly returned once the exercise was over. Never mind!

From another exercise we had to return by train, and the idea was to go to the nearest station, which was Tomintoul, I think, and ask for a train to be stopped. This the stationmaster declined to do, so he was promptly informed that if he wouldn't stop the train, we would. We had the equipment – we had railway detonators. After consulting his signalman it was agreed that the train would be stopped, and so we boarded it. To our surprise, the guard was so intrigued by us he placed us in the First Class compartment by ourselves. I have no doubt that eventually the unit paid, but this was real SAS stuff, and we loved it!

Our next billets was in Auchinleck in an ancestral home named Auchinleck House, which, I believe, had been the home of James Boswell, the famous Scottish author and lawyer. Here all the patrols were assembled, in order to have them all in one spot ready for the invasion of Europe.

The first two Phantom patrols to depart were those of Lieutenant Moore and Captain Sadoine, and we were left in sole charge, and able to draw rations for the whole outfit so no one would notice they had gone. I'm sure many local people benefitted from the excess food we had.

We continued to exercise until one day, over the radio, came the instruction to go forthwith to Prestwick Airport, where a plane was waiting to transport us south. And so we flew off, passing on the port side Blackpool Tower and my home town of Liverpool, before we flew steadily up the River Dee, where we were buzzed by two American Buffalo aircraft. Our pilot, ex-Spitfire, seemed unconcerned and continued on his steady course, and they got fed-up and left us.

Finally arriving at our destination, Rickmansworth, we were informed that we were going on an SAS operation to Northern France. Our job would be to observe traffic heading up from Southern France to the invasion beaches. Our patrol consisted of Lieutenant Johnsen, myself, Signalman Peter Bannermann and Trooper Bell. Fan Bateman, our driver, was due to go but there was no room for him in the aircraft. We moved south to a house at Pewsey which was adjacent to Fairford Aerodrome, and here we were briefed. (I've always been convinced that this place was run by a 'trick cyclist'.) After briefing we were taken and placed inside 'the cage', and once having gone inside you were there until your operation came up. It was not a very comfortable place, and the beer was like rusty water. I even remember the film that was being shown the night we arrived – *The Picture of Dorian Grey*.

After several alerts and stand downs we were taken out to the plane at Fairford that was to take us to our destination, and were handed our parachutes by the young WAAF who had actually packed it. I never knew her name but, God bless her, it opened!

Sitting on the deck in these four-engined aircraft was far from comfortable, but most of us dozed on and off and had coffee when it was brought. Eventually, we were told five minutes to destination, and we all assembled to hook up our static lines and have them checked by the dispatcher. I was to be the leader of the second stick and I remember standing there looking out into the darkness below thinking, dear God, what have I got myself into!

The descent was routine, but strangely the first thing I noticed about France was the aromatic smell. France seemed to have a smell all of its own.

We all landed safely and eventually set up the wireless set and got through to HQ without any difficulty. Everything seemed to be quiet all around and the SAS team set off to reconnoitre the area and observe what traffic there was on the roads heading to the invasion. This information we duly reported back to HQ, but what we did not know at the time was that we were in advance of General Patton's army, who surprised everybody by the speed of their advance south. A few days later we were overrun by the Americans and sent a message back to SAS HQ asking for jeeps to be dropped. This was denied, so we proceeded north east to join up with another SAS group at Le Mans. As we had no transport the SAS went out and commandeered several civilian cars, mostly Citroëns. We then proceeded to tear off the front and rear doors in order to have a good field of fire should this become necessary or to bail out of the vehicle without too much trouble. We travelled north east, mainly across country but also using some roads, towards Le Mans. As far as I can remember we did not hit any trouble on the way, although there were many areas of menacing forest to travel through. We did spot a German tank once, but managed to avoid it. Arriving at Le Mans we were billetted in what had been the local barracks and we Signals spent happy hours trawling through all the abandoned equipment. Le Mans by that time had no Germans of any strength in the vicinity but it was subject to a considerable amount of sniping, so we had to be pretty careful where we wandered outside the town.

It was while we were in Le Mans that we received the sad radio message that our companion Fan Bateman, who had been left behind in England, had been accidentally killed. Such, I suppose, is the fate of war. Our SAS group at that time was commanded by Airey Neave, later a Conservative MP and minister, who also died tragically in his car, many years later at the House of Commons.

We now heard that in excess of one hundred British PoW's were hiding in a forest to the south and it was decided that they should be rescued. Consequently, buses were commandeered and set off under an SAS escort to pick these lads up, which they successfully did.

Eventually, we were recalled to England and set off in the SAS vehicles for the journey back to port. In many of the villages that we passed through we were showered with flowers, and occasionally a bottle of wine, but one tragic scene remains in my memory. In one particular village a young lady was sat on a chair in the village square having her hair cut off, surrounded by a jeering crowd. We were told that this was because she had collaborated with the Germans. Who knows, perhaps she just went out with one of them. War is brutal!

We crossed from the Hook of Holland to Harwich and travelled by train to Rickmansworth. The thing that struck me at this time was how green England looked after the brown parched grass of Northern France.

At Rickmansworth we skulled about and did one or two exercises and the only incident I remember happening here was an RAF Mosquito crashing on a small copse next to the playground of the local school. We were called out to surround the area and see that the school was evacuated, but, of course, this had already been done. The area was strewn with live ammunition and the smell of petrol was invasive. We managed to get the two airmen out, who strangely enough were both elderly gentlemen. One was very seriously hurt, but the other one was okay and kept asking what had happened to his mate. All we could say was, 'Well, he's okay.' We collected up all the loose ammunition and on the arrival of the local fire brigade returned to camp.

This was followed by a period known to every soldier as 'a bit of work during the day and to the pub at night', until one day news came through to the unit that one of our patrols that was in the Vosges area of France with the SAS had suffered casualties and was out of communication. Eventually, they managed to get in touch with England through the French underground requesting to be re-supplied. The Phantom patrol that had run into trouble was that of Captain Johnny Hislop. Lieutenant Johnsen informed us that the colonel of the 2nd SAS himself, Lieutenant Colonel Brian Franks, had decided to personally drop into this operation, Operation *Loyton*, with a group of SAS and would require a Phantom communications team to drop with them. It appeared that this was going to be us! We were kitted out and were to take replacement wireless sets so that communication could be re-established with this SAS operation, whose objective was to harrass the Germans who were in front of General Patton's advancing army. Patton intended to drive straight through the Vosges to the port of Strasbourg on the Rhine.

We went through the same procedure as before, the house at Pewsey, the briefing by the 'trick cyclist', the cage where the beer was still lousy, and then collected our parachutes before boarding the plane, this time a Halifax. Just as uncomfortable. We flew over the Channel, the coast of France and on towards the DZ, only this time the scene over the DZ was different. Many signals blazed below and round we went once again. At this point one of the aircrew said he thought we were bloody mad, and we returned the compliment!

The same routine as before, red light, green light, out, but this time my exit was different. Having successfully got out of the plane and lowered my leg bag to the end of its rope, for some unaccountable reason it broke away and plummeted down to the DZ like a bomb. When I landed I was immediately surrounded by the French Resistance, who promised to look for my leg bag, although they never found it, and I was left with only the clothes I stood up in. In spite of having no clean socks and underwear, I did have less weight to carry on my back.

The story of Operation *Loyton* has been told in the foregoing pages so I will record some of my impressions of the operation.

During the day the wireless section's work was not too arduous. We spent our time encoding any signals to be sent out when we had a schedule and listening very carefully on the little portable receivers, that many of the officers and men had, for personal messages. Sometimes in code, sometimes in clear, these were preceded by a few bars of the tune '*Sur le Pont D'Avignon*' and our code name '*Romo*', which would come out 'Hello *Romo*. Hello *Romo*', in which case we knew that somewhere there would be a message for our group.

Our work really started at night, especially if there were to be drops. We were responsible for going to the DZ, and having ascertained the recognition signal for that night, flash it to the aircraft that was coming in. This could be dicey for we had no way of knowing if the aircraft was German or British, but we did have a Canadian pilot with us, who had been shot down and brought to us by the Resistance, who reckoned he could recognise the difference in the engine noise of aircraft. Give him his due, this worked. We also had a device called a '*Eureka*' and its companion in the aircraft called '*Rebecca*'. It was said that if this was switched on the plane could home in on it, but I'm not sure whether this damn thing ever worked. We preferred to use our own methods.

Once the loads were dropped we would assist with collecting the containers, these would be marked with colour symbols to indicate what was inside, and grouping them together. With the help of the local Resistance we shifted them off the DZ as quickly as possible to wherever they were to be stored. When this was done we would make our way back up the hill in the darkness to our camp, where we would send a message back to HQ indicating the success of the drop.

On more than one occasion, though, things did not go exactly as planned. Once, with a drop planned for that evening, we were informed that the enemy were approaching the DZ. With the utmost speed we had to dash up the side of the hill, set up the wireless set and send off the appropriate 'Q' message. This would indicate that the drop was to be aborted because the enemy were in control of the DZ.

On another occasion we were informed that an SAS officer was bringing his dog with him. Apparently, they had had a special parachute constructed for it. At this point the Colonel ordered us to go back up the hill, make contact with them again and tell them, in no uncertain terms, that a dog was the last thing we wanted when we were being pursued through the forest by the Germans.

It was not only messages for the SAS we sent, at one time an officer of the SOE joined us. Captain Gough had lost his operator and his wireless, so the Colonel authorised me to send his radio traffic back to SOE. This I did, using Captain Gough's crystal to get in touch on the correct wavelength direct with SOE. I also helped him to encode his messages, which seemed to be done on exactly the same basis as our system. Sadly, I later heard that he did not get out, he had been captured and shot.

When transmitting we very frequently moved our location so that the Germans could not detect the signal coming from the same spot. All the time we were in France they were continually on our trail. The SAS were out and about gathering intelligence of enemy movements and attacking railway lines and enemy installations, with the co-operation of the Resistance movement. Frequently, targets were detected, enemy strength was assessed and we would relay map references back to HQ in the UK to summon up an air attack by the Allied Air Force.

Many of the local Resistance fighters, men and women, sacrificed their lives in support of us and they must never be forgotten. Nowadays, visit any village in the area and there will be a stone memorial to those who lost their lives. Some indicating that many were from the same family.

The forest is like the sea, it is ever changing and in the Vosges the morning mists that swept in were uncomfortable. The forest is a funny place, sometimes it offered security and peace and at other times the aspect of a prison. I've never, ever liked any forest since those days. During the day when we were not doing anything operational people passed the time in their own personal fashion. Johnny Hislop I know found comfort in poetry. *'The Crock of Gold'* and *'The Golden Treasury'* being two of his favourite books. I, not having any such literary education, managed to perfect a scheme of blocking out all thoughts when it came time to go to sleep or doze. Each person had his own way of dealing with the situation, but towards the end I think overall the sense was of fear and trepidation. I have never been in favour of recording people's personal reactions, but I must say that our little group supported one another and within our little orbit each one felt that they were not alone.

Eventually, when Operation *Market Garden* was in progress at Arnhem in September, the number of aircraft available to drop supplies was restricted, so, in effect, we were out on a limb on our own. I think it was a great relief to us all when the Colonel decided that no useful purpose was being served by us continuing in this fashion, trying to perform a task for which we were not equipped or designed, and that the operation should be terminated. General Patton and his Army had stopped at Nancy and there was no news of when he would continue.

Colonel Franks required two Phantoms to remain to close up the operation, Johnny Hislop and myself. Lieutenant Peter Johnsen was told to take the other 2 Signalmen, Peter Bannermann and Jock Johnson, back through the lines and they departed two days before us. SAS men left at the same time.

With our work complete we were taken by the Americans to a bungalow that Phantom was using at Epernay as an HQ. By this time we were stinking and all sported vast beards that required the application of scissors before we could even start to shave. I swear that the water that drained off us in the shower was yellow.

Eventually, we were loaded onto a very ancient Dakota that lumbered its way across France and Holland before landing in England. Trucks took us to the HQ at Moor Park where we were very closely questioned as to where were Peter Bannermann and Jock Johnson. All we could say that they had left forty-eight hours before us, little knowing that they were already dead. When the news came through of what had happened to them, plans for highjinks on return from Operation *Loyton* just didn't go ahead.

The story was that they successfully reached, what they thought, were the American lines and sat down in a clearing strewn with empty *'Lucky Strike'* cigarette packets. What they didn't know, of course, was that the Germans had retaken this sector and that they were being observed by a German patrol who immediately opened fire. I understand that Peter Bannermann was killed instantly and Jock Johnson was shot and later died of his wounds. Lieutenant Johnsen was also wounded but managed to run off and escape. He eventually got back. Such is war, fate, destiny, luck, who knows!

Sergeant Gerry Davis was different, his group, including SAS were hiding from a German patrol when one of the Resistance men they were with raised his head and was seen, they came under fire and scattered. Gerry lost contact and went to a house for assistance. He was betrayed, captured and shot in the head, having, I understand, given no information away. He was the real hero. This happened early on in *Loyton* before I dropped with Colonel Franks.

This bloody operation had had everything – betrayal, murder, a beautiful spy, a parachuting dog, and death. For me war is bloody and can only end in tears and sadness for many people who are in no way responsible for what happened.

We returned to Rickmansworth, but not for long. After a few weeks we were told to stand by for another operation, this time with the 1st SAS under the command of Lieutenant Colonel Paddy Mayne. This was not a parachute job, we were going over to Germany to work in conjunction with the 4th Canadian Armoured Division with armoured jeeps. This was Operation *Howard* and was near Mappen, so off we went in convoys. We arrived at the Canadian HQ where we enjoyed such exotic foods as flapjacks and maple syrup for breakfast.

We were organised into patrols and I was to go with Colonel Mayne's patrol to provide communications. My opposite number was Sergeant Dave Danger, MM. As we set off down a forest track the jeep in front hit a landmine and I'm sorry to say a member of the SAS, Trooper Rose, was killed.

It was clear that this was a different kettle of fish, for the Germans here were fighting on their own soil for their homeland, not destroying somebody else's country as they had been doing for several years. The area was very dicey. There seemed to be thousands of German troops around the area who were well dug in in the fields. These commanded a field of fire over all the roads, and our jeeps, having tremendous fire power, were prime targets. Quite early on in the operation we went down a road and could clearly see in the distance German troops wandering about in the fields and they were obviously

Phantom 'L' Sqn. with detachment of American Signals, Selsey, June 1944.

Capt. Peter Stileman's 'L' Squadron Phantom patrol at Bastogne just prior to Battle of the Bulge, December 1944. *L to r:* back-row Pte John Campbell, Cpl Bill Joss, Pte John Tudor Evans. Front row-Pte Paddy Watson, Pte Pat Page, Tpr Alistair Clark.

Pte John Campbell with American MP beside wreckage of Me 109, Eupen, Belgium, early 1945.

Phantom Signals 'B' Squadron at Luneberg immediately after VE Day 1945. Hospital as background. (Lord Haw Haw - captured and wounded in ward above) *(Photo William Glazzard)*

Vadheim, Norway, 1945. *l to r:* SSM Seekings 1st SAS; not known; Trooper Harris 'F' Sqn Phantom; Arthur 'Chippy' Wood 'F'; Rifleman Ralli 'F'; Private Brinton 'F'; Sgt Terry 1st SAS.

Captains Bob Perret and Clem Skinner (right) 'B' Sqn en route to England across Channel, 1945.

'Phantomime', Christmas 1945, Bunde.

'Phantomime', Christmas 1945, Bunde.

Phantom 'A' Sqn No. 12 patrol, Denmark, 1945. *l to r (back)*: Ted Rourke; Ron Eaton; Fred Clarke. (front): Albert Bradbury; Paul Holdway; Andy Black.

Ron Eaton with captured Mercedes German Officers' Staff Car, Denmark, 1945.

No. 12 patrol's officer, Capt. Meade *(left)* with Major Russell, 'A' Sqn's Commanding Officer, Denmark, 1945.

Driver/operator Ron Jackson, 'L' Sqn, Richmond Park, 1945.

The Earl of Rosslyn *(left)* with Capt. Geoffrey Brain, Phantom's 'B' Sqn on the road to Nijmegan, March 1945.

'A' Sqn No. 12 patrol, Denmark, 1945.

Phantom No. 3 GHQL Reg. Officers, Richmond Park, August 1945.

No. 3 GHQ Liaison Reg. Magazine.

ensconced in slit trenches. It was on this road that the leading patrol encountered stiff opposition from a German strongpoint in a factory. During the exchange of fire the second-in-command, Major Bond, and his driver, Lewis, were killed. We buried them by the roadside in blankets and Paddy Mayne said a few words. Somebody found some wood and made a crude cross to mark the position. Paddy Mayne was incensed by this set back, and, calling for a volunteer driver, set off and charged down to this factory blazing away with twin-Vickers and a .5 Browning. After several attacks the opposition was finally silenced, due entirely to this unconventional officer.

After that we roamed through some of the local villages, destroyed an ammunition dump and rounded up quite a number of prisoners. This was not easy to handle for some of them were not just ordinary German soldiers, their uniforms were those of crack members of the SS. These lads needed careful watching. That night we were in the centre of a large forest and the prisoners had to be completely surrounded by armed guards all night. A dicey situation at any time.

All around we could hear the sound of German movement as some of their units were retreating and some, with horsedrawn transport, obviously aware that we were in the area, kept continuous fire upon this wood all through the night. Unfortunately, an SAS man had one of his testicles shot off. Despite the reassuring words of many of the officers, the rough soldiers, as usual, made such remarks as, 'Hell, mate, you'll have to spend twice as long and pump twice as hard now.' However, when someone started calling him 'Gooly', the matter was stopped. Poor sod!

It was at this time that Paddy Mayne did his famous walk. Some Bren-gunners had gone out to try to silence the enemy and Paddy walked out with them amidst a hail of fire armed only with a camera.

There was also an incident during the day when we had several seriously injured SAS men and an extremely seriously injured German officer. It was decided that these casualties should be loaded on a jeep and under a white flag be taken over to the nearest German troops. I understand that the officers who manned the jeeps were actually given a meal in the German officers' mess. One German officer, whose brother had been killed just that morning, wanted them all arrested and shot, but they were allowed to return safely with the promise that, when they moved on, the SAS troops, after medical treatment, would be left behind.

Eventually, much to our relief, Sherman tanks of the Canadians arrived on the scene and cleared the immediate area. Jeeps were not ideal for this sort of warfare and we were transferred to an independent brigade, which had armoured cars, and worked towards Oldenburg. Many of the prisoners that we took at that time were German Marines who were no more than teenagers. We worked with this unit for quite some time until the Germans had retreated out of this area, but at one point we were confronted by a noise that sounded like the whole of the German army. We retreated to a farm and armoured jeeps were posted round the outbuildings. I was manning a pair of twin-Vickers and expected at any moment the German troops to come over the rise in the ground in front, but it never happened although the noise continued. Eventually, we were able to get a message back and an hour or so later rocket-firing Typhoons came over and strafed the positions which we had given.

Thankfully, orders came through that we were to return to the UK, in order to go to Norway to assist with the evacuation of the German army there. So once again we set off across Europe and this time we embarked at the *Mulberry* Harbour. Fate again stepped in and the American landing craft that we were embarked on went ashore, and there we sat for a couple of days. By the time we returned to our units the attachment for Norway had already departed and so we were left to man the rear link at Moor Park. A pity, I would have liked to have gone on this operation!

After our travels it was a bit boring here. Work during the day and to the pub at night. Then volunteers were called for to go out to the Far East. The majority of us volunteered and we were transferred to Phantom HQ at Richmond. While there we were billetted in a large house, Wick House, overlooking the Thames, and it was in the pub opposite, The Roebuck, that we celebrated the end of the war in Europe several weeks later.

Things now happened in the Far East and we were informed that we would no longer be going there, the whole unit was to be transferred to Germany, to a place called Bunde in Westphalia. Bunde turned out to be a lucky place for me, because it was there that I met my future wife, Tess, who was serving in that area for the Control Commission for Germany. It was from Bunde that most of us would be demobbed. My time came in October 1946 when I returned to the UK to get married, Tess having preceded me on her release from the CCG.'

As a footnote to Joe Owens's story we would like to add what Captain Johnny Hislop had to say of him after Operation *Loyton*. 'He was as good a soldier and companion in time of stress as anyone could wish for. Short in height, he was squarely built, tough, intelligent, and sensible. Unselfish, cheerful and patient, he was a true gentleman by nature and earned the confidence and devotion as much of his officers as his men. I found Joe a great stand-by during the whole operation, and it was largely due to his skill and care that communication never failed.'

In mid 1946 a story appeared in the '*Soldier*' the army's own newspaper about joint Phantom/SAS missions, concerning Arthur 'Chippy' Wood and Len 'Joe' Owens. It read:

'Two of the most daring of 'F' Squadron's escapades while working with the SAS were those of Phantom Sergeants Wood and Owens who dropped behind the German lines in the mountains some 250 miles south-west of Paris. There they assisted in collating important information, most of which had been obtained by the *Maquis*, and passed it on to guide the RAF in bombing targets.

In the opinion of Sergeant Wood, the best piece of news that their mission obtained was the location of Army Group B's Headquarters at La Roche-Guyon under the command of *Feldmarschall* Erwin Rommel. This information confirmed the uncertain report which already lay on the table of the officer who eventually gave the order to bomb the Chateau and kill the German commander.'

This sortie was carried out by rocket-firing Typhoons made up from RAF Squadrons 198 and 609. Fortunately for the *Feldmarschall* he had left the Chateau sometime before, but he was not to be so lucky next time. On the 17th July, 1944, on the way to his headquarters from battle HQ, Rommel's escorted car was spotted by RAF Typhoons from 193 Squadron. Led by Wing-Commander Johnny Baldwin, they roared down to attack. Rommel's driver was struck down at the wheel as he raced for cover and the car crashed into a tree severely injuring Rommel himself. He was carried unconscious to a nearby village, which incidentally was called St Foy de Montgommery, where his wounds were dressed by a pharmacist before he was taken to a German Air Force hospital at the nearby town of Bernay. The accident had not killed the *Feldmarschall* but it had forced him to relinquish command of Army Group B.

Only two days before this incident, Rommel had sent an urgent memorandum to the *Führer* outlining the grave situation in the West. He forecast an Allied break-through in two to three weeks. 'The consequences will be immeasurable. The troops are fighting heroically everywhere, but the unequal struggle is nearing its end. I must beg you to draw the conclusion without delay. I feel it my duty as Commander-in-Chief of the Army Group to state this clearly.'

When Rommel's attempt to make Hitler grasp the seriousness of the situation failed, the *Feldmarschall* agreed to an assassination attempt on the *Führer*'s life. Even before the invasion had taken place Rommel had reached the conclusion that, if Germany was to be saved, Hitler must be got rid of. He was originally opposed to an assassination attempt on the grounds that it could make a *martyr* of Hitler but proposed instead that Hitler should be seized and tried before a German court. Hitler's handling of the Allied invasion only served to stiffen Rommel's resolve.

On the 20th July, Hitler was at the *Wolf's Lair* at Rastenburg in East Prussia. While in one of his headquarters' wooden huts listening to an account of the worsening situation on the Eastern Front a bomb exploded. The device, which had been left in a briefcase by one of a group of conspirators, *Count* von Stauffenberg, devastated the room in which Hitler and his generals had gathered. Hitler himself survived the blast with only minor injuries but four of his staff were killed and several were seriously injured. This became known as the '*July Plot*'.

Rommel lay unconscious in his hospital bed at the time of the assassination attempt but the *Gestapo* investigating the conspiracy implicated Rommel's involvement – although this was not wholly proved. Three months later on the 14th October, while recuperating from his wounds at his home at Ulm in Swabia, Erwin Rommel would be given the choice of taking poison or facing a public trial involving his family for his indirect involvement in the murder plot. He chose the former option and was pronounced dead on arrival at hospital the same day.

If the information supplied by Phantom's SAS detachment's Sergeant Wood had been acted on with more urgency, resulting in the bombing of Rommel's headquarters whilst he was still present, perhaps the course of events that followed would have reached a different conclusion.

Alan Hoe, in his authorised biography of David Stirling

which was published in 1992, quotes the words of the co-creator of the SAS: 'It is probable that during operations in France, Holland and Belgium, three seeds were implanted which have been nurtured by the post-war SAS. Firstly, there was very close liaison with Phantom, the field signals liaison element of GHQ, which proved that it was possible to combine a first-class standard of soldiering with a professional ability to communicate from inhospitable sites. Secondly, there was a dependence (on primary targets at least) on close liaison with, and trust in, a variety of intelligence agencies. Lastly, techniques for gaining the confidence of highly individualistic indigenous, irregular fighting forces were formulated.'

Praise, indeed, for Phantom!

The SAS was not the only special service that Phantom worked with, it also had contact with SOE (Special Operations Executive). In January 1944, Leo Marks, head of the code department of SOE, was visited at his Baker Street office by Major the Hon. Jakie Astor. In his book, 'Between Silk and Cyanide', Marks recalls the meeting, although he mistakenly refers to him as Captain Astor.

'On the 18 January, Muriel informed me that a Captain Astor was in her office. She added that he was a member of the SAS, and that he'd called on the off-chance that I'd see him without an appointment! Liking the sound of a captain who took off-chances, I told her that I'd give him a quarter of an hour as soon as she'd checked his credentials.

Five minutes later a fair-haired young captain appeared on the threshold, but at once turned to leave when he saw that I was on the phone. Unaccustomed to such consideration, I beckoned him to a chair whilst I finished talking to the Grendon supervisor in shorthand. He spent the time staring apprehensively at the blackboard, on which I'd written a famous quotation from Frances Croft Cornford for the coders to reconstruct at my next lecture (I'd produced no poems of my own since Xmas Eve):

*O fat white woman whom nobody loves,*
*Why do you walk through the fields in gloves,*
*Missing so much and so much?*

Replacing the receiver, I asked Captain Astor how I could help him.

He replied that the SAS needed an expert to advise them on codes, and if possible to supply them, and he'd reason to believe he'd come to the right person.

I knew nothing about the SAS except that they operated behind enemy lines and had been founded by a maverick young officer named David Stirling, who sounded as if he were SOE-minded.

So did Captain Astor, but before I could allow him to proceed there was one formality which had to be disposed of.

'Sorry to have to ask you this, Captain, but who gave you the authority to approach SOE?'

'Sorry to have to tell you this, Mr Marks, but I forgot to ask for it! Here's my CO's number if you want it.'

'I don't think it will be necessary.' His reply had ensured that he'd get all the help I could give him.

'What sort of traffic are you likely to pass?'

He produced a bundle of specimen messages (the first visitor who'd done so) but they were so carefully phrased I suspected they'd been composed especially for the occasion. Pressed for detail, he estimated that the average message would be fifty letters long and that most of the D-Day traffic would be between France and London, though in certain areas two-way communication between SAS units would save 'a lot of to-ing and fro-ing'.

We to-ed and fro-ed between ourselves for several minutes, and I decided that they could most safely pass their paramilitary-type messages in code-books and letter one-time pads. We'd also have to supply them with WOKs (worked out keys) for emergencies, of which I imagined there'd be plenty. Providing them with two-way communication as well meant that we'd have to dig into the last of our reserves. But so would the SAS when they reached the field. It was time to demonstrate the merchandise.

Pulling back the curtains (I knew by now where the light switch was), I explained the various systems and added that if the SAS proved to be temperamentally unsuited to code-books they could encode their messages directly on to pads.

Captain Astor had only one question for me: 'How soon can we have some for training purposes?'

'Would tomorrow be soon enough?'

The smile which parachuted from his eyes to his lips reminded me of Tommy's when he was still able to smile.

I then explained that I'd need an informed estimate of the quantities they'd require, and that he'd better leave the formalities to me as his approach had been somewhat irregular.

He shook my hand in silence.

Five minutes later he took a final glance at the 'fat white woman who nobody loves' and hurried away, probably to drop in on the Chiefs of Staff without an appointment.

The following morning I was assembling Astor's training codes when Heffer strolled in.

'Prepare yourself for a shock,' he said, an innovation which was a shock in itself.

He waited till his cigarette was aglow with excitement before making his announcement. 'We've been asked by the War Office to supply codes for *all* Special Forces.'

I had just enough strength to enquire what quantities this would involve.

'It'll make no difference! Nick's agreed that we'll do it.'

He watched my face slither (it hadn't the vitality to fall), and smiled. 'There's a bright side to it – you'll have the authority to supply Captain Astor with the codes you'd agreed to send him anyway. His CO (Lt Col A A Macintosh) took the trouble to phone Nick to tell him in detail how helpful you'd been."

Nick was, in fact, Brigadier F W Nicholls, head of signals with SOE, and the Executive Council had endorsed his decision to supply Special Forces with everything they needed. A decision that led to close co-operation between SOE, SAS and Phantom.

Major the Hon. Jakie Astor was not the only member of Phantom who visited the SOE offices in Baker Street.

George Starr, affectionately known by his army mates as 'Twinkle', had fought in the 1936 Spanish civil war with the International Brigade against Franco's Fascist's. Between then and 1939 he lived in France and Belgium and when the war broke out in 1939 was a taxi driver in Brussels, and one of Belgium's leading pigeon fanciers. Starr enlisted into the British Army in Belgium.

After Dunkirk, back in England, he joined Phantom, was promoted to Lance Corporal and with the jockey Gordon Richards, another Phantom, placed in charge of the pigeon lofts in St. James Park near Horse Guards Parade. '*Twinkle*' was multi-lingual, and this came to the notice of SOE. Consequently, he was summoned to the office of Special Operations Executive's Colonel Buckmaster in early 1942, and some hours later, after an interview, returned to the lofts to collect his kit and say goodbye to his pigeons and his mates. It has been said that he left the lofts in the morning a Lance Corporal and returned in the afternoon a Captain.

Little was heard of *'Twinkle'* for a while, but we can now reveal what happened.

In October 1942, as a fully trained SOE secret agent, George Starr dropped into occupied France behind the German lines with other SOE members. There he was responsible for organising and training a French resistance movement in the south-west of the country, this group of *Maquis* was known as *'Wheelwright'*. Starr's codename was *'Hilaire'*. *Wheelwright* was causing havoc by 1943 and its members, with Starr at the helm, were dealing the Germans massive blows one after another. In the days leading up to D-Day and after, his resistance fighters played a prominent part in harrasing the Germans, especially when they were rushing reinforcements to the Normandy front.

Starr ended the war as a Lieutenant Colonel with a DSO, an MC and the French Legion of Honour. George 'Twinkle' Starr had gone from a Lance Corporal in Phantom responsible for its pigeons to a Lt Col in SOE in three short years. In all his time behind enemy lines in France he evaded capture.

Not all operations involving SAS were successful. 'Operation Rupert' was one that went disasterously wrong.

On the night of the 23rd July, 1944, thirteen died when the aircraft they were in crashed near Graffigny – Chemin, Yonne, France. The aircraft flew past the first drop zone as there appeared to be 'no reception' party on the ground to guide them in. Whilst on route to the secondary drop zone it crashed into the mountain near Graffigny.

Amongst the dead were eight SAS members, including two SAS wireless operators, and five aircrew. Amazingly, there were two survivors.

CHAPTER XX

# Hitler's Answer To The Invasion Of France

*'The V-weapons will be decisive. I prophesy the imminent collapse of Britain under the V-bombs.'*
ADOLF HITLER, 10TH JUNE, 1944.

The *Reichführer's* response to the Allied landings was swift. Since the autumn of 1943 the Allies had been aware of the existence of Germany's experimentation with a pilotless flying-bomb. For months a silent war had been conducted by the RAF which regularly flew photo reconnaissance missions over occupied Europe. Together with information supplied by the French, Belgian and Dutch Underground movements and secret agent operations, British Intelligence were able to ascertain where the manufacturing and launching sites of these jet propelled winged aerial torpedoes were sited.

The whole Allied plan for the overall seeking out and destruction of the manufacturing and launching sites of these V-weapons was code-named 'Operation *Crossbow*'.

On the night of 17th/18th August 1943, 571 aircraft, out of some 600 despatched, had dropped 1,937 tons of bombs on the experimental station situated on the island of Peenemunde on the Baltic coast, where also the production of hydrogen peroxide was taking place; but the Nazis soon reorganized and adapted their launching methods sufficiently to send trial shots to London on the 13th June, 1944. Only one week after D-Day, the first V-bomb – *Vergeltungswaffe*, or revenge weapon – was spotted by a member of the Royal Observer Corps from his post in Kent. He incredulously reported, 'There's a new type of small aircraft approaching tremendously fast, emitting a bright glow of flame from its rear. It's making a noise like a model-T Ford going up a hill.' This bomb fell at Swanscombe, near Gravesend, just after 4am. During the next hour three more fell – at Cuckfield in East Sussex and Platt in Kent and on Bethnal Green in London's East End.

The author's father, Bill Parlour, by then demobbed from the army due to injury and living in nearby Hackney, recalled cycling to work that morning and hearing a loud thump. Wandering what on earth it could be, as he had not heard any planes overhead, he continued on his way. Soon after his arrival at work he heard the radio announcement that an unidentified flying object had fallen close by in Grove Road, Bethnal Green. A request was broadcast asking for volunteers to help in the aftermath of the terrific explosion. Bill made his way to the scene and gave whatever assistance he could. 'It was a scene of utter devastation,' he remembered. 'Nobody could understand what could have caused such destruction. Some thought at first that one of our own bombers had crashed. We were soon to realize the truth.'

At Bethnal Green, six people were killed and nine injured, the first victims of Germany's V-bomb, or *'Doodle Bug'* as the V.1 soon became known. Within an hour of the bomb falling its position had been announced on the radio, giving the enemy all the help he required in setting the range and direction for further attacks.

These impulse-jet-propelled pilotless winged bombs could fly at nearly 400 miles an hour so that only stripped down and polished Royal Air Force Tempests, Typhoons, Mustangs or Spitfires had any chance of catching them and shooting them out of the skies. The anti-aircraft guns situated all over southeast England also gained some success in bringing them down before they reached their targets, as did the cables of the barrage balloons. On August the 4th Flying Officer T D Dean, of 616 Squadron, flying a new jet-propelled fighter, the Meteor, attempted to shoot down a V 1. When his guns failed to function, determined not to be cheated of his quarry, Dean flew alongside and manoeuvred his wing-tip beneath the wing-tip of the *doodle bug*, tipping it off balance and causing it to spin down and explode its one ton war-head harmlessly in the open countryside below. This practise quickly caught on with other squadrons of the RAF and propeller driven aircraft also adopted this method of interception.

New Zealander Bruce Lawless, now living at Point Clear, Essex, flew with 56, 198 and 486 squadrons, when based near Saffron Walden, Essex. He remembers, when chasing V1 bombs over the Essex coast, flying alongside and tipping them over. The Germans soon caught on to this ruse and attached wires from the wings tips to the nose cone of the war head detonator, so that when the pilot attempted to tip the flying-bomb over, it exploded taking the aircraft with it. The pilots of the RAF now had to change their tactics.

Bruce recalls, 'Flying Hawker Tempests at the time, we could out-fly these Doodle Bugs so, once we spotted one, we would fly up behind it, get it in our gun-sights and let it have it. The best thing about the V1 flying bombs was they couldn't outrun us, they couldn't take evasive action and they couldn't fire back. This was great fun, although it was a bit scary at times when they exploded because we had to fly through their debris.'

These bombs were fired at Britain at a rate of one hundred a day for seventy-one days on end. At first, one in three got through but by September the ratio was down to one in eleven, such was the determination of Britain's defences not to let them undermine its morale and be the propaganda coup that Hitler, now on the brink of defeat, was so desperately seeking.

As the Allied invasion forces pushed forward into France, clearing the enemy out of the Cherbourg Peninsula, the Normandy coastal regions and the Pas de Calais, more and more of the V1 launching sites, extending from Watten in the north to Houpeville in the south, were being captured – thus stemming the flow of attacks on the English mainland.

On the 7th September, 1944, Mr Duncan Sandys, for the British Government, announced that the flying bomb menace was over. Seven days had passed since the last missile had been sent across the English Channel. The following day, however, the first two V2 rocket bombs reached England, falling on the outskirts of London. The first at Chiswick, West London, killed three people and seriously injured ten more; the second, less than a minute later, east of London at Epping, where fortunately there were no human casualties. Both V2's had been launched from a site in the Hook of Holland, less than two hundred miles away from their target. Owing to its speed and method of travel the projectile gave no warning of its approach. When fired it rose straight up in the air to a height of an incredible seventy miles, before curving gradually until it fell vertically downwards towards its goal at a speed ahead of its own sound. Thus, the first anyone in the area heard was the explosion as it hit the ground, followed by the roar of its progress through the air.

Churchill's War Cabinet, afraid that news of a new German terror weapon, in the shape of rocket bombs, falling on London might spread panic amongst the civilian poplation, at first explained the explosions as gas mains igniting. It was soon known that this was not the case, and as with the V1 flying bomb, and the *blitz* before, the Bulldog spirit of the British was not going to be broken by the V2 rockets.

There was no method of defence against this even more destructive form of weapon, so it was fortunate that within ten days many of the V2 launch pads had been wiped out. It was thanks to the Dutch Resistance Movement, aided by members of the Special Air Service, that much of the intelligence regarding the whereabouts of these secret rocket sites was discovered. This information was communicated by radio direct to London by a patrol of Phantom's 'F' Squadron working with the SAS and intensive bombing raids were then concentrated on these co-ordinates. By the 17th September, the German High Command ordered their remaining rocket-firing troops to move their sites eastwards in retreat of the advancing Allied forces.

Between 25th September and 3rd October, Norwich, in East Anglia, came under fire sixteen times and in the next eleven days a further thirty-nine fell on that city and on London. During the next six months more than one thousand rockets and five hundred flying-bombs were to fall on the Home Counties.

Hitler's original plan had been to start attacking Britain with his flying-bombs on the 15th December, 1943. The bombing of the launch sites by the Allied Air Forces had delayed his assault.

Supreme Commander General Eisenhower later had this to say of the V1: 'It seems likely that if the Germans had succeeded in perfecting and using these new weapons six months earlier than they did, our invasion of Europe would have proved exceedingly difficult, perhaps impossible. I feel sure that if they had succeeded in using these weapons over a six month period, and particularly if they had made the Portsmouth-Southampton area one of their principal targets, '*Overlord*' might have been written off.'

The first seven months of 1944, culminating in the assassination attempt on his life, had not gone well for Hitler. The new year had brought an intensification of the war on all fronts.

The fighting in Italy had seen the Germans steadily pushed northwards, with the Allies taking Monte Cassino in the middle of May and liberating Rome on the 4th June, the first European capital to fall to them. From then on, more and more Italian patriots, mainly communist led, had taken to the hills in the north of their country from where they played a major role in disrupting German communications. The British 8th Army was training and equipping Italian brigades to fight against their former Axis partners and the first contingent of the Brazilian Expeditionary Force had set sail from Rio de Janeiro on the 2nd July, to join the Allied forces in their battle to liberate Italy. Brazil had declared war on the Axis alliance in August 1942 and its navy had participated in joint Allied action in the Atlantic. Now it was coming to Europe. The five thousand South American officers and men who arrived in Naples were to operate under the strategic command of the Americans.

Their arrival helped to booster the depleted forces of the British 8th and the American 5th Armies as they faced the *Gothic* Line. Large numbers of American and French troops had been withdrawn from the Italian front to aid the coming invasion of southern France.

As the Allies in the west were planning the great invasion of Europe, in the east the Russian guns, tanks and men were crumbling the spirit of Hitler's forces. The Red Army was dealing great blows against the *Wehrmacht*. In January the Russians had freed Leningrad, in February they had crossed over the old Polish frontier and in March the Rumanian. After a pause for the spring thaw, the Red Army renewed its attacks. The German armies were stretched out in defence of lines that Hitler would not shorten and could not hold. In early June the Finnish Government was forced to seek an Armistice after over four years of confrontation with the Russians, and in the first half of July, Minsk, Vilna, Pinsk and Grodno all fell and were back under Soviet control. The Russians were now in a position to cut off the Baltic states and advance towards the province of East Prussia. The *Wehrmacht* was being forced to fall back to a new line of defence on the Polish border, just fifty-five miles east of Warsaw.

In the Far East and in the South Pacific Ocean the Japanese Imperial Army was gradually losing control. The Allied forces were winning vital battles against it in Burma and in India and on the 18th May, 1944, after a three month struggle that had seen them take Hollandia, the administrative capital of Dutch New Guinea, the US Army troops under General MacArthur finally realized their determination to cut off Japan's last supply routes to its South-west Pacific bases, at Rabaul and Kavieng, by wiping out the last pockets of Japanese resistance on the Admiralty Islands, off north-east New Guinea.

At sea, the 20th June saw the US Navy victory in the Battle of the Philippine Sea decide the fate of the Mariana Islands by giving command of the surrounding sea and air to the Americans. In this, the greatest aircraft-carrier battle of the war, the Japanese had so many aircraft shot down that the US pilots called it 'the great Marianas turkey shoot'. Japan had lost 480 of its aircraft, 218 shot out of the sky and the remainder wiped out whilst still on the decks of two Japanese fleet carriers, the *Shokaku* and *Taiho*, which were torpedoed and sunk by American submarines. In total three-quarters of the aircraft with which it had set sail, for what it proclaimed would be 'the decisive battle' in the Pacific, had been destroyed.

The Japanese land forces were aided by volunteers from the mainly Sikh prisoners-of-war who they had captured on defeating the British and Commonwealth Armies on their initial advance into Malaya. Major Mohan Singh, himself a Sikh prisoner-of-war, had agreed with Major Iwaichi Fujiwara of the Japanese General Staff, in December 1941, to set up a special unit for Indians, Burmese and Thais who did not want the British or French to return. The slogan that the Japanese suggested for this unit was 'Asia for the Asiatics'. Within a few weeks, Major Singh was prepared to lead an Indian National Army against the British. Between December 1943 and April 1944 a division of the INA was under the command of General Mutagachi and serving on the central front on the Indian/Burmese border, just prior to the collapse of the Japanese invasion of India.

Not only did the INA fight alongside the Japanese, they also fought with German troops.

Harry Binge remembers that part of his Phantom training consisted of the recognition of enemy uniforms and the identification of regiments, for a commander had to know the strength of the opposition and the fighting qualities of the men that his force was about to face. Harry was well-prepared to see Eastern Europeans, who had fought alongside the Germans, amongst the prisoners captured in Normandy after D-Day, but he was surprised to see men in turbans. These were men of the German '*Indian Legion*' who had manned the Atlantic Wall and put up much fierce resistance against the Allied invasion. They had been captured by the Germans as they fought with the British Eighth Army in the North African Campaign and had been promised that, if they changed sides, when Germany won the war, their Sikh nation would be granted independence from British rule.

By the end of July, Operation *Epsom*, the taking of Caen, had been accomplished and Operation *Goodwood*, the breakout from Caen, was well under way. Phantom was now to play a crucial role in the closing of the Falaise Gap, fifteen miles south of Caen.

CHAPTER XXI

# Closing The Falaise Gap

*'The 15th of August, 1944, was the worst day of my life.'*
ADOLF HITLER, AFTER THE FALL OF FALAISE.

When Poland had collapsed in the face of the German onslaught in September 1939, members of the Polish Army, as well as many civilians, escaped from the occupation of their country. They were determined to fight on. It is estimated that as many as eighteen thousand escaped to Britain where they were to join other Poles, or people of Polish ancestry, who had come from all over the world. These men and women were to form the Free Polish forces and to serve in all three services - Army, Navy and Air Force. Amongst the many army groups which were created was the Polish 1st Armoured Division under General Maczek.

The Polish 1st and the Canadian 4th Armoured were two of the five divisions that made up the Canadian II Corps as, under Montgomery's orders, they launched Operation *Totalize* down the Falaise road on the 7th August. Another of the five divisions was the Canadian 2nd Infantry Division whose Phantom patrol was Captain Ling's '*Kite*'.

From Captain Ling's diary we see where 'B' Squadron HQ had set up after Amblie and where they had remained whilst the battle for Caen was fought.

'Moved to LASSON. Static for over a month. Used bulldozer excavations as trenches. Whole camp below ground level. Operational set-up reorganised. Addition of R. vehicle (receiving vehicle). Coders transferred from tent to R.vehicle. Proposed move cancelled at last minute by heavy storm. Flooded out. Vehicles unable to move until mud dried.

Through CAEN to VERRIERES. Flat open common land. Under shell-fire. Filthy with German litter and some bodies. Mosquito ridden. Very hot. Health affected. Dysentery rife. Camp lit by enemy flames. J's caught in bombing by own planes. Came to us for refuge. Moved after about one week.'

The task of II Corps was to drive its way through to Falaise to complete a pocket that was rapidly forming about General Hausser's Seventh Army as it desperately fought to stem the Allied advance. On the west was the US First Army, on the south was the US Third Army and to the north was the British Second Army. With the Canadian II Corps filling in the northeastern side, the German Seventh Army and the Fifth Panzer Army would be trapped in the Falaise-Argentan pocket.

Harry recollects, 'We had been assigned to the Polish 1st Armoured Division and were having a job to keep up with all the information that was coming in. We were working like beavers to pass on the endless stream of wireless messages and sitreps that were coming in thick and fast from the most forward tank commanders. Our two motorcycle despatch riders, Ron Eagle and 'Robbo' Roberts, were continually back and forth between our position and HQ with leather wallets full of messages that could not all be transmitted by radio.

Our main duty at this stage was to listen in to the radio traffic between the most forward attacking tank commanders. As none of us spoke Polish, we had with us some Polish officers who spoke good English. They listened in to their own tank commanders and translated the messages coming through for us to send on. From the information that we picked up by this means, we could set the bomb-line down, often changing it several times a day, and so prevent our own heavy artillery from shelling our front-line forces. This information, decoded, enciphered and re-coded by us, would also be passed on to RAF through Phantom 'B' Squadron HQ, which had now moved to Lasson. The idea was that the RAF would know exactly where the Allied positions were and only attack the enemy, who were sometimes less than two hundred yards ahead. Unfortunately, everything did not always go according to plan.

When we reached the village of Bretteville sur Laize, just off the Falaise road, we set up base on the edge of a wood where we were surrounded by deserted British gun-posts. We built dugouts from empty ammunition boxes which we had filled with earth. From there, our patrol went into the Polish 1st Armoured Brigade Signals HQ, which was situated in an orchard just outside the village of Cauvicourt. On arrival there, we quickly set up our wireless equipment and made contact with Phantom 'B' Squadron HQ. The Germans had concentrated some of their Panzer Armoured Tanks and infantry just south of here in the Quesnay Woods. Following reconnaissance and observation reports, an RAF Pathfinder from the Mosquito Squadron, dropped a smoke bomb to indicate the target to the heavy Lancaster bombers, which had taken off from their bases in Britain and were on their way to blast the woods. We saw the red smoke rising from out of the woods and thought, 'they're going to cop it soon'.

As the first wave of bombers approached, the wind suddenly changed direction, blowing the smoke back towards us and the Poles. We stood there in amazement. At first, we could not believe it. Then we realized what would happen next. Our patrol captain, Mick Millar, quickly saw the seriousness of the situation and the danger that we were in. He shouted to us to leave all our equipment and run away from the direction in which the smoke was coming. We didn't need to be told twice and ran hell for leather as fast as we could. The Poles, meanwhile, had been ordered to stand firm. Mick Millar stayed with the radio car desperately trying to contact Phantom HQ to halt the bombing attack. He must have eventually got through because only half of the bombers, about two hundred and fifty, dropped their bombs before the mission was halted.

When we returned to the scene it was utter devastation and destruction, with a quarter of the Polish 1st Division wiped out. (I later heard that there were many Canadians included in the casualties, too.) Amongst all the chaos, standing in the middle of the crater-strewn ground, was our Dingo armoured radio car completely unmarked with Captain Millar still sitting inside, unbelievably, unscathed.'

Millar's 'J' was not the only Phantom patrol affected by this terrible event. Captain Michael Astor, brother of 'F' Squadron's leader, Major Jakie Astor, also witnessed the scene with his 'J' patrol, which was working with the Second Canadian Armoured Brigade. In his autobiography, he gives his version of the same incident as seen from his position.

> *'At ten o'clock one morning on the road to Falaise the Lancaster bombers of the Royal Air Force, from their bases in England, mistook a concentration of Canadian guns and tanks for their target. We were waiting on our start line ready to begin an attack which was to be preceded by a heavy bombardment of the enemy positions. I noticed, at first well to my rear, the dust and flashes and repercussions of bombs. To my flank an armoured car had drawn up, and inside it were the commander of the Tactical*

*Air Force, Air Marshal Coningham, and a colonel from the operations branch of the Canadian Army who had come to view the aerial assault. I hurried over and told them I was in wireless touch with corps headquarters. Would they, I asked, send a message by my wireless indicating what was going wrong. The precise-minded colonel, conscious of the bombing and even more impressed finding himself in the company of the Air Marshal, told me that what we were witnessing was artillery fire. We had another look through the binoculars. I told him that what we were witnessing was bombs not shells. It was quite obvious (I did not add) to anyone except a staff officer. He said it could not possibly be aerial bombing. I turned to the Air Marshal. He had fought in the desert and I felt he must have learnt the difference, visually and sonically, between shell fire and the explosion of enemy bombs. He remained silent. All this had occupied five minutes of our time. The report I sent back giving warning that our bombers appeared to be dropping their load behind our front line lacked, therefore, the supporting opinion of these two senior officers whose voices might have curtailed the extent of the catastrophe. I was a small cog in this vast machinery, too small on my own to call off a major bombing attack. Suddenly the full force of the raid, which continued with one brief interruption for forty minutes fell on us. My car and wireless were put out of action, but not before the armoured car from army headquarters had gone hurtling down the road. I told my men to jump under the nearest vehicles. We lay, crouching like insects, while the earth shook and roared all around us. We buried our faces while one thunderous percussion followed another. A bomb miraculously dug a deep crater beside my scout car, scorching us with its blast and pelting us with gravel, its full lethal effect carrying to some target further removed from its point of impact. I noticed the celluloid cover of the map case in my hand was burning. In an attempt to relieve the tension of the men crouching beside me I gave them, peremptorily, an order, telling them not to move from their positions. The remark, literally interpreted, sounded unnecessary. There was nowhere to move to in this inferno.*

*The start of my first battle, the first set-piece for which we had been so carefully trained, ended in anti-climax. Several hours later, in a scene of carnage, an officer from my squadron arrived to find out if there was anything left of us. Apart from my corporal, who had a fragment of steel in his shoulder, the few men in my patrol were unscathed.'*

The combination of the two Phantom officers transmitting

wireless signals had helped to prevent an even greater massacre from occurring on this day.

Michael Astor's re-formed and re-equipped patrol was now sent to the American sector to the American 3rd Army, to report on the progress of some of General Patton's forces. Harry's 'J' patrol, as recorded by Captain Ling in his diary, spent a week with '*Kite*', both patrols working with the Canadians as they fought their way towards Falaise. Harry's No. 23 patrol with the Polish was replaced by Captain Geoffrey Brain's No. 22 '*Gull*' patrol of 'B' Squadron. '*Gull*' had come over in June with the 4th Canadian Armoured Division, whom it was soon supplying with information about the fighting in the Orne Valley.

Captain Brain was to be with the Polish 1st Armoured Division, under General Maczek, when it played a vital part in the capturing and closing of the Falaise pocket.

On the 14th August, the Allies launched Operation '*Tractable*', the drive into Falaise itself.

Falaise, overlooked by its massive Norman castle with walls twelve feet thick, and the birthplace of William the Conquerer in 1028, was 916 years later to be the scene of bitter fighting as the Canadians and Poles finally battled their way into this ancient town on the 16th August, 1944. The so-called Canadian 'Mad Charge' was proving decisive in forcing the German 5th and 7th Armies into the tighter and tighter pocket. By the time the German Commander, *Feldmarschall* Gunther von Kluge, decided to defy Hitler's orders – to stand and fight to the last man – and pull out, it was too late. They were trapped. Continuous onslaught from the air by low-flying rocket-firing Typhoons decimated the rapidly retreating convoys as they desperately sought to get away.

On the 15th August, prematurely believing that Kluge had disobeyed him, Hitler ordered *Feldmarschall* Walter Model to take over Kluge's command. On the day that Canadian, Polish and American troops launched their final attack to close the Falaise pocket, Gunther von Kluge committed suicide. In his final letter of self-defence to Hitler, he advised him to end the war pleading, 'The German people have borne such untold suffering that it is time to put an end to this frightfulness.'

The high hedgerows and narrow lanes of the Bocage had always aided the German defenders but it now was to prove their downfall as the leading columns of armour and military vehicles were put out of action, thus clogging the Nazi Army's escape routes.

So terrified were the Germans of the rocket-firing Typhoons (incidentally the first aircraft to use this type of weapon) that they removed the doors from many of their vehicles in order to make it quicker to jump out and seek cover from these *'Tiffys'* that circled in the skies above at 3,000 feet, like a pack of killer sharks waiting to close in on its prey. In a system that became known as the 'cab rank', the pilots of the Typhoons awaited instructions of their targets. This information came in via forward RAF/Army Intelligence Liaison Officers in battle front armoured cars known as VCP's (visual control points) or VCU's (visual control units), sometimes working alongside Phantom patrols which were laying down the bomb-line. On being given map references and co-ordinates, the Typhoons would strike the enemy with awesome power. The 'cab rank', first pioneered in the North African campaign, was to prove one of the most effective examples of RAF/Army close liaison in ground to air co-operation.

Henry Maule's book, *'Caen'*, quotes Charles Best, Battery Sergeant Major of the 67th Anti-Tank Battery, who saw the results: 'Along the Vire-Falaise road I came to a stretch for two miles choc-a-bloc with German dead bodies and vehicles, even horse gun teams. It was the most terrifying sight I had seen – a massacre! The British rocket-firing Typhoons had caught them in close formation. There must have been a major traffic jam when they struck.'

And quotes Frederic Wilkinson, an RAF corporal of a ground crew Typhoon wing: 'The scene was terrible – overturned tanks, heavy armoured vehicles blasted out of recognition, upturned guns, even horse drawn vehicles, all blown up. The stench of death from all the decomposing bodies lying about was indescribable. I had the smell on my uniform for weeks.'

After such bitter fighting at Falaise the jubilant message received at 21st Army Group HQ from Phantom HQ on 18th August was met with great relief:

'Source Col G3 VII US Corps. Contact established between 11th British Armoured Division and 1st US Division at approximately 1100 hours. The gap is closed.'

On the 21st August, in what was left of the Falaise pocket,

the Germans, mainly comprised of the remnants of the SS Divisions, made one last attempt to break out of the trap as Hitler finally allowed Model to withdraw his troops. In the north-eastern sector, more than three hundred Poles were killed as they successfully defended and held their positions, taking a thousand Germans prisoner in the process.

In the aftermath of Operation *Tractable*, Harry's patrol was sent down to assess and report on the defeated enemy's losses. Identifying German regiments had been an important part of Phantom's training programme. During the Falaise battles a total of fifty thousand German soldiers had been taken prisoner and ten thousand killed.

The closure of the Falaise pocket completed the disaster of the Germans in France.

Harry recalls seeing David Niven, ex-Commander of Phantom's 'A' Squadron, in a wood south of Perrieres where his patrol had set up after Falaise. Now promoted to Lieutenant-Colonel, Niven had been seconded to General Eisenhower's Supreme Headquarters Allied Expeditionary Force from Phantom in the spring of 1943. Here he was able to make use of his invaluable liaison skills, learnt during his time with Phantom, to the full. Under the direct command of American General Raymond Barker, Niven was to travel extensively in France and beyond, communicating between the Allied commanders. When Harry saw him, Niven, in true showman style, was driving a battered German car, plainly labelled 'US NAVY'!!

In his book, '*The Moon's a Balloon*', David Niven recalls meeting other members of Phantom just after the breakout from Caen: 'I found 'B' Squadron (now part of the new 'A' Squadron) of Phantom hidden in a wood behind the Orne. Dennis Russell was still in command. Hugh (Tam) Williams, that fine actor, was still in the squadron. They told me that Hugh Kindersley had been badly wounded and 'Tam' and I agreed that if we had known about the German *Nebelwerfer* – a six-barrelled mortar – we would never have joined the Army in the first place!'

Tam Williams, newly promoted to captain, had come ashore at Normandy on the 17th June, 1944. Determined to make a success of his new command, at his own request, he had come on ahead of his patrol to make preparations for its arrival the following week. It was to work with the 21st Army Group commanded by Montgomery up to the fall of Paris and then transfer to the Americans.

While the German *Wehrmacht*, with ten of their Generals dead, had fought on in Falaise, the Allies had struck another blow. On the 15th August, seven hundred miles away on France's south coast, an Armada of ships landed a large force of American, French and British troops and vehicles at Frejus and other small Mediterranean ports between Cannes and Toulon. The seaborne invasion was preceded by British and American paratroops dropping from the skies and by aerial and naval bombardment to soften up the defences. Originally known by the code-name Operation *Anvil*, Operation *Dragoon* was launched against the wishes of British Prime Minister Winston Churchill, who believed that the troops could be better employed in Italy, which also was the opinion of General Montgomery. President Roosevelt would not be persuaded. In the event, the landings were to meet with minimal opposition and the combined Allied forces quickly made progress inland, moving up the Rhone valley to link up with the Allied troops advancing south from Normandy.

After Falaise, Captain Millar's patrol, back with the Canadians after their brief spell with the Poles, moved swiftly north-east, chasing the Germans towards the Belgian border, leaving Paris to the French and the Americans.

Captain Ling's diary tells us of '*Kite's*' progress during the following five weeks:

Wood south of PERRIERES. Green fields and woods without the usual layer of white dust. Found burnt out tanks and remains of crashed bomber on hill. Two of our men buried pilot whose body had been flung considerable distance. Moved after three days.

> 23rd AUGUST 1944. OUEN LE HOUX. Heather floored wood. Strange looking stone graves near R vehicle! Storm during night. Roads a sea of mud.

> 25th AUGUST 1944. LE PLANQUET. Orchard. Inconvenient owing to excessive distance from Corps. Jeep overflowing with men, used for meal shifts. Very friendly French farmers who gave us quantities of fresh milk.

> 27th AUGUST 1944. LA GROSSE LONDE. Bad site. R.vehicle got bogged. Met party of French Maquis men. Young French civilian used our sets for French news bulletins. Patrol's morale high due to rapid advance and continuous moves.

31st AUGUST 1944. Crossed River SEINE at LE CROIX. Only stayed here one night.

1st SEPTEMBER 1944. To AUFFAY via ROUEN. Patrol ate too many green apples from orchard! Corporal...helped Canadians to gather in some German PW's.

2nd SEPTEMBER 1944. LE MESNIL REAUME. Camped by main road. Huge concentration of PW's on opposite side. Moving now a set routine with the usual cheering crowds in every town and village.

3rd SEPTEMBER 1944. MOYENVILLE. A French dog joined us and we decided to keep him. Named him VIC as he answered to the whistle 'dot dot dot dash' (the letter 'V' in Morse code)

5th SEPTEMBER 1944. Crossed River Somme MONTREAUL. In tiny wood near large concrete German pillbox (empty). Roads strewn with German papers and books.

7th SEPTEMBER 1944 COLEMBERT. Our first 'billet' but only for one night. Fruit farm near huge Chateau. German stores in a barn. Crates of toothpaste and food. Huge bonfires of German cigarettes still burning.

8th SEPTEMBER 1944. HARDIFORD (nr. Cassels)

12th SEPTEMBER 1944. LICQUES. Camped in wood on top of hill overlooking Calaise. Watched bombing of Calaise and some men went in soon after to see destroyed guns etc. Cinema shows in middle of thick wood.'

Being in the heat of battle then pulling back to re-group and re-supply for the next assignment, was mostly very dangerous but was not without its lighter more humorous moments. Harry's patrol had its fair share of both.

As Captain Ling says the rapid advance was good for morale, but Harry recalls one member of his team who was not quite so happy about the continual moves.

'Dr Roberts, who was our cook and batman to Captain Millar, was getting really fed up with having to keep packing and unpacking the Captain's belongings. Slowly but surely, each time he packed up to move on, he was getting rid of some of poor old Millar's gear. Everything 'Robbo' thought was surplus to requirements would disappear. What he did with it we never knew. Eventually, the Captain was down to one small bag and one small tent. How 'Robbo' ever got away with it, I will never know. But get away with it he certainly did. I still had all the gear that I went across with, including a guitar, a piano accordion and the board game Monopoly. The Captain often used to borrow my accordion, which I didn't mind, but when he wanted to take my jeep, that was a different matter. I had come to consider it my own private property and had got quite attached to it. Besides, it seemed that every time he brought it back it had a puncture!

One particular incident, that happened at Auffay, was very scary. We had sought cover in one of the many orchards that made up the countryside in that part of France. As we had got down behind a thick stone wall and started to brew-up, we heard gruff muffled voices. One of the patrol said they sounded like Jocks. As we knew the 51st Highland Division was somewhere close by, we assumed that was who it must be. Darkie Watson stood up to look over the wall and stood there mortified for on the other side were three fully-armed Germans, only about twenty yards away. Before 'Darkie' could make a move they spotted him, whereupon they threw down their weapons, raised their arms in the air and surrendered. Quickly calling to the rest of us, 'Darkie' shouted, 'Grab your guns and stand up'. Captain Millar, who couldn't speak German, beckoned the three of them over. They obviously thought that we had the orchard surrounded, not knowing that there were only seven of us, and we certainly weren't going to let them know any different. I spoke a little German and asked the one in front who was the sergeant, 'Are there any more of you?' He turned his head and shouted into the trees behind him. Lo and behold, another twelve stood up from under cover and walked towards us with their hands held high. Captain Millar immediately radioed Corps HQ telling them of our new arrivals and was promptly told, 'If an enemy attack develops, shoot them and get the hell out of there as fast as you can.' Lucky for us, we managed to make contact with a forward Canadian patrol who came along and took them off our hands. What a terrible situation to have been in. It's all very well to shoot the enemy in the heat of battle but to shoot unarmed men would have been a different matter. Remember we were not a combat unit as such but a secret radio patrol.

The next day we moved on, but not before we scrumped

some of the green apples still hanging from the branches of the trees in the orchard. A move we regretted the following day when we all ended up with bellyache!'

Phantom patrols not only supplied information back to the Corps or Division that they were attached to, via their own Squadron HQ, they also, on occasion, came to the assistance of other regiments. Charles Jarvis, a captain in the RAOC (Royal Army Ordnance Corps) in France, relates a story concerning Phantom: 'I was in command of a convoy of about seven trucks that had just taken some supplies up to a forward infantry company just south of Caen. On the return journey we became lost in the high hedgerows and narrow lanes. You could easily become disorientated in these surroundings so we stopped to try to work out our bearings. We discovered to our horror that we were further forward than the troops we had just delivered to! Before we could get back into our vehicles, we came under shellfire. This, my sergeant realized, was coming from our own gun positions. I immediately ordered my R/T Operator to radio back to our HQ. He was having big trouble getting through, but, to his surprise, a voice from a radio unit operating nearby enquired, 'Are you in trouble? We'll sort it out.' Within a couple of minutes the barrage ceased. Luckily, we had suffered no casualties.

When we eventually got back to our HQ, without any more incidents, I reported to our major, who had been informed of what had happened. He said that the message that had come through to the Artillery that was firing on us was, 'If you don't increase your range in sector...by 400 yards, you are going to be minus one company of RAOC. Over and out, Phantom.'

That was the first time I had heard of Phantom and I would have liked to have met them personally to have thanked them.'

Phantom was not only responsible for marking out the bomb-line but, working in conjunction with the Artillery forward OP's (Observation Posts), in laying down the 'creeping barrage'. This was a system of warfare where the ground in front of the enemy was shelled creating dust, smoke and confusion, then the enemy positions themselves and, if they attempted to retreat, the ground behind them. Allied tanks advancing, followed by the close support of the infantry, could then press home their advantage.

The importance of close co-operation and liaison between all the Army and Air reconnaissance and communication services cannot ever be over-estimated in time of war and Phantom was always able to play its part when called upon.

At 2.30 on the afternoon of the 25th August, 1944, the German commander of the Paris area, *General* Dietrich von Choltitz, surrendered to Lieutenant Henri Karcher of the French 2nd Armoured Division. Commanded by General Leclerc, it was the first Allied unit to enter Paris. At the luxurious Hotel Meurice, where the Germans had their headquarters, Karcher asked Choltitz if he was ready to surrender. The German answered simply, '*Ja*'.

The French capital's own citizens had done much to speed the liberation of their city. A week earlier, as the Americans were making their way towards Paris, the Resistance had called for an uprising. This was supported by the 20,000 Paris police who went on strike, turning their arms on the Nazis who had occupied their great city since the 14th June, 1940.

As Leclerc's troops, together with units of the US 4th Infantry Division, entered Paris, great crowds of cheering French men, women and children packed the boulevards to give them a tumultuous welcome.

The German garrison had hurriedly capitulated and the main enemy forces were streaming back across the Seine, but a few fanatical German Nazis and French Fascists continued to snipe at the crowds. Following a triumphant victory march from the Arc de Triomphe, General Charles de Gaulle and other leaders of the Free French were fired upon as they walked towards the cathedral of Notre Dame to celebrate the liberation of their city. Luckily, they themselves were not hurt but, sadly, several, who moments earlier had been celebrating their freedom, were killed in the mayhem that followed.

Captain Mackenzie's No. 12 Phantom patrol of 'A' Squadron was working with the Americans as they fought to gain Paris. Ron Eaton remembers, 'After the Falaise gap, we were still with the Americans making our way towards Paris. This was the big objective for the Americans. The second night out on this dash for the capital, we spent the night in some woods with American HQ. One of our patrol took his shovel and walked off to relieve himself. All of a sudden he came running back and said, 'I've just seen three Germans!' He was rather shaken up as they had just seemed to appear out of nowhere. We armed ourselves while one of our patrol went down towards the Americans to warn them. They quickly took control of the situation and the outcome was that, between us and the Yanks, we rounded up just over a hundred German soldiers. A right mixture, not just from one unit, but several regiments. I think that they were glad that, for them at least, the war was over. This was another contribution we had made to the war effort.

When we reached the outskirts of Paris, we couldn't enter. The Americans held off so that de Gaulle could enter first. Also, I think they realized that if they let us loose in Paris, as we were such a small unit, they might not see us again for a few days. They were right, they wouldn't have done. Paris was a city full of celebrations, and we were all too eager and ready to join in. Our officer soon put paid to that idea though and we were ordered to stay put.'

War Office papers, published here for the first time, describe Phantom's early role with the Americans thus:

## THE SWEEP ACROSS FRANCE

'By August 5th, the control of all Phantom radio nets had moved over to France with 21st Army Group. 12th US Army Group became operational on August 1st but no Phantom information was as yet available to it; the FUSAG Detachment now assigned to it, moved with rear echelon and had not yet arrived. On August 11th, therefore, a detachment consisting of US and British personnel, commanded by Capt. M K Mainwaring was despatched to 12th Army Group. This detachment was in communication with Phantom HQ at 21st Army Group, who re-transmitted all messages from American and British patrols to the detachment. On August 14th another 'Allied' detachment was brought in to cover 12th Army Group Main while Capt. Mainwaring's detachment moved forward with Tac Echelon. By this time all the US Corps were covered by PHANTOM, including VIII Corps in the BREST Peninsula. In order to cover the swift movement of the armour, a patrol was sent to 7th and 5th Armoured Divisions to report directly back to 21st Army Group and through them to 12th Army Group Main and Tac.

During the early operations in BREST, owing to the poor communications which existed with VIII US Corps, the patrol at Corps HQ undertook to clear most of the urgent traffic in connection with air bombardments. On one occasion, while the bombers were on their way, the patrol was instrumental in postponing an infantry attack which had the same objective as the bombers. This patrol also passed the signal which brought the HMS *Warspite* to shell the BREST coast in support of ground troops.

After the fall of BREST until the beginning of the ARDENNES counter-offensive, PHANTOM in the US sector carried out its normal role.'

CHAPTER XXII

# Arnhem

*'It was very sad listening to the final messages coming out of Arnhem from Neville Hay's Phantom patrol knowing there was very little we could do to help.'*

HARRY BINGE, RADIO OPERATOR, No. 23 'J' PATROL

'B' SQUADRON PHANTOM.

After the successes of the Allies in France during the month of August, mainly the capture of Falaise, the landings and advance on the French Riviera front and the liberation of Paris, September 1944 proved to be a month of considerable mixed fortune. Apart from isolated pockets of enemy resistance, these not considered to be of great strategic importance, much of France was in Allied control. The push into the low countries of Belgium and Holland was now to begin and swiftly gather momentum.

During a ten day spell at the beginning of September, the British, Canadian and Polish forces raced across Northern France and into Belgium to liberate Brussels and capture the key port of Antwerp. At the same time, the Canadians were besieging the Channel ports of Boulogne, Calais and Dunkirk. Here the Germans were holding out to deny the Allies the ports closest to the front lines.

Only a shortage of fuel temporarily halted the advance of Patton's US 3rd Army within striking distance of Germany at the Moselle river, the US 1st Army nearing Aachen and Montgomery's 21st Army Group on the Albert Canal. On the 10th September, at the village of Roetgen, the first Allied soldier, American Charles D Hiller, crossed into Germany. A truly historic moment.

Sir Robert Mark, Commissioner of the Metropolitan Police from the 17th April, 1972, until 1977, was to see war service as a member of Phantom. He tells us in his autobiography, *'In the Office of Constable'*, how as a young man he joined the Army and how, on leaving Sandhurst Military Academy, he became a member of this elite communications regiment.

On leaving school in mid-1935, the young Robert Mark obtained a job at the Manchester office of James Templeton and Co of Glasgow, the largest firm of carpet manufacturers in Great Britain, but it slowly dawned on him that it was not really the life for him so, in 1937, he applied to join the Manchester police.

By the middle of 1942, with air raids on Britain's cities having fallen to an insignificant level, the government decided to release some of the police for military duties.

The newly-wed Robert Mark began his service in August 1942 at a Primary Training Centre, consisting of Nissen huts right outside HM Prison *Parkhurst*, on the Isle of Wight. Two months later, after basic training, he moved to Catterick, in Yorkshire. During a routine interview whilst there, he applied for a commission. His application was successful and he was duly posted to 100 (Sandhurst) Officers Cadet Training Unit.

From Sir Robert's book we quote his experiences after he left Sandhurst:

'I was posted to 108 Tank Brigade which was assigned to the 38th Welsh Division as Lines of Communication troops. Goodness knows I am no hero and never had the slightest desire to die on the battlefield – or anywhere else – but to go home and tell one's family of three years training to be a railway porter at the greatest moment in history. For God's sake! I was fortunate. My brother James, having served for some time in the western desert, had been posted to the War Office and I asked him if he could help. He arranged an interview for me with a Major J A T Morgan of Phantom (GHQ Liaison Regiment) of which I had never heard. I was both relieved and curious when he agreed to take me on.

I had better explain the purpose of the regiment. One of the most important features of warfare is communication. It is important for the high command to know where the enemy is with absolute certainty. This cannot be achieved by signals having to pass from platoon to troop to battalion, brigade, division, corps and army. Apart from time, something always gets lost on the way. Phantom was designed to overcome this. The officers were, with few exceptions, from fighting units. The other ranks, again with a few exceptions, were from the Royal Corps of Signals. We maintained a wireless net entirely separate from all other military formations and had our own code book for wireless transmission. The idea was to deploy patrols, each consisting of one officer and five other ranks, to every division, with listening stations at corps and army and with the headquarters at army group. In addition, one squadron was dropped by parachute behind the enemy and transmitted from special sets to a receiving station in Britain which re-transmitted the messages to army group overseas. I was one of a small group whose training was inadequate to enable us to take part in the *Overlord* operation on D-Day. We were called FLRs or first line reinforcements. We therefore trained hard at Richmond as the great day approached. Richmond Park, at that time, was closed to the public because it had in it a device to attract enemy bombers. It was also just at the limit of the range of the V1, the pilotless bomb used by the Germans before D-Day. They came over in considerable numbers, serving no useful military purpose, but spreading death and destruction indiscriminately. We had a splendid vantage point in the park and counted eighty in one day. One dropped just behind the '*Lass of Richmond Hill*' late one night when I was duty officer. The only casualty was a trooper who on diving for the floor had his leg penetrated by a sliver of glass from a shattered window.

At long last came D-Day and the dawn of the liberation of Europe. I was at Selsey Bill, where we had our rear link and to our immense satisfaction Phantom worked perfectly. Monty had without any delay an accurate picture, or sitrep, as we called it, of the British and Canadian front whilst the Americans, who were having a difficult time, had nothing. Thereafter a squadron, designated 'L' Squadron, was assigned to the Americans on a whole-time basis. It could not, of course, deploy to a level lower than corps, except for specific operations, because of a shortage of numbers, but as each corps or army entered the war zone it was assigned its Phantom patrol. In this way, not only was the high command sure of the disposition of its forward troops; corps and divisional commanders were similarly well informed. Situation reports were transmitted from army group twice daily so that every army commander was kept fully in the picture about the situation on his flanks. It was perhaps one of the most imaginative and successful planning operations of the war.

I did not join all this excitement until the end of July, when the Normandy bridgehead, manned by thousands of Allied Troops, was on the point of exploding. I disembarked at the *Mulberry*, the floating harbour created especially for the invasion, and joined Phantom rear headquarters in an orchard where the wasps were very much more threatening than the enemy. After only a few weeks came the breakthrough at Avranches, Patton's drive east and the butchery of the Falaise gap. Michael Astor, with an armoured brigade at the tip of the gap, had the terrifying experience of being heavily bombed on two consecutive days, once by the Americans and once by the RAF. He lost three men and two vehicles and was lucky to emerge alive.

The advance through France to Belgium, through Amiens, Mantes-Gassicourt and eventually to Brussels will never be forgotten by anyone lucky enough to take part in it.'

Lord Cullen of Ashborne, in 1944 a major and the senior Signals Officer with Phantom, was asked by his CO, shortly before they arrived in Brussels, to take charge of the advance party to set up signals communications.

In his book *'Phantom Was There'*, Reginald Hills, a quartermaster with Phantom and later commander of 'L' Squadron, explains how Lord Cullen searched for a suitable site.

'Every Phantom officer had a keen eye for country as regards wireless siting. None more so than Major Lord Cullen. It was no easy task to find a good site within reasonable distance of 21st Army Group. There was little doubt that he had selected the best. His choice also commended itself by its propinquity to a very pleasant officers' mess.'

Lord Cullen himself rather humorously describes, in correspondence with us, how he actually located the site eventually chosen and set up his headquarters.

'I set off with my batman/driver named Needham. We drove into the city and spotted the Metropole Hotel. I went into the bar and asked those present if they could suggest a place for our headquarters that would be suitable for wireless transmission. They unanimously agreed on the Waterloo Golf Club. We set off and on arrival there were greeted by the Secretary of the club. We immediately requisitioned it, together with several chateaux nearby for billets.

Our top priority was to get telephone communication with rear HQ. This was in due course established. Some officers and men of Phantom had by now joined us at Waterloo and many more were on their way.

At first, no calls were coming in so I told the Lance Corporal who was manning the switchboard to take lunch and I took over myself. Almost at once calls came in by the dozen. I plugged them in alright to start with, but it soon became too hectic. I ended up with Phantom patrols talking to each other in the field! So I pulled out all the leads and slowly started to sort them out again.

In due course, the Lance Corporal came back and I went to lunch. The cry came up, 'Who the bloody hell was manning that switchboard for the last hour?' I thought it wisest to come clean!'

It was by now the middle of September and the Waterloo Golf Club, the highest point in the area and ideal for the receiving and transmitting of wireless communications, was to be the headquarters of the General Headquarters Liaison Regiment for the autumn and winter of 1944/45.

On the 17th September, 1944, Operation *Market Garden* was launched. In an attempt to shorten the war, Montgomery, promoted to Field-Marshal as from the first of the month, planned to by-pass the heavily defended *Siegfried* Line by landing three airborne divisions behind German lines in Holland. The aim was for the Americans to take the German-held river bridges at Nijmegan and Eindhoven and for the British paratroops to take and hold the bridges on the Rhine at Arnhem. This, if successful, would in effect cut Holland in two and establish Second Army beyond the Rhine.

The three divisions chosen for this operation were the 101st American, the 82nd American and, under Major-General Robert Urquhart, the 1st British. The 1st and 82nd Divisions were to operate under command of HQ 1 British Airborne Corps commanded by Lieutenant-General Frederick Browning. A fourth division, 52nd Lowland, was available to be flown in by DC Dakota transport aircraft as soon as an airfield had been captured.

Just after 10am, on a brilliant Sunday morning, the greatest armada of troop-carrying aircraft ever assembled for a single operation took off from airfields all over southern England. In total, 3,887 aircraft, British and American, and some 500 gliders became airborne. Of these, 1,240 were fighters and 1,113 bombers. The huge columns these aircraft formed stretched for many miles.

The bridge at Eindhoven on the River Maas fell fairly easily to the Americans who had landed to the north of the river. Meanwhile, the Irish Guards of the Armoured Division were pushing up from the south through a corridor one mile wide along the Eindhoven road. From the air a constant stream of

Typhoons were skimming down to the tops of the trees before firing their rockets and machine-guns, clearing a path ahead and pushing the enemy further back. Typhoons from 174 Squadron, as part of 121 Wing, 83 Group were arriving every five minutes and as each aircraft made several strikes it appeared to those on the ground that the attacks were continuous. A 'cab-rank' of eight Typhoons was on call overhead all the time.

In his book, *'The Struggle For Europe'*, Chester Wilmot describes the scene:

'As the tanks of the Irish Guards rolled forward up the road, the Typhoon pilots were directed to their targets by radio from an armoured half-track, moving with the column. The white road, standing out against the dark pines, was easily identified, and all our tanks carried florescent orange screens which were plainly visible from the air and were soon hailed by the Dutch people as banners of liberation. The Typhoons were so efficiently directed that they were able to strike at targets within 200 yards of these tanks.'

(Phantom patrols working in close liaison with RAF ground control units were supplying much of the information on enemy positions that was being passed on to the Typhoon pilots.)

Those of the Panzer Grenadiers who were captured by the Irish Guards as they advanced up the Eindhoven road, at first refused to co-operate with their captors by giving information on the whereabouts of other German units further ahead, until they were placed on their own surviving tanks to be taken back behind our own lines. So terrified were they by the thought that they would come under attack from the Typhoons circling above in the 'cab-rank', they promptly revealed the positions of the rest of their battery. This information was relayed at once to the Typhoons and the medium artillery. By dusk, the Irish Guards, with the aid of the Typhoon pilots, had slowly overcome any remaining opposition and had reached their day's objective, Valkenswaard, five miles south of Eindhoven.

The following day the road was clear for them to drive on through the corridor to Nijmegan to link up with the American 101st Airborne Division.

The bridge at Nijmegan on the Waal was won only after a sharp struggle. The huge, multi-spanned Nijmegan crossing, together with its approaches almost half a mile long, finally fell intact into Allied hands after bitter fighting at 7.15pm on

September 20th. At Arnhem, only eleven miles away, it was to be a different story.

Thinking the area around Arnhem to be only lightly defended by old men and members of Hitler's *Jugend* (Hitler's Youth), British High Command sanctioned the operation, despite being informed by the Dutch Resistance and Allied photo-reconnaissance that this was probably not the case. *Feldmarschall* Model, commander of Germany's Army Group 'B', had recently decided to move his headquarters just north of Arnhem. *General* Wilhelm von Bittrich's battle-hardened 2nd SS Panzer Corps, after fighting against the Allied landings in Normandy, had been instructed by Model to rest up and regroup at Arnhem.

The British paratroops, who floated down out of the skies on the 17th, to land on the isolated Renkum Heath, eight miles to the west of the Dutch town of Arnhem, found themselves in the midst of German territory. Although the drops had gone well, without any initial enemy resistance, this was soon to change dramatically.

The man with the most important task on landing was Major Freddie Gough of the 1st Airborne Division Reconnaissance Unit. Leading a four-troop squadron in heavily armed jeeps, Gough was to make a dash for the bridge to reconnoitre and to report on the strength of the enemy positions. Also on their way to Arnhem were the three battalions of Brigadier Lathbury's First Parachute Brigade. Lieutenant-Colonel John Frost's Second Battalion and Lieutenant-Colonel Fitch's Third Battalion set off first to make their approach from different routes. They were swiftly followed by Lieutenant-Colonel Dobie's First Battalion who were to advance along the main Ede-Arnhem road and occupy the high ground north of the town.

Frost's Second Battalion had advanced for only an hour or so before they met their first serious German opposition, but managed to fight their way through to the first objective – the railway bridge over the Lower Rhine. This they were to take and hold but, as they arrived, they witnessed a German soldier run onto the bridge from the other side, detonate charges and blow it sky high. Frost's second objective, a pontoon crossing less than a mile west of the Arnhem Bridge, was found to have been sabotaged, and so now his only thought was, 'Now we've got to get that other bloody bridge.'

Shortly after 8pm, Frost and his battalion headquarters

reached the road bridge at Arnhem, which was the main objective of all three battalions, having endured ferocious enemy counter-attack as they made their way eastwards and into the town itself. Believing the bridge to be deserted, Frost ordered his men to move across. As they did so, the Germans sprang into action, pushing them back to the north end.

Frost, linking up with Major Freddie Gough and his squadron, had managed to secure the bridgehead that Montgomery so desperately sought but, almost immediately, experienced frantic enemy counter-attacks. Soon they were surrounded. They managed to hold out for nearly four days, repelling all attacks by German armoured cars and half-tracks across the road bridge, but were fast running low on food, water and ammunition. The main force, advancing from the south towards Arnhem, was held up at Nijmegan and just could not get through to them.

The First and Third Battalions, with Major-General Urquhart and Brigadier Lathbury, were held up by street fighting on the outskirts of Arnhem and pinned down by German snipers. They were unable to reach the bridge only two miles away. Urquhart was desperate to get back to Divisional HQ and told Lathbury that the two of them must take a chance and break out before they were completely trapped. As they tried to escape, climbing over back-garden fences, Lathbury was wounded and had to be left with a Dutch couple. Urquhart, did not make it much further before he too had to rely on the shelter of a Dutchman's home. Eventually, he was successful in making it back to Divisional HQ.

On the morning of the 20th, Major-General Urquhart was forced to order his troops to fall back into the Oosterbeek perimeter. The Germans had surrounded Frost and his men, held out at the bridge, and Urquhart, without reinforcements, was unable to do any more to help them. At 8am he managed to get through to Frost and Gough by radio link. Feeling he was abandoning them, Urquhart had the bitter task of informing his officers that their only hope of help was from the south.

The main British forces, advancing north from Nijmegan, had been unable to get through to help Frost and Gough at Arnhem and join the rest of the 1st Airborne, encountering impenetrable enemy resistance at Elst, a village half-way between the two rivers – the Waal and the Rhine.

Phantom's Lieutenant Neville Hay and his patrol had dropped at Renkum Heath with Major-General Urquhart and his 1st Airborne Division on the 17th. The following day, the 18th September, the British had requisitioned the Hartenstein Hotel at Oosterbeek, a small village to the west of Arnhem, to set up Divisional HQ. Urquhart, holed up on the outskirts of Arnhem, was not to learn for nearly two days where his headquarters was sited. Communications were bad. The Canadian No. 22 wireless sets of the division's Signals could at their best only transmit and receive within a radius of between three to five miles, whereas Phantom, by using a special kind of antenna, had been known to transmit a distance of a hundred miles or more using the same set. For this reason, when Hay and his patrol assembled their radio set on landing at Renkum Heath to give their position, he could not understand why he could not get through to Browning's Corps headquarters, set up a mere fifteen miles away.

Until contact could be made, Hay could not inform Browning of the progress of Urquhart's Division or relay Browning's orders to the 1st Airborne Division. Browning was becoming anxious. He could direct the 82nd and the 101st but he had absolutely no idea what was happening at Arnhem, until, at last, the news came through that the bridgehead was held, but that Frost was in dire need of reinforcements and supplies.

Phantom's 'A' Squadron commander, Major Dennis Russell, had ordered Captain Denys Brook-Hart at Nijmegan to take his No. 5 patrol up to Arnhem to find out what was going on. Brook-Hart left SHQ on the morning of the 19th equipped with the new Canadian No. 9 transmitter, but only got as far as Eindhoven before being driven back by German tanks and constant air attack.

'A' Squadron's No. 12 patrol NCO, Ron Eaton, recalls that Sergeant Vic Stump of No. 5 patrol, a good friend of Ron's, kept a diary of his version of events:

'19th September: Left Squadron HQ with new Command 9 Set, and a special job. To get up as far as possible to contact Airborne pockets. Crossed Dutch frontier and reached Valkenswaard at 1400 hrs. Then pushed on and reached Eindhoven. Stopped by civilians in centre of town, they reported enemy tanks advancing on outskirts of town. So we put vehicles on side road and took up defence positions. Then at 2200 hrs. large number of enemy aircraft attacked centre of town. Thought we'd had it, but patrol and vehicles all safe. All routes out of town were now blocked by blazing ammo and petrol trucks. Civilians took it well, but there's urgent need for bandages etc – having emptied patrol first-aid box. Eventually moved patrol to a field on immediate outskirts of town. There opened wireless and sent priority request message for ambulances.'

Three days later No. 5 patrol reached Nijmegan, and the following day Brook-Hart and his men crossed the bridge and were able to reach Driel where they transmitted from a water-logged ditch in pouring rain. After returning to Nijmegan once more to replace the wireless set, they set up in a barn at Homoet. They were to remain on the 'Island', the area of land between the Waal and the Rhine, for the final days of Operation *Market Garden*.

Just after 11am on the 20th, General Browning received the first clear picture of the seriousness of the situation at Arnhem. The Phantom message he received via Second British Army read:

'Source Patrol Officer, Airborne Div. SITREP at 191530 hrs. Elts senior formation still in vicinity NORTH end of main bridge but not in touch and unable re-supply. Part of 2 Bn now being concentrated SOUTH of DERBRINCK E7277. Next senior and junior formations now being reorganised to hold rd and rly crossing 699799 Pt 635 and 687785 – x-roads 688793. Third lift very hvy oppsn by Flak. ARNHEM entirely in enemy hands. Request all possible steps taken to expediate relief. Fighting intense and oppsn extremely strong. Posn not too good. TOO Not stated. THI 201105.'

Now information from the 1st Airborne was coming through well, and accurately, from Neville Hay. In fact, Phantom's radio link with Hay at the Hartenstein Hotel was the only contact now possible with the 1st Airborne Division trapped at Arnhem.

On the morning of the 20th, at the bridgehead, completely surrounded by the Germans and with no help getting through, Lieutenant-Colonel John Frost, himself badly wounded, agreed to a truce with the Germans for himself and his wounded men to be handed over. Major Freddie Gough and the remainder of the able-bodied men tried to make a run for it. Gough was subsequently captured, but a few managed to cross the river and escape to safety.

They had fought heroically against overwhelming odds, holding out for nearly four days, but had finally been forced to succumb to a far bigger force.

Back at the Hartenstein Hotel, Major-General Urquhart did not receive their final message, so was not aware of the total seriousness of their predicament, or the fact that the bridge was now back in German hands.

The Polish Parachute Brigade, due to join the beleaguered 1st Airborne, dropped on the 23rd over a wide area around Driel, on the south side of the river. Under the cover of darkness that evening, they managed to cross over in sixteen boats. They came under intense enemy fire and suffered heavy losses. Only two hundred reached the Hartenstein Hotel. The supplies, also dropped on that day and aimed at the grounds of the hotel, mainly fell into enemy hands. The situation there was rapidly becoming desperate.

The Phantom message sent to Phantom's Signal Headquarters at Waterloo Golf Club was:

'231605...Resupply by air; very small quantity picked up. Snipers now severely curtailing movement and therefore collection. Also roads so blocked by falling trees, branches and houses that movement in jeeps virtually impossible. Jeeps in any case practically out of action.'

Four hours later in his situation report relayed to Browning by Phantom, Urquhart reported:

'232015...Many attacks during day by small parties infantry, SP guns, tanks including flame thrower tanks. Each attack accompanied by very heavy mortaring and shelling within Div. perimeter. After many alarms and excursions the latter remains substantially unchanged, although very thinly held. Physical contact not yet made with those on south bank of river. Resupply a flop, small quantities of ammo only gathered in. Still no food and all ranks extremely dirty owing to shortage of water. Morale still adequate, but continued heavy mortaring and shelling is having obvious effects. We shall hold but at the same time hope for a brighter 24 hours ahead.'

On Sunday the 24th September, Lieutenant Neville Hay was called into Urquhart's room in the cellar of the Hartenstein. The General handed Hay a message to encode and return to him. The message, which Lieutenant Robert Mark took at Phantom's wireless receiving operation room at HQ, Waterloo Golf Course, read:

'Urquhart to Browning. Must warn you unless physical contact is made with us early 25 Sept, consider it unlikely we can hold out long enough. All ranks now exhausted. Lack of rations, water and ammunition and weapons with high officer casualty rate. Even slight enemy offensive action may cause complete disintegration. If this happens all will be ordered to break towards bridgehead if anything rather than surrender. Any movement at present in face of enemy impossible. Have attempted our best and will do so as long as possible.'

The order to abandon the operation was given by Field-Marshal Montgomery on Monday 25th. During the night of the 25/26th withdrawal south across the Rhine, Operation *Berlin*, took place. Less than 3,000 men out of 10,000 who took part in the operation got away, either in boats or by swimming across the river. 1,220 had been killed and 6,642 taken prisoner.

Lieutenant Neville Hay and his Phantom patrol were amongst the last to leave, having operated their wireless sets by candlelight until the last possible moment. Before walking down to the river, they hacked them to pieces, destroying the tiny charging engines.

Captain Denys Brook-Hart with his No. 5 patrol, on the south side of the River Rhine, had been able to establish contact with Neville Hay on the 24th. Hart, and other Phantom patrols not directly involved with Operation *Market Garden* but operating in a back up, listening and relay role, received reports of the evacuation of survivors over the following two days. One of those patrols involved was 'B' Squadron's No. 23 'J' patrol. Harry Binge remembers listening into, and even taking, some of these messages. 'It was very sad listening in to the final messages coming out of Arnhem from Neville Hay's Phantom patrol, knowing there was very little we could do to help.'

Some of these last sombre messages were:

> 'Source Div G Ops 1530 hrs. Intention. 4 Dorset and 1 Airborne Div will be evacuated SOUTH tonight crossing in area 6876 covered by arty fire and smoke screen if operation continues after first light.
> TOO 251550 THI 251825'

> 'Source BM 130 Bde 2100 hrs. 130 Bde plan for withdrawing force SOUTH of river.
> 2100 hrs. Arty barrage
> 2140 hrs. First boats reach NORTH side to collect 1 Airborne Div
> 0200 hrs. 4 Dorset start withdrawing to SOUTH side of river
> 0400 hrs. Heavy smoke screen

0600 hrs. Operation stop
TOO 252130 THI 260130'

'Source 43 Div 0925 hrs. General URQUHART here during night. He estimated 2,500 men to be evacuated. There are still approx 200 men on NORTH bank of river moving EAST.
TOO 261030 THI 261120'

'Source 43 Div 0845 hrs. Number of men evacuated 2800 repeat 2800. Operation stopped 0830 hrs. NOTE: The Phantom Patrol Officer with 43 Div believed this included POLISH Paratps.
TOO 260925 THI 261053'

Sir Robert Mark recalls, 'I was one of the staff in the Ops Room at Phantom Headquarters on Waterloo golf course when Operation *Market Garden*, the Arnhem drop, took place. The next ten days or so were traumatic. Towards the end the only messages coming out of the Arnhem pocket were from the Phantom patrol and there was a peculiar poignancy about them as the situation got more and more desperate.'

Phantom patrol leaders, Captain Denys Brook-Hart and Lieutenant Neville Hay were to be awarded the Military Cross for their vital communications role during the operation.

Although being decisively defeated at the Arnhem Bridge, Operation *Market Garden* had not been a total failure. The Allied forces, under Montgomery's command, had gained some fifty miles in a matter of nine days and the American links in the Airborne chain had successfully held the Maas crossings and were able to consolidate their positions.

The price they paid for these extra miles had been high. The Allies suffered more casualties in the nine days of *Market Garden* than they did on D-Day, the 6th June. The combined Allied forces of '*Market*', the airborne paratroop drop and glider borne landing part of the operation, and '*Garden*' the advancing ground part, suffered an estimated 17,000 casualties, either killed, wounded or reported missing.

We leave this chapter with the words of Lieutenant General 'Boy' Browning, deputy CO, 1st Allied Airborne Army and commanding 1st British Airborne Corps, on the eve of Operation *Market Garden*:

'We might be going a bridge too far.'

CHAPTER XXIII

# Battle Of The Bulge

*'If we reached the Meuse we should have got down on our knees and thanked God – let alone try to reach Antwerp.'*

FIELD-MARSHAL GERD VON RUNSTEDT.

September became October, October became November. The names of Liege, Brussels, Aachen, Antwerp and Metz all made the headlines of the newspapers back home in Britain as they in turn fell to the victorious Allied Armies in Europe.

October the 5th, 1944, saw British troops back on the Greek mainland after three years, fulfilling their promise to return and liberate Greece.

In the Pacific, the 24th October saw the US crush Japan in one of the greatest ever sea battles, set in and around the Philippine Islands. By the middle of November ships and submarines of the Royal Navy, released by their successes in the North Atlantic, had been sent to the Indian Ocean to join the British Eastern Fleet for sorties into the Pacific.

In East Prussia, the Red Army was closing in on Germany. Pushing up from the south through Hungary and from the west through Poland.

In Italy, the war reached a stalemate in the mountains as both sides got bogged down. The autumn rain turned to winter snow and the British tanks found the going impossible. The next couple of months were spent training for the Alpine warfare that was to come.

Mid-November saw Chinese and US troops in Burma, reinforced by the 36th Indian Division, force the Japanese Army to retreat northwards and take up defensive positions.

At the same time the Allies in Europe were preparing for a new drive into Germany whilst, at home, Hitler's secret long-range V2 rockets were continuing to inflict devastation on Britain's capital. At lunch time on the 25th November, one hit a Woolworth's store in New Cross, south-east London. Packed with Saturday shoppers, 160 people were killed and a further

200 injured.

On the 1st November, British and Canadian troops crossed the River Scheldt in an attempt to seize the German-held Walcheren Island, situated in the estuary of this great river. Until the enemy guns could be cleared from this Dutch island, Allied shipping could not reach the Belgian port of Antwerp, seventy miles inland. Four weeks previously British aircraft had attacked the dykes which protected the island, allowing the sea to rush in, and dropped eight thousand tons of bombs on German ammunition dumps, artillery batteries and radar stations. With these mostly destroyed, and with three-quarters of the island deep under water, a naval force of nearly two hundred vessels and landing craft carried out amphibious landings on Walcheren. For eight days the landings continued until, finally, the Canadian and British troops, joined by Dutch and French units, overran the last enemy defences, but only after savage and arduous fighting. Hitler had ordered his men to fight to the last and not to surrender. The German military command was well aware of the importance to the Allies of the strategic port of Antwerp for the continuation of their supplies as they fought their way towards the Fatherland. Antwerp, which had fallen to the Allies on the 4th September, could only be reached along the River Scheldt and supplies of vital war materials and troops were, meanwhile, being forced to rely on the long supply routes from the original Normandy beachhead. It was the 28th November before the first convoy entered Antwerp. For 85 days the Germans had denied the Allies the use of this great port.

Two Phantom patrols were used for the Walcheren operation. Those of 'B' Squadron's No. 19 *'Merlin'* patrol, under the command of Captain Ian Balfour-Paul, and Captain Roderick MacFarquhar's No. 6 of 'L' Squadron, both in the Flushing area of the island.

Harry Binge, by then at the 2nd Canadian Corps' winter headquarters at Wijchen, near Nijmegan, in Holland, remembers talking to a mate of his in *'Merlin'* patrol.

'It was pretty scary working on the Walcheren offensive because Jerry were fighting tooth and nail to hold on. We were sending back our reports from right up at the front line,' Harry was told. 'We were glad when we finally kicked the Germans out. We were sending a constant stream of SITREPS (situation reports), both day and night, on the progress of the battle.'

Before moving to Wijchen, *'Kite'* patrol spent four or five weeks in Belgium, and Captain Millar's 'J' patrol was with *'Kite'* for some of that time. From Captain Ling's diary we read:

> 'SEPTEMBER 30TH 1944. DESTELBERGEN nr Ghent. Great relief after France. Camped in orchard. Made friends with farmers. Many trips into Ghent. Amazed at quantity and quality of luxury goods in shops. Damp rising in tents. Constructed beds but finally forced to move into a barn. Monotony of work at last offset by congenial surroundings.'

Harry well remembers how they came by their billets.

'When we were staying near Ghent, in Belgium, the weather was awful. All it did was rain non-stop. We'd all had enough of it, so Captain Millar decided that we should go in search of billets. He took me with him because I could speak a bit of French and Dutch. We found what we thought looked liked the possible answer to our problem. A small farmhouse that had very large barns close by. The Captain knocked at the door and it was answered by an attractive middle-aged lady. In my faltering Dutch, I asked her if she had space in her barn for a British officer and six men.

She hesitated for a while before answering, *'Ja'*. Looking at the Captain, she nodded and winked at the same time.

'I have a room in the farmhouse for your Captain and,' pointing her finger towards the far barn, 'space in there for the rest of you.' Again looking at the Captain, she nodded and winked.

Our Captain, who was rather a reserved man, gave me a worried sideways glance. As we accepted her offer and set off back to the lads waiting in the orchard, he turned to me and said, 'Did you see her winking at me, Binge? What have I let myself in for?'

'You'll be alright, Sir. Don't worry. We won't be far away,' I reassured him as I laughed to myself. Here was a Captain of the British Army anxious about the prospect of being alone with a Flemish farmer's wife, after all we had been through since D-Day.

We threw everything into our vehicles and drove into the farmyard, parking up by the barns. 'Robbo' sorted out the Captain's stuff and took it over to the farmhouse with him. When he came back he couldn't stop laughing. 'She's still winking at him,' he chuckled.

We settled down for the night, sleeping well on the soft

warm straw and hay. Heaven after the cold, muddy sites we had been used to. In the morning, after breakfast, a very relieved Captain Millar came across to the barn. It turned out that the woman had a husband and three burly sons, and the nodding and winking was nothing more than an affliction – a rather bad twitch!

We ended up staying there for about a month, so made it quite homely. The 2nd Canadian Division was resting up and re-grouping so it was pretty quiet, we were just being used as a relay service. Intercepting and sending messages up to Phantom HQ at Waterloo. When we had to move on to Wijchen we were quite disappointed as we had made many friends amongst the locals. The patrol had even managed to wangle a few days leave in Brussels during this time. Captain Millar suggested we had our photo taken while we were there, and some of the '*Kite*' boys came along, too.'

Peter Ling's diary continues:

> '*NOVEMBER 8TH 1944. WIJCHEN nr NIJMEGAN. Winter billets. Arrived before previous Corps had gone. Colossal muddle for one night. Billets cold and miserable. Partly destroyed by Germans. Work dropped to absolute minimum. Front stationary. Snow, frost, skating. Flying Bombs roaring overhead continuously. Several dropped locally.*'

In the autumn of 1944, Hitler made up his mind that any new divisions being formed would go to the Western Front, not to the East. Eighteen out of twenty-three new infantry (*Volksgrenadier*) divisions were sent to the Rhine to join the Panzer and Panzer-Grenadier divisions already stationed there. Nearly three-quarters of the *Luftwaffe*'s already depleted force of planes would be used in their support as Hitler launched Operation *Grief*, German for grab, because that is just what he intended to do – grab back Antwerp. And all the Allied fuel reserves and supplies that his *Wehrmacht* were so desperately short of. By driving a wedge through the Allied front at the Ardennes, across the Meuse and on through Liege and by capturing this Belgian city, a key American centre containing vehicles and petrol, Hitler figured he would split the American and British forces as he reached his target. The British would be trapped between the rivers Meuse and Rhine with the North Sea behind them. He arrogantly believed that this would be the end of the British Army and, with the Americans denied their principal supply port, the beginning of the end for them too.

This last offensive by the retreating Germans proved to be one of the most threatening challenges to the Allies as it caught them completely by surprise.

At 5.30am on December 16th, the *'Battle of the Bulge'*, under the overall command of *Feldmarschall* von Runstedt, began with the thundering roar of an artillery barrage. The seven armoured divisions of *General* Dietrich's 6th and *General* von Manteuffel's 5th Panzer Armies led the attack and for the first few days the German Army made considerable gains before the stunned Americans, recovering their balance, made a stand.

*General* Hasso von Manteuffel expressed his opinion on the first day of the battle: 'My storm battalions infiltrated rapidly into the American front – like rain-drops. At 4 o'clock in the afternoon the tanks advanced, and pressed forward in the dark with the help of 'artificial moonlight'. Resistance tended to melt whenever the tanks arrived in force, but the difficulties of movement offset the slightness in this early stage.'

A special commando force, raised by the *SS Obersturmbannführer* (Major) Skorzeny who had in 1943 rescued the Italian dictator, Mussolini, from captivity in a daring raid, was to infiltrate behind the Allied lines. Disguised as American servicemen, their mission was to disrupt communications and cause chaos and confusion. In *'The Struggle For Europe'*, Chester Wilmot explains their plan and its outcome:

'The *'Trojan Horse'* plan miscarried but more than forty jeep-loads of 'American-speaking' Germans slipped through the crumbling front on the first two nights and some of them actually reached the Meuse before they were stopped. All except eight of these sabotage parties regained their own lines after cutting telephone wires, intercepting despatch riders and liaison officers, shooting-up radio stations and killing military policemen posted to direct convoys. One brazen German even took over a pointsman's duty and turned an American regiment down the wrong road.'

The German soldiers who were captured wearing American uniforms were treated as spies and executed by firing squad, as their *ruse de guerre* denied them the protection of the Geneva Convention on PoWs.

Shortage of personnel prevented Phantom from covering every sector of the American front, but the following official war office papers describe Phantom's role in the 'Battle of the

Bulge' counter-offensive and includes the first message received of the attack, this coming from a Phantom patrol.

## THE ARDENNES COUNTER-OFFENSIVE

'On the 16th December 1944, PHANTOM, like so many others, was caught napping by considering VIII US Corps 'the quiet sector', and had, as a result, no patrol with the Corps at the time. The following message from V Corps patrol at 0930 hrs on the 16th December, heralded the attack.

'Enemy arty fire along whole V Corps front this morning. 106 DIV report Counter-attack by approximately one company in area L-0393 and further small counter-attack area 0390. 99 DIV: CP Third Bn Regt area P-9799 receiving small arms fire. Unknown strength counter-attack made slight penetration against First Bn 393 Regt in area F-0304 but no details as yet. Third Bn 395 Regt repelled counter-attack area K-9516. Enemy patrol activity continuing.'

As soon as it was appreciated that the attack was in earnest, the patrol which had previously functioned with VIII Corps, and which was at the time with XV Corps in 7th US Army Sector, was sent up from the south. Until the VIII Corps patrol arrived the Phantom patrols at V Corps and XX Corps were able, through the information available at their HQ, to give a reasonable clear picture of events. By 0800 hrs on the 18th December a Phantom patrol had arrived at VIII Corps and opened a radio link to 21st Army Group. During the next few days the patrols around the salient sent back all information that was available to them, a large percentage of which gave the position of enemy troops as reported by various sources. From these reports it was possible to plot the advance of the enemy spearheads.

When General Montgomery took over the 9th and 1st Armies, it was decided to hand over the control of all PHANTOM in Third Army to Phantom Detachment at 12th Army Group Tac. By this arrangement Gen. Bradley's HQ was in direct communication with the Phantom patrols in 3rd Army, thereby reducing delay in retransmission. When 30th British Corps was deployed between 1st and 3rd Armies, two patrols were sent to it, one working to Phantom HQ at 21st Army Group Main and one to the 2nd Army Sqn in order that Gen. Montgomery's HQ and the Army Commander could have the information with the minimum of delay.'

(With reference to the message contained in the above war office paper, the letters L, P, F and K refer to the first letter of a village to be found in the following map square. Phantom avoided spelling out the full name into cypher but this would be inserted at Squadron, or Regimental, HQ Ops Room before forwarding the message to Army or Army Group Ops Room.)

Amongst the Phantom patrols that were deployed in the Battle of the Bulge, was 'A' Squadron's No. 12 patrol, now under the command of Lieutenant J T D Probyn, ex-Royal Tank Regiment, who had replaced Captain Mackenzie in early December. Ron Eaton, now promoted to Corporal, tells us how he came to be at Bastogne, right in the centre of the battle. His patrol was at Regimental HQ at Waterloo when the offensive began.

'About ten days before Christmas we came back to headquarters. We came in one day and the very next day were told that we were going out again. We were told that the Germans were breaking through from the Ardennes and that we were needed in the area. Picking up our supplies, including our Christmas dinner, we set out. First we had to go to the Belgian city of Liege and work with a unit of the French SAS who were patrolling the river in that area, I forget the name of it now. This lasted a couple of days. On the night of the second day we stayed at a monastery on the top of a hill that overlooked Liege. It was a very strange experience. We each had a little cell with a wooden bed in it and a stool. The window was a slit about three inches wide and the walls were about three feet thick, with a heavy old wooden door in one of them. All night long we could hear the monks chanting. A very unusual night's lodging.

Next day we went down south of Bastogne where the Americans were making a big stand. Here we worked with the division that was holding the line there. A few days later, things got a bit hairy there. After about three days, we had to take up a defensive position with the Americans there. When our headquarters back at Waterloo heard about it, they told us in no uncertain terms, 'You're not infantry. You're too valuable. Get out!'

We were only too glad to, the weather at that time was atrocious. I had never been so cold in all my life. It had been snowing just prior to this and I don't know what the temperature was but it was way below freezing. Everyone was moaning about it, so we weren't too put out when they wanted us to report back.'

By the end of the first day, despite their early successes, the Germans were held up in the north at Malmedy and in the south along the Luxemburg frontier, but the road to the key town of Bastogne lay open. The capture of this Belgian town was crucial as it was the focal point of seven major roads. It was here that several thousand lightly-armed men of the 28th Infantry and 10th and 101st US Airborne Divisions were to become trapped. They realized the importance of holding Bastogne to deny the entire road network of the Ardennes to the Germans. Bad weather, although it made slow going for Runstedt's tanks, protected the Germans from air attack. The Allies were unable to take off and use their superior air power to pound the enemy on the ground with bombs and rockets.

On the 18th the Germans came very close to Bastogne, after an advance of nearly thirty miles, but the following day they were stopped by the Americans. Another two days assault on the American defences proved fruitless, so Manteuffel decided to by-pass the town and push on to the Meuse. With one infantry division and two Panzer divisions surrounding the town, the Germans called on the Americans held out there to surrender. Brigadier General Anthony McAuliffe's scrawled reply which was handed to the German messenger read:

'To the German Commander: NUTS! From the American Commander.'

By 25th December, Christmas Day, St Vith and Houffalize to the north of Bastogne had been overrun and Libramont to the south likewise. Bastogne was in a pocket, but the tide of battle was about to change. Patton's 3rd Army was on the move and the General had promised General Eisenhower that he would soon reach Bastogne. By now the foggy weather had cleared, heralding the first of the Allied air attacks, which the scanty resources of Hitler's *Luftwaffe* could do little to counter. The Germans were now also experiencing problems with diminishing fuel supplies, rapidly slowing down their armoured advance.

The clearing weather also meant that the trapped men at Bastogne, running desperately short of food and ammunition, could be supplied by air.

As evening fell on December 26th, Sherman tanks of Patton's 4th Armoured Division, commanded by Major General Hugh J Gaffey, reached the perimeter of Bastogne. They had fought their way up from the south through Luxembourg. Patton had ordered the 4th Armoured: 'Drive like hell.' This they did, but not without coming up against stiff opposition from the German parachute troops, stubbornly defending the ground they had so recently regained.

The German armour had come under furious air attack from Typhoons of the RAF. Many American GI's were thankful that the Typhoons were British when they saw the devastation that these rocket-firing fighter-bombers were capable of. 'Gee, I'm glad they were on our side,' they were later to say.

It was also on this day that the deeply-penetrating German spearhead at Celles was smashed by the forces of Major-General 'Lightning Joe' Collins, supported by the British 29th Armoured Brigade. The Panzer force, without the reinforcements promised by Hitler, was forced to pull back. These reserves had in fact been released but, by now, there was no fuel available to continue their advance. Bitterly, Manteuffel said: 'It was not until the 26th that the rest of the reserves were given to me – and then they could not be moved. They were at a standstill for lack of petrol – stranded over a stretch of a hundred miles – just when they were needed.'

Ironically, on the 19th the Germans had been within a quarter of a mile of a huge US fuel dump at Stavelot, reputedly containing an unbelievable two and a half million gallons.

December 26th, was to prove the turning date in the *'Battle of the Bulge'* and the high point of the German Ardennes offensive. From this day on the Germans were on the defensive; the Allies had blunted the *Wehrmacht's* progress.

*Feldmarschall* von Runstedt, Commander-in-Chief of the German Army in the West, later wrote: 'I wanted to stop the offensive at an early stage, when it was plain that it could not attain its aim, but Hitler furiously insisted that it must go on.'

The Allies, who on the 16th December, had held a five hundred mile front, had come close to disaster by neglecting the forty mile stretch at the Ardennes. The Germans saw this as the Allies' weak point and made their move. Fortunately for the Allies the bad weather lifted in time for a counter airstrike, the shortage of fuel delayed the German advance and the Allied armies were fighting in freezing conditions with more food in their stomachs than their opponents. The German fighting man was having to live on less than a quarter of the daily rations of his counterpart. Having to survive on these meagre rations in such atrocious conditions inevitably led to low morale within the German forces.

Heavy losses in the Ardennes offensive, in reality, wrecked Germany's chances of any further serious resistance. They had opened their attack on the 16th December, 1944, and seven weeks later they were back where they had started. Hitler had lost upwards of 120,000 men killed, wounded or captured, about half of the manpower he had started with, 600 tanks and a thousand aircraft. The men and equipment he had squandered by refusing to pull back when he had the chance had left his army and air forces sorely depleted. Whilst the Allies were capable of replacing their weapons and equipment within a couple of weeks, the Germans' losses were irreplaceable.

Patrols of all Phantom squadrons had worked alongside the American Signal Corps and kept in close liaison with them throughout the Ardennes offensive. The US Army Signal Corps had always projected its map lines furthest ahead of the fighting troops and announced: 'Along this route we can give you wire communication.' They based this assumption, rightly or wrongly, on the civilian facilities, which they hoped the Germans would leave intact, or on wires strung up by their own Signal Corps linesmen. Phantom had offered the American commanders the use of powerful wireless communications. A Phantom receiving station had been set up near the racecourse just outside the French town of Verdun on the River Meuse, in a building the Germans themselves had used as a radio operations room before being overrun. The German *Swastika* still hung on the wall as the Phantom radio operators set up their equipment.

Eagle TAC, the tactical headquarters of the US 12th Army Group, was situated nearby on muddy fields in tents and trailers. General Omar Bradley, commander of 12th Army Group, had conducted the progress of the *'Battle of the Bulge'* from there, aided by much information from the battlefront supplied by Phantom.

Sir Robert Mark recalls: 'I was still at Waterloo when, on 16 December, six SS Panzer Army and five Panzer Army launched an attack in strength and burst through 28th and 106th US Divisions in an advance towards the Meuse. The stubborn gallantry of the Americans, especially at Bastogne, was sufficient to absorb the shock until the regrouped Allied Armies were able to attack the salient from north and south and eventually to restore the status quo. But it was a grim few days in which the Allied flags customarily displayed by each Belgian house were suddenly conspicuously absent. As the offensive lost its edge I was sent to join another Phantom officer at Eagle Tac, the forward headquarters of General Bradley. From there I was sent to take over the Phantom patrol with VII Corps of 1st US Army. I found them at Duren, on the Roer River, where the line had been stable for some time and there was no fighting, merely an occasional and desultory exchange between the artillery.'

Another patrol that served with the US 1st Army at that time was that of Captain Geoffrey Brain. His No. 22 Phantom patrol, '*Gull*', was briefly attached to it in the Ardennes. Brain's patrol had been with the Poles for the drive through Europe but now was to spend a short time with the Americans. Always known for his coolness under fire, when the building he was operating from was hit by a shell, Brain didn't flap. He was eating as the blast came and when the dust settled, he was seen calmly removing dusty chunks from his mess tin and licking them to see if they were glass or meat. If it was meat, he ate it, much to the amazement of the Americans! Harry Binge remembers, 'Captain Brain always was a cool customer!'

In Italy throughout the second half of 1944, things had been slowly moving towards the full amalgamation of Phantom and 'J' Service. As outlined in Chapter Fourteen, they had been working alongside each other, although in slightly different roles, since the Spring of 1943. Prior to the Allied invasion of Northern Europe, Phantom and 'J' had been integrated, with Phantom Squadrons having 'J' Troop patrols working to 'J' Service methods. Now, in Italy, Phantom and 'J', as they prepared to go into 1945, were to become No. 2 GHQ Liaison Regiment.

CHAPTER XXIV

# Across the Rhine and into Germany

*'It is quite devastating that the Americans should have succeeded in capturing the Rhine bridge at Remagen intact.'*
DR JOSEPH GOEBBELS, THE THIRD REICH'S
MINISTER OF PROPAGANDA.

On the 25th December, 1944, the people of Britain sat down to yet another wartime Christmas dinner. The optimism they had felt the previous year had not been fulfilled. Although since the great Normandy invasion in June, the Allied troops had pushed far into Europe, across France, Belgium and Holland, they had failed to penetrate into Germany itself. Hitler, recovered from the shock of the conspiracy against him and the attempt on his life, had, in the autumn, called for a complete reorganization of his forces in the West and raised a whole new army. Montgomery's gamble, Operation *Market Garden*, had not paid off. The war had not been won. The retreating German Army had made a stand, halted the victorious Allied armies and, only nine days before Christmas, mounted an offensive capable of destroying them. As we now know, December 26th was to be the turning point in the *'Battle of the Bulge'*, but on the 25th all did not look well.

On the 3rd December, 1944, in London, contingents of the Home Guard from all over the country, including an American section made up of US citizens living in London, held a moving farewell parade. With the threat of invasion now over, they were standing down. King George VI, accompanied by Queen Elizabeth and the Princesses Elizabeth and Margaret, took the farewell salute at the beginning of the march in Hyde Park, and cheering crowds thronged the streets as the three-mile procession made its way through the streets of the capital. In a broadcast to the nation the king said: 'I believe it is the voluntary spirit which has always made the Home Guard so powerful a comradeship... You have found how men from all kinds of homes and occupations can work together in a great cause. I am very proud of what the Home Guard has done and I give my heartfelt thanks.'

Three months previously, the creation of the *Volkssturm*, the German equivalent of the British Home Guard, had been announced in Germany. Hitler ordered the call-up of all able-bodied men between the ages of sixteen and sixty who were not already serving in the war. So, as the British Home Guard stood down, the *Volkssturm*, consisting largely of old men and schoolboys, prepared to fight. They wore armbands for uniforms and carried whatever weapons could be found. Hitler even ordered ground force personnel of the *Luftwaffe* to hand in their rifles and guns to equip his new troops.

To assist the *Volkssturm*, the *Führer* emptied his convalescent homes to form what became known as 'Stomach Battalions', because most of the soldiers in them suffered from stomach disorders. They were even allowed special convalescent diets!

The 5th December saw the call go out for all women over the age of eighteen to volunteer for the German services. They were needed as auxiliaries by the badly depleted *Wehrmacht* and *Luftwaffe* to free men for service on the front.

Despite all its new units, the *Wehrmacht's* counter-offensive in the Ardennes, after initial success, had failed. As 1944 became 1945 fierce strikes by the British in the north and Patton's 3rd Army in the south hurled the Germans back to their original positions by the 7th February.

Throughout the autumn of 1944 the planes of the Allied air forces had continued to *blitz* Germany's cities, factories, oil refineries, railway links and transport systems. While the American Air Force concentrated on the primary targets of oil and communications, Sir Arthur Harris, the Chief of RAF Bomber Command, reverted to sending bombers to wipe out cities. His methods met with much criticism from the Church and even the Chief of Air Staff, Sir Charles Portal, but Harris, insisting that it would shorten the war, was unrepentant and the bombings continued. 'Bomber' Harris threatened to wreck Germany from end to end.

For the first two months of 1945, the diary of events unfolded as follows:

> JANUARY 11th. Armistice in Greece.
> JANUARY 13th. The Hungarian capital, Budapest, in Russian hands.

JANUARY 17th. The Germans evacuate Warsaw as the Polish capital is taken by Polish and Soviet troops under Marshal Zhukov.

JANUARY 21st. Hungary declares war on Germany.

JANUARY 27th. In Poland, the Red Army take Aushwitz Concentration Camp and the Germans evacuate the Upper Silesian industrial zone.

JANUARY 31st. Marshal Zhukov's Soviet troops cross the river Oder north of Frankfurt. Only forty miles from Berlin.

FEBRUARY 1ST. In the Philippines US troops advance twenty-five miles into Japanese held territory and free over 500 prisoners of war.

FEBRUARY 2nd. Ecuador declares war on Germany.

FEBRUARY 4th. Start of the Yalta conference between Stalin, Roosevelt and Churchill.

FEBRUARY 6th. General MacArthur announces the capture of Manila and the liberation of five thousand prisoners of war.

FEBRUARY 13th. Anglo-American air attack on the ancient German city of Dresden. Troops from General Sir Henry Crerar's First Canadian Army finally win the battle for the Reichswald after six days, aided by the 1st Battalion, The Gordon Highlanders.

FEBRUARY 14th. Further air attacks on Dresden, city annihilated causing many thousands of civilian casualties.

FEBRUARY 22nd. Operation Clarion, to destroy all enemy communications throughout the Reich, launched by Allied bombers.

FEBRUARY 23rd. The American 9th Army launches an offensive from its bridgeheads on the Roer. Turkey declares war on Germany. US marines raise the Stars and Stripes on the top of Mount Suribachi, on the southern end of the island of Iwo Jima in the Pacific.

FEBRUARY 24th. Egypt declares war on Germany. (Seven days later Finland was also to declare war on Germany.)

Wherever the Allies advanced on the Western Front, Phantom went with them. The men of Phantom were liable to be switched at a moment's notice to another campaign or assignment, proving the flexibility of the men of this special regiment. Such was the case during the Rhine crossing. A fortnight before the river assault, a Phantom officer stepped out of a jeep and detailed certain men of a Squadron to report immediately to the nearest aerodrome. No questions were asked. The men landed in England, went through some refresher courses and fourteen days later dropped with the Airborne troops in the Rhine bridgehead. To Phantom it was just another assignment. In this, as in any campaign, secrecy was an indispensable part of Phantom's make-up for, as Phantom's Major Mackenzie put it, 'We were dangerously in the picture over momentous decisions, but none talked'.

Lieutenant Robert Mark had been sent to take over the Phantom patrol with VII Corps of the 1st US Army. He joined them at Duren on the Roer river.

'The high command had eventually agreed on a frontal assault to clear the western bank of the Rhine and 1st and 9th US Armies attacked on 23th February. We crossed the river without difficulty and during the next few days the only really uncomfortable enemy opposition was from newly encountered jet fighters, who did not seem to have mastered the technique of ground strafing. In the event they were more frightening than lethal and ten days later we duly arrived in Cologne with only minor casualties.

The night after we had captured that part of Cologne that lies on the west bank I was astonished to receive a wireless message from Phantom ordering me to take my patrol to a town called Remagen, to cross the Rhine and to report to the Headquarters of XVIII US Airborne Corps at Siegen, on the southern edge of the Ruhr. This arose from the unexpected capture of the bridge at Remagen on 7th March, by a platoon of 9th US armoured division, a military achievement of almost priceless value.'

On the 7th March the tanks of General Patton's 3rd US Army broke through the weak defences in the Eifel and reached the Rhine at Coblenz, after a sixty-mile drive in three days, to find their progress blocked. The bridges in that area had been blown up before they arrived.

Further north on the same morning, the 1st US Army, under General Courtney Hodges, reached the Rhine at Cologne and found all the bridges there down but, in between, thirty miles to the south of Cologne, the railway bridge at Remagen remained intact. Hitler had ordered that not a single Rhine bridge must fall into Allied hands but the Ludendorff bridge spanning the river at Remagen, one of Germany's great railway bridges built during the First World War, stood defiant, despite previously being damaged by Allied bombers. In fact, the Germans themselves, fearing it unsafe for heavy traffic, had spent the previous month endeavouring to repair it, in the event of them having to make a hasty retreat.

When Brigadier-General Hoge, commander of one of the combat teams of the 9th US Armoured Division, heard the news, he ordered his tanks and infantry across the bridge. American Intelligence reports had come in that the enemy intended to blow the bridge at 4 o'clock that day. As the Americans approached it, German engineers on the far bank were seen to set off the first of their explosive charges, but the bridge remained intact. The main charge had failed to go off. The emergency charge caused a big bang and both sides thought that it had now gone, but when the dust cleared it was still standing. The American soldiers set off across the bridge. Germany's *Major* Scheller, who had ordered the detonation of the bridge, decided to fight no more.

By early evening a hundred American soldiers had crossed the Rhine. No enemy or invader had done so since Napoleon in 1805. Hitler, furious at the failure to destroy the bridge, dismissed *Feldmarschall* von Runstedt from his post of Commander-in-Chief of the German forces in the West.

The War Office papers record the capture of the Remagen bridge: 'After the failure of the Ardennes offensive, all eyes were turned towards the Roer river. Apart from numerous reports regarding the depth and width of the river and the condition of the dams, PHANTOM traffic was of a routine nature. Operations '*Veritable*' and '*Grenade*' (the crossings of the Maas and Roer rivers) were fully reported.

The following message sent at 1735 hrs March 7th announced the beginning of the last battle. 'Source Maj. G3 III US Corps at 1735 hours. 9th Armoured Division. Unconfirmed report that Combat Command 'B' infantry elements are across Rhine River at F.6520 (Remagen) with RAILWAY BRIDGE INTACT.'

From then on the volume of traffic increased as the whole front burst into activity. Owing to the speed of advance the lag between the time of event and time of receipt of messages became noticeably greater.'

One message that did come through swiftly from Phantom, though, came that same evening soon after 9pm. It read: 'Source Maj. G3 III US Corps at 2030 hours. Three infantry companies over Rhine. Railway bridge at Remagen has been de-mined, is in good order and convertible.'

When Prime Minister Sir Winston Churchill visited Field-Marshal Montgomery at his army headquarters at Eindhoven that evening, excitement was high. 'Have the retreating Germans really left intact a bridge across the Rhine?,' he incredulously asked his commander. That night the Prime Minister and the Field-Marshal would not go to bed until confirmation came through. An hour later came the message 'Remagen bridge intact'. It bore the signature Phantom.

The great bridge finally collapsed ten days later, but not before the US 1st Army was on the far side of the Rhine and two pontoon bridges had been constructed alongside it.

No other Rhine crossing was attempted until the night of the 22nd March, when General Patton's men made a spectacular crossing at Oppenheim. He went across with heavy tanks against light opposition and swept down on Darmstadt.

Twenty-four hours later and one hundred miles further north at Wesel, after very heavy artillery fire and bombing by seventy-seven Lancasters had reduced the town to rubble, the British and Canadians crossed the Rhine. Montgomery's men met with more opposition than Patton's had and the Germans clung on for the best part of 24 hours, but, eventually, behind a smoke screen twenty miles long, the 1st Commando Brigade and the 51st Highland Division overran the town and managed to form a bridgehead on the right bank.

The German defenders on the far side of the Rhine had been blinded by tanks carrying specially designed searchlights, so powerful that they came to be known as *'Monty's Moonlight'*.

Hardly had the dust settled from the heavy bombing than, just before daybreak on the 24th, tugs and gliders carrying the British 6th Airborne Division and aircraft bearing the US 17th Airborne Division arrived in the skies above the battle area. The glider landings were very much on target and the twenty-one thousand paratroops of the two airborne divisions, who had been dropped to the north-east of Wesel ahead of the Rhine assault force, helped them clear the way.

Only at the riverside village of Rees, just north of Wesel, did the Allies meet any really stiff opposition. Here a battalion of battle-hardened Hun parachutists, who had been chased out of France, Belgium and Holland, stood their ground and held out for three days.

The Allies now had three bridgeheads east of the Rhine and from these, especially Remagen and Wesel, they would break out and surround Germany's Ruhr industrial areas. This was the plan of Field-Marshal Montgomery, for the Ruhr was the heartland of the German industrial war machine. To smash their supply of new materials with which to continue the war would mean the end of the once mighty *Wehrmacht*. For an army that cannot be re-supplied is a dead army. *Feldmarschall* Albert Kesselring, in overall command of the army in the West since the dismissal of Runstedt on the 7th March, frantically tried to re-organize his rapidly demoralizing army, without much success. It was too late.

Once the Ruhr was overrun, Montgomery wanted to push on to take Berlin, but Eisenhower, Allied Supreme Commander-in-Chief, disagreed. He was quite willing to let Stalin capture Berlin with his Red Army. Those who criticized Eisenhower's decision argued that the British, Canadians and Americans, now meeting little resistance, could easily arrive first. Montgomery was concerned about the political situation after the war if the Russians took not only Berlin but also the political centres of Vienna in Austria, and Prague in Czechoslovakia. In trying to persuade Eisenhower to change his mind, Churchill appealed, 'We should shake hands with the Russians as far east as possible.' Eisenhower, however, was not to be dissuaded and so Montgomery drove his army hard for the Baltics. His object was to prevent the Russians from getting up into Denmark and thus controlling the entrance to the Baltic. In the end Montgomery's army arrived on the 2nd May, only six hours before the Russians, and sealed off the Danish peninsula.

Ron Eaton's No. 12 Phantom patrol was working with the Americans as they crossed the Rhine, supplying Phantom HQ at Waterloo with a constant stream of messages and sitreps. These being immediately passed on to 21st Army Group HQ as the battle advanced. Once across the Rhine it was much easier for Phantom to supply accurate information on laying down the bomb-line as the Allies were advancing on a much wider front. Leap-frogging by the forward troops was less likely to occur, curtailing the accidental bombing by air and artillery shelling of its own forces.

Ron recalls: 'We serviced several American units in the beginning of 1945, until we eventually reached the Rhine. We crossed it on a basic floating bridge, made up of what looked like a row of little boats, but were in fact pontoons, with two tracks not much more than the width of a tyre going across it. The tracks had two little ridges on them that were supposed to keep you on the thing. Well, the Rhine is a pretty wide river and those two little tracks looked awfully small, especially if you were driving an armoured car. If you went off the tracks it would sink like a stone, besides smashing up the row of boats. It was a pretty hairy ride I had there and was thankful when I got to the other side safely.

We stayed the night in Dr Krupp's villa. There was no furniture in it, but there were still some lovely tapestries hanging on the walls. The Americans liked to stay in town if they could. They didn't like sleeping in tents under canvas or tarpaulins. Usually when we entered a town with them they would take the Party Members' houses. They found out who the Nazis were in town, threw them out of their houses and said, 'OK, Phantom, you've got that house over there.' That was your house and you went in it just as it had been left. The Americans just turfed them out without giving them time to take anything.'

Villa Hugel, the home of Doctor Gustav Krupp von Bohlen and Halbach, was just outside Essen where his 'Krupps Works' was responsible for producing massive amounts of war materials. Krupp, an extremely wealthy man, had been a personal friend of Hitler's since the thirties and had financed the Nazi party's rise to power and, consequently, much of the war effort.

Although under constant attack by Bomber Command since the beginning of the war this huge heavily-defended industrial area of the Ruhr had still churned out vital armaments. The continual bombing had not brought the German war machine to its knees, as predicted by Air Marshal 'Bomber' Harris, until February 1945, when its production of coal and steel had been reduced to a fifth of what it had been in the summer of 1944 and its production of arms and munitions to less than a half.

While Ron Eaton stayed with the Americans, his friend Harry Binge, with No. 23 patrol, was still working with the Canadians. They had spent Christmas 1944 with them at Wijchen, in Holland.

Harry recalls, 'I remember having Christmas dinner with the Canadians. They really did us well, and in the evening we started on a feast of our own. The Canadians had thrown a party for over five hundred Dutch children that day. It was a joy to see their smiling faces as they joined in the fun and games. On Boxing Day our patrol was lucky enough to spend the day on leave in Brussels. Here everyone was letting their hair down. After so long of enemy occupation, the newly-liberated Belgians were going wild as they celebrated their first Christmas of freedom for several years.

The task of the Canadians was now to clear Holland of the enemy. We ventured into Germany briefly, crossing over the Lower Rhine with a forward company of Canadian artillery at a place called Emmerich. Once again we were under canvas, camped in a field. We immediately set up the RT vehicle in which we carried our wireless equipment, using some of the remaining trees to hold our aerial antennae. Our patrol was now acting as a rear receiving relay unit as our forward patrols of 'B' Squadron were right up on the front line in the thick of it transmitting the progress of the current action. It wasn't always easy to hear the messages, which were now coming in at a tremendous rate, because of the noise of our artillery, plus the noise of German shells landing in the next field. They hadn't quite got their range sorted out, thank God. Next thing we knew a German reconnaissance spotter plane flew low over the camp. We had a pop at it with our small-arms. I don't know if we hit it at all but it flew on. After this the shells dropped nearer, but suddenly they stopped. Our forward patrols had located their positions and the Canadian artillery soon put an end to the Germans' fun.

The very next day, while on the receiving radio, I picked up, amongst our lads, German voices. It was lucky I could speak a bit of German because I soon realised it was coming from the commander of a Tiger tank, which was heading straight for us! I rushed to Captain Millar's tent, where he was grabbing a few hours sleep after having been up half the night, and told him what I had heard on the radio. He soon realised the seriousness of the situation and ordered us to pack up and get out of there quick. We weren't exactly a fighting unit so we again left it to the Canadians to sort out.

It was about this time that we managed to get a few days leave home in England. How great it was to see my Mum, family and friends again, if only for a few days. We knew by now the war would soon be over and couldn't wait for the day when we would be home to stay. But for now there was still a war to be fought.

When we returned to Germany we were still with the same Canadian unit, which was by now well dug in. The German family, whose farm it was we were on, had moved back in but they were no trouble. In fact, we got on quite well with them. They knew that the end was near and just wanted to get back to a peaceful life. One of normality. During this time we visited Nijmegan several times.

After some time we moved back into Holland and our patrol was told to report to a division of the 2nd Canadian Corps just outside Hilversum. We couldn't drive directly across Holland to Hilversum as Arnhem was still in German hands. Our patrol, together with the other Phantom patrols of Captain Ling and Captain Cohen, was to join the main battle group of the Canadians as they prepared for the push north-eastwards and, in so doing, encircle Arnhem.

I remember we stayed in the grounds of a big house near Hilversum, owned by the Yarlink family. On arrival we pitched our tents, and those of our officers, on the great lawns behind the mansion. The lady of the house was very friendly and even invited us in for showers, although there was no hot water. That night she held a party for the officers, who had by now been asked to take up quarters in the house, and, about 1 o'clock in the morning, she sent one of her house-servants to invite us, the other ranks, to join the fun. I was the only one who took up the offer. The others just wanted to get some rest.

Most of the officers didn't seem to want to dance, they were more interested in drinking. So the lady asked me to partner her and, although they didn't like it much, the officers didn't say a thing. I have always enjoyed dancing and I wasn't going to pass this opportunity up. The party went on until nearly dawn, by which time we were ready to get our heads down. The locals, who had made alcoholic drink out of apples and pears, or anything else they could get their hands on, were serving it out of glass carboys, large round bottles. I remember a Dr Stramrood telling everyone that what he had made was the finest.

One funny incident that happened while we were there concerned Captain Millar's batman 'Robbo', who was also our cook. It could have had disastrous results but, fortunately, there was no real harm done. 'Robbo' had built a field-oven. This was done by digging a trench and laying a grid over it. At one end of the trench stood a jerry can half full of petrol with a hole just above the level of the petrol in it. The fumes coming out under pressure were lit like a blow torch and would heat up anything placed on the grid above. A dodgy practice at any time.

I suddenly noticed that the jerry can was beginning to expand and shouted a warning to 'Robbo'. 'Get away quick, it looks like it's about to blow!' Robbo's answer was a nonchalant, 'Naw, that's alright', as he pulled on a pair of gloves, casually sauntered over and picked up the bulging can – just as it exploded! It went off with a loud bang and flames shot out. Luckily, there was a blanket nearby which I grabbed and rushed over to smother him with. Fearing the worst, I removed the blanket, and, lo and behold, the only damage to Robbo was a pair of singed eyebrows! He had a big grin on his face from ear to ear, he always did see the funny side of things. He was a lucky so-and-so.'

As the war continued the Germans were relying on their V-weapons as prime methods of counter-attack. The bombardment of Antwerp had revealed the limitations of the V1 and V2 as weapons of attack against military targets. When it ceased during the last week of March 1945, 5,622 V1s and 1,982 V2s had fallen in North-western Belgium and South-western Holland. Of these, only 242 had caused military damage or casualties. Of the 5,960 that landed within an eight-mile radius of the centre of Antwerp, only 302 fell inside the boundaries of the port. It was the civilian population of the town that had suffered the most. 3,470 civilians lost their lives compared to 682 Allied servicemen.

On the 27th March, the Germans fired their last V-weapons of the war at Britain. One of these rockets fell on London at 7 o'clock in the morning. Tragically, it killed 134 people in a block of flats at Vallance Road, Stepney, in the East End. Later that same day, at Orpington in Kent, another rocket fell, killing a local man. He was most probably the last civilian casualty of the war in Britain.

CHAPTER XXV

# Hitler Remains Defiant

*'It is written in the stars that the middle of April will be the turning point for us.'*
JOSEPH GOEBBELS, APRIL 13TH, 1945.

The autumn rains and winter snows that had held up the Allied advance in Italy were now over. A re-equipped and revitalized Allied army, which had spent much of the winter of 44/45 re-grouping and training, was preparing for a major new offensive. Field-Marshal Alexander, Supreme Allied Commander (Mediterranean), planned to trap and destroy the Germans south of the River Po in what he anticipated would be the last great battle of the Italian campaign. Alexander had lost the Canadian Corps to North-west Europe but he still had under his overall command Britons, Americans, Italians, New Zealanders, Poles, South Africans, Indians, Gurkhas, and even a Jewish brigade.

Before the ground troops made their move, air attacks prepared the way. First came 234 US medium bombers, which dropped 24,000 20-pound incendiary bombs. Next came 740 fighter-bombers of the US Tactical Air Force which swooped down on the German gun and mortar sites. These were followed by 825 heavy bombers which dropped 1,692 tons before the artillery opened up with 1,500 guns.

The advance of the Allied forces, when it came on the 9th April, was swift. As it pushed forward at a terrific rate, Phantom's 'H' Squadron, now part of No. 2 Regt, which had a patrol with nearly every division, was hard pressed to keep HQ up to date with the whereabouts of the forward troops, and the positions of the enemy forces as they retreated in huge numbers.

By the 17th the British V Corps had captured Argenta and two days later the US 5th Army broke out of the Appenine mountain area onto the Po plateau. On the 21st, when the people of Bologna woke up, they found themselves rid of the German garrison that had occupied their university city. In the

Post D-Day Invasion Monetary Notes issued by the Military.

Bunde, Germany, 1945/7. Back row 1st & 2nd left: Sgts Arthur 'Chippy' Wood & Len 'Joe' Owens.

Members of No. 3 GHQL Reg. Bunde, Germany, 1945/7.

Fraternizing with the locals at Bunde, 1945/7.

Phantom Sgts Mess, Bunde, 1945/47.

Phantom's Cecil Bramley in armoured radio patrol car, Bunde, 1947/9.

Phantom members posing at Lido, Bunde, 1945/7.

Phantom No. 3 GHQL Reg. Football Team, Bunde, 1945/7.

'A' Sqn Sports Day, 1945. Ron's patrol No. 12 won. Ron Eaton is seen collecting Cup.

Phantom patrol sent to Bremerhaven, Germany, to provide signals for the American Army, 1946.

Trooper Harry Binge's Record of Service, (note spelling mistake of surname).

Phantom's Ron Eaton and Harry Binge, 2002.

Pembroke Lodge, Richmond Park as it is today.

Richmond Hill Hotel, Phantom's Wartime HQ.

Phantom Memorial Garden. Opened at the National Memorial Arboretum at Alrewas, Staffordshire, on the 14th June, 2003, with a dedication service to those who lost their lives on Operation Loyton (France, 1944). This garden was made possible by Sgt Len Owens and the late Capt. Peter Johnsen (Phantom surviviors of Loyton) and the Allied Special Forces Association, Hereford.

Officers' reunion at Pembroke Lodge, Richmond Park, 2003. *l to r:* I R Mackrill; M B Ramage; D G R Oldham; C J Skinner; T H White; J H Randall; P M Luttman-Johnson; D Hearsum *(guest)*; P Gimpel; Col D T W Gibson, MBE; Col R S D Maunsell; *(behind)* A W Laurie; Col J P Fane, MC; A R M Sedgwick. *(Photo Daniel Hearsum)*

early hours of the morning, as advance units of the Polish II Corps neared the city from the east, the Germans left. As the Poles hoisted their flag on the town hall, American tanks arrived from the north. They were soon joined by Italian troops now fighting with the Eighth Army.

Within four days the towns of Mantua, Verona and Parma had all fallen to US forces. The Italian Committee for National Liberation ordered a general uprising through the areas still under German control and, on the 25th, the Italian partisan Brigade liberated Milan and Turin. Columns of German soldiers were seen everywhere as they retreated northwards towards Austria.

On the 28th April, 1945, the 5th Army in Italy captured Venice. This signalled the end of the fighting in that country for the following day the German surrender was offered. At midday on the 2nd May, after Field-Marshal Alexander had accepted the surrender, more than one million men from twenty-two German divisions and six Italian Fascist divisions, in Italy and Austria, lay down their arms. A vast area of former Axis territory was now in Allied hands. It had taken twenty long months for them to fight their way up the Italian peninsula.

Back in Germany, with the Allied armies across the Rhine in force, Eisenhower ordered a general advance.

General Hodges' 1st US Army and General Patton's 3rd Army were to drive east to isolate the Bavarian mountains. In the north, General Crerar's 1st Canadian Army was to clear the Dutch coast while General Dempsey's 2nd British Army was to advance eastwards with General Simpson's 9th US Army. As March became April this great force moved forwards, encircling *Feldmarschall* Walther Model's Army Group B on the Ruhr by the 3rd.

Hitler, to save face, insisted that Model had intentionally consolidated his army in the 'fortified area of the Ruhr'.

The task of caving in this huge pocket of German resistance fell to General Bradley. Prisoners were being taken at a rate of between 15,000 and 20,000 a day as the Americans pressed in. A counter-attack by *General* Karl Student had to be cancelled as his tanks ran out of fuel. It took the Americans only three weeks to clear the Ruhr of Model's army. 325,000 prisoners were herded away to join the rest of the two million captured in the West since D-Day. Twenty-nine generals were amongst those taken on the Ruhr, but Model was not one of them. In despair, he committed suicide in a wood near Duisberg.

In the West an organized German front no longer existed, and on the evening of the 11th April the Americans reached the Elbe near Magdeburg in the very heart of Germany. There had been no stopping the Allied forces as they rushed towards Bremen, Hamburg and Hanover. White flags greeted them as they raced across the German plain through a collapsing country.

On the 12th April shocking news reached the American forces all around the world. Their president, Franklin Delano Roosevelt, was dead. The only American president to be elected four times, had died suddenly at the age of 63 at his home in Warm Springs, Georgia. Although his health had not been good for some months, his death came as a complete surprise. Battle-hardened soldiers, sailors and airmen wept when they heard the news. That same evening, Harry S Truman, the vice-president, was sworn in as the 33rd President of the United States of America at the White House in Washington.

The report of Roosevelt's death was greeted with joy by Germany's Minister for Propaganda, Josef Goebbels, a believer in astrology, who called for champagne as he rung Hitler: 'My *Fuhrer*, I congratulate you! Roosevelt is dead. It is written in the stars that the second half of April will be the turning-point for us. This is Friday 13th April. It is the turning-point.'

Their rejoicing was short-lived. Reports from the front showed that Roosevelt's death had not upset the Allies' performance. In fact, it had quite the opposite effect as the Americans fought on, determined to fulfil their president's hopes for victory and peace.

The 6th April had seen the Russians break through into the suburbs of the Austrian capital, Vienna. A week later this magnificent cathedral city was liberated by Marshal Tolbukhin, seven years after the *Wehrmacht* had marched into it. Austria, because its people had helped the Red Army fight the Germans, would not be treated as a conquered nation.

After the war, Austria would be controlled by the four conquering nations of Great Britain, America, France and Russia for several years before being granted independent statehood.

It was during this time of intense activity that Phantom was to be involved with the RAF and reconnaissance from the air. Flt Lieut Bentley, 264 Mosquito Squadron, recalls missions he flew accompanied by British and Dutch Army officers. One was with Captain Maurice Macmillan, 'B' Squadron Phantom, who was transmitting to Phantom patrols on the ground.

'There were three Dutch officers, Jaap Ludolph, Leo Fleskins and Hilda Bergsma. We were to spend some time with them on the ground and they were good company. But it was important that we knew little of what they were doing in case we were shot down and captured. On their uniform they wore a cloth badge with three witches.

I think our guns were still in the Mosquito but we had no ammunition. It was thought rather desirable that the aircraft were as light as possible in case we had to escape from any of their fighters, but in fact I never saw one, because they weren't coming up at this stage of the war, but it was good to know that you could go a bit faster. We used to manage nearly 300 knots. I was flying these tasks from 18th March to 14th April. We flew most days – it wasn't particularly hard work. Once we got over the target area the officer would only need fifteen minutes or so and I'd just circle around. I never felt vulnerable because we were jolly high at about 20,000-25,000 ft.

I did one night flight with Captain Macmillan so there must have been some British involvement. He was trasmitting as well, doing the same job as them. I flew Hilda Bergsma only once. She was older than us, about twenty-eight and rather nice looking. She just did her job and we came straight back. She flew more often with Flt Lieut Moss or Flt Lieut Brooke. It was an interesting month, one of the best bits of the war really. One was on one's own and it was quite fun. However, it was only after the war that we saw and realised the terrible suffering of the Dutch under the Germans.'

From about the middle of March until the middle of April things were very busy for the members of Harry's Phantom patrol. They were now regularly crossing the Rhine, sometimes back and forth two or three times a week. One day into Holland, the next into Germany, then back into Holland again. Always on the move, keeping up with the most forward division of the Canadian 2nd Corps that they were assigned to. Sometimes they were only a hundred yards from where the action was taking place! They watched the tanks go forward, all the while listening in as tank commanders passed a constant stream of messages between each other. Gathering all this information, which was coming in thick and fast, was one of the hardest tasks that the Phantom radio operators had to perform. All the years of training were paying off. Sometimes four or five operators were listening in at the same time. What one missed the other picked up. It was Captain Millar's task to sort out these messages and decide what was priority. This he would de-code and relay to Squadron HQ. This information would give the battle commanders an up-to-the-minute picture of what was happening at the front line, and form the basis of laying down the bomb-line for the Allied Air Force.

The tanks were followed closely by the infantry as they sought out the pockets of stiff German resistance, mainly the crack *SS* units who never knew when to give up. Some of these were members of the Hitler Youth, young boys of only fifteen years of age and less.

During this period of high activity, No. 23 'J' patrol was moved back from the front to regroup and re-supply. Harry remembers how they managed to grab a couple of days rest: 'We had been out on continuous patrol for what seemed like an age. Messages had been coming in thick and fast as the Canadians worked in this sector, clearing it of the enemy. We had been working non-stop, getting very little sleep or rest, so when we were told that we were being pulled back for a couple of days, we were very relieved. We managed to get a night's sleep in a cellar of a large house in Bedberg, Germany. We all felt that the war would soon be over anyway and that we would all be going home. The following day we set up camp about three or four miles back from the front and were just lying about when Captain Millar emerged from his tent with instructions for Ron Eagle, one of our operators who doubled as a motorcycle despatch rider, to take a water can and find some fresh water. We were running a bit low. Strangely, I found myself offering to go along with him for the ride. It's funny isn't it, I had really been looking forward to relaxing, doing nothing for a while, but after all the activity of the past weeks, I was finding it difficult to unwind.

I jumped on the back of Ron's bike and, with the can in the pannier on the back, we set off in search of a farm. We were heading west as we knew that the Canadians had cleared that area of any Germans. We had only gone about two miles when we found a deserted farm. We quickly found the well in the yard at the rear of the house. The well, luckily, had a cover on it and lifting this we peered down into the darkness to make sure that there had been nothing thrown down it, such as a dead animal. Seeing nothing, we dropped the bucket and pulled it up again. It was full of clear, fresh, ice-cold water. We hastily filled our can and started back to camp. We had only gone a few yards when I shouted to Ron, 'What's that over there to the right?' He stopped the bike and we both stared in amazement, for no more than 100 yards away was this bloody great Tiger tank, heading straight towards us. He must have spotted us, for we saw the turret slowly turn around and point its massive long gun-barrel in our direction. 'Crikey. It looks like he's going to have a pop at us,' Ron yelled, as he opened up the throttle, threw the bike around and roared up the lane away from the tank, nearly throwing me off. Just as he did so there was a flash and a loud thump as the tank fired at us. The next thing we knew the barn, that we had seconds before been in front of, disappeared in a ball of flames and dust. There were bricks flying everywhere. We weren't going to hang about there. Ron turned the bike into some woods, out the other side and across a field, with me hanging on for all I was worth.

When we got back to the camp we were still shaking as we told our Captain what had happened. The Captain knew what damage a rogue German Tiger Tank roaming about out there could do if it got amongst us. He immediately got on to Phantom Squadron HQ to report it. They ordered us to stay put and to report any further sightings. About twenty minutes later we saw two RAF Typhoons fly over, just above tree-top height, in the direction of where we had seen it. I don't know whether they got it but, thankfully, we never saw it again. I think that was the nearest I ever came to copping it during the war.'

Meawhile *'Kite'* patrol, which had also been rested for a couple of days, was very soon back in action. From Captain Ling's diary we read:

'APRIL 2nd 1945. HOLLAND AGAIN. ZEDDAM. Crossed Rhine at Emmerich. Camped on high ground. Almost lost tents in gale.'

'APRIL 4th 1945. VEEN. Only two miles from front line here. Dutch people flocked to us with eggs to barter for soap, chocolate and cigarettes. Very busy.'

'APRIL 13TH 1945. GERMANY AGAIN. BORKEN, near MAPPEN. Dull site. Germany like a prison after Holland. Near river. Fishing. Patrol browned off. Tempers edgy.'

Harry continues his story: 'After a busy month, to-ing and fro-ing between the two countries, we found ourselves in Germany again. This must have been about the middle of April,

I suppose. We set up camp at a place named Borken. Not much happened for a while and we were all getting a bit fed up when things started to warm up again. We all cheered when we heard that Arnhem had been captured by the Canadians at last. It was seven months since we had first tried and lost so many men.'

No. 23 patrol was working with the 5th Canadian Armoured Division at that time and Harry's patrol officer, Captain Millar, wrote of the eventual fall of Arnhem in his log: 'The operation was to clear Arnhem and encircle and cut off remaining enemy west of the River Ijssel, by striking north-west to reach the Zuider Zee. The enemy was being attacked by two Canadian infantry divisions westwards across the river to the north of us.' His log contains a few messages about the 'famous battle of Otterloo, 17th April, when Divisional Headquarters and two companies of infantry repulsed an attack by one regiment of enemy infantry plus artillery, with another regiment in the offing. Luckily the enemy was of low morale. I didn't have much time for message writing as I was messing around in the bushes most of the time.'

Harry remembers this incident very well. 'We were so close to the fighting, near the front line, we had to find some heavy cover. We ended up in a thicket, and from there we were getting the messages from the tanks coming in thick and fast.'

Harry continues: 'By now, the German army was in total confusion and disarray. We all knew that they couldn't resist for much longer, and so did they. Well, most of them anyway. They were surrendering in droves, they knew that to resist any further was useless. Bedraggled and un-fed bands of men were walking into Allied camps carrying white flags of surrender. They had had enough. Like us, they just wanted to go home. But still there were the diehards, isolated pockets of fanatical Nazis who still thought that they were the 'master race' and would go on to win the war. Because of them we still had a lot of work to do. The Canadian detachment that our patrol was assigned to had the job of mopping up these pockets in our sector. I think we were with the Winnipeg Light Infantry Grenadiers at that time. Anyway, they and the other Canadians were a great set of men. When they had come over to Europe some of them were only eighteen-year-old lads, but now they were men. They had been more-or-less fighting non-stop since June 1944, and never knew when to give up. They only managed to grab a few days leave here and there, but never going home. At least we had managed to get back home to

England a couple of times.

One of our main duties at that time, apart from continually receiving and transmitting messages on the whereabouts of the enemy and setting down bomb lines, was to report the capture of German prisoners. Their numbers had to be collected and reported to HQ. It was Captain Millar's job to collate the information on the German officers, especially those of the most senior ranks. As part of our training, we had all been taught to recognize the enemy's insignia and badges and to what rank, units or regiments they belonged.

One day Captain Millar had been ordered to go to a holding camp to get this info and I was detailed to be his driver. We went out in the patrol's jeep and, when we reached this camp, we found a mass of bedraggled men, just milling about, amongst them were many high-ranking German officers, with a look of utter disbelief on their faces. Not so long ago, they actually thought that they were still going to win the war and now here was I, a mere private in the British Army, telling these officers what to do. Their rank didn't mean a thing. They were like all the rest now - just prisoners-of-war. After we had gathered all the information we required, we began to make our way back to base. We had only gone a short way when we passed some Canadian infantry coming out of the line. Some were wounded and making their way back to the Army field hospital at the rear. As we came round a bend in the road, we saw two soldiers on foot who were not too badly hurt but were having difficulty carrying their equipment. The Captain told me to stop and offer them a lift to the first-aid post that we had passed on the way here. They were only too pleased to accept and threw their rifles and kit in the back of the jeep before clambering in on top. The road was terrible, what with the mud and the potholes. It had been attacked by the RAF several times as the Germans had retreated down it, and there were bomb craters everywhere. And lots of wrecked vehicles all over the place. I was weaving in and out of all this mess when, suddenly, Millar, conscious that there was something wrong, turned round and saw that there was no-one sitting there. 'Crikey, Binge, they've gone!' he exclaimed. I hit the brakes and swung round. About two hundred yards back up the road we saw them hobbling towards us. They weren't very happy. They said that I had hit the edge of a bomb crater a bit sharp and they had been chucked off. They were more hurt now than when we had picked them up. We had done more damage to them than the Germans had! I promised I wouldn't let it happen again and they climbed back in. I drove very gently the rest of the way.

The funny thing about what happened is that Captain Millar just sat there and never said a word until we had dropped them off. And he was the officer. But when we left the first-aid post, he just burst out laughing and didn't stop until we got back to camp.

That night when I told the rest of the lads they all said, 'It could only happen to you, Bingey!"

Of all the receiving and transmitting radio sets used by Phantom, which included the no.9, no.11 and no.22 (Canadian) which were all very successful in their own right, none was to achieve such a high standard as the Golden Arrow. War Office records describe its role thus:

## THE GOLDEN ARROW

The use of the *Golden Arrow* Highpower Transmitter was one of the most successful departures from normal routine introduced into PHANTOM throughout the operations. After midnight each day sitreps were written by Regimental Headquarters giving the latest information available throughout the whole front.

These sitreps were encoded in a cipher breakable by every Phantom detachment and patrol and were broadcast twice on the 4 Kilowatt *'Golden Arrow'* Transmitter. Transmission started at 0400 hrs each morning. This system made it possible for every Corps to give an up to date briefing on the whole Allied front at 0800 hrs. Although this information was at first only of interest value, towards the end, when the whole front became active, the result of operations on one front had a direct bearing on the enemy reaction in another. Knowledge of what was going on throughout the whole front became an operational necessity. In some cases the Phantom officer was made responsible at the Corps commander's daily briefing for dealing with the situation of flanking formations.

CHAPTER XXVI

# Victory

*'Every man who served with Phantom rates it
as a high honour.'*

THE SOLDIER. 1946.

Swift and dramatic was the fall of Germany in the April and early May of 1945. The Fatherland was being attacked from all sides. The Russian Red Army was deep into Germany on the outskirts of Berlin to the east, and the British and Americans were rapidly overcoming the isolated German armies in the west.

Eisenhower and the Allied strategists deduced that, with the Russians on his doorstep, Hitler would call a surrender and negotiate a peace deal with the British, Americans and the French, rather than let the Soviet Army capture and control Berlin. They were wrong. Hitler would not surrender. As long as the Fuhrer was alive the fanatical forces within Germany, the Nazis, would fight for every foot of land with their lives.

The Allied armies, knowing that this most destructive and devastating conflict the world had ever seen must surely soon be over, raced forward with a determined spirit. German soldiers were surrendering in their thousands or simply laying down their arms and walking back home.

Vic Stump, of Phantom's No. 5 patrol 'A' Squadron, records:

> '7th April: Today 22nd Armoured Brigade made long advances to reach the River Weser in the Bucken and Hoya areas. Total PoWs now claimed by this division since crossing the Rhine is fifty-seven officers and 3,583 men. Today our Armoured cars in the Bassum area, encountered Hitler Youth aged eight to twelve armed with rifles. Yesterday I went out and 'acquired' a 4-cylinder Mercedes Benz saloon, as a replacement for our trailer.
>
> 10th April: The ancient capitals of Konigsberg and Hanover have fallen. Russians are in Vienna. General Patton within fifty miles of Czechoslovakia. In Italy the Eighth Army has started a new offensive. 53rd (W) Division has established a bridgehead over the Weser at Hoya and have reached Rethem.'

Stump's Captain, Denys Brook-Hart, remembers his patrol

accompanying the jeep of the General commanding the 82nd US Airborne Infantry Division, as they dashed towards the Baltic coast. As they crossed the north German plains, they could make out what looked like a low grey cloud on the horizon. As they got nearer, the cloud turned into a solid mass of thousands of German soldiers, intent on surrendering to the Americans or British rather than the Russians.

By a strange coincidence, amongst the Allied PoWs who were making their way westwards from the camps that had been overrun and liberated, Brook-Hart was surprised and elated to recognize some old army friends of his who had been captured at Calais in 1940.

Back in Berlin, Hitler had not made up his mind where to make his final stand. It had been thought that he would gather around him his most loyal diehards and retreat to his mountain-top fortress at *Berchtesgaden* in the heart of the Bavarian Alps, the homeland of the Nazi movement. By the 20th April, his fifty-sixth birthday, as a few of those still faithful to the cause attended to pay their respects, the *Fuhrer* had still not decided what to do. On this, the day that the Soviet artillery opened their bombardment of Berlin, Hitler called a conference in his '*Fuhrerbunker*', which was housed in the massive two storey air-raid shelter buried fifty feet below ground in the gardens of the Chancellery. Gathered around him for the last time were his Nazi henchmen. Should Germany be split in two by the approaching forces, he appointed *Admiral* Dönitz to assume responsibility in the north and Kesselring in the south, if he didn't take charge of the war from the south himself.

The following day, Hitler ordered an all-out attack on the Russians, and, on the 22nd, he proclaimed in a letter to the people of Berlin that was published in the newspaper *Der Panzerbar* on the 23rd:

GRAVE WARNING FROM THE FÜHRER. MARK WELL!

> Anyone who proposes or even approves measures detrimental to our power of resistance is a traitor! He is to be shot or hanged immediately! This applies even if such measures have allegedly been ordered on the instructions of *Reichsminister* Dr Goebbels, the *Gauleiter*, or even in the name of the *Führer*.
>
> Führer's Headquarters, 22/4/45<br>Signed: Adolf Hitler

Hitler had believed that while he was still alive he could save the Thousand Year *Reich* and its capital, but when he finally realised that the '*Battle for Berlin*' was about to be lost, he was determined to lead its final defence from his bunker and shoot himself at the last moment. Ranting and raving, he proclaimed that, since the Army, the *Luftwaffe*, the *SS* and the Party had betrayed him, he would not now go to the *Berchtesgaden*. His mistress, Eva Braun, who had joined him during the last week, was adamant that she should remain at his side to the end. On the night of the 28th/29th April, Hitler, still believing that the loss of the war was not his fault but that of his Generals' treachery, wrote his last will and testament and married Eva Braun in the map-room of the bunker, which was usually used to hold small conferences. That evening, he had reacted furiously when he received a Reuter report to the effect that *Reichführer* Heinrich Himmler, Commander of the *SS*, had been in touch with *Count* Bernadotte at the Swedish Consulate in Lubeck for the purpose of negotiating peace terms.

During the night of the 29th news reached Hitler that Benito Mussolini (*Il Duce*) and Clara Petacci had been caught by the partisans in Italy and shot on the shores of Lake *Como*. The bodies of the man who had ruled Italy for more than two decades and his mistress were now hanging in the Piazza Loretto in Milan.

This news sealed Hitler's fate. He resolved to commit suicide now and, determined that his body and that of his new wife should not be allowed to fall into the hands of the Russians and suffer the same fate as that of his former Axis partner, Hitler ordered that their remains should be burnt. During the afternoon of the 30th April, 1945, Hitler coolly bade farewell to his staff and retired to his suite with Eva. A short while later a single shot rang out. The *Fuhrer* was dead. By his side lay the body of Eva, she had swallowed poison. Earlier in the day he had ordered that his faithful Alsatian bitch, Blondi, be destroyed.

On the 1st May, the news of Hitler's death was broadcast, implying that he had died fighting to the last against *Bolshevism*, and announcing that the *Fuhrer* had appointed *Grossadmiral* Dönitz as his successor.

Many of the Nazi members, both men and women, in the bunkers round the Chancellery attempted a mass breakout, some successfully, but Dr Josef Goebbels did not join them. He shot his wife Magda and himself, after poisoning their six children who had been living with them in four rooms in the bunker. Goebbels and his wife had both written letters of farewell to Magda's son, Harald.

On the same day that Hitler's death was announced, General Chuikov, Commander of the Russian 8th Guards Tank Army, and a veteran of the defence of Stalingrad, was approached by four German officers carrying white flags, as he stood in the city of Berlin. *Generaloberst* Hans Krebs, the Chief of the German General Staff, was calling for a truce in the fighting in order to negotiate the surrender of the city. Krebs' conditions of surrender were not acceptable to the Russians and he returned to the Bunker and committed suicide. The first moves towards ending the war in Europe had been made and the following day, the 2nd May, *General* Karl Weidling, who had advocated capitulating earlier to save any further loss of life, surrendered unconditionally his garrison of seventy thousand troops. The *Battle of Berlin* was over.

As the Second World War in Europe came to its close, three very historic meetings hit the headlines.

The first was at Torgau, seventy-five miles south of Berlin on the River Elbe, on the afternoon of the 25th April, 1945, when patrols of the American 69th Division of the V Corps linked-up with elements of the Red Army's 58th Guards Division. Germany was now cut in two.

Phantom was present at this momentous meeting, and not to be outdone in the celebrations. Two patrols of 'L' Squadron, those of Captain Brent Hutton-Williams and Captain Peter Stileman were there, as was Corporal Ron Eaton, NCO with No. 12 patrol 'A' Squadron. Ron's patrol was now under the command of its third officer, Captain Meade, ex-Welsh Guards, who had taken over from Lt Probyn mid-March. Captain Meade was to be No. 12's patrol officer until the end of the war. Ron's patrol was now with an advanced unit of the American XVI US Corps.

Ron remembers: 'When we met up with the Russians at the Elbe, there was lots of celebrating. We got hold of an abandoned German Army staff car, a Mercedes Benz, and decided to make a bonfire out of it. We threw five cans of petrol into the back of it, but it didn't explode at first. The seams on the cans just melted and jets of fire came out. Then, all of a sudden, up it went. All very spectacular. There was great camaraderie between us and the Russians at that time.'

This is how official Phantom papers recorded its role in this historic event:

'About April 23rd a Phantom patrol was sent forward of V US Corps in order to report when contact was made with the Russian forces. For two days many reports from civilians and other unofficial sources regarding the position of the Russians were sent back. These reports, though unconfirmed, made it possible to plot fairly accurately the position of the Russian forward troops.

At 1815 hrs this patrol, which was then with the 2nd US Inf Div reported:- '69 Div: 273 Regt made contact with Russians early this afternoon.'

The patrol officer immediately moved to 273 Regt CP and crossed the gap between the US and Russian forces where he opened wireless communication and reported all details that were available to him.

After this meeting the situation in the South became fluid. Patrol officers, though moving two or three times a day, were able to send back reports well in advance of normal communications. Reports continued to come in from the US sector until each Corps had reached its stop line. Reports were then reduced to details of enemy units surrendering.

PHANTOM operations with the US Army ceased at 1400 hrs May 7th, 1945.'

The following is the conclusion of Phantom's work with the US Armies, although some Phantom patrols with Corps HQs stayed a few days longer, but their operational duties were finished. 1st US Army HQ packed up on 7th May and the senior officers left at once for the USA to assist in the plans for the invasion of Japan.

## CONCLUSION

1. In the US Army with one Phantom patrol at Corps HQ as much can be achieved as by having one with Division. Though it is not the case in the British Army, in the US Army one of the chief functions of Div HQ is to report to Corps immediately information becomes available. It was therefore found that a Corps patrol often had information at the same time as it was available to the Div patrol. Under special circumstances, however, where the speed of advance made communication forward of Corps difficult, or during assault landings or airborne operations, it is necessary to have Phantom with the forward echelons. Under these conditions, while the information is being transmitted to the rear, it can at the same time be made available to Corps.

2. The Air Forces working with the Armies or Army Group

should have some means of obtaining Phantom information without delay. During operations in France and Germany, the G-3 Air Section at 9th Air Force was continuously using Phantom information for the position of forward troops.

3. Without the support of the staff at the formation where the Phantom patrol is working, the patrol officer can achieve nothing. The policy of leaving the same officer at headquarters is essential.

4. Lateral liaison between Corps is an important secondary role. The Corps patrol officer can do as much for the Corps as they can do for him.

5. At Army Group level the individual messages from divisions of a flanking Army Group should be withheld by the Phantom Detachment and consolidated into Periodical Sitreps except where the information immediately affects its own formation.'

When news of the historic meeting of the US Army and the Russian Red Army at the River Elbe reached New York, crowds danced and sang in Times Square, and in Moscow 324 guns fired a salute in celebration.

The second significant meeting was at Wismar, Northern Germany. Churchill and Eisenhower were both anxious that Montgomery's army should reach this German town on the Baltic before the Russians, to prevent them from getting into Schleswig-Holstein and occupying Denmark. This the Allies did. The 11th Armoured Division of the British VIII Corps arrived at Wismar and Lubeck on the 2nd May, six hours before the Russians, and sealed off the Danish peninsula. The third notable meeting was at the Brenner Pass on the Austrian/Italian border on the 4th May, when a column of the American 7th Army, advancing southwards in Austria, pushed through the Brenner Pass to make contact with the American Fifth Army, advancing northwards in Italy. The war in Italy and Austria was already over when this meeting took place, for Field-Marshal Sir Harold Alexander had accepted the German surrender two days earlier. At Caserta, on the 29th April, *SS General* Karl Wolff, representing *General* von Vietinghoff, Commander-in-Chief, South West, had signed an armistice and fighting ceased on the 2nd May.

Phantom No. 23 patrol was assigned to the 5th Canadian Armoured Division for some weeks and, on the 4th May, one of the Canadian's Intelligence Officers reported: 'The German Army is dying, the slow death of a thousand pockets. Adolf is '*kaput*' and Benito '*finito*'. Berlin, Hamburg and Munich have fallen, the escape route to Denmark has been closed. The junction of the Western Allies and the Russians on the Elbe and on the Baltic have been established, two German armies have surrendered unconditionally in Italy and two have been smashed against the Austrian Alps. During the first twenty-six days of April 1,300,000 prisoners were taken including over one hundred Generals – the scene is one of rout and round up.'

On the 4th May, in a tent at Montgomery's Tactical HQ on Luneberg Heath, south of Hamburg, *Admiral* von Friedeburg and other representatives of the German High Command signed an armistice providing for the surrender of all the remaining German forces in Holland, North-west Germany, Denmark and, surprisingly, Dunkirk. This port, scene of the great British evacuation in May 1940, had remained in the hands of the Germans as the rest of France was overrun, as had the ports of St Nazaire, Lorient and La Rochelle on the Atlantic coast.

Phantom's Captain, the Honourable Michael Astor was at Luneburg Heath when the surrender was signed. He had been posted there some weeks earlier. From his autobiography '*Tribal Feeling*' (John Murray) we quote:

'My next posting was to Field-Marshal Montgomery's Tactical Headquarters where, for a change, I was on the receiving end of the information which was being sent by the Phantom patrols at all hours of the day. Almost immediately after I had reported to this small headquarters, which controlled the plans and decisions of two armies, the Field-Marshal summoned me to his caravan for a briefing. He then proceeded, with the help of a large map, to explain just how he had conducted the operation of his armies since his leading troops had landed in Normandy on D-Day. After this he told me to go away and read all his operation orders and his various instructions to his staff still stationed in Brussels. Some of these were formal documents, some were highly secret, others were engagingly colloquial, showing his use of a trite form of slang, revealing some of his candid and unpublishable opinions. Immediately I was made to feel in a position of trust.'

Captain Astor remembers the surrender thus: 'My last view of 21st Army Headquarters was of the surrender of the German Army. Its delegates arrived, one and two at a time, and were then followed by some very senior German officers. There was nothing more military than a German general and the British junior staff officers of my age and rank seemed strangely affected by their presence. It was now the end of the war.'

Captain Michael Millar's Phantom patrol had moved up from Enschede in Holland, where rumours of an imminent surrender were breaking, to Bad Zwischenahn, near Oldenburg in Germany. Alongside them went Captain Peter Ling's *'Kite'* patrol. These two patrols had worked with the Canadians since D-Day, often together.

Captain Ling records in his diary:

'MAY 6TH 1945. BAD ZWISCHENAHN. Not far from Oldenburg where Canadian Army have taken over all the best theatres and cinemas. Near large lake. Swimming and boating. Tension high. Surrender expected.'

On the 7th May, Harry Binge, on duty at his radio transmitter, heard the jubilant news coming through his headphones that the war was finally over and that all hostilities would cease as from midnight May 8th. 'I always considered myself lucky that I was the operator on duty when the message came through,' Harry proudly remembers. 'This communication was then passed on to the Canadians who we were with. At last the war was over. I was also the one who took the message, when we were at Enschede a few days earlier, announcing that the Germans had surrendered their remaining forces in Holland.'

Winston Churchill, the British Prime Minister, broadcast a victory message to millions of listeners in Great Britain and the British Empire on Tuesday, May 8th, 1945. He begun his speech with the words:

'Yesterday morning at 2.41 am at Headquarters, *General* Jodl, the representative of the German High Command, and of *Grossadmiral* Dönitz, the designated head of the German State, signed the pact of unconditional surrender of all German land, sea and air forces in Europe to the Allied Expeditionary Force, and simultaneously to the Russian High Command.'

The Prime Minister continued: 'Hostilities will end officially at one minute after midnight tonight (Tuesday), but in the interests of saving lives the 'Cease Fire' began yesterday to be sounded all along the front, and our dear Channel Islands are also to be freed today.'

The Channel Islands, the only part of the British Isles to fall into German hands, had suffered almost five years of enemy occupation when they were finally set free on the 9th May. The document of capitulation had been signed in the early hours of the morning and the islanders rejoiced as a body of Royal Artillerymen went ashore at St Peter Port on Guernsey to hoist the Union Jack.

While most of the Phantom patrols were now stood down to await further orders, Captain Millar's No. 23 patrol was ordered back to Enschede, in Holland, headquarters of 2nd Canadian Corps. Before doing so they managed a few days leave in Brussels and Nijmegan where they were able to soak up the euphoric atmosphere that victory had created. The Belgians and Dutch had suffered so much under German rule that their new found freedom was being wildly celebrated throughout their countries.

Phantom's Captain Peter Ling, officer of *'Kite'*, speaks for both patrols when he ends his diary with the entry:

'During our stay with Corps a fine relationship grew up between the Canadian boys and the fifteen British Phantoms, in spite of the usual title - THOSE BLOODY LIMEYS.'

At Enschede, *'Kite'* patrol and Harry's 'J' patrol broke up, before reassembling at 'B' Squadron HQ at Apeldoorn, still in Holland. Their next task was of a civilian nature as they moved near Hamburg to work with the British Red Cross and its German counterparts, organizing the massive amounts of food and medical supplies that were now needed to feed and help the starving population of this devastated city. Harry's knowledge of the German language, although not fluent, was to prove invaluable in co-operating with the civilian relief agencies in the distribution of the aid.

Harry relates, 'Our patrol was billeted in the village of Zeven, between Hamburg and Bremen. We took over a hotel which was run by a woman and her helper and we gave them our rations which they cooked for us. The woman's son had been a soldier in the German army and had been killed. Nearby was a hospital for both German and British military who had lost limbs during the fighting. We were not supposed to fraternize with the locals, but we did. They were just as glad as we were that the war was over, and were very grateful for the work we were doing. It's funny, isn't it, that the radio and wireless equipment that we had so recently been using to fight the war was now being used to help our former enemy.'

While Harry remained in Germany, Ron's Phantom patrol was one of four which went up into Denmark, to use its experience in communications in the service of the SHAEF Mission to that country.

'After the surrender,' Ron tells us, 'we went up into Denmark and worked for about three weeks with some relief organization, providing the communications. We had a rather nice time there.

The people were very friendly and we had lots of invitations to their homes.

The Germans called Denmark the 'cream cake country', and they weren't wrong there. The bakeries were bulging with them, large and small. From Denmark we went back to Bad Oeynhausen, just south of Minden in Germany, where the regiment was fast running down. We had a short stay there before we returned home once more to Phantom HQ in Richmond, taking our vehicles with us.

At Richmond there was some demobilization, the older people getting preference over us younger people. When we joined the regiment Harry was twenty-six and I was only twenty, so I got the short end of the stick there. We were being reorganized into another unit, No. 3 GHQ Liaison Regiment, to go to the Far East and I was given twenty-eight days embarkation leave. During that time the Americans dropped the Atom bomb, which ended the war with Japan and changed my life and the lives of millions of others. When I returned from leave, there was no more talk of going to the Far East and I was once more sent back to Germany. Here I languished for a couple of months before I was demobbed from Germany. I had been visualising another couple of years overseas and was beginning to feel like a professional soldier, but I was glad the war was over. Harry and I had done our bit and we picked up our lives back at the upholstery firm of Greaves and Thomas in East London.'

Another member of 'A' Squadron, whose patrol was sent to Scandinavia when the war was finally over, was radio operator H G Allen. He had originally trained as a wireless operator with the Royal Armoured Corps in 1942 and was later seconded to Phantom. In June 1945, he found himself in Norway, helping American soldiers with a very important task. Here he explains his role.

'When Germany was on the brink of defeat in Europe early in 1945 allied armed forces were flown from Scotland at night to retake Southern Norway. It was a disaster. Several of our airplanes filled with troops of all ranks were lost simply because they flew straight into mountain sides. An inquiry uncovered a most disturbing and unusual fact, the maps of Norway used for flight navigation were not in perfect alignment with the rest of Europe. The error, although small, was sufficient to mislead airforce navigators flying in the dark to steer straight at mountains instead of flying between them, causing the deaths of several hundreds of men.

In June 1945 my Phantom unit was flown to Stavanger and thence travelled by road to a village named Amli north of Christiansand in Southern Norway. There, together with soldiers of an American army survey unit, we set up survey and wireless equipment on top of a mountain. From 10pm to 2am nightly for about six weeks we watched flares, clouds permitting, dropped from aircraft flying up and down over the Skagerrak between Norway and Denmark. Similar units in Sweden, Denmark and Scotland listened and watched, each taking a bearing on a flare at an exact moment of time. The information recorded was then used to realign the maps of Scandinavia with Britain and rectify the errors that had caused the invasion disaster.

1945 was a memorable summer; we walked for miles through silent forests and ate wild strawberries, humped heavy batteries and generators up mountain tracks and sometimes lay on hot rocks in the middle of a small river and slid into the ice cold mountain waters when the heat became unbearable.'

Early on the morning of the 6th August, 1945, the American B-25 Liberator bomber, the *Enola Gay,* dropped an 'Atom bomb' on the Japanese city of Hiroshima, wiping the city centre from the face of the earth and with it eighty thousand people.

As early as June 20th, American Intelligence had learnt that the Japanese Government wanted to negotiate peace with the United States but that it was not prepared to accept unconditional surrender. This knowledge had made the Americans all the more determined to bring Japan to its knees.

A second atom bomb was dropped on the 9th August, this time on the city of Nagasaki, creating similar devastation to that of Hiroshima, and immediately killing forty thousand. This action was confounded by the announcement from Moscow the previous day that Stalin had declared war on Japan.

Six days after the second bomb was dropped, the 15th August, 1945, Japan surrendered unconditionally to the Allies. The Second World War was over.

This conflict had been the most devastating in the history of the world. Between September 1939 and August 1945 a total of fifty-eight million people, both military and civilian, perished. A figure comparable to that of the whole population of Great Britain today, the year 2003.

The General Headquarters Liaison Regiment, Phantom, originally founded as the General Headquarters Reconnaissance Unit in 1939, never numbered more than fifteen hundred officers and men up to the time of its disbandment at the end of

1945. By VE Day the GHQ Liaison Regiment in North-western Europe totalled about 105 officers and 800 men.

The article, 'P stands for Phantom', published in the British Army's paper 'The Soldier' on the 8th June, 1946, best sums up Phantom's role in World War Two:

'As 'the eyes and ears of the British Army', Phantom secured the ever growing confidence of the Americans and French commanders. Cherished possession of the regiment today is a stack of telegrams and congratulatory messages from men like General Crerar, Canadian Army, and Generals Patton and Bradley. When the war ended the Americans were, in fact, in the process of forming their own Phantom regiment.'

General Bradley's message read: 'The Phantom patrols provided a special means for procurement and transmission of tactical and intelligence information from Corps to Army Groups and furnished most timely and accurate knowledge of the front line tactical situation that would not have been available through the normal channels of communications. Working frequently under great stress and for excessive periods of duty, improvising effectively at times to cover deficiencies of equipment and men, and co-operating closely with the staffs to which they were assigned, these officers and men conducted themselves with great credit to their service.'

The article continued: 'The Germans, aware of the existence of Phantom, tried unsuccessfully to break down the code system. It is on record that the enemy could never make head nor tail out of anything which, allegedly, had been intercepted from Phantom. How useful it would have been to the enemy if he could have made sense out of the highly complex bulletins which were collected and transmitted daily to Allied Commanders on the powerful transmitting set nick-named '*Golden Arrow*'! This set was the only type of its kind in Europe. The job of marking Field-Marshal Montgomery's personal map at Tactical HQ was entrusted to a Phantom officer, Captain A S Davies, assisted by Sergeant Nicholson.

Every man who has served with Phantom rates it as a high honour to have been associated with the outfit that was something of a mystery to the outside world. They alone shared the knowledge - hitherto unpublished - that Field-Marshal Montgomery moved his HQ twenty-eight times during the European campaign. The regiment, too, must be classed as unique in that, according to 32-year-old Sergeant Major Hopper, who grew up with Phantom, no man has yet been put on a charge.'

In his excellent book '*Das Reich*', published by Pan Books in 2000, Max Hastings wrote:

'An impeccably-bred Englishman who fought with distinction in Europe said afterwards: 'The great thing about the 1939-45 war was that everybody did what they liked.' By this he really meant that a few thousand Englishmen with access to the bars of the great St James's clubs proved able to organize their own military destinies – sometimes even their own campaigns – in a manner impossible in any war before or since. The Special Air Service was among the most celebrated of the array of 'private armies' that emerged during the war. Almost all were conceived and partly officered by those with privileged access to high places. A posting to Phantom or the commandos was passionately coveted by a dashing young man. If the risks were greater than those of regimental soldiering, so were the fun and the company and the opportunity for extraordinary adventures.'

Lieutenant Robert Mark, who had been ordered to take over another Phantom patrol in the last weeks of the war, remembers his final days with Phantom:

'I was ordered to take over a patrol of XII US Corps, which was part of Patton's 3rd Army and was on its way across north Bavaria to the Czech frontier. Memory gets a little dim, but I caught up with them, I think, at a town called Viechtach and remained with them until we reached the Czech frontier facing a town called As. We were prevented from crossing the frontier by the Yalta agreement but were later allowed by Stalin to make a limited advance well short of Prague.'

Lieutenant Mark was eventually summoned back to 21st Army Group, imagining that his military days were over, but no such luck. Tom Reddaway, the Adjutant of Phantom, knowing that Mark was a former policeman, asked him if he was prepared to volunteer for service with military government.

'My reply was an unprintable version of 'Not on your nelly'. I should have known better. Within twenty-four hours I was presented with an order promoting me to Staff Captain and posting me to military government. This meant the compulsory freezing of my entitlement to demobilization. It was a bitter pill.'

From June 1945 until January 1947, Robert Mark remained with the Control Commission at Bad Oeynhausen, during which time he was promoted to major. On demobilization he returned home to England where he resumed his police career. He rose through the ranks to become Commissioner of the Metropolitan

Police, being knighted in 1977.

The Astor brothers, Michael and Jakie, were both to enter politics after the war, serving as Conservative Members of Parliament.

Harry Binge and Ron Eaton even now remember their days with Phantom with pride and affection. Harry, now in his nintieth year, still lives in London's East End, while Ron sought a new life in America, emigrating with his wife and family to Los Angeles, California. Even today Harry and Ron remain great friends.

Captain Charles McDevitt was promoted to Major and was Phantom's last Commanding Officer, having succeeded Major Morgan, when as No. 3 GHQ Liaison Regiment they were stationed at Bunde. Jock McDevitt stayed on in the army as his words in a Phantom News Letter dated July 1949 show: 'I've had a nice round trip so far. Phantom finished up in Germany in June 1948 and I had July in the UK, sailing for Port Said then returned via Malta to Tripoli, where I took over this Squadron on September 2nd. Finally, 2 AGRA moved to Egypt in October and Mrs McDevitt flew out to join me in December. This job I have is quite interesting – running communications for 3 Regiments of RA – but, of course, it isn't like Phantom and we often dream of our adventures in Deutschland with 'P'.'

Tam Williams and David Niven both continued with their acting careers, but Tam's career was to blossom more as a playwright, with several notable stage successes.

David Niven returned to California to resume his film career. At his home in Beverly Hills, Hollywood, a terrible tragedy occurred. His wife, Primmie, who he had married in 1940, fell down some stairs in their new home and as a result of this accident she died, aged only twenty-five.

A few weeks later David Niven was presented with a boxer puppy by fellow film-stars Rex Harrison and Lili Palmer to help keep him company. In fond remembrance of his days with the regiment, he named her *'PHANTOM'*.

CHAPTER XXVII

# Phantom Officers Remember

PHANTOM SIGNALS 1940-1941.
*by Colonel (Rtd) David T W Gibson. MBE.*

I was commissioned into the Royal Signals in August 1937, and did the twenty month Qualifying Course after RMA Woolwich, which gave us all a very good grounding. In keeping with the attitude to engineering in Britain, we were cautioned against being too 'technical' in outlook, as this was likely to prejudice our careers as regular officers. Despite this, it roused our interest in how things worked.

I commanded an Independant Artillery Section during 1939; we served 1st Medium Regiment, with 6-inch howitzers, still on wooden wheels, short range, but most efficiently served by the very professional Gunners. As OCs of Signal Sections we had remarkable freedom of experiment, and we set up unofficial radio nets between our Signal Sections over ranges up to several hundred miles, using No.1 and No. 11 sets, low power HF, a watt or so, that gave all concerned invaluable experience.

We went to France with the BEF early in September 1939 to endure the uncomfortable monotony of the 8 month 'phoney' war. Radio silence was imposed most of the time because German intercept was feared, so training was stultified. I realised the need for really accurate 'netting' if radio links were to work in war, so I practised carrying a small frequency meter round with me to tune sets by visiting them one by one.

The Germans attacked, and we rumbled into Belgium up to the small river Dyle, beyond Brussels. British artillery was most effective during the retreat to Dunkirk, despite our old weapons, and we were in action until we had to abandon our guns. Most of the time we managed to lay field cable to link up the regiment, but, by visiting as many detachments as possible with the frequency meter, we did achieve radio links when needed.

I had been posted to 'GHQ Liaison Regiment' (Phantom) just before the German attack, so in July 1940, a month after getting back to England, I reported to the redoubtable 'Hoppy' (Lt Col Hopkinson) in the Richmond Hill Hotel, and took over the Signal Section, then about fifty men. After three years as a Second Lieutenant, I became a Lieutenant in August 1940, and soon afterwards the post was upgraded to Captain to match the steadily growing 'Section'.

It was obvious that if Phantom was to survive in the rather fluid situation after Dunkirk, it must use radio communication more efficiently than normal Army units. At that time, 'getting through' over any distance was a hit or miss affair that sometimes took hours, or even failed altogether. There were three main reasons for this. First, the vehicle sets available (No. 11 and No. 9) could not be precisely tuned to allotted frequency, so operators had to search for the expected signal. Second, due to fear of being intercepted, control stations only sent out short 'tuning calls', before searching, hopefully, for a relatively long time for a reply while confidence leaked away. Third, there was too often little understanding of how low power HF radio waves travelled, so that planning was weak.

If confidence was not to leak away, accurate timing was essential. The pocket watches supplied were rarely accurate. Our rugged Signals Storeman, Cpl Landells, seemed to have friends in all the useful supply depots, and the ability to use the same indent more than once, so we soon acquired enough watches to be able to rate them carefully and give accurate ones to patrols. I decided that a thirty second tuning call was justified to guarantee first time detection by outstations. Another point was the rather cumbersome British procedure, at that time, that also gave away which was the control station. I found out about the German 'link-sign' procedure, and reduced it to a single letter callsign, because the scale of the unit (six squadrons) was small enough. We used only hand speed morse, so this speeded up messages as well as concealing the control station. At that time only armoured units that 'netted' before moving off were getting through as reliably.

The next problem was to discover, more precisely, how the H.F. radiowaves travelled between low power sets separated by distances from five to 100 miles. At that time there was remarkably little understanding among the 'experts'. Amateur radio fans and long range commercial link planners knew a lot about 'skywaves' sent over several thousand miles, and broadcast engineers, using huge power, used 'groundwaves' on relatively low frequencies up to a few hundred miles.

I visited experts at the Dollis Hill (Post Office) research station who were busy with slide rules planning links to islands in the Pacific, and university researchers who explained their radiosounds. As the picture cleared, the reason for mysterious experiences, like those of some units in East Anglia who had marked certain woods on their maps 'unusable for radio', became clear. The reason was that the low power vehicle sets had a far shorter groundwave range than anyone suspected, perhaps a mile. Operational ranges were from two to 100 or more miles, and were sometimes being obtained, but were by good luck on skywaves. These, of course, depended on reflection from the ionosphere, which weakens during the night.

Using data I got from the experts, my admirable Royal Signals operators lay in muddy meadows by the Thames for several weary watches, day and night, using different aerials to test these ideas. The 9 set had a frequency range of 2 to 5-MHz, with a power up to 10-watts; the 11 set 4.2 to 7.5-MHz. The noisy cumbersome 9 set was used from RHQ in St James' Park to Squadrons; the 11 set, power about a watt, was used out to patrols in cramped Daimler scout cars.

Both sets had been designed during a sunspot maximum period, so that ranges obtained, especially in the evening, had been deceptively great. By 1940 we were in a sunspot minimum phase, so that the 11 set in particular could only hope to get the skywave ranges we needed from about 8 or 9 in the morning to about seven in the evening on the lowest frequency on the 11 set, and rather longer on the none.

I got copies of the overall frequency allotment for UK by friendly liaison in War Office, and was able to make my own Phantom frequency allocation between the official allotments.

Hoppy fully supported me in my work, although sometimes arguments were needed to convince him. eg 'David, operators haven't got psychology.' Arguments that were tactfully smoothed by Tony Warre, Hugh Kindersley and, the wise and always understanding adjutant, Tom Reddaway.

Hoppy arranged for me to visit Gambier Parry's exotic establishment in a country mansion, where mysterious agents got their low power radios, and I learnt more about throwing wire aerials into bushes and their results. They were masters of the art of using HF skywaves, and had established a supernatural reputation. I remember Hoppy looking hard at me when I explained what I had learnt from them. 'You mean they are using ordinary wireless sets like us, David?' he said. 'I don't believe it.' But he did in the end, when we got results, and he gave me the floor at some full unit meetings to enable me to explain to everyone how shortwave radio worked, and the need for really precise timing using rated watches and BBC time signals.

During daylight the full unit frequency allocation was to be used, then, as the signal got louder and began to break up, operators were to change to the lowest frequency – 4.2-MHz on the 11 set. Finally, when the signal went again, they were to roll up their blankets with a clear conscience: their alarm clock was to be set for the first call at 0800-0900 hrs, as experience showed us to be sensible during that sunspot minimum period.

Phantom operators sometimes worked near relatively more powerful Army terminals, amd this successful 'drill' sometimes exasperated the operators of other units who had 'toiled all night, and caught nothing', and then saw the speed and confidence with which the fresher Phantom operators, who were drawn from a delightful mix of regiments, established their link!

Some of our characterful patrol officers exchanged fruity stories over the air when bored on patrol, and our unique, but basically secure, link-sign procedure resulted in monitoring reports being sent to us with comments like: 'We suspect this must be yours'. I remember one rich story bore the comment: 'This message was intercepted by a lady operator'. Her blushes could be imagined, but I am afraid it quickly became a best-seller inside RHQ.

The next challenge came when it was decided to send a detachment to Greece. I got some books and reckoned that 10 watts output, into a large directional aerial at as high a frequency as the ionosphere would stand, should give clear results to a small aerial in Athens. The provision of some 'suitcase sets' was arranged, and Gambier Parry's experts agreed to design a simple transmitter (crystal oscillator, 807 power amplifier) to feed efficiently an 'open-wire' (telephone like) feeder, so that I could site a van in a convenient place well away from the aerial.

After searching, I found that Leith Hill, near Dorking, had no other users, and sent off Cpl Landells on a search for as many 'masts, seventy-two foot, steel' as we needed. He started with the 15-cwt truck, but soon phoned for the 3-tonner, and all stores were collected. I designed a six-wavelength side *Vee* aerial, which we built, and walked over the heather with a homemade meter on a stick to iron out the standing waves on the feeder, which mystified my loyal driver as he helped me. As we had no funds, I 'paid' for the transmitter, a communications receiver and other gear by bartering for them with a load of No.11 set equipment.

The establishment of the link to Greece vindicated all our work and ideas. A message through diplomatic channels said they would transmit at 0800 hrs on a Sunday morning. Their first call came through clearly, exactly on time. Sgt Young had tuned his receiver to a crystal and he did not have to adjust, so a sound link was established in less than thirty seconds, as planned. A calm but triumphant phone call from Sgt Young to Richmond Hill then followed.

Our operational HQ was in wooden huts in St James' Park, near the drained lake. Hoppy disapproved of slit trenches, he felt they encouraged cowardice, so we had some anxious moments during air raids. As far as I know, neither our staff nor the pigeons (part of the Signal Section) suffered any casualties, so we were all lucky and Hoppy felt justified.

I laid a cable along the Mall, and across to the bandstand in Green Park, and had mains power put in to supply our transmitters. I wonder whether that power supply has been any use since then? The Commissioner for the Royal Parks took me to task for hanging our cable from his trees, and risking their health. Fortunately, they survived both my misuse of them and the German bombs!

After nearly a year and a half, I was posted to Marine Divisional Signals (later 1st Army Signals) in Scotland. It was heartbreaking to leave such a fascinating unit and so many delightful colleagues.

## PHANTOM REMINISCENCES

### by Lieutenant-Colonel T A (Rtd) Peter Luttman-Johnson

To be invited to recall memories of fifty-five or more years ago is tantamount to being asked to use one's imagination, for there will be all too few to offer corrections; so I will try very hard not to be 'economical with the truth'.

I was a very late recruit to Phantom, having joined the 15th/19th Hussars, newly back from Dunkirk, and served for eighteen months or so as Regimental Signals Officer, training driver or gunner/operators in wireless and morse code, and then as a Troop Commander before going off to do a Staff job at Brigade HQ. But come the D-Day invasion of Europe I was instructing, again wireless, at an OCTU, the very one I had been commissioned from four years before! So there was every chance of my serving out the whole War without leaving the UK. You can imagine the delight when a recruiter for Phantom arrived, with the comforting news that if Phantom applied for an officer that officer would be posted to them, no matter what the job he was filling at the time. This shows how very highly the top brass thought of Phantom at that stage of the war; and, to be accepted, I was very happy to loose my third pip and revert to the exalted rank of Lieutenant once more – and to find myself being instructed in wireless and morse all over again at the Training and Holding Unit on Richmond Hill, with HQ in the requisitioned Hotel. It may amuse readers to know that the telephone number there was RIC (for Richmond) 6806, which, in London at least, could be reached by dialling PHANTOM (unless I have forgotten the lay-out of the telephone dials of that era); this was reputed to be 'for security', though in practice it merely muddled callers who couldn't easily comprehend that those letters produced the number they wanted. It was during this time that the first V2 landed, the explosion being seen, and very much heard, from the terrace of Pembroke Lodge. This reminded us that we were at war!

For some months there was no place for me in the extensive Phantom organisation operating in Belgium and France, but ultimately I went to the Regimental HQ in the Golf Club at Waterloo, on the second floor, with the Officers Mess in a stately chateau next door. At last, just after Christmas 1944, during the German counter-attack in the Ardennes, I was sent for and, having had four or five days learning how messages were received, mapped, checked and passed on to Army Group Headquarters, found myself despatched to join Captain Brent Hutton-Williams with a new Phantom Patrol with Headquarters 1st US Army at Spa. There had been another Patrol with 1st US Army but it was felt essential to replace them because the Americans, not unnaturally, were a little touchy on their hasty withdrawal from Spa when it seemed that the Germans might recapture it. But to a fresh Patrol the Americans couldn't have been kinder. I found we were handed snow-boots (worn over the top of one's ordinary footgear, like enormous galoshes), unlimited chinagraph pencils and talc and a huge map-board; and the officers were given an entitlement to a monthly bottle of whisky from the PX (or Post Exchange, the American version of NAAFI). As we got one from RHQ occasionally as well, we didn't do badly; but it is fair to say that we didn't drink it all ourselves; to be able to offer a drink to one's hosts is not a bad thing for a Liaison Officer. The French Liaison team 'liberated' ten-litre carboys of white wine, which the American officers were very chary of imbibing. Of course, they were in their own Headquarters, under the eyes of their superior officers who, being regulars, were very 'regimental' minded. All US forces in a battle zone had to wear tin hats at all times; I don't remember that I had one at that time and luckily we, as visitors, were allowed to walk about with no greater protection than a beret; though in General Patton's Army, to the South of us, that wasn't the case, and the Phantom chaps there were constantly getting arrested as spies, or for 'being incorrectly dressed'.

Pretty soon after Brent and I joined the First Army, the German assault was halted (though not, you understand, by us) and we then stayed with them while gradually advancing into Germany. At Duren, in a fine German barracks, the Americans decided to show what they thought of German militarism by pitching the latrines for the whole of their Army Headquarters staff, including enlisted men (GIs), slap in the middle of the parade ground. This proved to be embarrassingly public and a considerable nuisance to those off-duty soldiers who fancied a game of soft ball.

It was here that we were asked if we could help deal with two soldiers of the Indian Army who, somehow or other, had been prisoners of war and had been released by the retiring Germans. This seemed to the Americans to be an unlikely situation and they were delighted, and surprised, when Brent, who had been a merchant in Calcutta for some years, and still proudly wore the cap badge of The Calcutta Light Horse, was able to communicate with them in their own tongue (more or less, I think he spoke *Urdu*) and assured the Americans that they were what they claimed to be. There was, at this time, a very popular book circulating among the US officers, written by an American purporting to give the low-down on British rule in India. The Americans, proudly remembering how they had thrown off the yoke of King George III, believed we were brutal occupiers of a poor land struggling to be free, and they were very surprised to find a British officer willing to help a couple of these subject people, and able actually to speak with them.

We received messages in our office, when allotted one in a building, or, later, in a tent in a field; but our transmitter had to be sited, with the American sets, on their transmitter site two or three miles away. Their Signal Corps laid us a remote control telephone line which was always ready when we arrived on a new site. One day our transmissions disappeared and I went down to the transmitter to see what was wrong. It transpired that an American signaller had erected his aerial over the top of ours, on the ground that Phantom were always through and therefore ours must be the best position!

In fact, Phantom communications were extremely good. The groundwork for this had been done in the months immediately after Dunkirk, with extensive experiments with different types and lengths and heights of aerials on different frequencies, so that the difficult range from just beyond ground-wave to the first reflection from the Heaviside layer of sky-wave could be covered; wireless operators will know what I'm talking about. And they will also appreciate that we had this type of operator who could suck a signal out of the thinnest of breaths, even through interference, and get it down so that the deciphering came out into English rather than Chinese.

*En passant*, I deplore the dropping of the morse code which, using hand-speed signalling, could almost always get a message through. I trust the modern methods, though infinitely more efficient when they work, cannot be ruined by jamming.

To revert to our American transmitter site, very quickly they asked if they might lend us a set which they knew how to operate and which was a good deal more powerful than ours; need I say, we accepted the offer.

When to everybody's surprise, the bridge over the Rhine at Remagen was found to be inefficiently blown, and crossable even by tanks, there was naturally enormous excitement. One could not but admire the urgency with which the Americans brought up their heavy bridging equipment and pushed every soldier who got anywhere near the bridge across to form a bridge-head. This was effective but took days to sort out when battalions found their platoons were spread out all over the countryside. But on they pushed, South of the Ruhr, until finally General Patton's tanks came to a halt through lack of petrol. With no power, they couldn't even traverse their turrets, and if the Germans had been able to mount any sort of offensive there would have been some sitting ducks to be found. But perhaps my criticism is unkind; though I well remember a nice American Liaison Officer, Major May, complaining to me at about midnight that he had, since 5am that day, motored in his jeep two hundred miles over terrible roads to the leading troops, and back again, to find the senior officers who had sent him off safely in bed and asleep.

It was after we had caught up with the advance that we had a puncture and were advised that it wasn't worth trying to mend it; much easier to get a replacement wheel from the forward vehicle store. Off went the Patrol Corporal, with spare driver fortunately, to return not only with a spare wheel but also with another jeep! The NCO in charge of this depot envied the Corporal's battle-dress blouse and was quite happy to swap a jeep for it! This was useful, providing I kept on good terms with my Patrol NCO, especially as at about this time Brent was directed, by our RHQ, to go forward to cover the meeting of the Russian and American armies near Torgau. In one way we were glad to see the German civilians frightened, and they were, with reason, terrified; but it wasn't pleasant to be begged for help. One day, from Marburg, I was able to 'swan' over to the Eder Dam, or what was left of it. I was very glad not to have been below it when it burst. The ruination was still extensive.

At Weimar we visited Buchenwald concentration camp. Bodies of dead soldiers one can stomach; after all, that's the risk a soldier runs; but bodies, piled up, of starved civilians; and cremating ovens still containing half consumed corpses; and a torture chamber with hooks on the wall and wire nooses; and living corpses, hairless, fleshless, almost sightless; these brought home to us very strongly what we had all been fighting for.

I think it must have been here that I was told by the French Liaison team that a British officer was in their office. I should say that these Frenchmen had been connected with SOE (Special Operations Executive) or with the Free French agents in France, matters I knew nothing of, and they were very happy to have discovered the White Rabbit, Wing-Commander F F Yeo-Thomas, DSO, whose fantastic adventures in SOE were fully described in a book published forty or more years ago. He had been captured in March of 1944 and imprisoned in Buchenwald. I had never heard of him, of course, which made the French think I was a complete ignoramus, which on this subject I most certainly was. I offered him what help I could give, but the French had already seen to his evacuation to Paris and my role was limited to sending a message telling of his escape. Whether this ever got re-transmitted to the addressee, General Gubbins (commanding SOE at that time), I have no idea.

The day before VE-Day, First US Army handed over its formations to the flanking Armies and closed down, the senior officers being sent back to the USA in order to form a new Army which would be used for the invasion of Japan. Brent was still away and I was told to return to RHQ as soon as possible.

There was then an unreal few days of idleness. When Headquarters ceased to move, Royal Signals connected them all up by telephone and, in a flash, there was nothing for Phantom to do. However, we were soon asked to supply about ten wireless stations to help with the de-mobilisation of the farmers and farm labourers in the German Army; they were required to help with the summer's harvest. This took me, with a new Phantom Patrol, up to Schleswig-Holstein where a company of *SS* Engineers were constructing a temporary holding compound in which local soldiers from the two main areas to which the Germans had been confined (against the Frisian Islands and in the Ruhr) would spend a night before being dispersed to their home villages. I was most impressed by the discipline shown by these soldiers, both the SS and the men to be sent home, and also by the efficiency shown in building this wire stockade. It transpired that at this time, about a week after the cessation of hostilities, many Germans believed that we would re-form and re-arm the German Army and fight with it to throw the Russians out of Europe, or anyway out of Germany. No way would a single officer or man of either the British or American forces have joined in such a campaign and the Germans were severely shaken when at last they realised it. I was able to commandeer the use of an eight cylinder Mercedes-Benz car, ex-*Gestapo*, that had a siren which started when the accelerator pedal was flat on the floor. The car would have been going at about 100-mph by this time, had it been firing on all eight cylinders. Fortunately for me, it only fired on four, and thus I didn't succeed in killing myself. It only went four miles to every gallon of petrol, so back into the car pound it went quite quickly.

In early June, I suppose, we were told to form a new Phantom Regiment (No. 3, No. 2 having been in Italy) to fly out to India to cover the re-occupation of Malaya, which it was believed would have to be done by an invasion across the beaches between Penang and Malacca, so all the younger members of Phantom came back to Richmond Park, to a tented camp just inside Star and Garter Gate. We were given a new CO, Lieutenant-Colonel Sleeman, RTR, who found that he was taking on a unit that knew its job a great deal better than he did; so he sensibly organised visits to the Zoo (to familiarise the soldiers with tropical fauna) and to Kew Gardens (ditto flora) and arranged cricket matches (perhaps there was only one) and gave us a lot of local leave. We were to fly out to Colombo, Ceylon, on the 15th August, and collect vehicles, wireless sets and so on on arrival. I hate to think how ghastly this kit would have been, desperately second hand and probably out of date models, but we were saved by the bell as on the 15th August Japan surrendered. When the first Atom-bomb was dropped I well remember the sense of relief that we all felt in the sure knowledge that this would mean the end of the War; but I also remember the awe, and fear, when we realised what this dreadful weapon could accomplish. However, Churchill said: 'Let the bells ring! Let there be bonfires!' There was a large dump of packing cases and other inflammable material not far from our camp, and somehow or other this suffered from self combustion, to spectacular effect! At that time the public were not admitted to the Park (because of the decoy in the middle of the Park which could be ignited to attract bombers during night raids on London) and the gate was manned, after 6pm by our soldiers. One of them had the initiative to open the gate wide enough to admit one person at a time – and took his beret off and held it out. He made enough money for his Patrol, or maybe the other men on guard that evening, to have a jolly good celebration!

With our Far Eastern adventure cancelled, we had a summer and autumn doing nothing in Richmond Park, and we were relieved when Colonel Sleeman was ordered to take us back to Germany, where the remnants of Phantom were beginning to demobilise themselves and go home. No. 3 GHQ Liaison Regiment settled in a building estate on the edge of Bunde, not far from HQ 21st Army Group, and quite soon had a job sending a Patrol to Helmstedt, where the railway to Berlin left the British sector of Germany and entered Russian occupied territory. But there was little else to do and Colonel Sleeman left us, sensibly, to be replaced by a CO who broke his leg falling off a table at his own dining-out party and so didn't arrive for some time. I don't recall that this made any difference. At Christmas we still put on a stupendously successful pantomime in conjunction with the young ladies of the Control Commission, while our soldiers became expert at the rates of exchange on the various black markets, cigarettes and coffee being the most popular media of exchange. One man went AWOL, holing up in a tent twenty yards 'out of bounds' with a German girl and a rifle; he came back after two days because he was hungry (and the girl, sensibly, had gone home); the fact that we didn't get heavy-handed and send people to arrest him shows that we too were beginning to count the days, well anyway weeks, before our own demob. An attempt by me, as Adjutant, to re-introduce a little soldiering in the form of foot drill did not go down at all well. Those last months must have been pretty boring for our soldiers; for the officers, we had a good club in Bunde and a better one at Bad Oeynhausen, and a better one still at Bad Salzuflen, where the pretty girls of the Special Liaison Unit (receiving messages from *Ultra*, as at last I know) were to be found.

I managed to take up a vacancy on a good-will skiing holiday at Chamonix, offered by the French Army and necessitating a three day rail journey, each way, through Brussels and Paris; I don't think my absence was noticed, which shows how busy we were.

Less than a year after demob I joined the Kensington Regiment TA, who were being reformed as a Phantom Regiment, after a distinguished War as a Machine Gun Regiment. But that, as they say, is another story.

## RECOLLECTIONS OF PHANTOM
### by Major (Rtd) Mark Ramage

I first heard of Phantom in the summer of 1943. With a number of friends I had joined the 60th Rifles (KRRC) a year earlier, straight from school. We were commissioned in June 1943, and posted to the 'holding' battalion in Yorkshire. There we would stay until needed as replacements. The number of junior officers awaiting more active employment seemed to be growing, and when a notice appeared asking for applications for the GHQ Liaison Regiment (Phantom) it had immediate appeal, despite no one having any idea of what Phantom did.

The first two of us to get our names in were summoned to London for an interview with Lt Col Mackintosh, the Commanding Officer, a territorial from the Fyfe and Forfar Yeomanry. It proved an unusual job interview, as he saw us both together in public, over tea at his club. He was most agreeable, though not very informative, as he politely asked us about our histories, which were of course not dissimilar. Finally seeming satisfied, he said he would be glad to have us. He added as an afterthought that he assumed that we did not propose to make a post-war career in the army. He feared that to have served in what he described as a somewhat irregular unit might not help a regular soldier subsequently. While thoughtful of him this ruled out my friend, who went on to be a very successful regular soldier indeed.

Luckily, another old school friend was selected the following week and we reported together to Phantom's HQ in Pembroke Lodge, Richmond Park. It had, I believe, once housed Royal mistresses, perhaps suiting it for the irregularity of Phantom.

With a number of other newcomers, some of whom seemed considerably older and more experienced, we embarked on a three week course, in what had, I think, been a hotel, half-way down Richmond Hill. We learnt what Phantom was, what it did, and how it did it. Its 'patrols', of an officer, a sergeant, and half a dozen or so men (wireless operators, coders, mechanics and dispatch riders), were to keep army commanders, and their RAF equivalents, constantly informed of what was happening.

We needed, therefore, to learn the use of the Phantom code book and one-time pad cypher system (unbreakable), which provided absolute security for our wireless messages. We were taught how standard army wireless sets, using morse and suitable aerials, would work over improbable distances. We were introduced to the ins and outs of the British army as a whole, and to the organisation and methods of the US army as well, just in case we ever ran into it.

I think we now understood why Lt Col Mackintosh was not very informative at our interview. Phantom worried about security to a probably unjustified extent. But our founder, Lt Col Hopkinson, had decided, quite rightly, from the start, that the less anyone knew about us the easier it would be to do and get what we wanted.

We grew accustomed to the most striking peculiarity of Phantom as a regiment. Everyone wore a black beret, as Phantom by now belonged, loosely, to the Royal Armoured Corps, and everyone wore a 'P' sign on their sleeve. But cap badges, and officer's uniforms, remained those of regiments of origin, making as colourful a display as is possible on a base of khaki, from kilts to trousers.

At the end of the course we were sent off to join different Squadrons, at that time scattered all over the country. Two of us went to 'F' Squadron at Largs, on the west coast of Scotland. It had taken part in the Dieppe raid in 1942, and was assigned to the corps earmarked for the initial assault in the forthcoming invasion of Europe. It had, therefore, been training in landings in Scottish lochs, but had finished this by the time we arrived.

This Squadron was commanded by Major J J Astor, Life Guards, who held 'stables' first thing each day, inspecting the vehicles instead of horses. It was held that kicking the tyres was as good a test as any. We were equipped with Humber Light Reconnaissance Cars (a pre-war civilian chassis with an armoured body). The increased weight had not been matched by better brakes, making for some exciting drives.

Having been allotted a patrol, I was sent on a training expedition to Stranraer, about a hundred miles south. 'Come back when you've established wireless contact,' I was told.

'What shall I do if I can't establish contact?'

'Phantom always does.' And indeed we did.

In the evenings I helped Captain John Hislop trace the family trees of racehorses on rolls of wallpaper. He claimed that this would greatly assist him in breeding them after the war. It may well have done, given the number of his winners.

At the end of the year we drove south to Frimley in Surrey, and on New Year's Day, 1944, the Leader (as our Squadron Commander was always known) told me that for the invasion there was an officer too many in the Squadron. I could, therefore, become a first line reinforcement or move on to 'B' Squadron, which was short of officers. I chose the latter, feeling slightly disloyal.

'B' Squadron was at Redhill, also in Surrey. It was twice the size of 'F', formed by the amalgamation of two Squadrons to serve the entire Canadian Army. It had, therefore, inherited two Majors, and I was never entirely certain which was actually the commander. But I was not amongst strangers, since several members of my initial course were there. It had the same small family atmosphere as 'F', but instead of being cut off in a remote part of Scotland, it was in easy reach of London. A fact of which undue advantage may have been taken by certain *'blackbutton'* officers older than I.

Before I was led too far astray however, in April we took the field on a mammoth exercise called, aptly enough, 'LAST'. We had a memorable party first, our guests including some most attractive members of a FANY (First Aid Nursing Yeomanry) unit nearby. I was by this time a Lieutenant, second officer to Captain Peter Ling in the Canadian Corps patrol, working with the Tac HQ of General Simmonds, the Corps Commander, the only

Canadian I have ever met with an English accent. (His father had been in the British army.) Our job was to keep the General informed of what the other Phantom patrols were telling Army HQ. At the end of the exercise we stayed with them and moved to a wood near Dover, while the rest of the Squadron returned to Redhill.

We camped in this wood until June, and a detachment from Phantom HQ moved into Dover Castle. At the same time, the harbour filled with very realistic dummy landing craft made of rubber. We did not know it but we were part of Operation *Fortitude*, the deception plan that successfully persuaded the Germans that the main invasion would be in the Calais area.

We were by now equipped with the American White Scout Cars and Jeeps, and when we started waterproofing them it was clear that movement was approaching. When D-Day arrived we were able to go down to Phantom in the Castle, and obtain a complete picture of the one Canadian division involved, temporarily under British command. The one gap was the situation on the two US beaches, since there were no Phantom patrols with the US Army, and no other information seemed to be coming through.

This was remedied on D+1 when two patrols were hastily scratched together and dispatched to the Americans. One was assembled from the detachment in Dover Castle, and we waved it goodbye from the harbour. We ourselves however, rather oddly, were to sail from the London docks, and after nearly a fortnight drove off on what was a long journey for waterproofed vehicles.

In every village and town the inhabitants turned out to cheer us on our way. I suppose we must have been the first to proceed to Normandy on such an odd route. We embarked on a Liberty ship, a US freighter not designed for carrying people, and sailed off down the Thames. Unfortunately, by this time a severe storm had begun to hold up unloading in Normandy, and we were delayed at sea day after day, only reaching the Straits of Dover after a week. If it took a week to get to where we started, this was going to be a very long war!

There must have been half a dozen Canadian officers, headed by a Lieutenant Colonel, and Peter Ling and I in our party, and we ate our pack rations sitting on boxes on deck. After a week of this, one major said to me, only half in jest,

'This is what you get if you come to rough it in the colonies.' I think this was the only time, in what for me was to be six months with the Canadians, that anyone commented on us being British.

We then waited several more days off the Normandy beaches, while the crew complained to the captain that they had only been hired for a voyage, not to sit around in a war. But finally the vehicles were unloaded into landing craft, and we climbed down after them. It still looked an astonishing traffic jam of shipping. We drove off the landing craft in deeper water than expected, and Peter, in the jeep, looked in danger of disappearing beneath the waves. The White rose above the problem and I landed dry.

We had arrived where we were supposed to, and found our way, without trouble, to the wood where Tac HQ was to establish itself. As we all arrived, holes were dug, tents put up, and in no time at all, Tac HQ and its Phantom patrol looked exactly as it had in the wood at Dover. It was, however, much noisier.

The next fortnight saw us in a sort of limbo. The main body of Corps HQ was even more delayed than we had been, and it was far from clear what units would be under its command when it finally did arrive. The best we could do in the meantime was to provide Tac HQ with the best general picture we could of the entire front, with more detail of the one Canadian division so far engaged, still under British command. The basics we got by wireless from Phantom, and for anything specific we took it in turns to go to the nearest Phantom patrol in person, doing our best not to get in the way too much. We extended this later by visiting units where we knew we had old friends. Some of the latter returned the compliment by visiting us in an excellent site (after our initial wood) where a large hole dug by a bulldozer provided a sort of underground map room with maps of the whole of Normandy on the walls, with which they could satisfy their curiosity about how things were going.

My most vivid memory was of driving the jeep down a strangely empty road on my very first expedition, and learning that the roadside warnings 'dust brings shells' were accurate.

Once the Canadian Corps became operational we were fully equipped in what became fairly routine work, making sense of the mass of Phantom information constantly streaming in. The load on the wireless operators, tapping out and receiving morse, and the coders, adding and subtracting numbers, was immense.

I can now only remember the unusual events. The first major use of heavy bombers on Caen was spectacular, and quite unlike shelling. Having been bombed out of my room at school in 1940, I could imagine what it must have been like, but the inhabitants appeared to show no resentment when we later drove through the ruins of their city on our way south.

Then, south of Caen, there was the first large-scale tank attack by night, with infantry carried in self-propelled guns from which the guns had been removed, to provide the first ever proper tracked and armoured personnel carriers. The dust clouds as the columns assembled made it astonishing that heavier Bomber Command support (1,000 heavy bombers) still fell in the right places, and that the tanks found their way. Tracer shells marking routes and artificial moonlight from search lights made an unusual sight.

By the third week of August what had become known as the Falaise gap was closed. Falaise itself was flatter than Caen had been, but what I remember most clearly is the roads where German horse transport had been destroyed from the air, blocking them completely with dead horses. It was a hot August, and I have never smelt anything like it.

The Canadian Corps then went north again, and began the clearing of the channel coast. I remember crossing the Seine, because of the length of the bridge, but from then, the end of August, until we reached Ghent at the end of September, I can only remember constant moving and the capture of Calais. Perhaps because that was preceded by another massive performance by Bomber Command, which was as spectacular as ever.

We spent October outside Ghent, where 'B' Squadron HQ was established. The Corps was by now stretched out all along the coast. We visited Squadron HQ fairly often, and they organised a number of parties where the skills of Captain Michael Oakeshott, the administrative officer, in finding new friends (female) became clear.

Preparations were being made for amphibious operations in very strange vehicles, but towards the end of the month I was told that I was to proceed to RHQ at Brussels to take over a new 'American' patrol.

I have already mentioned that the day after D-Day two new Phantom patrols had been 'scratched' together for the American beaches. Having seen what they could do the Americans asked for a complete Phantom squadron of their own. L, then in Scotland training in mountain warfare, was rapidly pressed into service. Since General Montgomery was in command of all troops in Normandy, this proved no problem. But, at the end of August, he ceased to command the US armies, which passed to the US General Bradley. He and his US Air Force equivalent wished to retain their Phantom, and indeed enlarge it, as more and more American troops arrived. It was agreed that a Phantom patrol would, so far as possible, be supplied for each US Corps, but this wasn't easy to arrange. 'L' Squadron HQ was abolished to provide two more patrols, and raiding the other squadrons became necessary. Captain Michael Astor was first to go from 'B' Squadron, on the grounds that his American ancestry might help, and I followed in his footsteps, perhaps because a second officer in a patrol could now most easily be spared.

The 'American' Phantom patrols had no Squadron HQ to report to, only an enlarged patrol at General Bradley's HQ. Messages to it went through RHQ most of the time, but sometimes directly. RHQ delivered one-time pads as necessary (and mail) but otherwise left the patrols to their own devices, without supervising them as squadron HQ's did. Indeed, one patrol officer left with the Americans besieging Brest feared for a time that his existence had been completely forgotten!

I duly set off for Brussels to present myself to RHQ, established in the golf club at Waterloo. There I learnt that I was now a Captain, which was pleasing, but that I had only two days to get a 'scratch' patrol together from a selection of bodies spared from here and there. Luckily, the new patrol sergeant was experienced, and had seen something of the Americans at Nijmegen in the unfortunate Arnhem operation. We collected a White armoured car and a Jeep and wireless sets (motorcycles had been abandoned for 'American' patrols) and managed to be ready on time. We were to take over from the patrol of Captain Bill McIntosh-Reid, MC, covering US VII Corps outside Aachen, which had just been captured.

Bill's patrol was established in a house at Kornelimunster, on a good wireless site, and not too far from the Command Post of General 'Lightning' Joe Collins, commanding US VII Corps. (His staff did not like their Phantom patrol too near, believing that constant morse transmission in cypher attracted enemy shellfire. I doubt if this was ever true.) It was one of the two first 'American' patrols post D-Day, and after an initial dispute with the General on '*Utah*' beach Bill never had subsequent problems. (The General hadn't been warned of his arrival, and did not take kindly to what seemed a British spy on his beach.) Bill himself was an impressive figure. Extremely tall, he had been with Phantom in North Africa and seen a good deal of the US army there. He took me into Kornelimunster and introduced me to the General and the main members of his Command Post, who were all most welcoming. In the meantime, his patrol sergeant was introducing mine to the vital sources of supply for food, petrol and other necessaries. (We were supposed always to be self-supporting for four days.) Then Bill and his patrol were gone, leaving us to sort ourselves out.

It was probably just as well that VII Corps was entering on a quiet few weeks. (My very first message was: 'Light shelling on whole Corps front. Otherwise nothing to report.') The routine was to send daily a first thing and last thing situation report, topped up by any developments in between. But the day came for us to send a very long message indeed – plans for a major attack towards Cologne. This started off promisingly, but soon became bogged down in the dreadful ground of the Hurtgen Forest. Heavy rain turned it into an ocean of mud. Paschendael with tree bursts, as someone described it. Even jeeps became stuck. Casualties were appallingly heavy and progress slight. The situation was often obscure, but there was no way one could get to it, so I remained outside Kornelimunster, reporting on a dismal situation which did not change much.

After a month Duren had still not been taken, let alone Cologne. Then in mid-December Captain Peter Stileman, covering V Corps on our right, reported a German counter-attack. I visited Peter who did not like the look of things, since he had now learnt that on his right, in the Ardennes, VIII Corps was being attacked. This was supposed to be so quiet an area that no Phantom patrol was covering it, so information was scarce.

That night, after some light bombing, a small number of German parachutists were dropped near us, but quickly rounded up. In the morning it became clear that they had dropped in error, as their main body had landed in the V Corps area. It was evident by now that something serious was happening, and the news from Peter was not encouraging. That night a Phantom patrol arrived at VIII Corps, and its first messages were not encouraging either. The next two days saw things go from bad to worse, and then we received news of two major developments. First, all US troops north of what was now clearly a German breakthrough had been placed under Monty's command, including us. I was far from sure how well this would go down, but apart from a perfectly friendly 'The British riding to the rescue, eh!' no one I met seemed to pay much attention.

The second development did concern all. General Collins was told to hand over his existing divisions to the corps to his left, and move southwest at once to take command of a counter-offensive force yet to be assembled. I was to follow him, and go on wireless silence, along with his Command Post and the new force. After sending a message to say that no more would be heard from me for the moment, I briefed the Phantom patrol to our left on the situation I was leaving behind, and set off after VII Corps Command Post and the General himself. The Command Post was to be established in the area of Marche. This looked comfortably far behind the furthest point the Germans seemed to have reached.

It meant, however, quite a long journey, gravely complicated by thick snow and ice. The jeep twice ended up in a ditch and had to be hauled out by the White. We were not alone in having difficulties. We ran into one of the armoured divisions destined for the new VII Corps, driving down from even further north, and they seemed to be losing vehicles and even tanks on both sides of the road.

The second problem was the employment by the Germans of a regiment disguised as Americans, in real American uniforms and American vehicles, to spread as much confusion behind the American lines as possible. They were extremely sucessful, one jeep getting as far as the River *Meuse*, and as a result we were continually stopped by US road blocks, convinced we must be Germans. This was particularly hazardous, making our way through a new division that had come straight from the US without having seen any British troops before. It is very difficult at gunpoint to explain that the British do not play baseball, when an inability to answer questions on the game is regarded as clear proof of being a German in disguise!

The General himself experienced difficulties, since troops who had never heard of him thought a General in a jeep looking for his Command Post seemed very suspicious.

The final problem was that by the time we got to the area of Marche, it was apparent that the Germans had got there before us. General Collins had found his Command Post some miles to the north, and was already visiting his new divisions and issuing orders. The weather was making the laying of telephone lines difficult, and we were all still on wireless silence. It was only to be broken if the enemy made contact. It was far from clear where either the Americans or the enemy were. However, we found a farmhouse, well sited for wireless, still inhabited by an aged farmer's wife, who at once invited us in and made us warm.

On Christmas Eve the American armoured division nearest the River Meuse was engaged with 'enemy tanks'. Wireless silence was broken. Unfortunately, it turned out to be British tanks that had been engaged. There was a certain amount of recrimination over this, but we could now reopen our wireless set and report positions as I knew them. We in turn received the picture as known at RHQ.

There was now a whole British Armoured Brigade on the Meuse (the tanks the Americans had met) acting as a long stop. There had also, pending their arrival, been three Phantom patrols covering the main bridges, to warn of any possible enemy crossing. These, I believe, were sent on Monty's own instructions! Even more surprisingly, a squadron of British armoured cars had been sent to more or less where I was going, to act in a Phantom role. (ie Where were the Americans? Where were the enemy?) And, finally, another Phantom patrol, Captain Barry Coward's from 'B' Squadron, was coming to join me, to report directly to Monty's Tac HQ (My messages were still going to Phantom RHQ.) It was clear that we were right in the middle of events.

On Christmas Day, I sent a message which suggested that the Germans would get no further. A dozen or more enemy self-propelled guns had been captured, out of petrol. A little further investigation revealed that there were considerable numbers of similarly stranded vehicles. The Germans had got as far as they would.

That night our kindly farmer's wife cooked us a wonderful Christmas dinner, with a splendid goose. A great change from our 'K' rations!

General Collins' attention now turned to the delayed counter-offensive. We were visited by one of Monty's personal liaison officers, who, without wireless, reported back to him in person each night, with not only news but also their impressions, something forbidden to Phantom. Later Monty himself visited us. There was some difference of opinion between him and General Collins as to where the offensive should take place, but all went off well, and by the end of January a large part of the 'Bulge' had been cut off.

Many years later, I was pleased to read, in the official US Army history of the Battle of the Bulge, that, throughout, Monty's best source of information had been his Phantom officers, and that Phantom had been particularly welcome at General Collins' HQ. Later still, I was less pleased to read, in the General's autobiography, that he thought Monty placed too much faith in the reports of Phantom officers, instead of listening to the US Generals. I hope he was confusing Phantom officers (GHQ Liaison Regiment) with Monty's personal liaison officers, a reasonable error.

Once the 'Bulge' was cut, VII Corps was withdrawn for a rest. The patrol had a week's holiday in Brussels, the Command Post went to Paris, and the General himself did best of all by going to Cannes.

We returned to a site outside Duren, while a fresh VII Corps attack on it was planned, but, after a fortnight, a message arrived to say that I had qualified for leave in England, and that a Captain Mark, whom I did not know, was coming to take over the patrol in my absence. (I think that leave was based on a combination of time in France and Germany, and a lottery.) This caused a certain amount of mirth, and envy, amongst my American friends. 'Could you fix me a transfer to the British army?' etc.

I returned in March to find that all had gone well in my absence with Captain Mark, the patrol, and generally. Indeed, Cologne had finally been taken, and, more dramatically still, a bridge had been captured over the Rhine at Remagen. General Collins was again given new divisions, and asked to take over the northern side of the bridgehead. We duly moved south, and crossed the Rhine on the, by now, famous bridge, actually a railway bridge on which a wooden road had been laid. An engineer Major said it had taken a lot of punishment but might last a little longer. It actually collapsed the next day, but pontoon bridges were already finished, and a few days later a drive north started.

By the end of March the leading armoured division had met a unit of the 9th US Army division coming south at Lippstadt. This cut off around 300,000 Germans in what became the Ruhr pocket. The corps became very spread out, as its exposed left flank was over 100 miles long, and small parties of Germans were trying to break out. I stayed with Command Post which kept on the move, trying to stay roughly in the middle, but General Collins used a small light aircraft, landing in any available space, in his daily tour. This was just as well for the armoured Division Commander was killed when his jeep met a German tank.

We now turned East, and in about three weeks reached the River Elbe at Dessau, where we met the Russians coming the other way. Then another fast drive, for there were still pockets of German resistance in the area making one last stand. I remember little else of this time as the total recall of Nordhausen blotted everything else out.

We had just gone through Nordhausen and set up shop when an officer from the armoured division, who knew me, stopped on his way to the Command Post and said there was something north of the town that I ought to see. I took the jeep with the patrol sergeant and drove out of town. Nordhausen is just south of the Harz mountains, and I could see from a distance two tunnels led into a steep cliff face. As we approached we came to a barbed wire enclosure packed with what looked like skeletons covered in skin, with what looked like striped pyjamas on top. Many were dead. More lay around the tunnel entrances. A small party from the armoured division was trying to organise food with the aid of a small medical section. The US Army Officer in charge had established the basic facts. This was DORA, the underground V2 rocket factory, run as a concentration camp with SS guards with whips acting as foremen. The prisoners came from all over Europe, topped up as necessary from the Buchenwald concentration camp, not far away. All the German staff had fled at the American army's approach.

The officer directed me to the left hand tunnel. Here the rocket assembly line stretched into the distance. More skeleton bodies lay alongside. There was no ventilation. I came out for air and he showed me some windowless buildings outside the tunnel. Two looked like giant shower rooms, but were apparently gas chambers. They were empty. The others were crematoria, and had not been keeping up with the load. Nearby there were gibbets, from which corpses had been cut down. We drove back in silence, it was difficult to convey to the rest of the patrol the horror of what we had seen.

Only after the war did I learn that over 20,000 men had died working on the construction and making of the rocket bombs in that factory.

Werner von Braun, the German rocket king, and *Herr* Rudolph, the factory manager, had fled in good time, and later negotiated a deal with the American Government. They went on to live in the USA, and played a leading role in the American rocket programme, culminating in the first US moon shots. Only many years later did Rudolph's past catch up with him, even then he was allowed to return to Germany without prosecution.

After meeting the Russians on the Elbe operations were over for VII Corps and my last message was about the dispositions of the Russian troops opposite. We moved to Leipzig with the Command Post. The patrol occupied a large apartment, and we embarked on several weeks of celebrations, with American parties for the Russians and vice versa. The inhabitants soon learnt that the city would end up in the Russian zone, and one girl asked if we could smuggle her out with us. I felt obliged to decline. I still wonder at the amount the Russians drank, and indeed how they had ever managed to achieve what they had when they so seldom seemed able to stand up. Perhaps it was simply the celebrations.

After reuniting with our fellow-countrymen, several ex-'American' patrols were sent north to pass messages about prisoners of war and other such problems. On the way, or rather on a detour, some of us visited Arnhem, where Captain Neville Hay, MC, who had been one of the Phantom officers with the airborne division there, took us through the battle like a military historian.

My patrol then went up to the Danish border, and while the wireless operators worked hard, we had a pleasant boating holiday as we camped by a lake.

At the end of June a new squadron was formed, made up of those not due for early release from the army, for the war against Japan in South East Asia, and we returned to Richmond and leave again. Some of us were then summonsed back to go on a parachute course, as it was thought that this might be valuable in jungles. We had first to endure a 'hardening' course, and having taken no exercise for a year I was far from fit. After a few days it was clear that we would never survive, and a quick-thinking officer thought of explaining our problem to Richmond. RHQ rose to the occasion and, exploiting Phantom secrecy, claimed that it was vital we were rushed straight to the parachuting, which we were.

All was going well when the atom bomb brought the war against Japan to an end, and in the afternoon jump on VJ-Day I carelessly broke my ankle.

In hospital I was visited by an old B Squadron friend, George Cohen, now a Major and second-in-command of the South East Asia Squadron. He brought the good news that as the holder of a university scholarship I qualified for early release from the army. I duly went home in plaster, and was in Cambridge for the autumn term to start finishing my education.

My time in Phantom had itself, of course, been educational, and I had come away with an abiding regard for America and Americans. Against this, the fact that the mighty US Army had found Phantom of such value, irregular as it was, may have left me with a perhaps not wholly justified belief in British superiority.

## RECOLLECTIONS OF PHANTOM
*by Major (Rtd.) John Randall*

My first meeting with Colonel Hopkinson was in the summer of 1940. My uncle Captain Billy Newan, who was the MT Officer at RHQ, Richmond Hill Hotel, introduced me to him and I expressed a keen desire to join Phantom. It seemed a much more attractive occupation in the Army than being an ACK ACK gunner. Colonel Hopkinson advised me to come back and see him again when I had obtained my Commission and he would see if there was a vacancy in the Regiment. In June 1941 I again went to see Colonel Hopkinson and he then accepted me and I was posted to 'G' Squadron in Northern Ireland.

This posting was one of the most enjoyable of my army career. The Squadron Commander Major Terry Watt was a pre-war regular soldier in the Life Guards. He was efficient, charming and all who served under him had the highest regard for him. Our Second-in-Command was Captain Lord Charles Banbury, a 12th Lancer and a great character of enormous charm and good humour. Other most engaging were Captain E L Rich, a University Don, Captain Dougan Webb of the Welsh Fusiliers, Captain Charles Stewart Liberty of the Royal Ulster Rifles, Mick Millar, Roddie Pannell, John Sadoine and Mick Lockett.

During my time in Northern Ireland the Americans entered the war. The first US troops landed in Northern Ireland and we were delegated to liaise with them and make them welcome. We did not realise 'fraternisation' was to cost us quite a lot. We lost all our girlfriends – it's surprising what the girls would do for a pair of silk stockings and some chocolate bars!!

My next assignment was to go with Phantom to North Africa. On the troop ship outward bound we were employed as 'look out' and wireless communications. It relieved the tension of the long voyage and gave us a real job to do. We landed in Algiers after what seemed a long and tedious journey, dodging the U-boats in the Atlantic occupied the mind quite a bit.

While most of the Squadron, under the command of Major Tony Warre, went and joined the 1st Army advance I was left behind with Lieutenant Cuming of the Seaforth

Highlanders. Later we joined the Squadron in the final advance on Tunis. Victory day in Tunis was a great occasion. King George VI and Winston Churchill attended and a great party followed. Among the Squadron were some charming characters: Hugh (Tam) Williams the actor was great fun and a great entertainer; Percy Pennant, who after the war became a country parson; Hugh Fraser, brother of Lord Lovat of Commando fame; Captain Julian Fane and Norman Reddaway. Soon after our return to the UK in December 1943 I was invited to join 1st SAS as their Signals Officer. I assumed that this was a direct result of the training course that I had done with them in North Africa. It was an opportunity that I could not refuse.

My days with Phantom were happy ones even if I never really felt I did a worthwhile job. Mostly charming people in the mess and a great bunch of men in the ranks from all the units in the British Army.

## CHAPTER XXVIII

# Stories from the men of Phantom

### HOW I CAME TO BE IN PHANTOM
*by Private Arthur Austin, 'B' Squadron*

My name is Arthur 'Bunny' Austin, I was a radio operator in the 59th Infantry Division the South Staffordshires, and went over to France on 27th June, 1944, three weeks after D-Day. Our division was one of the leading assault groups in the battle of Caen. The bombing, as part of Operation *Goodwood*, that started on the 7th July, lasted for nearly an hour, then we were ordered in. Little did we know we were up against the crack German 12th SS Panzer Division, so had a real fight on our hands. We took a lot of casualties before Caen was finally taken.

More savage fighting followed the next week at Villers-Bocage, and on the 6th/7th August, at Haut des Forges as we fought to oust the Germans and secure a crossing over the River Orne; this we achieved by the 9th.

Within six weeks of arriving in France our division had been decimated, having lost over 1,000 men, killed or wounded, at Caen alone. Being the junior division we were disbanded. I have kept the 'order of the day' which was read out to all the troops on parade.

> The shortage of trained reserves, particularly in the Infantry, has made it necessary to disband one Division in the Second British Army. The 59th (Staffordshire) Division has been selected solely because it is the junior Division.
>
> I wish to take this opportunity of thanking everyone of you for the loyal support which you have given me since I took over command.
>
> By your efforts you have earned for the Division a magnificent fighting record and reputation in NORMANDY. You may well be proud of this.
>
> Though it is inevitably a sad moment for all of us to see the Division and Units to which we belong being broken up, we must

look at it from the wider aspect as a step to help materially to bring the war to an early end.

I know that you will all take with you to your new Units the spirit of unselfish comradeship and high endeavour which has been so characteristic of this Division. GOOD LUCK TO YOU ALL.

19th AUG 1944<br>
(Signed) L O LYNE,<br>
Major-General,<br>
Commander 59th Inf. Division.'

We were split up and sent to different units, and as I was a radio operator I was told to report to Phantom's 'B' Squadron HQ at Amblie near Caen, which was attached to General Montgomery's Tac HQ about a mile away. I remember one of our officers was Lieutenant Phillips, ex-RAC. At Amblie I was on the receiving end of countless messages coming in from our Phantom patrols up at the front. These messages had to be prioritised and re-transmitted to the various Army Divisions who could act on the information.

While at Squadron HQ I often saw Lieutenant-Colonel David Niven who at one time had been the CO of Phantom's 'A' Squadron but was now liaising between the British and American Armies as part of SHAEF.

In September, during Operation Market Garden, the battle at Arnhem, we were taking messages that were being transmitted from the Phantom patrols engaged in the fighting there.

My mate Dave Brundritt and I stayed with Phantom right through till the end of the war. We finished up in Bunde, as part of No. 3 GHQ Liaison Regiment, where I got married to Sylvia who was in the ATS, and Dave gave her away.

I enjoyed my time with the Phantom regiment and was de-mobbed from Bunde in 1946.

## MY TIME WITH PHANTOM

*by Adrian Bazar, 'F' Squadron Phantom SAS*

I joined the RASC in 1941 and after the usual basic training, various schemes and postings, ended up in a BSD (basic supply depot) which was earmarked for the Middle East. Our final training included some crazy 'war games' and unfortunately, or perhaps fortunately, I fell off a high wall and fractured a bone in my foot. I was hospitalized in Manchester for a few months and then transferred to a 'Physical Development Centre' in Richmond, which after a few months turned me into a very fit soldier indeed, except for my foot. I was classified as A2, discharged to a holding unit in Oxford and, like many others, waited for a posting to a unit. It was now discovered that I was a musician and the camp CO gave me leave to collect my guitar and play in the camp band for the 'Sergeants and Officers' mess dances. This kept me here for some considerable time. Eventually I went through a series of aptitude tests, one of which was a paper on morse code, which meant listening to, I think, twenty questions on morse code signals. After the tests, I was interviewed by an intelligence officer, who informed me he had never received an all-correct paper on morse codes before and that he had the perfect posting for me. I thanked him and explained that being a musician, the test seemed quite easy.

Soon after, I received my posting orders and travel documents indicating that I was being sent to join the General Headquarters Liaison Regiment, which meant nothing to me at the time. I quickly learnt its pseudonym was Phantom. I was sent to the Special Air Services Regiment at their Headquarters at Moor Park, Rickmansworth, Hertfordshire. I was met at Ricksmanworth Station, to my great surprise, by a corporal with SAS insignia, in a jeep with a white 'P' on a black background painted on it. I still remember thinking at the time, surely I couldn't be posted to the SAS with the medical grade of A2. But I was now part of 'F' Squadron Phantom Regiment attached 2nd SAS, commanding officer Major the Hon. J Astor, second-in-command Captain John Hislop, and we were under canvas at Moor Park golf course. I soon became aware that the beautiful white mansion at the top of the course was part of the SHAEF organisation. It was all very thrilling. I was soon brought down to earth with a whirlwind of intensive training as a cypher operator, (though I was supposed to be a W/T operator!) various field training; guns, knives etc. I enjoyed it all and was progressing well. I was thoroughly at home with cypher and I think, looking back, felt being Jewish, I had to be at least as good as or better than others doing the same duties.

As time went on I knew I was now encoding and decoding traffic, including some from *Popski's Private Army*, faster than anyone else could. This was noted by control, Cpl Plato, who, by the way, was also Jewish. I explained that I had inadvertently remembered most of the two-letter combinations on the main reference card, so very rarely did I have to stop and check from my five-letter code pad. I must have had, at the time, an excellent memory and I was now very confident of myself – and others in charge were very sure of me.

One day I was on orders to see the MO. He told me there was a problem, because of my medical grade A2. He said the CO wanted to keep me and, therefore, he had arranged for me to have physiotherapy twice a week, in my rest period, at the local hospital. I was very relieved, and flattered, as sometimes my foot was quite painful, but for obvious reasons I never complained. The MO was going to do his best to be able to pass me A1. Unfortunately, rumours had started that I was malingering and there was a lot of strained feelings. After a while I made a request to the CSM to stop any treatment, but was told in 'army' language to do as I was ordered. Soon after the atmosphere around me improved and I'm sure he must have had a quiet word.

It was all academic anyway. D-Day had arrived and we were on the move. Next stop was Halstead in Essex. This time not under canvas but in a huge house, and we were soon operating normally again. My medical regrading was now forgotten and although my foot was occasionally painful, I certainly wasn't going to mention it to anyone! There must have been some covert arrangements though, because whenever there were route marches or country runs, I was always found some special tasks which prevented me from joining in. Just as well!

Instructions came on standing orders one day to report to the CO's office and I found Major Astor and Captain Hislop sitting at their desks, both drawing horses on their message pads. (Major Astor and Capt. Hislop were both very well connected in the racing world and were top amateur jockeys.) Major Astor announced grandly, 'You will be attached forthwith to the 82nd American Airborne Corps in France – see the CSM.' I remember I felt as though I had won a holiday competition, as there were so many others who could have been chosen.

A couple of days later I was at 'Mushroom Farm', the nearest American airbase, and after a couple of cancelled flights due to fog, found myself with other SAS personnel, from different units, in an uncomfortable DC3 piloted by two cigar-smoking Americans.

We landed in Rheims and were then taken on by jeep to

Epernay, 82nd Airborne's HQ. On our way we drove through two small villages on the outskirts of Epernay aptly named Boozy and Tizzy, for we were in the heart of 'Champagne Country' now.

I met my W/T operator at 82nd HQ, and we were soon transmitting. The HQ was a small hotel and we were working and sleeping in one of the top rooms. My memory's a bit hazy now, but I remember lots of messages regarding supplies and drop zones; sometimes travelling in a jeep with a mounted Bren gun; sending and receiving messages in open country – no idea where; endlessly winding the handle of the field generator powering the radio for wireless transmission; eating 'K' rations and sometimes drinking champagne instead of water; and listening into the BBC at certain times to wait for the tune '*Sur le Pont d'Avignon*', which apparently was a signal for us to tune into a special frequency for messages. I don't really remember what most of them were about but I do, however, remember decoding a couple of interesting messages. One, from the French Maquis, read: 'AMBUSH TO KILL *GENERAL* VON RUNSTEDT ABORTED'. The other, quite amusing, read: 'SGT–SMITH–KILLED–SNIPER'. We sent back: 'WHO WAS KILLED?' The reply was 'SNIPER'.

It was now late Autumn, there seemed to be a lull in the war, and all the transmissions seemed very mundane.

Ever since we had arrived at the hotel our W/T room was off limits to all ranks, other than Phantom officers. Late one night we were sending and receiving and I didn't hear the the door opening, but the next thing I knew was a heavy blow to the back of my head. I didn't remember what had happened but apparently I was hit by the butt of a rifle. My W/T partner managed to disarm the attacker and call for help. Of course I was stunned but not badly injured, except for a large bump on the back of my head. The person involved turned out to be a driver corporal in the SAS, but not anyone I had ever had contact with. I was asked later by an American officer whether I wished to press charges against him, but I preferred to speak to him directly myself, and ask, why me?, as I didn't know him at all. We did talk and he was very apologetic. He said he had been drinking too much and had somehow found out that I was Jewish. He had become violently anti-semetic because his sister, a nurse, had been killed by a bomb attributed to Jewish terrorists in the fighting in Palestine. I decided there and then not to press charges and we talked a lot, getting to know one another well and becoming good friends. I was pleased that there was now one anti-semite less in the world. This was, by the way, the nearest I came to personal injury during the war – except, of course, my foot in training.

It was now the middle of December, we were all thinking about Xmas and those back home when our normal routine was interrupted by the appearance at HQ of one Captain (Count) Sadoine. I cannot remember the details, but the W/T operator and myself were to be ready the following day for a secret mission into Belgium. I still remember the first day I saw Capt. Sadoine, he was dressed immaculately in the uniform of a Belgian Army Captain, with so many shining buttons he looked like a performer in some opera, but the next day he was dressed just like us – in red beret and camouflage jacket and trousers.

We set off as arranged with Capt. Sadoine driving the jeep and, as far as I can remember, not disclosing where we were going. It was bitterly cold and foggy and we finally ended up in Brussels. We were left at an Army Hostel and told by Sadoine that he was going on to Phantom HQ at Waterloo for further instructions because of the fog. Early on the morning of the 15th December, the Captain met up with us again and we all went back to Waterloo to pack code-books and W/T equipment in our jeep and, despite appalling weather and driving conditions, we were now on our way to somewhere! I don't think at the time I knew where we were heading. I remember passing Namur and Dinant, then we were travelling very slowly on secondary roads, then nothing more than country lanes, climbing it seemed all the time. I also remember so well all was completely silent apart from the engine of the jeep, and it was like being in the cockpit of an aeroplane flying through clouds. The jeep was an incredibly reliable vehicle and would go over any sort of terrain and obstacles. It was a very long and uncomfortable journey before we reached our objective which was the small obscure village hamlet of 'Froid-Fontaine'. There, we met up at a red brick school house with a Phantom patrol, I don't remember what squadron they were but we were relieved and glad to see them. We set them up for transmission with appropriate code-books and wireless equipment and wished them luck. It was now not only foggy, but dark and so cold, but we were on our way.

We stopped several times to consult our maps and when I now think of it I wonder how Capt. Sadoine knew which route to take. We arrived back in Epernay very late on Friday the

15th and the Captain left us. We set up transmission once again and on the morning of Saturday the 16th, received snippets of news that there had been some German activity in the Northern Ardennes area. No significant appreciation was given at the time to this news but later information made the situation look much more serious. Rumours were rife that a major German offensive was taking place. We knew that US 82nd airborne was involved in this area and I remember that by Christmas Day the situation had become very grave – the Germans were steadily pushing forward. We were ordered to pack up, as was the whole of the HQ, and be ready to move at a moment's notice. We remained on 'stand by' for quite a while, until gradually the position in the Ardennes improved. The weather had cleared over Christmas which allowed our air forces to strike at the Germans and they were pushed back to where they had started. I did realise at the time we were lucky to have moved from Froid Fontaine when we did, but still, even now, wonder what happened to the Phantom patrol that was working so close to the German lines. I did try and find out through various official channels, but no luck. I have often thought it strange that Phantom patrols were set up in the Ardennes at that particular time. Coincidence or planning? Later we were to learn that the German offensive was originally planned to start on the 15th December, but due to bad weather was postponed until the following day. Had we not left when we did we would have been trapped in the midst of the battle area.

With the *'Battle of the Bulge'* over we could now all relax a little. I don't remember much of interest after this, except transmitting to Phantom patrols in Norway, until the war in Europe finally came to an end.

We eventually arrived back in Halstead, Essex, travelling by jeep and then across the channel from Cherburg in an LST (Landing Ship Tank). Gradually, one by one, we were becoming obsolete and were posted to Holding Units, without any fuss or recognition. We had finished our assignments and done our duty.

No. 3 GHQ Liaison Regiment was now formed at Phantom HQ Richmond for action in the Far East, but the dropping of the atom bombs on Japan put paid to this. The war was finally over.

## FROM THE 4TH ROYAL TANK REGIMENT TO PHANTOM

*by Driver Stan Bennion, Phantom 'K' Squadron*

It was 1940, and a bright, sunny June day in France. My mates and I, a 19-year-old tank driver, said our prayers and were blessed by a padre – then we tucked into strawberries and cream. We were some of the remnants of the British Expeditionary Force, the BEF, sent over to France the year before. We were going into action in our Matilda tanks, but before we went we all had to hand in the page from our paybooks reserved for our wills. I wrote on mine that in the event of my death everything should go to my wife. The Dunkirk evacuation was over but there was still the rearguard action to be fought to protect the last remnants of the British army. Captain Colan of the 4th Royal Tank Regiment had hastily formed the Lines of Communication Unit in the Northern Division of which I and my two mates Fred Burgess and Ron Southcott were a part. We were now the Independent Tank Company, Beauman's Division, and were attached to the French General Gaillard of the 10th French Army. I was the driver of a *Matilda* Mk I tank to Captain Colan. During the second week of June 1940 the battle for France raged until, with all hope gone and the Germans entering Paris, we were ordered to withdraw from our position near Beauvais towards Rouen. It was then that our tank was hit by an 88-mm shell and had to be abandoned. Luckily, the CO and I weren't hurt and managed to run back to the *Matilda* Mk II behind us. Under heavy fire we climbed in and retired towards Brittany and headed for Cherbourgh. We returned to 'Blighty' on the 21st June as France capitulated to the Germans.

What a surprise our families had when Fred, Ron and myself arrived home, for they had received telegrams to say that we were 'missing in action, believed killed', little knowing that we were still fighting in France. On the 17th June the British passenger Liner *Lancastria* with five thousand soldiers and civilians on board had been sunk as she left the French port of St Nazaire. A German bomber struck and nearly three thousand of those on board lost their lives – and we were presumed to be amongst them.

We were given eight days 'survivor's leave', and on the 30th June, returned to the 4th RTR at Farnborough, but there were no tanks available so the next day were sent to join a new unit being formed at Lechlade in Gloucestershire. Together with Fred and Ron, I became a member of the GHQ Reconnaissance Unit, sometimes known as 'Hopkinson's Mission'. We were all mixed regiments, Artillery, Signals, REME, Rifle Brigade, Cameron Highlanders, Middlesex Regiment and the Prince of Wales Volunteers. After some months, early in 1941, we became the GHQ Liaison Regiment, based in Richmond, Surrey. We retained our original regimental uniforms but all had to wear a black cloth square with the letter 'P' in white on the right sleeve at shoulder. We were code named Phantom. I became Patrol NCO Corporal to 'K' Squadron's No. 2 patrol, led by Lt the Hon J J Astor, and on occasions our patrol officer was Lt Fulke Walwyn, who later became a trainer of the Queen's horses.

We were sent on various training schemes all round the country and I became a motorcycle despatch rider. In August 1941 we had our regimental motor cycle trials at the Devil's Punchbowl, Redhill, Surrey. I had a brand new BSA 500 and won the fastest hill climb for the second year running, but this year I had the bonus of wearing a RAF flying suit for all over protection.

In the Spring of 1942, still with 'K' Squadron, I was stationed down at Llanerchydrol Hall in Welshpool. Major Spicer was CO of 'K' Squadron. Later in 1942 we also spent some time at Chatham in Kent.

I was with Phantom until I was de-mobbed in June 1943. The reason for my discharge was 'Permanently unfit for any form of military service'. The German 88-mm shell that had hit our tank near Rouen in 1940 had caused me partial deafness, from which I was not to recover.

## PHANTOM IN GERMANY 1946-1949

*by Private Cecil Bramley, No. 3 GHQ Liaison Regiment.*

My time with Phantom was after hostilities had ceased, so was not as exciting as those who spent their time at war. Nevertheless, it was still a marvellous experience. This is how I came to be part of the No. 3 GHQ Liaison Regiment.

I was conscripted into the army in 1947 and after my initial army training at Bury St Edmunds and Catterick, I found myself on a ship bound for the German port of Cuxhaven. From there I was transported to a holding unit in Bielefeld.

After several weeks, myself and four others were told to report to the orderly room for an interview. After a short wait I found myself standing in front of an officer with a white 'P' on his arm, who asked me several questions and gave me a number of tests to do. I suppose to determine my IQ. The other four went through the same procedure and we were then given a basic outline of Phantom and its role. The officer finished by saying that we may or may not hear anymore from him, we would have to wait.

For three weeks we didn't hear a thing, we were beginning to think we hadn't been accepted into this regiment, when suddenly we were told to collect our kit together and be outside the orderly room at 2 pm. Within half an hour we were on our way to Bunde/Ennigloh – and Phantom. Expecting to be taken to another barracks, we were most surprised when the lorry dropped us off in the tiny village of Ennigloh, east of Osnabruck, and left us standing in the road. The place was deserted. There was no sign of any army personnel, no sign of any movement at all. We stood there for a while wondering what to do when round the corner came a soldier. He came up to us and asked what we were doing. Seeing the crown on his sleeve we quickly realised that he was a Sergeant Major and stood to attention.

'We've been posted to Phantom, Sir,' we answered in unison.

'Well, I don't know anything about you,' he stated. 'I'll have to find out what's going on. Go down the road there and you will see a swimming pool on your right. Wait there for me. And by the way you don't have to call me Sir, my name's Rabbetts. Just call me Bunny.

When we arrived at the pool most of Phantom was there, officers and men all together. We began to wonder what we had walked into, but we soon found out.

With the war over there were only about eighty Phantom personnel left in the regiment, for most had been demobbed or were waiting to go home to the UK. From the Regimental HQ at Bunde we were divided into patrols of six men, with GMC armoured cars complete with radio sets. We were employed in various trouble spots, reporting back to HQ, but when not out on patrol led a life of comparative ease in Ennigloh. The atmosphere was mostly very relaxed, but 'on parade' meant 'on parade', and every now and then we were reminded of this.

Major Morgan was the CO when I first joined Phantom but was later replaced by Major Charles McDevitt. I was detailed to be his driver, a job I really enjoyed. I remember on one occasion, in the summer of 1947, I was driving the major in his Humber Tourer, a big old square car built like a tank but capable of over 100-mph, to Travarmunde. The whole regiment was there on an excercise. As we drove through Hamburg the whole city was completely flattened, and I drove about twenty miles without seeing one house or building standing. And it wasn't just Hamburg, many towns and cities had been laid to waste.

When we came to the officer's club, which was in one of the few buildings left standing, Major McDevitt told me to pull in, because he needed a drink and refreshments. The NAAFI, for the other ranks, was in the Victory Club which, unfortunately for me, was over four miles from the officer's club.

'I don't know what to do about you,' he said. Then, after a minute's thought, he told me to get out of the car and handed me his battle dress jacket, saying, 'Put this on, keep quiet and follow me.'

As we passed through the doors of the Club the two MP's at the door gave me a terrific salute. I responded by touching my beret, as officer's do. When we came back out McDevitt said to me, 'That made your day didn't it. Now take that jacket off.' My moment of glory was over. It could only have happened in Phantom.

I remember another occasion when I was driving the major. We were on an autobahn in the big Humber staff car touching 100-mph when I suddenly felt Major McDevitt's hand grab the crease of my trousers. Without saying a word, he slowly lifted my leg off the accelerator – until the car had slowed to fifty.

I had three wonderful years with Phantom, attached to the 7th Armoured Division 21st Army Group British Army on the Rhine, until one day we were told that the Regiment was coming to an end. Those of us who were left were sent to the British Army barracks in the German town of Herford where we were shortly demobbed. Had Phantom remained I think I would have signed on as a regular soldier, but it was not to be.

Whilst in Bunde I had started courting a young German girl, Elfriede, whom I eventually married, and we have been together fifty-four years now. I was not the only Phantom soldier there to marry a local girl, so did my mate Peter Bloomfield. I have been back to Bunde nearly every year since 1949, to visit Elfriede's family, and each time I recall the happy memories of my days there as part of Phantom.

## MY SERVICE WITH PHANTOM.

*by Private John Campbell, The Gordon Highlanders serving with 'E' and 'L' Squadrons, GHQ Liaison Regiment*

I registered for military service at the Labour Exchange in Coatbridge, Lanarkshire, in the autumn of 1939, following the introduction of the Compulsory Training and Conscription Act. Sometime after I received orders to report to a Royal Artillery unit in Carlisle. That would have been in September 1939. A few days before I was supposed to leave for Carlisle I received word to join the 8th Battalion, The Gordon Highlanders at Aberdeen. I enjoyed the training and was put in the Signal Section in HQ Company. I learnt the Morse code and also signalling with one flag. We had to wear our civvy clothes until the end of December because there were no uniforms. We were still forming up on parade in fours whilst the rest of the army were forming up in threes. During that time the battalion moved to Craigellachie, Dufftown, and then Huntly. It was in Huntly when we learned the battalion was to be changed from Vickers machine guns to Royal Artillery. We were told we could stay with the battalion, transfer to another battalion of the Gordons or go to an Infantry Training Centre. Sometime before this some of my pals and I had put our names to a sheet asking for volunteers for GHQ Liaison Regiment. We were called to the COs office and given the opportunity of withdrawing our names. Bill Joss, Ian McAuley, Freddy Watt and Sandy Fraser are the only names I can remember, and so we travelled south together to regimental headquarters in Richmond. Here we were interviewed by Major Vernon, Grenadier Guards, and accepted into 'E' Squadron Phantom.

Training consisted of practice with Bren guns and rifle drill, some of it in the grounds of the Tower of London by a sergeant of the Irish Guards. Once the squadron was made up to strength we moved to Edinburgh. Here training started in the use of No. 11 wireless sets and speeding up our morse code. We trained as a patrol, each patrol having an officer, corporal, wireless operator, driver and two dispatch riders. Sometimes I would be in a patrol under Lt Mackinlay and sometimes it would be Lt. Stileman. The commander of 'E' Squadron was Major Vernon, second in command was Captain the Hon. Hugh Fraser, the Lieutenants were MacDonald, Fraser, Stileman, Mackinlay, Baring, McIntosh Reid, Adam and

Beckwith Smith, who left the squadron before we went to North Africa.

During the training we got to know each other and the officers. We were billetted in what had been Cranley Girls School and there was an assault course round two sides of the school. We also had a loft full of homing pigeons under the care of Taffy Jones. I don't think he knew how to care for them and the idea was abandoned. At least in 'E' Squadron.

In addition to training as a patrol we had one exercise as a squadron and all travelled up into the mountains. I can't remember exactly where but it was very isolated and we bivouacked on the moors. We paired off and using our ground sheets made a little tent. Someone suggested using Bog Myrtle to keep the midges away, but I'm not sure if it was effective or not. One pair who thought they had one over on the rest of us lit a small paraffin lamp to keep themselves warm, but they hadn't thought to trim the wick properly. The result being that the lamp smoked all night, covering everything in soot. Including themselves!

One day Lt MacDonald sent for me and asked my advice about a No. 18 wireless set he had difficulty with. Apparently, someone had told him I was an expert, which wasn't true. However, suspecting that someone was having a joke at my expense, or Lt MacDonald's, I asked what was wrong.

'It stops working and starts when I kick it,' he answered.

'Well, in that case, I suggest you kick it again, Sir,' I said. This he did, it started up again and he thanked me for my advice.

Later on he sent for me again because he had lost his spectacles. I asked why his own patrol couldn't search for them, but he said they already had, but with no luck. To humour him I asked him to think back to when he last had them, and what he was doing. He struck a pose and then his right hand started to circle round and round. When he described where he was standing, I looked up and there they were, stuck on a low branch of the tree he was standing under. He again thanked me, saying he knew he could depend on me. He may have been told that I had been sent on an exercise practising the use of No. 18 sets in street-fighting below the floors in a row of houses in the commercial part of Leith.

The squadron had Daimler Scout Cars for some time in Edinburgh until these were replaced by Humber Armoured Cars which were bigger and offered a little more protection. Each one had a metal frame welded to the rear which held a charging unit to charge the radio batteries which were heavy and awkward to handle. Our No. 11 wireless sets were replaced by more modern No. 19 sets which worked very well. We used these when we took part in an exercise off the west coast near Troon.

When the time came to leave for North Africa, as part of Operation Torch, a despatch rider and myself were sent down to the King George V docks at Glasgow to oversee our equipment being loaded onto ships. These ships had been especially built in Canada and America for carrying troops, transport and cargo. They were called Liberty ships and ours was named the SS *Fort Pitt*.

During the voyage to Algiers, whilst in the South Atlantic, our convoy was attacked by German U-boats and we could see ships being blown up. Our naval escort responded by dropping depth charges, but I don't know if they hit their target. It was a really frightening experience.

Sometime after the U-boat attack there were loud banging noises on the ship's sides, just like the sound of depth charges. The first mate asked for volunteers and four of us went down into the hold to see what was happening. It turned out that the noise was field kitchens that had broken loose and were hitting the sides of the ship. The mate was very concerned that the continual pounding could damage the ship, so, after several attempts, we managed to work out a strategy to secure the field kitchens which worked, and we slept peacefully until we reached Gibraltar.

The docks at Gibraltar were very busy, and we remained here for several days while deck cargo was off-loaded. Some of these crates contained stripped-down aircraft, which a couple of days later we actually saw flying off towards Algiers.

One duty we had to perform whilst in Gibraltar was to keep watch in shifts armed with a bomb. If we saw large amounts of bubbles surfacing near the ship, we had to light the fuse and drop it overboard. This was to counteract any attempt by the Italian Navy mini-subs, which were coming up from Spain, to plant limpet mines on the sides of the ships. These would explode when the ships were at sea.

But it wasn't all work. We were allowed to go ashore and it was a very welcome break. Some of us even managed to borrow clothes to go ashore at night to see a cabaret in a club.

It was while we were in Gibraltar that we began to hear news of the landings on the North African coast, and so we set sail again for Algiers.

The ship we were on had twin *Oerlikons*, anti-aircraft guns, and these were maintained by the army. I was told to familiarise myself with these in case the gunner got shot. I also had to try on an asbestos suit in case we had to rescue people from fire on board, and if shipwrecked had to be able to work the small radio. Thankfully, none of this was needed and we landed safely in Algiers in early November 1942.

For several days we were stationed adjacent to a big sports field, whose underground changing rooms made great air raid shelters. We were regularly being bombed by the Germans and Italians flying from North Africa and Italy. After a short time we moved to a place outside Constantine, where for a while we operated as a radio station to Phantom patrols working in forward positions. For some time I, along with Bill Joss, Freddy Watt and Ian McAuley, manned a radio set keeping in touch with these patrols, but we worked on a part of the band that shut down at night. A radio frequency amplifier was shipped out from Pye Laboratories in England, which we tried out, but it was a waste of time. If we were to maintain twenty-four hour contact with patrols we would need a better allocation of the radio frequencies.

'E' Squadron now formed into new patrols, and I was chosen to work with Captain Mackinlay, although once or twice I went out with Captain Stileman. The officers had all been promoted to captains by this time to make them more acceptable in the map rooms of the various formations we were attached to. During this time we were thin on the ground and our patrols were in great demand so were sent where needed most. We were despatched to wherever any action was planned or was taking place and would have to hurriedly leave one unit and travel as fast as we could to another. We all worked well together. Corporal Reg Wilsher helped Mackinlay with encoding and decoding and then handed the messages to me for transmission. We also had two despatch riders, one was called Stuka Pitts and I can't recall the other, and an armoured car driver, Bill Reynolds, who was an Eastender from Whitechapel in London. We had quite a few scary times when we were shelled, although we were never expected to go too far forward. On the whole we depended on getting news from Division or Brigade, or sometimes Battalion, but it never ruled out the chance of being bombed and strafed from the air by the horrible Junkers Ju 87 '*Stuka*' dive bombers. That was some experience, I can tell you.

Once when we were with the the French 19th Corps, along with eighteen American Honey tanks, they were to feign an attack on Pichon, while the main assault was carried out by the French from the rear. The road we were on, a track really, was mined and one of the Honey tanks hit one. Fortunately, no injuries were sustained and the damage was confined to the front track, so our officer called out, 'Jump out quick, Campbell, and get some petrol from them. We don't have very much and they won't need it!' So I jumped out and he shouted, 'Campbell, mind the mines!' How I could be careful of mines I couldn't see, I don't know. Anyway, I managed to somehow avoid the mines but as I approached the tank a big American sergeant stuck his head out with a Colt-45 in his hand, I think he thought I was a German. When he realised who I was he willingly allowed me to take his petrol.

We took shelter behind an outcrop of rock and I started to erect my aerial. This was a long wire held up by two nine foot wooden poles slotted together to make a single pole eighteen feet high. Captain Stileman questioned my siting of the aerial in full view of the German artillery and before it was properly erected shells landed. Fortunately, it was solid shot, and I was able to move to a safer spot.

The French soldiers we were with had a different radio system from us, a bit antiquated but just as practical. It was like an upturned bike with one soldier turning the pedals with his hands to power their radio set.

It was at this French HQ that we watched arabs lining up a few yards apart just before sundown, and as the sun disappeared they started walking towards enemy lines. One poor soul, not many yards into his walk, trod on a mine and was killed. We never knew how many came back each morning.

The assault was a great success and Pichon was taken on the last day of March 1943. Phantom had worked well!

Back with Captain Mackinlay we moved on to another town near Souk-el-Abra with the French and camped up in a farmyard. We were covering the French 9th and 19th Corps and I was sending many messages, mainly at night when the rest had bedded down. '*Stuka*' Pitts, who doubled as the captain's batman, for no reason at all removed the gearbox from of his motorbike and took it apart. Only trouble was he couldn't get it all back together again properly. The clutch didn't work any more, so the only way he could change gear after this was by using the engine revs.

It was not long after this incident that I noticed that *'Stuka'* was no longer with us, but I did spend most of my time on the radio in the armoured car so missed some things. Finally, I asked one of the other patrol members where *'Stuka'* was and was told that he had malaria and had gone to hospital.

It was about this time that anti-malarial tablets were issued, and we all took one with plenty of water. I was violently sick during the night and spent two days vomiting. I thought I was going to die. I remember Taffy Evans looking after me. Captain Fraser came out from HQ and it was decided I should take a small piece of a tablet and gradually increase the amount. That didn't work, I was sick again, so I never took the risk after that.

As well as the French we also worked with the Americans in North Africa and one of the best things about working with them was the great rations they supplied us with; flapjacks, maple syrup, pancakes and fried eggs, but most of all we appreciated the American cigarettes.

When hostilities ceased in North Africa the patrol packed up and headed east towards Tunis, where we watched the amazing sight of thousands of Germans and Italians coming in to be locked up in prisoner of war camps. We were billetted at Cap Bon for a time and then went west to a small place called Bugeaud, in a cork forest 3,000 feet up in the mountains west of Bizerta, where we were under canvas until the invasion of Sicily and Italy took place.

I was sent from Bugeaud along with others to train with the SAS near Phillipeville. The training in the heat and dust of North Africa was gruelling. Near the end of our training we were supposed to go to an airfield to do parachute jumps but the wind was too strong, so it never happened. Then, early one morning we were awakened and told to pack up as we were leaving for a drop on Sicily with the SAS. This frightened the life out of me, I had never done a parachute jump. Luckily, soon after, orders were changed and we were told to stay put until a truck arrived from squadron to take us back to Bugeaud.

Preparations were well under way when we arrived in Bugeaud and soon we headed east towards Bizerta. There we were told we were going to be deck cargo on two Navy cruisers, HMS *Aurora* and HMS *Penelope*, bound for Italy. The journey to Taranto was uneventful, except when we met the Italian Navy heading for Tunisia to surrender. At Taranto we were taken ashore by a small boat, where we had difficulty in unloading as the tide was going out, but when finished we marched inland to an olive grove where we bedded down for the night. At Captain Mackinlay's request, I played a few tunes on my mouth organ to help everybody settle. It was now September 1943.

The main body of troops that was going in at Taranto was the Airborne Division, commanded by Major General Hopkinson, who originated Phantom in France during the last days before Dunkirk. He was the type of person who always led from the front and was sadly killed soon after the invasion.

While the main body of paratroopers was sent up the west coast of Italy, Phantom, along with *Popski's Private Army* and the Long Range Desert Group, headed off to the east coast, to see where the Germans were. We set off for Bari and when we were about halfway there, as I was sending messages and listening to the radio, I heard on the BBC that a strong line of British troops was holding a line between Taranto and Bari. I repeated this to Captain Stileman and said, 'We haven't got anything to worry about, then, Sir.'

He laughed out loud and replied, 'Look around you, Campbell, that strong line is us!'

When we arrived in Bari the Germans had just left so there was no exchange of fire, and the Italians were delighted to see us. So much so that they showered us with gifts of wine, almonds, walnuts and ice cream.

From Bari we moved up the coast to the town of Trani where we were bivouacked in the grounds of a large house. The squadron had been asked to find out where the Germans were which meant the patrols had to go out. First on foot and then by jeep. I wasn't with Captain Stileman's patrol when they had to ambush a German convoy, but I remember when they returned they were pretty excited. Their baptism of fire.

I went out with a two jeep patrol, our driver was Bombadier Vicery but I don't recall the officer's name. I sat in the back of the jeep at the wireless set with my earphones on in case the jeep following wanted us. I began to get a bit worried as the officer sitting in the front was busy cracking walnuts on the floor of the jeep with the butt of his revolver. We ran into what we thought was a German motor cycle patrol and there was an exchange of fire. The jeep stuck when it reversed over some rocks and was left behind. It was returned the next day by Italians.

That night Captain Mackinlay asked me what had happened.

I gave him my explanation and added, 'You can shoot me if you like but I'm not going out with that officer again!' I heard nothing more about the incident.

The next day I was taken to an Italian hospital, I was in agony. Not as a result of enemy action but by my own foolishness. Before we had set out on patrol the previous day I had been splashed with diesel oil, and not being able to scrub my hands properly, plus sitting in the strong sunlight, both my hands were swollen and blistered. Our despatch rider took me along to the local hospital, where they took blood samples and announced that I had dermatitis. The result was that I ended up in the Italian military hospital in Bari, along with a member of the LRDG, who was having his piles treated, and an Italian Sergeant Major, who befriended me whilst taking great delight in tormenting an Italian pilot who had been shot down. In addition to the blisters on my hands, I had ulcers on my knees, caused by chafing ropes when training with the SAS. My treatment was high doses of Epsom Salts.

An interpreter, Giovanni, looked after me, and as I began to feel better he would take me out in the town with him when he ran his errands. He introduced me to his friends. Everyone was very friendly, except for one particular nun at the hospital. Every time she passed my bed she would scowl at me, so eventually I asked Giovanni what her problem was. Apparently, the Germans had told her that when the British came they were going to kill the Pope, and being a devout Roman Catholic, she thought this was terrible. I assured her that we had no intention of harming the Pope, it was just German propaganda, and that my next door neighbours in Scotland were catholics. After that she changed her attitude towards me completely, even giving me extra titbits. By the time I was well enough to leave hospital we were firm friends and she gave me a small religious medal which she said would protect me throughout the war. I lost it, but I still got home safely!

In June of 1943, Major Vernon had left 'E' Squadron and returned to Phantom HQ at Richmond. He was replaced by Major the Hon. H C P J Fraser.

I can remember a patrol with Captain Stileman when a landing was made further up the coast at Termoli. We were with the force that was supposed to break a way through and join up with this landing force. For some time it looked as though we would be overrun when the Germans counterattacked. As Captain Stileman had been away for some time and I was getting concerned, I asked Taffy Evans to try and find out what was happening. The mortar shells coming in were getting closer and more frequent. When Taffy came back he was looking scared and said, 'They are burning the code books and the Squadron Major was standing with a revolver in each hand ordering troops back to fight.'

Fortunately, the enemy counterattack was beaten off and Major Fraser and Captain Simon, Radio Officer, were both very lucky to get back. On their way through to Termoli Captain Simons had given me a few cigarettes, now he asked me if he could have one back. Major Fraser was still our CO when we were recalled to England in November 1943.

We left Taranto by Greek ferry and sailed for Bizerta. Our next journey was to a place near Algiers. During the journey, by train in horse boxes, there was an incident when we were stopped in a siding to let another train go by. It was a special train, with every window barred. The officer in charge asked if some of us would stand guard while his men rested. He told us all the men on board were criminals, rapists, murderers and deserters, and if they attempted to leave the train to shoot them. Since then I have often wondered if the men on the train were the members of the Scottish Regiment who were involved in mutiny.

The only other incident on the journey was when our train was rammed by another. Some who saw it coming managed to get out in time, but I was in the doorway ready to jump when the other train struck and landed head over heels on the ground.

Eventually, we ended up in a winery near Algiers, where some of the lads practiced their carol singing. Well, it was nearly Christmas, after all!

On Algiers Docks we were entertained by a group of French soldiers as we waited ages to embark. There were two guards stationed at the 'gangplank' who turned away everyone without permission from an officer on board. One officer who attempted to board was stopped, but even when he called out that he was a King's Messenger and demanded to be allowed on board, the answer was still no. I think had he been allowed on there could have been trouble, because the mass of men moved forward as if given a signal.

Eventually we boarded, and the worst part of the journey home to Liverpool was having to sleep in a hammock!

When we returned from leave we joined 'L' Squadron at

Dollar in Scotland. We spent a lot of time in the hills, either sleeping out on the snow or running from the camp out over the hills to Aucharder, about sixteen miles away, where Captain Stileman paid for tea and scones before a truck came to return us to Dollar. We also marched over the hills to try out our new equipment; rucksacks, sleeping bags, windproof trousers and smocks and, of course, heavy woollen sweaters. We went out as a patrol to different places up both the east and west coasts, with our new No. 22 wireless sets which had replaced the No. 19 sets.

I enjoyed the training and felt good in myself, the exercise, the better food and, of course, no fear. We weren't living in an area where we were about to be bombed at any time. We had no worries and could all relax a little. Our patrol was now Captain Stileman, patrol officer, Bill Joss, promoted to full corporal, John Tudor Evans and Alistair Clark, despatch riders, Pat Page, armoured car driver, Paddy Watson, jeep driver, and myself, radio operator.

In May 1944 our patrol was asked to move up into the Highlands, to transmit messages supposedly from formations moving north to the east coast. These messages were all in plain language in the hope that the Germans would think the Allies planned to invade Norway. The ploy worked because German troops were taken away from the defence of the Western front in Northern France to reinforce those in Norway.

One day in early June the Commanding Officer of Phantom, Lieutenant Colonel Macintosh, came up from HQ in Richmond to Dollar in Clackmannanshire especially to see 'L' Squadron. We assembled in the dining-room and Macintosh told us that the invasion of Europe had begun, but there would be no place for us.

Anyway, no sooner had he left than an order came through to pack up quickly and move south – we were going on the invasion after all. We moved down to an army camp near Guildford in Southern England, where there were other Phantom patrols. Our Humber armoured cars were taken away from us and were replaced with American White scout cars, superb vehicles. We spent a few days water-proofing them and all our equipment before driving down to a south coast port and being loaded on to an LST for the trip across the channel. On reaching the Normandy beaches we were lucky enough to have a dry landing. There were plenty of explosions going on on the beach but it was not German shells, it was our own engineers clearing a pathway through the wreckage left over from the D-Day landings. Phantom Regimental HQ had been set up alongside Army HQ, and we were there for a couple of days. At night we were being bombed, and it was quite frightening. That was our baptism of fire in France!

In the first few days of the invasion all the reliable information that was coming in came from Phantom. When the Allied Supreme Commander, General Eisenhower, realised this he requested a Phantom squadron be assigned to the US Army. 'L' was duly attached, and remained with American formations for the rest of the war. Our patrol was with elements of Patton's 3rd Army in Pilzen, Czechoslovakia, when the war ended in May 1945.

We were now idle for some time before we started supplying communication for the Berlin Military Government. In early June our patrol flew from Osnabruck aerodrome to Templehof in Berlin, where we saw Field Marshal Montgomery decorated by the Russian *Marshal* Zhukov.

Being among the first into Berlin was quite a thrill, and more so when I read in R J T Hills' book '*Phantom Was There*' this message sent from British Headquarters in Berlin: 'In spite of facilities for 54,000 groups per day provided by Signals, it has been found that Phantom is still the best means of getting a quick answer to a question. There is no intention of removing this patrol in the near future.' I like to think we were chosen as the best patrol rather than just being available.

Some time later I learnt that Major General Clarence Huebner, commanding officer of the US 5th Corps, had sent a letter of commendation to Phantom Regimental HQ in recognition of the work we had carried out whilst with his army.

We were all extremely proud to have served with Phantom – a very special regiment.

I was offered promotion to stay on but refused, but at the same time declined the offer of early release, which as a former building trade labourer I was entitled.

## MY MEMORIES OF PHANTOM
*by Paul Holdway, No. 12 Patrol 'A' Squadron*

I joined the Army in August 1942, or rather I was conscripted into it. By early 1943 I was a member of the General Headquarters Liaison Regiment – PHANTOM, and was stationed at the Army Training Ground at Swaffham Prior, near Newmarket. We were there for some time in training for the invasion of Europe.

I remember on one occasion we walked across the heath to the Newmarket racecourse, where I had a bet on a complete outsider called *Real Estate*. To my astonishment it won, at 30-1! Pity was I only had a shilling on it, but remember our pay was only about thirty shillings a week at that time, so it was probably all I had.

By the time I went over to France on D-Day plus 1, I was part of No.12 patrol 'A' Squadron. Our Commanding Officer was Major Dennis Russell and our patrol officer was Lt. Mackenzie. The patrol was made up of NCO Ted Rourke and the men were Ron Eaton, Freddy Clarke, Albert Bradbury, Andy Black and myself.

One of our first assignments was to work with the 6th Airborne who were holding Pegasus Bridge and we were all the subject of heavy German shelling, mortaring and bombing. It was completely a matter of luck whether you became a casualty or lost your life, and this in your first few days in France. After Pegasus we were withdrawn and joined the 51st Highlanders, who we were originally intended to be with, but after a couple of months we were assigned to the Americans as the Allies were preparing for the breakout from Normandy. It was during this time that Lt Mackenzie left us and he was replaced by Captain Meade. He remained our patrol officer all the way through.

Two scary moments I remember in particular. The first one was when on a pitch black night I had to take a message on my motorbike to Corps HQ. I, of course, had no lights, and neither did the Churchill tank parked in the lane. How I managed to stop in time I shall never know. When I had recovered from the shock the crew of the tank told me that I was heading straight for the German lines. So, I was quite lucky, I suppose!

On the second occasion we were with an American Corps HQ and I had to open up on the radio early in the morning. I had a little time to spare and decided to walk into the woods to obey a call of nature. I had gone about 200 yards when, to my horror, I could see fully-armed Germans with jackboots and several days growth of beard watching me. One of them lunged at me with a bayonet – he missed and I dived through blackberry bushes and God knows what else to escape as fast as my legs would carry me. When I got back I could hardly speak but, fortunately, the Americans believed what I was trying to tell them. I had to lead the way back and the Americans rounded up about 200 Germans – all fully-armed. I think that one or two Germans were shot as they did not want to surrender. I believe that our patrol officer got a medal out of it from the Americans.

We remained with the Americans until the end of the war, crossed the Rhine into Germany with them, and were well looked after all the time we were with the US Army.

Our patrol all got on remarkably well and stayed together until the end of the war when we went up into Denmark for a while before coming home to the UK in preparation for the invasion of Japan. By this time we were No. 3 GHQ Liaison Regiment.

I wasn't demobbed until 1947 and for the last five months of my service in Germany I worked for the Control Commission. I had volunteered for this so that I could get some clerical experience – just as well, as within a fortnight of leaving the Army I was working in the City for a merchant bank. I worked there for nearly thirty-three years until I retired at the end of 1979.

## MY DAYS WITH PHANTOM
### *by Trooper Ron Jackson, 'L' Squadron Phantom*

I was called up in September 1942 and spent six weeks at Nelson Barracks, Norwich, where I did basic training before being posted to 5th Royal Tank Regiment at Farnborough. I can't recall displaying any 'Phantom' attributes during my training but was, nevertheless, sent to Wootton, near Woodstock, to join 'L' Squadron in the spring of 1943.

The Squadron Commanding Officer was Major Reggie Hills, who had an obsession for vehicle maintenance, so every morning at 7.30am, although the squadron vehicles rarely left the car park, we carried out a daily 'task' on the hapless lorries. Tyres were inflated, nuts tightened and nipples greased, irrespective of their need. The fitters were horrified and spent an awful lot of time rectifying the damage we had caused. This operation was officially called '*stables*', a name that had been carried over from the cavalry regiments. It was at Wootton that I got my first wireless tuition. It was the No. 19 set and my tutor was Capt. Michael Astor.

Next to Dollar, Clackmananshire, where I spent a year – and £1 for wrecking a 15-cwt Bedford truck. I was taking Sgt Collis Marchant to Edinburgh to collect some batteries at about 6am on a dark morning when suddenly he said, 'Turn right!' Not being a very experienced driver, I did so and ran straight into the wall of a bridge over the River Forth. I turned to speak to Collis, but he wasn't there! I peered over the wall and saw a bewildered sergeant staggering about in the mud some eighteen feet below. Luckily the tide was out and Collis wasn't hurt. There were no proper doors on the truck, just canvas half-doors. We were later told that this section of wall was often hit and the workmen had only finished repairing it the day before. I was fined £1 for the loss of the vehicle, and relegated to drive the cook's truck! Collis was a lovely man and was my patrol sergeant until the end of the war. Whilst at Dollar I qualified as a driver-operator.

After spells in Paisley, Richmond and Thames Ditton our patrol, I think it was No. 4, was sent to SHAEF at Cosham, Portsmouth, to be assigned to General Patton's 3rd Army. At this time the patrol personnel were: Captain Speed-Andrews; Sergeant Collis Marchant; Trooper Les Durham, D/Op; Trooper Dickie Baker, D/Op; Trooper Ron Jackson, D/Op; Dave Parker, DR; and 'Colonel' Budd, driver, cook and man-of-all-trades. We had a US White armoured car (with only a canvas roof), a 15-cwt Bedford truck, a Jeep and a motorcycle.

We landed on '*Omaha*' beach about six weeks after D-Day and followed the US 3rd Army on the famed '*Red Ball Express*'. I remember on one occasion we had stopped for some reason on this road and another jeep stopped behind us. A five star general stepped out and strode up to our patrol leader, now Capt. Pannell, and demanded to know why we were blocking his 'goddamned highway'. It was none other than General Patton himself, and as a penalty he ordered us to park up a side-road and stay there for two hours!

The American Corps HQ held an early morning briefing each day where the current state of the front was reviewed, and an important document discussed was the summary of reports from Phantom patrols all along the front. These were re-transmitted by the '*Golden Arrow*' radio net from Phantom

HQ at 4am. On the day after our brush with Patton, the Corps HQ, to which we had been en route, had to postpone their briefing because Phantom was not ready due to our late arrival. I don't know whether this was by accident or design, but we got a lot more respect henceforward.

We stayed with 3rd Army and crossed the Rhine at Remagen with them. I was the duty operator at the time the first crossing was made and sent the message to Phantom HQ.

It was at this time that I suffered two perforated eardrums, and was told by an American doctor that if I were in the US Army I would be sent home.

The second week of December we were assigned to the American 101st Airborne Division at Bastogne and arrived on the outskirts of the town in the evening in thick fog. There was no sign of any other units anywhere and after a long wait Capt. Pannell decided to withdraw a few miles and wait until morning when the fog may have cleared. Next morning the enemy had encircled Bastogne and we were unable to join the Americans. Never mind, I nearly got a Purple Heart, and anyway 'Nuts' was not in our code book!

Towards the end of the war we were near Munich and I strayed into the American wireless compound of the Corps we were now with. I was impressed by the array of equipment set up in four massive trucks. I asked one of the operators how far they were transmitting. 'Oh,' he said, proudly, 'twenty miles.' I showed him our tiny No. 22 set, but was unable to convince him that I was working to Brussels – 400 miles away!

After VE Day we returned to Richmond awaiting shipment to the Far East, but when this was no longer necessary we set up in Bunde, Westphalia, taking over a German housing-estate which had a swimming-pool and a hall which became our cookhouse. This luxury ended when our patrol was sent to Fallingbostel on the Luneburg plain to work for the Coal Commission. This was in the winter of 1946/7, one of the coldest on record, and Fallingbostel must have been the coldest place outside the Arctic Circle!

In March 1947 I was demobbed and returned to find that Britain was also in the grip of the big freeze.

So ended my four and a half years in the Forces. I never considered that I did anything dangerous, as we had little choice as to where we went and what our duties were, but like good soldiers we followed orders. I met a lot of interesting people in Phantom, and writing this has revived many memories.

APPENDIX ONE

# General Headquarters Liaison Regiment Phantom: A brief record of this very special regiment

*by Military Historian the late Philip Warner*

During the Second World War Pembroke Lodge was requisitioned by the Government and allotted to be the Regimental Headquarters and Training Centre of 'PHANTOM', the code name and designation for the (secret) GHQ Liaison Regiment.

Phantom had been created in France in November 1939 with the specific purpose of obtaining the latest information about the 'bomb line', that is, the areas of a battlefield not occupied by our own troops and therefore containing suitable targets for bombing or shelling. In the First World War the position of our own and enemy troops had been fairly clearly defined by trench systems but in the more mobile conditions of 1939 onwards it would be difficult to avoid killing our or allied troops by 'friendly fire' as soldiers and vehicles, both camouflaged, frequently changed their positions, in the forward area.

Phantom was drawn from volunteers, usually very good linguists and always good motorcyclists. All were trained to a high level of sending and receiving morse code and were equipped with appropriate radios. Their task was to visit forward locations, obtain interviews with the battlefield commanders, ascertain their intentions, and then radio the latest state of the battle directly back to the Commander-in-Chief, at GHQ.

This would give the Commander-in-Chief an accurate picture of the progress of a battle as it was taking place and therefore enabled him to take vital decisions or change his plan if necessary. It was therefore far faster than the former method of relaying information by radio or line through the various formations, eg Battalion, Brigade, Division, Corps and finally GHQ, although that was still used for non-urgent signals traffic.

Collecting information was, of course, a difficult and

dangerous task, for it meant moving around in forward areas, travelling on motor cycles or fast, light vehicles over roads which might be mined or be within range of snipers, and making contact with isolated units in the middle of battles whose commanders might be too harassed and busy to want to be interviewed by a member of Phantom. It also involved listening to the radio transmissions of our own and enemy troops. An adventurous, determined, forceful personality was essential if the right information was to be obtained.

In consequence Phantom was a varied team of highly-talented personalities. Among them was David Niven, the actor, who had been a regular soldier and was as enterprising, brave and amusing in real warfare as he is in his many successful films. Another well-know actor was Tam Williams, who was amused to find that when he landed in enemy territory in Italy the local cinema was showing a film in which he was the star.

Three members became Professors: B Simon (Leicester University) and Michael Oakeshott (London School of Economics), and Brian Reddaway (Cambridge); two members became famous in the horse-racing world: John Hislop and the Hon. Sir J J Astor (who was also a Steward of the Jockey Club), and one member (Lord Bridge) a Lord Justice of Appeal.

Norman Reddaway became Ambassador to Poland. Sir Robert Mark became Commissioner of the Metropolitan Police, and Laurence Whistler became a poet and a renowned engraver on glass. Several became MPs: they included Jakie and Michael Astor, Sir Carol Mather, the Rt Hon. Sir Hugh Fraser, the Rt Hon. Maurice Macmillan, and Lord Christopher Mayhew.

Five, including Lord Cullen and Lord Reigate, took hereditary seats in the House of Lords. Kenneth Rose and Peregrine Worsthorne became well-known newspaper columnists and E E Rich became Master of St Catharine's College, Cambridge. A number of Phantom members became successful business men.

There were notable athletes, such as P Hincks, the Cambridge University shot-putter, and G O'B Power of Rugby Football fame. John Morgan, Chairman of a Publishing Company, who eventually commanded the regiment, made himself an expert on baseball in the cause of Anglo-American liaison and was the only Englishman who was ever asked to give a commentary on a broadcast of a top-level game in the USA. Sir Gordon Richards, the famous jockey, was in charge of the pigeon loft in St. James's Park: pigeons carried a number of important messages for Phantom when other lines were temporarily unavailable, and often flew through gunfire to reach their destinations.

The driving force behind the successful creation of Phantom here at Pembroke Lodge was the Commanding Officer, Lt. Col. G F Hopkinson, universally known as 'Hoppy'. Phantom had proved very useful in the Battle of France in 1940, but had ceased to exist after the Dunkirk evacuation and Hopkinson was determined that it should be recreated. He obtained permission to recruit forty-eight officers and 407 other ranks, set up a pigeon loft with 500 pigeons, acquired vehicles which were adapted to travel at high speeds, and established a training unit here in Richmond Park (which at the time was closed to the public). He was a relentless taskmaster. He trained Phantom to get up in the middle of the night and begin a complete working day, or work through a day, a night, and the following day, as they might be required to do on active service. Sometimes they would enter a period of working all night and sleeping (if possible) in the daytime. In air raids, however bad, he refused to let men take cover in slit trenches. He said that 'taking cover could make cowards'. Detachments were sent out all over the United Kingdom. Later, 'Hoppy' was promoted, became a Major-General, and was killed by a sniper while watching one of his companies attacking the enemy in Italy.

In Spring 1941 Phantom sent a squadron to Greece, but lost many men in that disastrous campaign. Later that year 'H' Squadron, consisting of five officers and fifty-one other ranks, was sent to the Middle East where the members learnt the art of desert navigation and survival (the North African desert is approximately the same size as India) and then sent detachments to operate with various units in the 8th Army.

During 1941 and 1942, Phantom was responsible for maintaining detachments in parts of Britain where they could give early warning of any invasion by the Germans. The regiment was now 900 strong and sent detachments to Palestine, Iraq and Syria, through which it was thought the Germans might try to reach the Middle East oilfields. When the Phantom members were in Mosul, Iraq, the temperature was 120 degrees by day and ninety degrees all night. Water was short and flies were innumerable, even settling on food as you conveyed it to your mouth.

When the Germans were defeated in North Africa the Allies

invaded Sicily and then Italy, giving much work to Phantom. Meanwhile, in 1942 Phantom had been used in a disastrous raid on Dieppe, mainly attached to Commandos, and sustained many casualties.

By 1944 Phantom's reputation was so high that everyone wished to have a detachment working with them. This included the SAS in France, the Canadians, the Americans, the Free French and the Poles. The Phantom presence was particularly valuable in France, notably in the closing of the Falaise pocket when the entire German armies were surrounded and annihilated (10,000 killed, 50,000 taken prisoner) by converging British, Canadian and American forces. Unless Phantom had been able to identify the exact position of allied forces, casualties from 'friendly fire', i.e. shelling and bombing, would have been enormous. In December 1944 when the Germans made a surprise counter-attack in the Ardennes and broke through the American sector, Phantom was soon on the spot, enabling the Higher Command to make the necessary moves to prevent temporary defeat turning into major disaster.

Although Field Marshal Montgomery had initially been sceptical about Phantom's ability to help him in his decision-making, he learnt by experience to value it very highly and said it was indispensable.

After the war ended in Europe, Phantom prepared to go to the Far East where the Japanese still had nearly five million men under arms and still occupied vast territories ranging from Malaya to China. However, the atomic bombs dropped in August 1945 caused them to surrender and Phantom's services were not required.

At the end of the war in 1945 Phantom was disbanded, but in 1947 was reborn as Army Phantom Signals Regiment (Princess Louise's Kensington Regiment); however, as technology continued to improve in the nuclear age, this was discontinued in 1960, on the basis that there would be no future request for Phantom. Whether that decision was the right one or not, time alone will tell.

Although Phantom, like many other regiments, has now ceased to exist, its contribution to winning the Second World War will not be forgotten. It had a vital part in all the campaigns from the Middle East to Europe, and at the same time managed to be one of the most cheerful, colourful and unorthodox units the British Army had ever contained – and its home was Pembroke Lodge.

APPENDIX TWO

# Letter from David Niven

With the kind permission of Daniel Hearsum, the present owner of Pembroke Lodge, Richmond Park, we print a letter by David Niven, containing three anecdotes. The letter was sent by the actor, and ex-Commander of Phantom's 'A' Squadron, from his home in Switzerland in 1982 to the late military historian Philip Warner.

Dear Philip,
Forgive rush, I'm catching a plane for California.

Yes, it is true. When 'A' Squadron was doing intensive training around Dartmoor, I did answer an SOS from the Navy, who were trying to handle the enemy E-boats which had twin *Oerlikons* guns popping off from an armour-plated bridge, and all they had were 3-pounder salute guns off, I suppose, the Victory, or something like that, with which to cope. Anyway, they had their eyes on our anti-tank rifles so I called for volunteers, hoping that nobody would suggest that I went too, but, unfortunately, everybody wanted to have a few nights at sea, so off we went, but, thank God, apart from endemic sea-sickness and the squadron's cook losing his teeth overboard, nothing happened. No E-boats showed up, or if they did, thank God, nobody noticed them.

The other saga was the pigeon. Hoppy gave us baskets of these foul beasts to carry messages when all else failed. I think General Paget was the Commander-in-Chief Home Forces and an elaborate loft was constructed outside his headquarters in St James's Park. Hoppy told him with great pride that messages would soon be arriving from the far-flung squadrons. Paget waited expectantly and at last a bird slapped in through the intake box. It was from 'A' Squadron. A massive exercise was in progress all over southern England and the message was ripped off the poor bird's leg and read in an expectant hush as follows: 'That beast Major Niven sent me away because he said I had farted in the nest'. I understand there was not much happy laughter in St James's Park!

I have forgotten the name of the Scandinavian actress I brought to the Richmond party who pinched everybody's cap badges, but I do remember organizing a concert in Richmond for the entire outfit, which included Flanagan and Allen, Nervo and Nox, Frances Day, Zoe Gale, Norton and Gold, Teddy Brown and his xylophone, Naunton Wayne, Arthue Riscoe, Lesley Henson and Debroy Sommers and his entire band. I believe the show was a hit, though as master of ceremonies I was too drunk to be able to assess it properly, and afterwards, in the officer's mess, one of the Crazy Gang asked Hoppy what the sandwiches had inside them. Hoppy pointed to the flag on the pile marked 'sardine'. Whereupon, Jimmy Nervo ate the flag, brushed the sardine sandwiches to the floor and broke the plate on Hoppy's head.

They were wonderful days which I would not have missed for anything.

All good wishes,
David Niven.

APPENDIX THREE

# An outline of the development of Wireless up to World War II

*by Colonel (Rtd) Cliff Walters, Director,
Royal Signals Museum, Blandford, Dorset.*

The term 'wireless' began to be used for transmissions of intelligence through space. The term remained in vogue until it was later changed to 'radio'. Wireless waves were first made in 1888 by Heinrich Hertz but it was Guglielmo Marconi, an Italian, who developed one of the first wireless equipments in the mid-1890's. The British military were immediately interested and the first demonstration took place on Salisbury Plain in 1896. Amongst those present was Captain JNC Kennedy RE (Royal Engineers) who subsequently helped Marconi with further experiments in the Bournemouth area and then took five sets to South Africa when he was deployed to fight in the Boer War.

Marconi's equipment was a rudimentary 'Spark' set in which an induction coil and a 14-volt battery produced a spark across a 250 mm gap which was connected to an antenna. There was no tuning device and any selectivity relied entirely on the length of the antenna. The receiver was a 'coherer' (it did not use valves which had not yet been invented) placed between the receive antenna and earth which produced an electric current from the received signal. The Morse code was then displayed on paper tape with an ink printer. This worked quite well in tests and distances of 136-km were achieved.

Tests commenced in December 1899 in South Africa but Marconi and Kennedy could not achieve consistent results; communications were very intermittent and unreliable. The wirelesss sets were deployed at various stations along the railway line from Mafeking, through Kimberley to De Aar. It is now known that their problems were caused by incorrect antennae, bad atmospheric conditions due to thunderstorms and dry desert conditions. On 12th February, 1900, the

Director of Army Telegraphs ordered the sets to be dismantled. Nevertheless, all had not been lost and the engineers then moved to Cape Town where further trials with the Royal Navy were more successful. One outcome of this was that the Navy were more advanced than the Army in the use of wireless by the time of the First World War.

Experiences in South Africa fired a few signals officers with enthusiasm and a small experimental team was set up in Aldershot in 1903. In 1905, wireless telegraphy was accepted as a distinct part of the Army Signals organization and the first Wireless Section was formed. Unfortunately, the rate of progress was not maintained and by 1914 the use of the wireless for military purposes was not proved. Its use was therefore confined to a few specific purposes particularly concerning operations of the independent cavalry. The General Staff looked upon wireless with suspicion. No army wireless set had yet been established for trench work.

Very few wireless sets were deployed by 1914. At GHQ there was the motor wireless set and three portable wagon sets. The latter had a normal range of eighty miles and were drawn by six horses similar to the cable wagon. The Cavalry Division had three more wagon sets within the Signal Squadron. Cavalry Brigade HQ was served by the Marconi pack set arranged in a limber wagon with a range of thirty miles. There were only three sets available at the outset of war for the four brigades. One was lost in the initial retreat so sets had to be deployed as circumstances dictated.

The sceptical attitude of the General Staff was partly justified for two main reasons. First, the primitive types of portable wireless were unreliable, bulky and took too long to set up and draw down. Second, the enemy could overhear what was being transmitted. This required important messages to be coded which was time consuming. These objections persisted throughout the First World War and wireless telegraphy was never established as an effective means of communicating during the conflict. It remained fourth-rate behind visual signalling, the despatch service and electric telegraphy which gave rise to significant problems for command and control. The chief instrument of generalship was the telephone which in a mobile warfare situation is unsatisfactory.

Whilst the work on the forward set went on, search was being made for a more powerful set for use at Corps level. It was to be as portable as possible and would be used to direct (control) the wireless network. This was solved by the use of the Wilson spark transmitter combined with a Mark III receiver. Together with the BF Set it was destined to become standard equipment for forward wireless working in the area between corps and brigade HQ for the remainder of the war.

Improvements were brought about by continuous wave (CW) technology; the invention of the valve. Its advantages over spark wireless were its selectivity leading to greater range for the same power; CW was much more efficient. Sets also required smaller aerials which was very much appreciated by troops in forward areas. The early sets were delicate but improvements were made and CW was used extensively by the Artillery by the end of the war. In June 1917, two continuous wave wireless sets were in constant communications between Corps HQ and a corps observation post about 12,000 yards away. For some time when the telephone was not available the stations handled up to 60 messages per day. This became well known by other organizations and in December 1917 an order was made for 882 sets. Subsequently, it was used by Divisional Observers, the Railway Operating Division and by anti-aircraft units.

Towards the end of the war a wireless chain was set up between Corps and Divisions. This comprised the main directing (control) station at Corps HQ, an advanced station at Advanced Corps HQ and sets at Divisions. However, the chain was only used as an outlet of messages if the advance ran ahead of the line. This demonstrates the scepticism that existed about wireless, at this level, to the end of the conflict.

In the more forward areas there was less scepticism especially during the later mobile phases of war. The traffic dealt with in the brigades down to battalion was often of the order of twenty to eighty messages per day using the 'Loop' sets. The disadvantage was that only clear messages were sent so anything of a secret nature could not be transmitted. CW had not reached down to this level before the war ended.

The policy after the First World War was to assume that no major outbreak of conflict would take place within ten years. As such there was little funding for any research and development of military equipment. Thus the late twenties and early thirties arrived to find that the wireless equipment available to the Army was still based largely on the First World War equipment with some minor advancement. For general usage there were the 'A' sets and 'C' sets which were designed for short range in brigades and divisions respectively. For

Corps and Army communications there were Light, Medium and Heavy Signal Troops equipped with the 'C' sets, 120-watt sets and 500-watt sets. None of the general usage sets had a radio telephony (RT or voice) capability.

*Cavalry, Artillery, Infantry and Tank Signals.* There was little progress in the communications capability of these other Arms, the communications for which were independent of the Royal Signals. An attempt to provide the Artillery with a short range portable wireless in 1928 failed. The 'MA', 'MB' and 'MC' sets had been designed with crystal tuning and had voice facilities. The 'MA' sets were used at Regimental level, the 'MB' sets (range of five miles) at Squadron level and the 'MC' sets (range of two miles) in armoured vehicles.

The problems were threefold:
The ranges of the sets were too short for the operational deployments.
The sets were designed after the vehicles so they were limited in size.
The frequency ranges were too restricted.
Nevertheless, progress was made and these Arms realised fully the potential of wireless communications and particularly voice.

A new policy was evolved for wireless in 1929. Due to the lack of funding it took a further four years for equipment to start becoming available. It laid down 6 new types of wireless sets. These were the No. 1 set for brigade and artillery: the No. 2 for division to GHQ and Army: the No. 3 for Corps: the No. 4 for GHQ and Army: the No. 5 for lines of communications: and the No. 6 for Army strategic communications. Priority was given to the No.s 1, 2, 3 and 4 sets.

*The Jackson Committee.* In 1936, General Sir Henry C Jackson chaired an Army Council committee which was to review the whole subject of communications for the field army, including the requirement for wireless sets. The committee also decided that the target for re-armament was April 1939. The downside was that the Treasury did not see fit to fund the essential projects to ensure that the British Army was adequately equipped with wireless equipment at the start of the Second World War. Thus, there were three main problems. The Division was the largest formation that could operate independently on wireless; the range of wireless sets was inadequate; there was no provision for administration communications.

*Summary up to 1939.* Despite the recommendations of the

Jackson Committee, in regard to wireless, the general system of equipment development in the Army did not keep pace with the rapid progress of a relatively new science. The restricted funds had been put to some good use in the development of mobile equipment for the forward areas. The main omissions were in the medium and longer range equipments for which the available wireless sets were woefully inadequate. Moreover, the equipment supply situation was in danger of failing. The available sets were often not deployed in sufficient numbers to meet the requirement. The British Army went to war in 1939 inadequately equipped with wireless communications – just as it had done in 1914.

## DETAILS OF SPECIFIC WIRELESS SETS

There was a whole range of about 15 radio sets in service or developed and brought into service during World War II and some of these had a number of variants. Not all of them were regarded a success and some of them did not remain in service for very long. Some of the sets that played an important part on the battlefields are outlined below.

*The No. 9 Set.* The post World War I development of the 'MA', 'MB' and 'MC' tank and AFV (Armoured Fighting Vehicle) sets in the late twenties, and the No. 2 and 7 sets in the thirties were not very successful. In 1934 the War Office decided to make improvements and further development was put in hand to produce the No. 9 set. This ended up being primarily for tanks and other armoured vehicles but due to the difficulty in mounting it into medium and small tanks it was later used as a general purpose vehicle station. It was an HF radio 1.875-5MHz, maximum power 10-watts with a range of ten miles for Morse code and five miles voice. It was expensive and difficult to manufacture in large quantities and production ceased in 1941 when about 4,000 were in service. Together with the No 11 set it formed the backbone of short and medium range communications in the first part of World War II, notably in the Western Desert. It was eventually superseded by the No. 12 set and by the No. 19 set in AFVs.

*The No. 11 Set.* This was a general purpose set for short distances. It superseded the No 1 set which could not be mass produced. Its development commenced in 1936 and it was in service by 1937. By the time production ceased in 1942 over 19,000 had been manufactured. It was an HF radio 4.2-7.5MHz, with a range from 3 miles voice to 20 miles Morse code. It was the first radio in which the transmitter and receiver were automatically tuned to the same frequency.

*The No. 19 Set.* This was primarily for use in tanks and AFVs. It had both an HF and VHF variant and, manufactured by PYE, it came into service in 1941. The HF version remained in service until the 1960's when it was replaced by the LARKSPUR range of equipment. During this time it underwent several major development modifications. It operated in 2 bands, 2-8MHz and 229-241MHz. Its range was from 1 mile voice to fifteen miles Morse code. Its power output varied from 400m watts to 5 watts. This set was used extensively in most theatres of war and was the primary set for tanks and AFVs, and was used by Commanders to command their battles.

*The No. 22 Set.* This was a general purpose station intended primarily for use in vehicles, but utilised widely, which could be quickly dismounted for use in static locations. It was an HF set using voice or Morse code and operating 2-8MHz with a power output of 1.5 watts. Its range was up to twenty miles and it could operate with a wide range of aerials. It was developed by PYE in 1941 to replace the No. 11 set and about 50,000 sets were manufactured in all. It was adopted by the Canadians and Americans from whom some were purchased when supplies ran low.

*The 'Golden Arrow'.* The use of the 'Golden Arrow' high power transmitter was introduced into Phantom (General Headquarters Liaison Regiment) during the war and is therefore worthy of special mention. The 3 kilowatt transmitter was the Marconi SWB8E and the whole outfit therefore ended up with three names: the 'SWOB 8', 'Phantom' or *'Golden Arrow'*. The station had a crew of twenty-two radio operators and was completely self-contained in vehicles. It was highly mobile and could be moved within 4 hours. The transmitter was carried in a large semi-articulated wagon. The valves were air-cooled and the masts were 70 feet high to allow for a large di-pole to cover all frequencies. Messages were usually encoded and sent twice by telegraph at a frequency range of 3 to 21.4MHz. The power and capability of the station enabled every Corps across the allied front to give a regular update. In some cases the Phantom Officer at Corps level was made responsible at the Corps Commander's daily briefing. This was a most successful operational responsibility that was carried out by Phantom.

# Bibliography

| | |
|---|---|
| Astor, M | *A Tribal Feeling*, Murray 1963 |
| Badsey, S | *D-Day: The Illustrated History*, CLB 1993 |
| Bickers, R T | *Air War Normandy*, Leo Cooper 1994 |
| Bowman, G | *War in the Air*, Evans Bros. Ltd 1956 |
| Buckton, H | *Forewarned is Forearmed*, Ashford, Buchan & Enright 1993 |
| Bullock, A | *Hitler: A Study in Tyranny*, CBC 1954 |
| Clostermann, P | *Flames in the Sky*, Chatto & Windus 1968 |
| Cocks, A E | *Churchill's Secret Army*, The Bookguild 1992 |
| Cookridge, E H | *Inside SOE*, Arthur Barker 1966 |
| D'Este, C | *Decision in Normandy*, Pan 1984 |
| Edwards, D | *Normandy Diary*, Manuscript 1996 |
| Eisenhower, D | *Crusade in Europe*, Doubleday 1948 |
| Gilbert, M | *Second World War*, Fontana 1990 |
| Harrison, Shirley | *The Channel: Dividing Link*, Collins 1985 |
| Hastings, Max | *Das Reich*, Pan 2000 |
| Hills, R G T | *Phantom Was There*, Arnold 1951 |
| Hislop, J | *Anything But A Soldier*, Joseph 1965 |
| Hoe, A | *David Stirling: SAS'*, Warner 1996 |
| Howarth, D | *Dawn of D-Day*, CBC 1959 |
| Hunter, R | *True Stories of the SAS*, Weidenfeld & Nicholson 1985) |
| Ingersoll, R | *Top Secret*, Partridge 1946 |
| Kemp, A | *The SAS at War:1941-1945*, Signet 1993 |
| Lewis, Jon E (ed) | *True from the SAS and Elite Forces*, Parragon 1995) |
| Liddell Hart, B H | *History of the Second World War*, B.C.A. 1973 |
| Mackenzie, Maj. Gen. J J G & Holden Reid, B (ed) | *The British Army & The Operational Level of War* Tri-Service Press 1989 |
| Mark, Sir Robert | *In The Office Of Constable*, Collins 1978 |
| Marks, L | *Between Silk And Cyanide*, HarperCollins 1998 |

| | |
|---|---|
| Maule, H. | *Caen*, David & Charles 1976 |
| Mercer, D (ed) | *Chronicle of The Second World War* Longman 1990) |
| Montgomery, Viscount B L | *Memoirs*, CBC 1958 |
| Niven, D | *The Moon's A Balloon*, Hamish Hamilton 1984 |
| Phillips, C E L | *Alamein*, White Lion 1973 |
| Pimlott, J | *Atlas of World War II*, Viking |
| Ryan, C | *A Bridge Too Far*, Coronet 1976 |
| Saunders, H St G | *Royal Air Force 1939-1945* (HMSO 1954) |
| Soucek, L | *The Story of Communications* (Mills and Boon 1969) |
| Stainforth, P | *Wings of the Wind*, Falcon 1954 |
| Stein, G H | *Waffen-SS*, Cerberus 2002 |
| Strawson, J | *The Battle For Berlin*, Batsford 1974 |
| Strong, Sir R | *The Story of Britain*, Hutchinson 1996 |
| Trevor-Roper, H | *The Goebbels Diaries*, Secker & Warburg 1978 |
| Warner, P | *Phantom*, Kimber 1982 |
| Watney, J | *The Enemy Within*, Hodder 1946 |
| Watson, P R with Andy & Sue Parlour | *Tiger Moths to Typhoons*, Ten Bells 2000 |
| Wheeler, H | *People's History of the 2nd World War* Odhams |
| Wilmot, C | *The Struggle For Europe*, RPS 1954 |
| Unnamed authors | *Arnhem - Diary of a Glider Pilot*, Pilot Press 1945 |
| | *Return Via Dunkirk*, Hodder Stoughton 1945 |
| | *The Victory Book*, Odhams |
| | *The Daily Express: Extracts*, 22$^{nd}$ May 1945 |
| | *The Evening News: Extracts*, 22$^{nd}$ May 1945 |
| | *The Scotsman: Extracts*, 22$^{nd}$ May 1945 |

# Index

## A

*Adam*, Cpt. William, 103
*Adam*, Lt, 103, 306
*Alexander*, General Sir Harold, 21, 88, 118, 119
*Algiers*, 94, 308, 314
*Allen*, Major, 118
*Allen*, Pte Henry, 262-263
*Anderson*, Pte James, 57
*Antwerp*, 15, 209, 222, 223, 225, 243
*Ardennes*, 15, 208, 227-232, 234, 236
*Arnhem*, 179, 209, 213, 215-218, 220, 221, 242, 250, 292, 296
*Ash*, Pte Oscar, 170
*Askew*, Cpl Alf, 144
*Astor*, Major the Hon. Jakie, 76, 79, 81, 152-156, 161, 166, 171, 172, 185, 187, 197, 266, 281, 297, 298, 303, 322
*Astor*, Cpt. the Hon. Michael, 79, 106, 144, 197, 199, 212, 259, 266, 285, 309, 322
*Auchinleck*, Gen. Sir Claude, 68-71, 87
*Auchinleck*, 153, 161, 173
*Austin*, Pte Arthur *'Bunny'*, 295-296
*Auxiliary Unit*, 40
*Averill*, Sgt 57

## B

*Baker*, Pte Dickie, 319
*Balfour-Paul*, Cpt. Ian, 138, 223
*Banbury*, Cpt. Lord Charles, 63, 153, 161, 293
*Bannerman*, Pte Peter, 172, 174, 179, 180
*Baring*, Cpt. R.W., 306
*Bateman*, Pte *'Fan'*, 172, 174, 175
*Bazar*, Pte Adrian, 296-301
*Beardsall*, Pte Francis, 57

*Beckwith-Smith*, Lt, 307
*Bell*, Cpt. Graham, 69
*Bell*, Pte, 174
*Bennion*, Pte Stan, 302-303
*Berlin*, 7, 46, 97, 258, 256, 259, 316
*Binge*, Pte Harry, 47, 52, 61-63, 81, 83-86, 106, 107, 144-147, 152, 167, 194, 196, 199, 201, 203, 209, 220, 223, 224, 232, 241, 251, 252, 260, 261, 266
*Black*, Pte Andy, 129, 317
*Bloomfield*, Pte Peter, 305
*Bradbury*, Pte Albert, 129, 317
*Bradford*, Cpt., 165
*Bradley*, Gen. Omar, 149, 227, 231, 232, 245, 264, 285
*Brain*, Cpt. Geoffrey, 199, 232
*Bramley*, Pte Cecil, 303-305
*Brinton*, Pte, 162, 167
*Brook-Hart*, Cpt. Denys, 107, 110, 135-137, 153, 217-221, 253, 254
*Browning*, Gen. Sir F., 213
*Brundritt*, Pte Dave, 296
*Budd*, Pte *'Colonel'*, 319
*Bunde*, 169, 182, 270, 296, 304, 305, 320
*Burgess*, Pte Fred, 302

## C

*Caen*, 124, 126, 138, 146, 147, 150, 194, 205, 284, 295
*Calais*, 16, 17, 125, 127, 209, 254
*Campbell*, Pte John, 306-316
*Chamberlain*, Neville, 8, 10, 11
*Channel Islands*, 39, 40, 260
*Churchill*, Rt. Hon. Winston S, 7, 9, 11, 17, 18, 21, 39, 40, 45, 55, 59, 65, 68, 74, 87, 93, 100, 101, 123, 202, 235, 238, 239, 258, 260, 277, 294
*Clark*, Pte Alistair, 315

*Clark*, Gen. Mark, 117, 120
*Clarke*, Pte Freddy, 129, 317
*Cohen*, Major George, 242, 292
*Collins*, Major Gen. Joe, 147, 148, 230, 286-290
*Coward*, Cpt. Barry, 289
*Craggs*, Pte William Ley, 77
*Cullen*, Major Lord, 212
*Cuming*, Lt, 103, 294
*Cunningham*, Lt Gen. Sir Alan, 68, 70
*Cunningham*, Admiral Sir Andrew, 64, 66, 95, 102

## D

*Daley*, Major Dermott, 69, 71
*Darwell-Smith*, Cpt. John, 152
*Davies*, Cpt. A S, 264
*Davis*, Sgt Gerry, 159, 171, 180
*Davis*, Pte 'Jock', 172
*Devine*, Pte, 165
*Dieppe*, 75-79, 281
*Douglas*, Pte 'Duggie', 144
*Dover*, 18, 21, 28, 29, 124, 137, 283
*Druce*, Cpt., 158
*Dulley*, Major J E, 114
*Dunkirk*, 16-21, 26, 28, 29, 54, 55, 153, 187, 209, 267, 268, 272, 274, 302, 312, 323
*Durham*, Pte Les, 319

## E

*Eagle*, Pte Ron, 144, 248
*Eaton*, Cpl Ron, 47, 52, 61-63, 84-86, 112, 129-137, 146, 147, 150, 155, 167, 169, 206, 217, 228, 239, 240, 256, 261, 266, 317
*Eden*, Sir Anthony, 40
*Eisenhower*, Gen. Dwight D, 8, 93, 95, 105, 123-126, 148, 192, 229, 239, 245, 253, 258, 316
*Enigma*, 88, 125
*Epernay*, 179, 300
*Evans*, Pte 'Taffy', 311, 314
*Exercises*:

Colombus, 113
Eagle, 153
Spartan, 100

## F

*Fairweather*, Wing Commander, 25, 26, 28, 29, 105, 107
*Falaise*, 194-201, 209, 212, 284
*Fane*, Cpt. Julian, 76, 103, 105, 294
*Farren*, Major Roy, 109
*Franks*, Lt Col Brian, 69, 156, 159, 176, 179, 180
*Fraser*, Major Bill, 67, 162, 163
*Fraser*, Major the Hon. Hugh, 108-110, 294, 306, 313, 314, 322
*Fraser*, Pte 'Sandy', 306

## G

*Gamelin*, General, 9, 12, 106
*Gammell*, General, 113
*Gibson*, Col David, 271-275
*Godwin-Austin*, LtGen. A., 68, 70
*Goebbels*, Josef, 233, 244, 246, 255
*Goering*, Hermann, 41, 42, 45, 46
*Gort*, Lord, 12, 16, 25
*Grant*, Major G, 102, 103, 118
*Graziani*, Marshal, 54
*Greece*, 54-58, 64, 68, 270, 271, 323

## H

*Hamar*, Cpt. Rex, 57
*Hannay*, Major John, 94, 114
*Harris*, Pte George, 162, 167, 172
*Harrison*, S S M, 152
*Hay*, Cpt. Neville, 209, 216-221, 292
*Herbert*, Cpt. Edgar, 69
*Highland*, Pte, 172
*Hignett*, Lt Col Derrick, 113, 144
*Hillerns*, Lt Michael, 76, 77
*Hills*, Major Reginald, 212, 316, 318
*Himmler*, Heinrich, 125, 255
*Hincks*, Cpt. P, 322
*Hislop*, Cpt. John, 152, 153, 156-

159, 176, 179, 183, 281, 297, 298, 322
Hitler, Adolf, 7, 12-22, 41, 45, 47, 53-56, 64, 65, 70, 73, 89, 91, 95, 97, 103, 104, 123, 184, 189, 192-195, 215, 222, 223, 225, 229-231, 233, 234, 237, 240, 245, 246, 248, 257-260
Holdway, Pte Paul, 129, 317-318
Home Guard, 40, 41, 233, 234
Hopkinson, Major Gen. G F, 23, 25-32, 43, 52-55, 58, 70, 94, 102, 105-108, 144, 268, 270, 280, 293, 312, 323
Hopper, Sgt Major R, 172, 264
Hovey, Pte, 137
Hutton-Williams, Cpt. Brent, 256, 273, 276

## J

'J' Service, 24, 57, 103, 110-114, 118, 232
'J' Troop, 113, 144
Jackson, Cpt. John 28
Jackson, Pte Ron, 318-320
Johnsen, Lt Peter, 156, 172-176, 179, 180
Johnson, Pte 'Croome', 170
Johnson, Pte 'Jock', 179, 180
Jones, Pte 'Taffy', 307
Joss, Cpl Bill, 306, 309, 315

## K

Kindersley, Cpt. Hugh, 201, 269
King George VI, 11, 14, 90, 99, 233, 294

## L

Landells, Cpl, 268, 271
Lane, Pte, 137
Laurie, Lt A., 103
Lawless, Bruce, 190, 191
Lechlade, 32, 49, 154, 303
Lewes, 'Jock', 66, 67

Light, Major H., 85
Ling, Cpt. Peter, 144, 145, 195, 199, 202, 203, 224, 225, 242, 249, 260, 261, 282
Lockett, Cpt. Mick, 293
Long Range Desert Group, 66, 312
Lovat, Lord, 77, 294
Luttman-Johnson, Lt Col Peter, 276-283

## M

McAuley, Pte Ian, 306, 309
McDevitt, Major Charles, 49, 52, 54, 167-169, 266, 304-305
MacDonald, Lt, 306-307
MacFarquhar, Cpt. Roderick, 223
Macintosh, Lt Col Alexander, 113, 144, 153, 284, 285, 315
Mackintosh-Reid, Capt. W S, 149, 285, 286, 306
Mackenzie, Cpt. John, 129, 206, 228, 236, 317
Mackinlay, Cpt. A, 306, 309-312
Macmillan, Cpt. Maurice, 149, 247, 322
Mainwaring, Lt Col Hugh, 24, 111, 112
Marchant, Sgt Collis, 319
Marconi, Guglielmi, 4, 327, 328, 332
Mark, Lt Robert, 209-213, 219-221, 231, 236, 265, 289, 322
Marks, Leo, 185, 186
Masterson, Cpl, 77
Mather, Lt Carol, 69, 322
Mayhew, Cpt. Christopher, 322
Mayne, Lt Col Paddy, 67, 156, 164, 166, 180, 181
Meade, Cpt. J A, 260, 317
Melvin, Cpt. Donald, 69, 70
Millar, Cpt. Michael, 144, 145, 197, 202-204, 224, 225, 241, 243, 248, 250-252, 260, 261, 293
Montgomery, Field-Marshal Bernard, 20, 23, 26, 57, 88, 91, 95, 102-105, 110-113, 123, 153, 195,

202, 209, 213, 216, 220, 221, 227, 233, 238, 239, 258, 259, 264, 285, 296, 316, 324
*Moor Park*, Rickmansworth, 154, 155, 157, 166, 174, 176, 179, 180, 182, 297
*Moore*, Lt Tom, 156, 158, 161, 166, 167, 173
*Morgan*, LtGen. Sir Frederick, 123
*Morgan*, Major J.A.T., 113, 210, 266, 304, 322
*Morse code*, 2, 3, 50, 61, 62, 70, 321, 327, 331, 332
*Morse*, Samuel, 2, 3, 50
*Mountbatten*, Lord, 79
*Mussolini*, Benito, 11, 45, 53, 54, 71, 103, 104, 115, 220, 255

# N

*Nicholson*, Brig. Claude, 16, 17
*Nicholson*, Sgt, 264
*Nijmegan*, 213-218, 223, 225, 242
*Niven*, Major David, 51, 52, 79, 83, 84, 94, 106, 107, 152, 154, 201, 266, 296, 322, 325, 326
*Northern Ireland*, 52, 58, 83, 85, 152, 293

# O

*Oakeshott*, Cpt. Michael, 285
*O'Connor*, General, 54, 56
*Operations*:
    Avalanche, 104
    Barbarossa, 65
    Battleaxe, 68
    Baytown, 104
    Clarion, 235
    Cobra, 149
    Crossbow, 189
    Crusader, 68, 69
    Demon, 57
    Dynamo, 18
    Epsom, 194
    Fall Greb, 13
    Fall Rot, 21
    Fortitude, 125, 282
    Gomorrah, 100
    Goodwood, 147, 194, 295
    Grief, 226
    Houndsworth, 158, 160, 165, 166, 172
    Howard, 180
    Husky, 101, 102
    Jubilee, 75, 77
    Loyton, 158, 159, 172, 176-180, 183
    Marita, 56
    Market Garden, 179, 213-221, 296
    Overlord, 124-143, 192, 211
    Rupert, 188
    Sealion, 41, 44, 45
    Shingle, 119
    Torch, 92, 93, 308
    Totalize, 195
    Tractable, 199, 201
    Trojan Horse, 226
*Owens*, Sgt Leonard 'Joe', 159, 169-183

# P

*Page*, Pte Pat, 315
*Panchen*, Pte, 172
*Pannell*, Cpt. Roddie, 294
*Paris*, 21, 53, 106, 159, 202, 206, 207, 278, 290, 302
*Parker*, Pte Dave, 319
*Parlour*, Bill, 44, 98, 189
*Patton*, General, 94, 125, 175, 176, 179, 199, 202, 209, 212, 229, 234, 236, 238, 245, 264, 316, 319, 320
*Pattrick*, Major P D, 114
*Pennant*, Lt Percy, 294
*Petain*, Field-Marshal, 21, 22
*Phantom Patrols*:
    No. 5 'A', 217, 218, 220, 253
    No. 12 'A', 129-137, 146, 147, 206, 217, 228, 239, 256, 317
    No.19 'B' (Merlin), 223

No.20 'B' (Kite), 144, 145, 195, 202, 203, 223-225, 249, 260, 261
No.22 'B' (Gull), 144, 199, 232
No.23 'B' (J-patrol), 144, 197, 203, 209, 220 224, 248, 250, 258, 261

*Phantom Squadrons*:
  'A', 55-58, 79, 80, 81, 86, 101, 106, 113, 114, 124, 129-138, 147, 150, 151, 154, 155, 201, 206, 217-221, 228, 239, 253, 256, 262, 297, 317, 325
  'B', 81, 86, 101, 113, 114, 144, 150, 155, 195-199, 201, 209, 215, 220, 223, 241, 247, 261, 285, 296, 297
  'C', 81, 101, 114
  'D', 81, 101, 114
  'E', 81, 93-95, 103, 109, 110, 114, 154, 306, 307, 313
  'F', 81, 114, 150, 151, 154-188, 192, 281, 296, 297
  'G', 52, 58, 61, 81, 83-86, 293
  'H', 68-71, 76, 81, 102, 105, 118, 244
  'J', 76-79, 81, 118, 152, 161
  'K', 94, 95, 103, 105, 114, 303
  'L', 114, 143, 150, 211, 212, 223, 285, 306, 315, 316, 318

*Pitts*, Pte 'Stuka', 309-311
*Plato*, Cpl, 297
*Power*, Capt. G., 318
*Plum*, Pte, 172
*Popski's Private Army*, 108, 109, 297, 312
*Probyn*, Lt J T D, 228, 256

# Q
*Quisling*, Vidkun, 9, 10

# R
*Rabbetts*, Sgt Major, 304
*Ralli*, Pte, 162, 166
*Ramage*, Major Mark, 280-293
*Ramsay*, Admiral Bertram, 18, 102, 124

*Randall*, Major John, 293-294
*Reddaway*, Cpt. Norman, 28, 107, 294, 322
*Reddaway*, Major Tom, 152, 265, 269
*Reid*, Major Miles, 55-58
*Remagen*, 233, 236-239, 290, 320
*Reynolds*, Pte Bill, 63, 309
*Rich*, Capt. E, 293, 322
*Richards*, Lance-Cpl Gordon, 187, 322
*Richardson*, Pte, 77
*Richardson*, Pte Frank, 170
*Richmond*, 49-52, 85, 107, 182, 211, 262, 268, 272, 277-280, 292, 293, 297, 303, 306, 323, 325, 326
*Roberts*, Pte 'Robbo', 144, 203, 204, 243
*Rommel*, Field-Marshal Erwin, 15, 55, 64-71, 87-95, 112, 125, 127, 163, 183, 184
*Roosevelt*, President F.D., 8, 73, 101, 202, 235, 246
*Rose*, Lt Kenneth, 322
*Rourke*, Cpl Ted, 129, 317
*Runstedt*, General von, 17, 125, 222, 226, 229, 230, 237, 239
*Russell*, Major D L, 113, 114, 217, 317

# S
*Sadoine*, Capt. John, 152, 156, 158, 173, 293, 300
*Salter*, Capt. Keith, 137
*Sedgewick*, Capt. Alistair, 76, 77, 102
*Seekings*, Sgt Major Reg, 163
*Sicily*, 101-103, 115, 170
*Simon*, Capt. B, 314, 322
*Skipworth*, Pte, 172
*Sleeman*, Lt Col J, 277, 278
*Southcott*, Pte Ron, 302
*Special Air Service* (SAS), 66, 67, 109, 151-188, 296-299, 311, 313
*Special Operations Executive* (SOE), 162, 164, 178, 185-188, 275, 276
*Speed-Andrews*, Cpt. A, 319

*Spicer*, Major J, 303
*Stainforth*, Capt. Peter, 97, 102, 108
*Stalin*, Josef, 7
*Stapf*, General, 39, 41
*Starr*, Cpl George 'Twinkle', 187, 188
*Stewart Liberty*, Capt. Charles, 293
*Stileman*, Capt. Peter, 256, 287, 306, 309-315
*Stirling*, Lt Col David, 66, 67, 163, 184, 186
*Stump*, Sgt Vic, 136, 217, 253

## T

*Taranto*, 104, 105, 108, 109, 311, 312, 314
*Tedder*, Air Chief-Marshal, 101, 124
*Tobruk*, 54, 64, 69-71, 92
*Trew*, Lance Cpl, 172
*Tripoli*, 55, 87, 92, 266
*Tudor*, Evans, Pte John, 315
*Tunis*, 93, 95, 112, 294, 311

## U

*Urquhart*, Maj. Gen. Robert, 213, 216, 217, 219, 221

## V

*Vernon*, Major Mervyn, 93, 154, 306, 313

## W

*Walwyn*, Lt Fulke, 303
*Walters*, Col Cliff, 327-332
*Waring*, Cpt. John, 144
*Warner*, Philip, 321-324
*Warre*, Lt Col Tony, 26, 94, 105, 269, 294
*Waterloo*, 212, 213, 219, 221, 225, 228, 231, 239, 272, 286, 300
*Watson*, Pte 'Darkie', 144, 204
*Watson*, Pte 'Paddy', 315
*Watt*, Pte Freddy, 306, 309
*Watt*, Major, Terry, 52, 61, 85, 293

*Wavell*, Field-Marshal Lord A, 53, 55, 64, 68
*Webb*, Cpt. Dougan, 62, 63, 293
*Webster*, Cpt., 119
*Weygand*, General, 16, 18
*Williams*, Capt. Hugh '*Tam*', 94, 159, 201, 266, 294
*Wilsher*, Cpl Reg, 309
*Wood*, Sgt Arthur '*Chippy*', 158, 160-167, 172, 183, 184
*Worsthorne*, Lt Peregrine, 322

## Y

*Young*, Sgt, 271